Reason's Neglect

Rationality and Organizing

Barbara Townley

OXFORD

UNIVERSITY PRESS

OXFORD

UNIVERSITY PRESS

Great Clarendon Street, Oxford OX2 6DP

Oxford University Press is a department of the University of Oxford.
It furthers the University's objective of excellence in research, scholarship,
and education by publishing worldwide in

Oxford New York

Auckland Cape Town Dar es Salaam Hong Kong Karachi
Kuala Lumpur Madrid Melbourne Mexico City Nairobi
New Delhi Shanghai Taipei Toronto

With offices in

Argentina Austria Brazil Chile Czech Republic France Greece
Guatemala Hungary Italy Japan Poland Portugal Singapore
South Korea Switzerland Thailand Turkey Ukraine Vietnam

Oxford is a registered trade mark of Oxford University Press
in the UK and in certain other countries

Published in the United States
by Oxford University Press Inc., New York

British Library Cataloguing in Publication Data

Data available

Library of Congress Cataloging in Publication Data

Townley, Barbara, 1954–
    Reason's neglect : rationality and organizing / Barbara Townley.
        p. cm.
    ISBN 978–0–19–929835–8 — ISBN 978–0–19–929836–5
1. Industrial management.   2. Organization.   3. Corporate culture.   I. Title.
HD30.19.T69   2008
302.3'5—dc22   2008009961

Typeset by SPI Publisher Services, Pondicherry, India
Printed in Great Britain
on acid-free paper by
Biddles Ltd., King's Lynn, Norfolk

ISBN 978–0–19–929835–8 (Hbk.)
ISBN 978–0–19–929836–5 (Pbk.)

10 9 8 7 6 5 4 3 2 1

Dedicated to my mother, Elsie Townley (1924–1996), and to my father, Norman Townley.

⬜ ACKNOWLEDGEMENTS

The debts incurred in writing a book are considerable. I should like to thank friends and colleagues at St. Andrews for their support and patience with a book that took a little longer than anticipated to complete. Research for the book was supported by the Economic and Social Research Council (ESRC) Advanced Institute of Management Research (AIM) Public Service Fellow grant (RES 331 25 0013). I thank those on the committee who supported a non-traditional management research project. I hope they find their confidence well placed. I am extremely grateful to Gibson Burrell, Karen Dale, Rosemary Doyle, and Nic Beech for putting friendship first and reading earlier drafts of the book rather than choosing to take advantage of extra summer holidays. Their comments have been extremely useful in guiding revisions. Karen and Gibson were party to early discussions when the argument of the book was first mooted, and I thank both for all their help and encouragement. I would like to thank Rosemary Doyle and Elizabeth Gulledge for searching for references and Elizabeth for the work she did on preparing the bibliography with such diligence. I am deeply grateful to Barbara Porter for all the help and support she has given me, both in preparing this book and in my other roles at St. Andrews. I am also very grateful to all those who gave of their valuable time to talk about the empirical content of this book. For reasons of confidentiality, they remain anonymous.

The ability to write is built on a vast hinterland of advice and support from friends and colleagues throughout a career. I should like to thank Stephen Ackroyd, David Cooper, Dame Sandra Dawson, Mahmoud Ezzamel, Royston Greenwood, Karen Legge, Alan McKinlay, Paul Marginson, Tim Morris, and Paul Willman. Last, but certainly not the least, I have been blessed with the friendship of wise women, many of whom have been seriously neglected in the book's writing. By way of redress, I should like to thank Dallas Cullen, Erna Dominey, Tricia Findlay, Carol McCallum, Helen Newell, Leslie Oakes, and Stephanie O'Donohoe.

There have been several journeys during the writing of this book. The intellectual journey reflects reading undertaken during my time in Canada and here in Scotland and the friends, colleagues, and students who helped frame this. Many physical journeys have been between France and Scotland, parties to that auld alliance. I should like to thank my love and partner, Dominique Martin, an arch Cartesian. I first thanked Dominique twenty years ago when writing my first book. Together again, I am thankful once more.

Another journey has been from Edinburgh to St. Andrews. That I should start a book on reason and rationality in Edinburgh, heart of the Scottish Enlightenment, is appropriate. The move to St. Andrews takes us along the coast to East Neuk, with its long tradition in witchcraft and opposition to Edinburgh's dominance. St. Andrews, a mediaeval centre of learning and pilgrimage, saw the establishment of Scotland's first university and lies in contrast to the solid rationality of Edinburgh's predominant New Town-inspired architecture and the confidence of eighteenth-century science and professions. Its old stones are imbued with a different form of rationality. But the latter too may be sensed in the preserves of Edinburgh's Old Town, especially when the *haar* descends. It is then that the confident all-knowing presumption of a modern rationality is mocked by a deeper, older, and more grounded reason.

Barbara Townley
St. Andrews
November 2007

☐ CONTENTS

⬚ FIGURE

☐ LIST OF BOXES

1 Foucault and rationality

I have three reasons for writing this book: theoretical, political, and autobiographical. Theoretical interest stems from forays into teaching organization studies. Organization texts are traditionally content based, discussing concepts such as organizational culture, change, technology, and structure (e.g. Dawson 1996); paradigm- or theory based (e.g. Hatch and Cunliffe 2006); or historical, taking a synchronic analysis of subject development (e.g. Jaffe 2001), although a few have moved outside these traditional approaches (e.g. Fineman and Gabriel 2000). But the question remains. What is the subject matter of organization theory? What topics are to be studied and what is their ordering? What constitutes an organizing framework for understanding topics traditionally addressed under this subject heading?

Politically, the argument is put by Clegg (2002b: xxvi): 'there is an ethical dimension to ... organization studies ... the organization analyst has a responsibility towards the subjects of that science. When we investigate organizations ... we address the impact of major structures of society on the lives of ordinary people.' While we might agree with the centrality of organizations for our lived experience, what impact does our writing on organizations have? How can we speak to, and address the concerns of, 'ordinary people' in the work context? What is organization theory's political import and hence its ethical weight? In other words: for whom do we write and why?

These two sets of questions are not independent. They inform each other. For a theoretical framework to have political purchase, it must be able to engage with those to whom it speaks. It must address the question, 'to whom do I speak and why?' If theory has any role, it should be that of providing a framework for understanding that which is experientially understood by the 'practical experimentalists' who work in organizations. 'If we cannot effect a conversation, a dialogue, between the two, then it is not clear what we are doing is useful' (Clegg 2002b: xxvi).

In trying to address these two sets of issues, I am guided by two principles: to avoid a focus on the object 'organization' and to try and avoid the contending debates in social science, the prism or prison of 'isms'. A focus on organization tends to lead to its anthropomorphization ('the organization acts ...'), while the championing of particular theoretical paradigms has, to date, led to an impasse. Instead, I focus on the activity, organizing, and on one of the core concepts of organization theory. The core concept I interrogate is rationality. The nominal 'organization' focuses on the presence or absence of the adjectival form, 'rational', spawning a number of antitheses: the rational versus political, rational versus irrational, rational versus emotional, etc. A focus on activity indicates that purchase may be gained from an analysis of the 'forms' or 'types' of reasoning involved in organizing, thus entailing a move away from dualistic categories, and the recognition that 'rationality is not a unitary measure of behaviour; it has many degrees, multiple dimensions' (Boden 1994: 188).

In an age when reason has been dismissed as the failed project of the Enlightenment, a book on rationality and its relevance for understanding organizing may appear somewhat anomalous. Why reason? The answer is twofold. First, reason is foundational to social coordination and organizing. Social coordination requires the ascertaining of reasons. In order to understand what is being said or done, there has to be some understanding of the underlying reasons for an action or statement. 'As humans we expect each other to be reasonable. Without such an assumption, everyday life would be impossible' (Boden 1994: 179). Reason and the need for action to be rendered rational are thus essential dimensions of any collective endeavour. Second, rationality has been foundational to definitions and historical analyses of organizations, defining the subject of its study, the rational organization. It has been a central or core concept that has structured our analysis, either as a positive characteristic or from a critical perspective. Of late, however, organization studies seem content to relegate rationality to economics and the colonizing tendencies of rational choice theory, preferring to present positions 'in opposition to'.[1] The dominance of a means–end concept of rationality is so prevalent that it has become taken for granted. This does not, and cannot, exhaust our understanding. Here, I argue that rationality should be seriously engaged with as a concept and that all facets of this multifaceted concept need to be explored.

As a means of addressing rationality, I argue that Foucault's work provides both an entrée into its analysis and a template with which to approach its use in organization studies. Why Foucault? Appeal to that supposed anti-rationalist may, at first glance, appear surprising, his work often being associated with the postmodern turn that eschews meta-narratives of 'liberating' reason and progress. This, I argue, would be to misunderstand the focus and intent of his work and its place firmly within the intellectual tradition of responding to Kant's *What is Enlightenment?* (Gutting 1990). Foucault's work allows us to engage with rationality in a theoretically fruitful and ethically engaged manner. It challenges us to see rationality as a form of labour and as an activity that structures identities, and through these effects acts as a subtle form of the exercise of power.

And why is this important? It is important for its political possibilities. As an approach, it addresses the political project of writing about organizing with the ability to directly address the experiences of those in the workplace, not merely a restricted stratum of management. Although challenging the organization of topics and subjects as they are traditionally examined, a focus on rationality and the way it informs individuals' responses provides an individual with the means to be able to negotiate their experiences in organizations. It is a means of giving individuals, as they enter an organization, an entrée into a subject.

The focus on rationality also addresses the autobiographical, the third of my reasons for interrogating the rational. Historically, 'deficiencies' in 'women's reasoning' has laid the foundations for the exclusion of women from the public sphere, denying them access to learning and positions of power and influence (Noble 1992).[2] Women's advances notwithstanding, organization still remains a male construct. Entering the domain of organizations and not benefiting from the advantages of wealth, privileged class, networks, or connections, it is disquieting to learn that even with the faculty for rational engagement, one is never quite a full citizen of that country, one is always something of the stranger in its domain. What counts as being rational is a highly contested terrain.

What follows is thus an excursus into reason and rationality and its modes of expression and use in organization studies.

Why rationality?

Having staked a claim for an analysis based on rationality, it must be acknowledged that the use of terms thus far has been loose, with reason, rationality, reasons, and reasoning having been used interchangeably. Although much used and intuitively understood, rationality does not, like many meta concepts in social science, lend itself easily to simple definition. Rationality denotes a 'mode of reasoning', 'having reasoning power', 'acceptability to reason', and 'a process of constructing knowledge' [*Oxford English Dictionary (OED)*]. It is an ambiguous word. Translated from Greek, it reflects the double meaning of *logos*. [Logos comes from the verb *legein*, meaning to gather, chose, or pick out (Toulmin 2001).] It incorporates 'word', 'speech', and 'account', as in being able 'to give an account of' or being able to formulate (Taylor 1985: 136). It refers both to the furnishing of accounts or reasons, that within contexts count as 'reasons' or accounts of actions, behaviour, and occurrences, and to *ratio*, that which is measurable or accountable. The former is context dependent, being 'reasonable'. The latter, linked to the use of computation, apportionment, calculation, or calculative judgement, lies in formal procedure or order, being 'rational'. Thus, the term has within it rationality, and its links to certainty, and reasonableness, which for Toulmin (2001) involves living without certainties. As we shall see, the rational/reasonable tension informs its history and use.[3]

It is with the common place and intuitive understanding of reason as the 'furnishing of accounts' that I begin my initial comments and the starting point for my argument. I begin with the simple premise that reason is a necessary yet neglected element of social organization and coordination. Reason is the foundation of social interaction in that its premise is that social encounters will be reasonable, that is, they will be capable of being understood at some level. We expect each other to be reasonable in the sense of our actions being amenable to some form of rational explanation. Without this, there is no way to predict how to act or respond. Reasons provide the basis, justification, or explanation of a belief or action. 'To say that someone acts rationally, or that a statement is rational, is to say that the action or statement can be criticized or defended by the person or persons involved, so that they are able to justify or ground them' (Giddens 1994: 98). To deny giving a reason is to remain unaccountable and tears the social fabric (Scott and Lyman 1968).

This is as true of the organizational sphere as elsewhere. People approach organizations and management expecting them to be rational. This may be more recognized in the breach than in the observance, but any discrepancy has to be explained, as for example, being 'political' or 'cultural'. People expect to act rationally in organizations, in the sense that actions have to be rational or intelligible both to the situations in which people find themselves and to others involved. Reasons must be given for decisions taken, policies adopted, and power exercised. They may not be adequate, well thought out, based on viable analyses, believed or credible, but they must be offered. As Foucault (2002: 324) says in an aside that offers some comfort, 'There is always a little thought even in the most stupid institutions.' To fail to offer reasons is to coerce. It is the exercise of overt power and the failure of authority. For authority to be granted, as opposed to power being exercised, engagement has to be based on reason.

This latter point indicates that how we proffer reasons is an important dimension of how we relate to the other. To proffer reasons is to acknowledge the status of the other as a subject:

I may propose a course of action to someone either by offering him reasons for so acting or by trying to influence him in non-rational ways. If I do the former I treat him as a rational will, worthy of the same respect as is due to myself . . . To treat someone as an end is to offer them what I take to be good reasons for acting in one way rather than another, but to leave it to them to evaluate these reasons—not to influence them except by reason. It is to appeal to impersonal criteria of the validity of which each rational agent must be his or her own judge . . . to treat someone as a means is to seek to make him or her an instrument of my purpose by adducing whatever influences or considerations will be effective on this or that occasion . . . an attempt at non-rational suasion embodies an attempt to make the agent a mere instrument of my will, without regard for his rationality.   (MacIntyre 1981: 46)

Engaging in reasoned argument, leaving the other to reach their own judge-ment, is to see ourselves and others as ends, not means.[4] It is to construct the other as subject rather than object.

A focus on reason allows us to decentre an analysis that takes as its starting point different 'isms' informed by different schools or paradigms: positivism, symbolic interactionism, structuralism, deconstructionism, critical realism, phenomenology, ethnomethodology, and critical theory.[5] This is not to argue that they are not important (although sometimes abstract and obtuse writing owes more to competition among academics than to illumination for those engaging with organizations), but that they should not be the primary lens through which life in organizations is approached, an obligatory passage point before anything of value about organizations may be said. Are we going to claim that access to understanding such a central activity is to be open only to those who have engaged in sufficient social theory that they are able to locate themselves in one particular paradigm or another before debate and practice may begin? Or are we to argue that if social theory has any role it should be that of providing a framework for understanding that which is experientially understood by those in organizations: 'the knower to whom our texts should speak'? (Smith 1987: 142).[6] My argument is that the concept of rationality and its centrality in social coordination is intuitively experienced by those in orga-nizations, and it is thus with this concept that we should begin our analysis.

Placing the reasoning individual as central, however, is to argue neither for a subject-centred analysis of organizations nor a subject-centred under-standing of reason. The focus is rationality not the individual. But this is not to argue that rationality is individual or transcendental. Reasoning is learnt, and because of this, is eminently social. That which is understood as being 'reasonable', the 'reason' within an encounter, is the consequence of a process learned through social engagement. The ability to function successfully within the constraints of what is taken to be reasonable, that is, capable of being explicable to oneself and others, is indicative not only of a rational person but also of a socially competent individual. Because of this, rationality is ascribed. Something is rational from the point of view of the actor. Rationality is a relational concept. It is attributed. 'Rationality does not inhere in things . . . a thing can be rational (or irrational) only from a particular point of view, never in and of itself' (Brubaker 1984: 35).

Whose reason?

Having identified reason as the focus of analysis, the complexity of its meaning results in there being a plethora of riches from which to choose in engaging with it.[7] Within social science, Weber's work, in particular, has been concerned to engage with 'the multi-faceted nature of the concept—the rational—that only appears to be a simple one' (quoted in Kalberg 1980: 1156). Weber draws the distinction between substantive and instrumental rationality (Eisen 1978; Kalberg 1980; Mouzelis 1975; Mueller 1979; Sica 1988; Swidler 1973). *Zweck-rational* action is 'determined by expectations as to the behaviour of objects in the environment and of other human beings; these expectations are used as conditions or means for the attainment of the actor's own rationally pursued and calculated ends'. *Wertrational* action is 'determined by a conscious belief in the value for its own sake of some ethical, aesthetic or religious or other form of behaviour independently of its prospect of success' (Weber 1978: 25). Zweckrational and wertrational actions are two forms of social action. Social action may also be affectual, determined by an actor's feeling states, or habitual, determined by ingrained habituation. The latter two, however, do not constitute rational action as they are not conscious actions. Weber's analysis of rational action cannot be divorced from his overall project of tracing the rationalization of Western societies, that is, the displacement of magical and religious views by a view of the world that may be mastered by technical means, nor isolated from his work tracing the rationalization of actions, the deliberate adaptation to situations in terms of self-interest rather than the unthinking acquiescence in customary ways. Weber's work identifies the underlying processes of rationalization, the mapping of human activity around purpose, and the segregation of this from other 'irrational' aspects of life. The dominance of a formal or instrumental rationality is what is 'specific and peculiar' about Western social order (Lash and Whimster 1987; Horowitz and Maley 1994).

Weber's analysis subsequently structured debate. It informed analyses of the Frankfurt School and their depictions of the dominance of an instrumental rationality, the legacy of the Enlightenment as the triumph of zweckrational-ität (Horkheimer and Adorno 1995; Horkheimer 1994). In contrast to Weber, however, Habermas sees Western logocentrism 'not as an excess but as a deficit of rationality' (Habermas 1992: 302). He wishes to escape the dominance of a subject-centred philosophy of consciousness, a non-social concept of rationality, that he sees informing Weber's analysis of reason. His position is that rationality is linguistic and discursive and hence social. He posits a communicative reason, with interlocutors being guided by the assumptions of sincere, truth-governed speech. His concept of communicative rationality was to counter what was seen as the unidimensional presentation of rea-son, the instrumental rationality of Weber's analysis (Habermas 1984, 1987).

Discourse is not solely a matter of power and self-interest. The devaluation of rationality denies the emancipatory potential of reason (Bernstein 1994; Brand 1990; Cooke 1997; Meehan 1995). For Habermas, rationalization as the domination of an instrumental rationality is merely one form of reason. Rationalization is also a process whereby the 'taken-for-granted' can be brought into language, and its assumptions thereby become criticizable. As the 'guardian' of reason, Habermas's critique is of the domination of instrumental rationality, while resisting the overarching critiques of rationality that he identifies with postmodernism. The 'perversions' of reason, its distortion through the domination of a one-sided conception, must be challenged through critical or reflective reason. Within his framework, reason may be instrumental, practical, or emancipatory. Technical reason, with an interest in production and control, is counter-posed to practical rationality, aimed at mutual understanding. Emancipatory interests seek to expose the 'unreasoned givenness' of social arrangements and develop more critically rational social institutions.

Thus is debate structured, as being either 'for' or 'against' reason. Faint echoes of this debate are also reflected within organization studies. On one level, organization studies may be understood as the working through in theoretical and practical terms of the dimensions of rationality; organizations as a conceptual and material space within which various dimensions and facets of reason and rationality are worked out in theories and in practice alongside and through the organization of production.

Rationality is explicit in early functionalist definitions of organizations, reflected in the classical model of the formally rational organization: Taylor's (1911) scientific management, Fayol's (1949) administrative systems, Weber's (1948) bureaucracy, and Simon's (1947) administrative behaviour (Reed 1996; Scott 1981). The model is of the organization as a consciously planned, rationally designed system which develops in response to both internal and external forces (Aldrich 1972; Pennings 1992; Thompson 1967). Having established organizations as the epitome of rationality and organization studies as the concern with rational systems, subsequent approaches challenge what are seen as overly rationalist accounts. The Human Relations School, the next chronological development, presents the 'unconscious' or 'non-logical' reality of organizations lying just below the surface of the formally rational. Explanation is posed in terms of binary oppositions: 'as we inspect these formal structures we begin to see that they never succeed in conquering the non-rational dimension of organizational behaviour' (Selznick 1948: 51). Rationality subsequently becomes modified by a bounded-rationality as is reflected in the work of March and Simon for whom the organization is a decision-making entity.[8] Simon's (1978b) work identifies procedural rationality, that is, the effectiveness of procedures to choose actions, as well as substantive rationality, the extent to which appropriate courses of action are taken. Such a focus is later eschewed in favour of the behavioural theory of the firm, and the ascendancy of the political or the cultural (Cyert and March 1963; Pettigrew 1977). Rationality is now the province of specialized analysis of decision-making, game theory, and rational choice.

The focus on rationality is now taken to characterize a particular historical period of theoretical development, dismissed as no longer having pertinence except for a historical sociology of knowledge.[9] Despite this, rationality still has multiple meanings and multiple uses in organization theory (Townley 2005c), and modern organizations continue to be presented in rationalist terms. Production is the rational organization of resources and people. Management is assumed to behave rationally, albeit within bounded terms, to secure overriding organizational or individual objectives. Organizations are presented as pursuing rational goals. As Halpern and Stern (1998: 1) note, 'rationality is a fundamental concept that is assumed rather debated'.

An alternative to the rational mainstream and managerialist perspective is offered by European, particularly the UK, analyses. These reject the depiction of management as a rational activity to achieve organizational goals. Adopting a critical perspective, the dominant motif is that of power, 'understanding of the use and exercise of social power and ways in which political forces, conceived very widely, shape, govern and even determine human life' (WOBS 2001: xxxi). Organizations are instruments of power. This control perspective is an analysis informed by the metaphor of property, contract, or conquest, the opposition between the interested and the disinterested, an economistic or sovereign concept of power.

Although both paradigms may be seen as diametric opposites, in effect they represent twin sides of the same coin. Both engage with the concept of control. Both engage with reason. On the one hand, management control is authoritatively coordinated action, the rational requirement for the successful purpose of organization. Control is rationally apparent. On the other hand, control is also the prerequisite for the successful rational purpose of organization. The latter, however, requires the appropriation of economic surplus and subordination of labour, hence the need for control. 'Rationality' is dismissed as a post hoc rationalization. Opposition is between the rational as reflecting 'the real' and 'pure' knowledge versus its being a camouflage for power.[10] Organization theory, especially when viewed through the lens of characteristic or stereotypical 'North American' and 'European' presentations, has set up a dominant motif of 'reason versus power'.

In many senses, what this represents is an engagement with Enlightenment discourse: what is it to be rational? What are the constraints of rationality on power and power on rationality? This harkening back to the Enlightenment project constitutes the 'positive unconscious of knowledge' (Foucault 1970) of organization theory. It constitutes what Foucault terms the 'positive unconscious of knowledge', the implicit philosophies subjacent to it. However, one might not reframe this dichotomized perspective of 'reason versus power' and suggest that it needs to be engaged through a Foucauldian lens, not as an antithesis, but rather the 'rational' needs to be examined for its power effects and power for its inscription in rationality. Rationality is one of the most subtle but neglected forms of power/knowledge relations with which we engage. We need to explicate the dimensions of rationality rather than dismiss these as 'rationalizations'. What are the power/knowledge effects of the concept of rationality and how have these been promulgated within the domain of organization studies and practised within organizations?[11]

Having argued that reason and rationality remain salient yet opaque in organizational analysis, in need of further elucidation, how to proceed?

Why Foucault?

The appeal to Foucault may appear problematic. Foucault's work has been criticized for its apparent denial of the efficacy of reason, as it has been for a denial of truth and objectivity. This, however, would be to misunderstand Foucault's work, placed firmly by Gutting (1990) within the tradition of responding to Kant's *What is Enlightenment?* and offering critique of reason[12]:

I think the central issue of philosophy and critical thought since the 18th century has always been, still is, and will, I hope remain the question: What is this reason that we use? What are its historical effects? What are its limits, and what are its dangers? How can we exist as rational beings, fortunately committed to practicing a rationality that is crisscrossed by intrinsic changes? One should remain as close to this question as possible, keeping in mind that it is both central and extremely difficult to resolve.

(Foucault 1984*c*: 249)

Foucault identifies contemporary debates as caught in a binary 'for' or 'against' reason, perfecting, criticizing, or trying to escape it. This he sees as the blackmail of the Enlightenment. 'My basic preoccupation isn't rationality ... I don't believe one can speak of an intrinsic notion of "rationalization" without positing an absolute value in reason' (Foucault 1981: 9). Rather than assume a priori concepts or universal structures that are relevant at all times, Foucault highlights the importance of the historical and the contingent. It is for these reasons that Gutting (1990: 265) concludes that 'Foucault's philosophical project is rationalist in the sense that it involves an acceptance of reason as the primary means of human liberation'. However, as reason is a historical phenomenon, its norms are always open to challenge through critical analysis. Such an analysis is the exercise of reason.

Foucault's work is important in three respects.

First is his focus on *rationalities*. Critical of an 'invariant' understanding of rationality, the sovereignty of consciousness or rationality as the *telos* of mankind, Foucault does not dismiss the value of examining rationalities (Foucault 2002). In *Omnes et singulatim: Toward a Critique of Political Reason*, where he engages with the role of reason in political structures and the excesses of rational systems, he denies any value in contrasting reason with non-reason or excessive rationalism with irrationalism. Foucault denies a universal rationality and the universal validity of rational judgement. Reason has its history, its genealogy. It is not a disengaged 'view from nowhere' that offers an absolute, historical body of theoretical truth (Gutting 1990). The historical and the contingent influence the conditions of possibility of reason:

[reason] was born in an altogether 'reasonable' fashion—from chance; devotion to truth and the precision of scientific method arose from the passion of scholars, their reciprocal hatred, their fanatical and unending discussions and their spirit of competition—the personal conflicts that slowly forged the weapons of reason.

(1977b: 142)

Valuing the work of the Frankfurt School's investigation of the rationalism specific to Western culture, he advocates an analysis, not of rationalization, but of rationalities that are grounded in fundamental experience, for example, madness, illness, death, crime, and sexuality. 'It is not "reason in general" that is implemented but always a very specific type of rationality' (Foucault 2002: 313). He writes:

one isn't assessing things in terms of an absolute against which they could be evaluated as constituting more or less perfect forms of rationality, but rather examining how forms of rationality inscribe themselves in practices or systems of practices, and what role they play within them because it is true that practices don't exist without a certain regime of rationality.   (Foucault 1991: 79)

He says, 'the history of various forms of rationality is sometimes more effective in unsettling our certitudes and dogmatism than is abstract criticism' (Foucault 2002: 323).

Second is the importance of *analysing* rationalities. Foucault denies Nietzsche's position that there is no rationality and that there are only the effects of power. Nor does he dismiss reason as post hoc rationalization. 'Rationalization of government does not mean that a logical facade is affixed to unconsidered practices in order to justify it. Rather practices "rest" on "modes of thought".' Rationality is 'always embodied in institutions and strategies and has its own specificity' (Foucault 1988: 161). He writes:

the government of men by men—whether they form small or large groups...or by a bureaucracy over a population—involves a certain type of rationality...Those who resist or rebel against a form of power cannot merely be content to denounce violence or criticize an institution. Nor is it enough to cast the blame on reason in general. What has to be questioned is the form of rationality at stake. (Foucault 2002: 325)

Those who oppose 'must be able to recognize and challenge the particular form of rationality whose logic justifies violence and organizational procedures' (Foucault 1981: 8). While membership of a group can explain why such a person chose one system of thought over another, the condition enabling that system to be thought never resides in the existence of the group. 'Types of practice are not just governed by institutions, prescribed by ideologies, guided by pragmatic circumstances—whatever roles these elements may actually play—but possess up to a point their own specific regularities, logic, strategy, self-evidence and "reason"' (Foucault 1981: 5). An analysis of how agents use forms of rationality, in what situations and for what purposes, is the analysis of power. For Foucault, this is analytically separate from an analysis of what forms of rationality are available for use. Analysis of the latter illustrates the power/knowledge effects of rationality and how it constructs the subject positions that inform action. That is Foucault's contribution.

Third, Foucault's analysis of rationalities offers an alternative to dichotomized choice by which reason is defined or defines itself: the rational/ arational, rational/non-rational, and rational/irrational. To pose in opposition through a binary division is to posit a confined or bounded universe. One is either/or; rational or irrational. In his analysis of rationalities, Foucault introduces the term 'unreason' (its only remnant now being 'unreasonable'). In *Madness and Civilization* (Foucault 1967), he traces how an 'undifferentiated experience' becomes differentiated into madness and reason through the operation of disciplinary power.[13] He writes (1967; quoted in Sheridan 1980: 80), 'the ascendancy of reason and science brought with it a certain impoverishment of human experience...a Reason that banished unreason in order to set up its own undivided rule becomes defensive and constantly exposed to attacks from the outside.' It is this 'other' of reason that continually disrupts the supremacy of reason, requiring it to be subordinated or dismissed through the operation of numerous binary oppositions.

Foucault's concept of unreason is an important one. The contrast reason/ unreason has several implications. It supposes that the boundaries of unreason remain unknown and potentially unknowable. It is also to conceive of reason as something which is carved, or fashioned, out of unreason. Reason is not a pre-given object, a pre-existent entity, the function or purpose of which is to make itself known. Rather, reason is hewn from unreason. It involves labour, an ongoing labour. Learnt strategies or tactics are employed or worked upon to construct reason and to keep unreason at bay. It is because of this that reason remains un- or ill-defined. Its nature is dependent on the circumstances of its creation. Perhaps most importantly, reason as hewn from unreason introduces a metaphor of depth. It shifts the focus from a restricted dichotomy or dualism that circumscribes how rationality may be understood. It introduces rationality as labour. There is work involved in being rational and ascribing rationality, and what this book traces are the various labours that are engaged in, in hewing its form.

Foucault's analysis also casts a different light on another area of the debate on reason, its relationship to the individual and identity. From Kant, rationality has been intimately linked with individual identity; maturity is ensured through the exercise of reason. Foucault's analysis of Kant also draws upon the intimate relationship between reason and the subject, not in terms of the search for universal principles of reason, but the way that reason constructs a particular form of subject position. For Foucault, autonomy involves a recasting of the original instruction of Aude Sapere (dare to know). What characterizes the Enlightenment for Foucault is not the establishment of, or the attempt at, a set of doctrines as to what it is to be rational, but rather its heralding the philosophical ethos of critique. For Foucault (1984*b*), modernity is an attitude rather than a period of history. The Enlightenment project requires work on oneself, entailing a critical interrogation and engagement with the 'natural or inevitable' of one's own identity. Centrally, modernity presents the relationship that one has with oneself as a task. He argues, 'we must try to proceed with an analysis of ourselves as beings who are historically determined' and to engage in a series of historical enquiries 'not towards the essential kernal of rationality', but towards 'what is not or is no longer indispensable for the constitution of ourselves as autonomous subjects' (Foucault 1984*b*: 43). Autonomous subjects are free, not because of the exercise of rationality, but because they are able to explore and transgress the limits that constitute them as they are (Simons 1995). Freedom or autonomy lies not in the liberation of an autonomous self but in following the 'possibility of no longer being, doing, thinking what we are, do, and think' (Foucault 1984*b*: 46).

What Foucault's reformulation does is make us aware of a different approach to the relationship between reason, rationality, and the individual. Foucault uses a form of analysis that derives from Nietzsche's (Schacht 1992) analysis of a promise. For Nietzsche, the analysis of a promise does not begin with 'the individual' and thereafter see promising as the function of a particular individual faculty, for example, the capacity to develop a memory, remembering the past and anticipating the future, leading to the ability to make and to keep promises. Rather, analysis is reversed. The act of promising requires individuals to anticipate eventualities, think causally, calculate, and compute. It is the act of promising that requires this form of identity be adopted rather than the individual being responsible and reliable and thus being able to promise. The practice of the activity creates the individual or subject. The individual or subject is the 'product'. Thus with reasoning. The practice of reasoning in a particular manner structures the individual allied to the mode of reasoning.[14] Rationality structures the individual in a particular way. This is one of its power/knowledge effects.[15]

This rather reverses the traditional depiction of the individual vis-à-vis the exercise of reason. Analyses of rationality in rational choice theory, for example, take the individual as a given, and then consider the rationality that informs this individual's action and behaviour. It is the individual who reasons and thereby acquires a rational understanding of an external world. Reason is the individual's tool honed in the process of acquiring and perfecting knowledge, validated by means of its correct deployment. Foucault reverses this. And informed by this, the position adopted here is that forms of reasoning are forms of making or crafting a self. Rather than starting an analysis with 'homo economicus' who exercises 'rationality', a means–end rationality constructs 'homo economicus'. This construction is then hidden from view, to be presented as 'rational man' exercising 'individual' reason. It thereby denies that reasoning is necessarily a social function rather than an individual function. Reason positions the self and constructs or structures the functioning of this self. Rather than the subject who reasons to know the world (objects), reasoning positions both subjects and objects.

Foucault . . . how?

Having established that reason and rationality are in fact quite central to Foucault's work, the question then becomes: how to proceed in terms of its relevance for organizational analysis? The three axes of Foucault's work can help in this respect. Foucault identifies his work as being concerned with 'the correlation between fields of knowledge; types of normativity and forms of subjectivity' (1990: 4). He sees this as a way of examining what he identifies as three axes of practical systems or three broad areas of relations: control over things, action upon others, and relations with oneself. These correspond to the axis of knowledge (savoir), the axis of power, and the axis of ethics (the subject). Thus, in any field of activity, there are the formation of sciences (savoirs) that refer to the field; the systems of power that regulate its practice (connaissance); and the 'forms within which individuals are able, are obliged, to recognize themselves as subjects of this field' (1990: 4). These domains identify the knowledge, power, identity triad that he sees as organizing action. Foucault identifies this as 'how are we constituted as subjects of our knowledge? how are we constituted as subjects who exercise or submit to power relations? and how are we constituted as normal subjects of our own actions?' (Foucault 1984*b*: 49).

In his own work, these three axes may be identified in his analysis of the discursive practices that articulate the human or empirical sciences (*The Order of Things*, *The Archaeology of Knowledge*); analyses of specific rationalities, the 'games of truth within power relations' (*Madness and Civilization*, *The Birth of the Clinic*, *Discipline and Punish*); and his later work where he traces the formation of the self (*The History of Sexuality* vols. 1, 2, 3). *The Order of Things* and *The Archaeology of Knowledge* detail the nature of the disciplines of 'scientific' knowledge, or knowledge in general (*savoir*). *Madness and Civilization*, *The Birth of the Clinic*, and *Discipline and Punish* offer analyses of specific practices sustained by local rationalities (*connaissance*). *The History of Sexuality* offers analyses of the constitution of the subject as the individual engages with disciplinary regimes.

Foucault's work would indicate that within any field of knowledge there are three axes or foci: the field of knowledge (*savoir*), relations of practice (*connaissance*), and individuals' understandings of themselves. Modelling the three axes, we can understand that there are specific rationalities that underpin each of these areas: rationality that informs a *savoir*; rationality as a localized or specific *connaissance* that informs rational behaviour in particular contexts; and rationality that informs the way in which the subject is to understand himself or herself. Because rationality constructs a particular mode of engagement for the subject, we can further assume that each of these rationalities constructs a particular identity through which the subject engages with the world.

Foucault's three axes may be used as an organizing framework with which to approach organizational analysis: the 'science' or knowledge of the subject, the positions informed by power relations, and the understanding of the self. These correspond to three dominant rationalities and necessarily to three identities. I label these three the disembedded, the embedded, and the embodied.[16] A disembedded rationality constitutes the *savoir* or science of the field. Its corollary is a disembedded identity. A disembedded rationality is identified in the economic, bureaucratic, and technocratic rationalities that sustain the 'savoir' or 'science' of organization studies. The disembedded position that they inform requires the subject be removed from the specificities of context. All inform a disengaged, 'oversight' subject position. This concept of self, presented as divorced from a historical, cultural, or political context, 'stands back' to take an 'objective' view of a situation and pronounce judgement. This disembedded self is fictional in that its requirements are an impossibility, but it is a socially required fiction. Its appearance and enactment are a necessary part of social competence. While adopting this disembedded position, conventional dualisms or distinctions between subject/object, self/world, and objectivity/subjectivity remain obvious and apparent, only to fade, however, the more embedded in a context one becomes. An embedded rationality recognizes the importance of rational behaviour taking place within a particular context. The contexts that are identified in organization studies are the institutional, contextual, and situational rationalities that organizing responds to. These require the adoption of an embedded self in order to function rationally within these spheres. An embodied rationality recognizes the location of reason within the physical body of the reasoning subject and as such recognizes the importance of the tacit, emotional, and psychoanalytical as dimensions which inform the rational. There are thus several identities constructed in various situations and positioned in relation to the reasoning that is deemed appropriate, or 'reasonable'.[17] This is the power/knowledge effect of rationality.

These rationalities and identities have been used to frame the following discussion. The pertinence of each, the disembedded, embedded, and embodied, their historical location, and the subject position they support, is discussed in the introduction to each section. I then illustrate how each dimension of these rationalities, the economic, bureaucratic, technocratic, institutional, contextual, situational, and embodied, has been understood, developed, and used in the organization studies literature, mainly in relation to a few classic or exemplary texts. To illustrate these rationalities, I also consider research material from those who are faced with the introduction of a 'rational' management technique. This analysis of modes or forms of rationality proffers a critical analysis, in the Foucauldian sense of the term, of the operation of power manifest in modes of rationality, illustrating its disciplinary effects.[18]

The importance of analysing practice

As argued, analysis should be able to speak to organizational lives. This is the 'practical' element of 'theory'. This is its political role. It should be able to give a framework or perspective that opens up a way of seeing that allows the adoption of a more reflexive position and a position from which, if necessary, to contest the more egregious aspects of practice. This is the practical and the political purport of theory and why its engagement with operational practice is essential.

As part of a political project of addressing the 'lived experience' of people in organizations ('for whom do we write?'), I wish to consider some empirical material to illustrate how a conceptual framework based on modes of rationality can help illuminate this. The empirical material is drawn from those who are employed in the criminal justice system (CJS): lawyers, police, judges, court clerks, etc. The empirical material is *not* about criminal justice. It is about work: the organization of work, incentives, bureaucratic structure, socialization, culture, etc., the 'normal' or usual concerns of management and organization texts, as understood by those who work in the arena of criminal justice. This empirical material neither assumes nor requires any technical knowledge of CJS on behalf of the reader. It is chosen because it is an area that is relatively accessible to the reader. The police, courts, lawyers, etc. is an arena with which people have some degree of familiarity, if only through the media. The CJS offers a range of work contexts with different task and skill requirements and varied occupational mix. It is also relatively uncharted by those who write on organizations and work (see Appendix).

More specifically, the focus is the role of performance measures within the CJS. The reasons for this choice stem from Foucault's work. It is perhaps apposite to remind ourselves that *Discipline and Punish*, possibly the most frequently cited text in Foucauldian analyses of management and organization, begins with the analysis and contrast of the execution of Damien, the regicide, and an examination of the timetable. Thus, the initial starting point for what follows is an examination of practices or technologies. Not a sovereign subject. Not interests. Foucault begins his analysis with the 'how', not the 'who' nor the 'why', of power. From this starting point, Foucault then elaborates the concept of disciplinary power, the point being that disciplinary power may be used by a variety of agents for a variety of purposes. The latter is a matter of examination in a particular locus, at a particular juncture of time. For Foucault, an understanding of power comes through the analysis of 'how'. The empirical material here equally addresses the 'how'. It is also perhaps apposite that the CJS continues with the substantive theme of Foucault's text.

Performance measurement systems are a disciplinary technology, the creation of a power/knowledge system with disciplinary, that is, positive and negative power effects. Introduced in many organizations as a 'rational' managerial technology, part of the panoply of effective management and organizational functioning (Townley 2002a), the idea of performance measures is that they 'cascade' through organizations, linking front-line work activities to the highest echelons of those within, and those observing, organizations and the 'system', to give a snapshot 'picture' of performance and progress. The experience of performance measures is used to illustrate the different modes of rationality, as they are engaged with by those trying to make sense of them as a 'rational' thing to do. The essence of rationality, it must be remembered, is that it does not inhere in that which is described, but is ascribed.

BOX 1.1. THE CRIMINAL JUSTICE SYSTEM

Criminal justice has traditionally referred to the stages through which criminal behaviour is dealt with through the state agencies: charge, prosecution, trial, sentence, appeal, and punishment. The agencies responsible for these stages are referred to collectively as the criminal justice system. A number of different agencies are involved: the police, the prosecution service, the courts, solicitors, lawyers and barristers, the judiciary, prisons, criminal justice social work and voluntary agencies dealing with victims of crime and offenders.

Under the Scottish system, crime is investigated by the police under the direction of the Procurator Fiscal Service (PFS) (the Prosecution Service). After the crime has been investigated and an individual has been charged by the police, the case is then passed to the PFS which determines what action to take—no further proceedings ('no pros', where there is insufficient evidence to warrant further action), a warning, a fine, mediation, or a prosecution before a Sheriff Court or the High Court—depending on the seriousness of the crime. Cases are allocated court time by the Court Service, cognizant of the legal requirements under Scottish law that criminal cases are to be heard within certain stipulated times, if not they must, by law, be dismissed. The PFS prosecutes cases in Sheriff Courts which are defended by solicitors. (In the High Court, the equivalent personnel are Advocate Deputes for the prosecution and Advocates or QCs for defence.) Sheriffs and judges hear cases and are responsible for the conduct of cases before the court. Sentencing can include non-custodial drug treatment orders (heard before a special drugs court), community service orders, and imprisonment. This is at the discretion of the sheriff or judge, although it takes place within general sentencing guidelines. Social work reports on the accused are often required before sentence can be passed. Appeals against sentence, either on grounds of leniency or harshness, are heard by the High Court.

The criminal justice system refers to an institution, but is in fact a number of institutions and agencies and reflects a number of tensions: between criminogenic or welfare orientations; private, local authority, or central government sources of funding; and managerial versus practitioner emphasis. Operationally, there have been a number of problems with the coordination and effective joint working in the delivery of what has been termed 'end-to-end' justice, that is, from the point of detection of an offence to case disposal. These include delays in cases coming to trial; the non-attendance of the accused and witnesses at trial; late pleas, adjournments, and delays in court proceedings, all impacting on witnesses, victims, and jurors. As governments of all political persuasions have been increasingly excised by crime, crime levels, and the incidence of recidivism or reoffending, a number of questions have been raised concerning the effectiveness of the criminal justice system. In Scotland, a review of operational difficulties (hereafter the Normand 2003 report, after its Chair) recommended the establishment of a National Criminal Justice Board to oversee the operation and performance of the CJS against overarching aims, objectives, and performance targets. Local Criminal Justice Boards were also recommended for coordination and liaison at a local level. Similar proposals have been implemented in England and Wales.

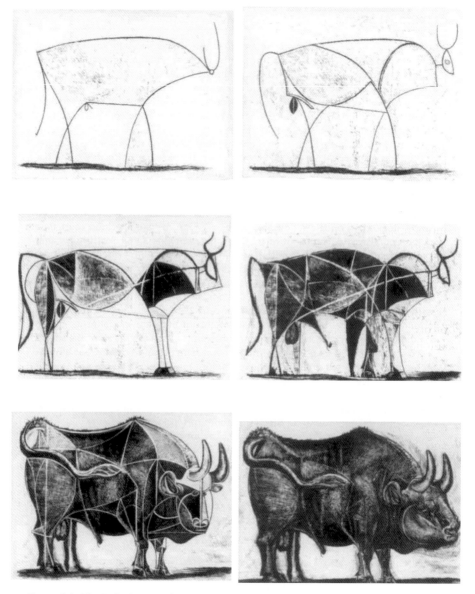

Figure 1.1. The Bull: six states from one stone © Succession Picasso/DACS

The argument: A pictorial representation

The emphasis thus far has been on text, the reasoned exposition of position, as a means of accessing the structure and argument of what follows. A more immediate and visceral means to the same end is provided by Picasso's sketches of *The Bull: Six States from One Stone* (Figure 1.1). This outlines the process of abstraction from that which is the most immediate and easily identifiable representation, here of a bull (although it draws upon symbolic and iconic associations rather than more naturalistic representations), to that which is the most rarefied representation of a large, male, animal that may or may not be identifiable as a bull. These series of sketches are evocative for several reasons. They illustrate the argument of the book on several levels. They parallel the abstraction of reason from its most embodied through to its more disembedded or abstract forms. They also illustrate the abstraction of performance measures through organizations as they move from those most immediately and directly associated with the work context to those taken to 'represent' the 'broader picture'.

This pictorial representation raises important questions: what is lost, and equally what is gained, from moving from one state to another? Are the traces of one state represented in another or do each represent independent and autonomous states? Is it possible to 'understand' one state without seeing the whole and the relationship between them? What is understood by a representation when only one state is accessed? What determines the choice of what is kept and what is omitted in the movement from one to another? Perhaps, most importantly, and echoing Foucault's (1982*b*) use of Magritte's painting *C'est ne pas une pipe*, what is the relationship between these representations and the large, male bovine eating in a pasture, or, perhaps, charging towards the observer? It is these questions that will guide us as we trace through the modes of rationality that are presented in the following pages.

Part I
Disembedded Rationality

Introduction

Rationality is a relatively modern institution. Its origins lie in changes in class realignment, the rise of the middle class, and urban bourgeoisie. Belief in the capacity for individual reason provided the foundation, first for the challenge to the power of the established Church, and later to the State (MacIntyre 1988; Toulmin 1990, 2001). Linking philosophers such as Voltaire, Montesquieu, and Diderot, the supremacy and liberating role of individual reason fed into the philosophical grounding of the American and French revolutions (Lukes 1973).[1] The supremacy of reason and the capacity of humanity to perfect itself through the power of rational thought were the guiding principles of the Enlightenment and a defining characteristic of modernity (Porter 2000).[2]

The Enlightenment legacy is of a rationality informed by the mind/body split (from Descartes) and the principle of universality (from Kant). Herein lays the foundation of a disembedded and disembodied rationality. It is a rationality that informs many taken-for-granted contemporary 'truths', namely, that reason is the natural disposition of the human mind; that truth or an objective reality can be known independent of the subjective knower and accessible through the operation of reason; that these truths are sufficient in themselves to ensure intersubjective agreement among like-thinking or right-thinking individuals; that reality operates according to universal laws generalizable across time and place, accessible to human reason; and that human history can be seen as the gradual progression to the full realization of human capacities for reason.

This disembedded and disembodied rationality, and with this a disembedded and disembodied self, is a construction formed over several centuries (Bloor 1991; Lukes 1973; Toulmin 1990). The seventeenth century, particularly under the influence of Descartes, saw reason as attainment. It was an intellectual skill to be learnt, 'a distinctively methodical way of thinking, sharply differentiated from other kinds of thought' (Lloyd 1995: 39). It was an abstract or ordered mode of reasoning. It heralded a concern with rigour and exactitude; the decontextualized rather than studies rich in context and content; an emphasis on geometry, mathematics, and logic rather than ethnography, history, and poetry (Toulmin 1990). This new philosophy narrowed the scope of rational debate. Indeed for Toulmin (2001), the language of reason, the meaning of key words such as reason, rational, and rationality, changed dramatically in this period. Rationality became limited to theoretical argument independent of context, away from an earlier Aristotelian influenced approach where the subject and circumstance dictated the degrees of formality and certainty of 'reasonable' debate. This shift was reflected in the privileging of the written over the oral; the universal rather than the particular; the general and the timeless rather than the local and the timely. Rationality was confined to 'abstract, timeless methods of deriving general solutions to universal problems'; rationalism was an abstract core of theoretical concepts (Toulmin 1990: 35). The certainty and stability of this new philosophy promised the prospect of stability in social organization, particularly pertinent given the religious conflict of the sixteenth and seventeenth centuries. It was part of the 'quest for certainty' that characterized the development of natural philosophy and the study of natural sciences from the mid-sixteenth century onwards (Toulmin 2001).

The rationality that came to the fore in the seventeenth century has dominated Western thinking ever since. The ideas promulgated 'gained the understanding of common sense for the next 100, 150, or 200 years' to the extent that from 1700 they 'go without saying' (Toulmin 1990: 107). That modern knowledge focuses on rationality, validity, truth, and objectivity is part of the taken-for-granted institutionalized understanding that we have derived from Enlightenment thought. Rational argument does not depend on its reception by an audience. Rather, it is judged by formal analysis and 'proof', usually in the form of 'facts'. It deals in abstract, general ideas and principles, and the most effective way of stating and solving problems is to decontextualize them. The methodological style that came to dominate was an emphasis on the individualistic and atomistic, whereby wholes and collectives are the equivalent to their constituent parts; a static, timeless, and universal emphasis; abstract deductivism; allied with a strong moralizing or prescriptive emphasis, 'general principles whose very distance from reality can serve as a reproach to the latter and a goal for action' (Bloor 1991: 63). The pillars of thought are certainty, systematicity, simplicity, and intelligibility (Toulmin 1990: 179).

The 'rational method' is a precisely ordered way of reasoning, abstract theorizing from disengaged principles, focusing on logical rules, principles of consistency, coherence, and non-contradiction, specifying rules of inference, and appropriate means of reaching conclusions. The most effective way of stating and solving problems is to divide more complex operations into their simplest forms and recombine them into an orderly series (Bloor 1991). This specialized and highly abstract way of thinking is detached from thinking that is ordinarily engaged in. It is 'pure thought', an enquiry into 'truth', applicable to any subject matter, but more significantly, separate from practical matters and the practical concerns of 'ordinary' life (Lloyd 1995). Rationality is a determinate mode of thought proffering the ideal of objective knowledge; clear, unequivocal knowledge stripped of contextual confusion (Bordo 1987). It is reasoning that marks off that which is to be known and makes it independent of the knower. The 'object' 'speaks'. Logic and rationality are endowed with an asocial, aperspectival objectivity (Daston 1992).[3]

Whereas Descartes had seen reason as a method, the essence of reason for Kant is that its principles are universal, categorical, and internally consistent (MacIntyre 1981: 45).[4] What he aims to determine are the conditions under which the use of reason is legitimate; the limits to pure reason (as opposed to practical moral or scientific reasoning); the limits that would prevent speculative errors and excesses of judgement; and the private and public uses of reason. Moreover, for Kant, the exercise of reason also becomes an important source of identity. It is allied to maturity, defining humanity's passage to adult status and the awareness of oneself as a free and responsible subject. From Aristotle onwards, the exercise of reason has been associated with autonomy (the life worth living is that in which human abilities, especially human reasoning, is fully realized). In Kant, however, the full realization of rational abilities requires, and in turn sustains, the exercise of individual autonomy. To be unduly reliant on another in decisions is to fail to exercise one's reason, not to be fully autonomous. Thus, rationality is intimately bound to the independent social actor. Truth 'can only be achieved by means of proudly independent, solitary Reason. We pursue it rationally and we pursue it alone' (Gellner 1992: 8). Autonomy is founded on separation, and reason is autonomous when it is separate from others. As an abstract process, engaged in by a socially disembodied being, rationality is the property of individuals apart from, and prior to, their entry into social relations.

A rationality transcending historically contingent circumstances promotes the idea of rationality as common to all, a universalism.[5] These claims to universality become incorporated not only into concepts of truth but also into what it is to be a person. The identity that is promulgated is that of an 'impartial self'. Impartiality, however, is not restricted to being fair, open minded, even handed, or balanced, considering others needs as well as one's own. Rather, it is to be neutral, independent, objective, detached, unprejudiced, and disinterested, disembedded from a context and a society. It is to be 'outside' or 'above' the situation about which one reasons. It is the self that takes the 'view from nowhere' (Nagel 1986), 'a transcendental ego sitting at a height from which it can comprehend everything by reducing it to a synthetic unity' (Young 1987: 68).[6] It is not reasoning informed by giving reasons or giving an account, the intelligent reflection on a situation. It is reasoning derived from *ratio*, the reduction of objects to a common or universal law. All situations are treated to the same rules. Following a disembedded rationality, one may be fully rational without being reasonable.

In the Enlightenment's rhetoric, autonomy, objectivity, and universal reason are indelibly linked; knowledge may only be acquired through dispassionate, disinterested, value-free, and context-free objective enquiry, unswayed by spatio-temporal considerations.[7] The legacy is of a disembedded and disembodied self that adopts a disengaged stance to the self and others. It is the construction of the individual as sovereign, autonomous, with clear boundaries. The sovereignty of reason brought with it a scepticism of accumulated custom, fashioning a division between rationality and culture (Gellner 1992). Its heavily individualistic characterization reinforced a separation between the individual and the collective. It sustains and is sustained by the 'presumption of a singular reality, pre-existent representational categories, an unambiguous language of representation, produced and utilized by a singular, rational, and unified knowing subject, unhampered by personal concerns' (Grosz 1993: 205). Its apotheosis lies in the scientific method, the one true means of attaining truth. The sciences became a model for all knowledge, and scientific rationality the foundation of objectivity. The literary and humanistic lose their legitimacy as a source of knowledge, thus informing the hierarchical positioning between the natural and the social sciences, science, and art. Aperspectival objectivity, a non-situated, distanced position, is taken to be the epitome both of accessing knowledge and of discharging the moral position.

This disembedded rationality has come to the study of organizations in many forms. It informs organizations' *savoir*, a disembedded knowledge that gives itself the status of science. Pugh (1966), for example, describes organization theory as the unified science of man (sic) in organizations, specifying organized and organizing behaviour in the provision of goods and services. Rationality is incorporated into the understanding of what it is to be a manager, the character in pursuit of rational knowledge for the purposes of control (MacIntyre 1981). Indeed, Toulmin (2001) argues for the need to see in management how ideas of rationality developed and were refined.

Three elements of a disembedded and disembodied rationality are found in organization theory: the economic, bureaucratic, and technocratic. In the economic, rationality is the means–end calculation of efficiency based on individual interest. It is the rationality of homo economicus. Rational decision-making involves the processing of information and the choosing among alternatives. A bureaucratic rationality denotes the application of a 'veil of ignorance' (Rawls 1971); rule application without fear or anger, thus ensuring a depersonalization of the administrative process so that the organization may efficiently achieve its goals. A technocratic rationality reflects a scientific rationality founded on semantic clarity, rules of procedure, and acting according to a body of scientific knowledge (Schutz 1962). Its epitome is the application of the scientific, neutral algorithm.

These rationalities are presented in organizational texts as singular, universal, and trans-historical. They constitute the 'fundamental codes' (Foucault 1970: xx) of organizational rationality that guide understandings of action. Idealized rationalities that have considerable consequences for how individuals proceed and the accounts they give of their actions. They are presented like Newtonian theory of matter in the physical sciences: 'a law that behaviour would obey if not for various disruptive influences…behavioural analogues of friction, wind, measurement error etc.' (Boden 1994: 182).

Differentiating between them allows for different aspects of the organization theory literature to be engaged with. An economic rationality is the matching of means efficiently to ends. Action is judged in relation to consequences as compared with other alternative courses of action. No action is right or wrong as such. This is distinct from the rationality that is assumed to reside in rules. It is to recognize a distinction, often not clear in Weber, between 'rationalization' as calculation and rationalization as bureaucratization (Brubaker 1984; Udy 1959). The classical model of organization, represented by Taylor, Fayol, Gulick, and Urwick, has an implied assumption of economic rationality or maximum efficiency as a value in itself. This is distinct from the rationality of Weber's bureaucracy, most often associated with public bureaucracies. An economic rationality conceives of homo economicus who, given a monetary incentive, could be engineered as an instrument. It informs agency theory, transaction costs analysis, and the organization as a 'nexus of contracts' (Jensen and Meckling 1976). This is distinct from Merton's (1940) 'methodical, prudent and disciplined' bureaucrat who may occasionally act as a 'trained chicken'.

Technocracy rationality is an authority grounded in facts and techniques (as Knorr Cetina 1981 reminds us, facts comes from the Latin, facere, to make). Impersonal techniques and systems substitute for the personal exercise of authority as decision-making is programmed into a system. This disembodied and disembedded management is supported by a proliferation of techniques; ones that have universal relevance and may be introduced in any organization, anywhere. Abstracted from context, and disembedded, homogenous, and ubiquitous, it 'can be applied in any time and place and activity setting' (Meyer 1994: 53). As such, management becomes 'a portable technical skill, divorced from specialized experience and knowledge about particular subjects, applicable to the private and public sectors, and primarily concerned with the efficient use of resources' (Power 1997: 169). It is to these practices of a disembedded rationality that we now turn.

2 **Economic rationality**

Economic rationality (Weber's 'goal rationality' or the 'instrumental rationality' of the Frankfurt School) is a part of the taken-for-granted assumptions of how organizations are understood and studied. Organizations have economic purpose and intent; organizational structures, systems, and policies are designed to achieve goals or ends. Ergo, organizations are rational. All this notwithstanding the abundance of literature illustrating that organizations often follow purposes and objectives which do not make strict economic sense; that structures, systems, and purposes are rarely designed and often fail to achieve stated intent or purpose.

Although economic rationality is often presented as a discrete, coherent, and readily identifiable mode of rationality, it elides a series of confusions and contestations: disputed definitions of rationality; disagreements as to what behaviours typify it and how it may be identified; and strong objections to the characterization of its dominant actor, homo economicus. Its genesis, both from debates about the nature of individual autonomy and the disciplinary development of economic thought where rationality arrives as a relative latecomer, reveals a series of discrete strands of literatures and debates that coalesce in a generic, rather fragmented, understanding. These various strands and how they have impacted on organizations form the basis of this chapter.

Purposeful individuals

The building block of rationality is the purposeful individual: human action as purposeful or intentional. Purposive action is conscious, foresightful action guided by intent, aimed at the achievement of ends. From this initial premise of 'man' as a purposeful animal, there has been an elaboration from purposeful action to rational action and from choice, to rational choice, to rational choice theory (Goldthorpe 1998), involving an ever more elaborate panoply of the requisite relationships between preferences, beliefs, expectations of consequences, and action. Not only this, but there is also an ever more elaborate depiction of the rational actor who engages in such action.

Rational action is a more circumscribed form of purposeful action. Rational action specifies that for actions to be rational, there must be reasons for action; reasons must cause the action; and they must cause the action in the intended way. Every condition must be satisfied. Davidson (1980) gives the example of a man intending to murder another: the taking of a gun and firing it with the intent to kill is a rational action; firing the gun and accidentally causing a stampede of some suitably located cattle killing the intended victim is not, even though the reasons and actions are the same. Equally, according to this understanding, sticking a pin in a doll with the intent of killing someone would not constitute rational action (although the extent to which it would be so in another society is a contentious issue in debates about the rationality as will be seen in the introduction to Part II).

The initial conception of rational action portrays a minimal elaboration of the rational actor and a minimal specification of the relationship between preferences, beliefs, and action.[1] An extension of this, instrumentally rational action, is premised on further elaborations of the nature of the rational individual. This individual is a rational pursuer of self-interest. He or she also calculates the most efficient means to a goal. Having goals and alternative means to achieve these ends, the actor must weigh probable costs and benefits in choosing actions. This conception of rational action modifies the original understanding by conceiving of rationality as efficiency, stressing the assessment of the means adopted to achieve desired ends and the importance of efficiently securing one's self-interest.

This lies at the foundation of Weber's zweckrationalität, or instrumental rationality, 'action is instrumentally rational . . . when the end, the means and the secondary results are all rationally taken into account and weighed. This involves rational consideration of alternative means to the end, of the relations of the end to the secondary consequences, and finally of the relative importance of different possible ends' (Weber 1978: 153). Note that here Weber recognizes the importance of weighing secondary consequences and evaluating ends, points often overlooked.

Rational choice further elaborates the original premise of rational action. Choice arises from preferences (desires) and expectations (beliefs) and is guided by a calculation of the costs and benefits accruing to alternative actions and their likely outcomes. Rational choice also elaborates the individual who engages in it. It presumes self-interest and a calculating individual, and also a self with a number of stable preferences. Rational choice aims to maximize these preferences. This requires that preferences are ranked and that these preference rankings fulfil a range of conditions with regard to their completeness and consistency.[2] Preferences that satisfy these axioms are coherent and the individual rational. Armed with a ranking of preferences, the individual is then equipped to engage in the calculations required to ensure that preferences are maximized. The ability to make a calculation between alternative actions and outcomes, however, requires a calculus, a metric or common coinage, through which comparisons of preferences and outcomes may be drawn, and the apportionment of activity decided.

This elaboration first graced the pages of writings on utilitarianism, with its psychological thesis that 'man' has two motives, the maximization of pleasure and the absence of pain, and the recommendations of Bentham to engage in a 'felicific calculus of "utiles"' (MacIntyre 1981). Although utilitarianism has lost some of its philosophical import, it has bequeathed us 'utility': a fiction, as MacIntyre (1981: 68) notes, but a 'fiction with highly specific properties', 'a quasi-technical term...designed to make plausible the notion of summing individual prospects of pleasure and pain' (MacIntyre 1981: 70). Rational choice gives the individual the single goal of maximizing utility. The reasonable actions of the purposeful individual are thus transformed into the rational calculation of the maximization of utility.

From rational action as reasons causing actions in an intended way, rational action is now determined by the value or utility of the decision outcome (choice) as calculated by the maximization of benefits and the minimization of costs when making a comparison between alternative actions. The maximization of an expected utility is taken to be the criterion of rational choice. More elaborate calculation sees choice optimization as a function of complete and consistent preferences, the consequences of feasible actions, and their likelihood and constraints as represented by costs. Calculation based on the future consequences of current actions (their probability) and the future preferences of consequences (their expected utility) gives expected utilities and guides action. Here, however, we are not far removed from rational action having been transformed into calculations based on fully ordered preferences, complete and accurate information, and perfectly calculated outcomes (Hollis 1987). From a subjective or 'internalist' assessment, in which the individual is assessed only for the consistency of preferences and the match between desires, beliefs, and actions, comes an 'objective' or 'externalist' assessment, about the rationality of preferences, the accuracy of information, the choice of means, and the correctness of calculation of what a fully rational agent would do (Hollis 1987).

The instrumentally rational pursuit of self-interests and utility maximization has assumed many manifestations. It informs social contract theorists and public choice theory in politics, liberalism in political economy and utilitarianism in public policy, neoclassicism in economics, expected utility theory in psychology, and rational choice theory in sociology. Substantive ends, their formulation, and choice, are not addressed: *De gustibus non est disputandum.*

The original premise of individual action being purposeful and rational has engendered a very specific conception of the rational individual and what it is to have a rational self. Giving birth to such a rational individual, however, generates its own difficulties, not least the nature of this rational self; how this individual relates to other individuals; and if, and how, this individual develops through time.

While recognizing its value as a general approach, some are critical of the presentation of this rational individual. Sen, for example, is disparaging of 'this rational fool decked in the glory of his one purpose preference ordering' (1977: 335), the latter designed to capture individual interests, individual welfare, actual choice, behaviour, and what should be done, as well as the incipient tautology of choice demonstrating preference. Others dismiss the model of rational calculus entirely. For MacIntyre, 'human happiness is not a unitary, simple notion and cannot provide criterion for making key choices'. Of necessity, it involves incommensurability. 'The objects of natural and educated human desire are irreducibly heterogeneous and the notion of summing them either for individuals or for some population has no clear sense' (MacIntyre 1981: 70).

As rational choice is based on individual calculation, the unit of analysis is the decision made by the individual rational decision-maker. Interaction only explicitly enters into calculation in game theory. Methodological individualism offers the social only in terms of aggregation (see Chapter 9). Certainly, rational choice theory eschews the appeal to causal properties of structures or institutions on the grounds that sociological explanations are expressible only in terms of the properties and actions of individuals, acting in accordance with what is rational in the light of knowledge and preferences. Society is the aggregate effects of decisions. For its critics, this renders links to social action and 'society', and considerations of power, trust, legitimacy, solidarity, and values problematic. They point to the context dependency and social embeddedness of preferences and argue that the extent to which rational choice has to be adjusted to a feasible set of realistically possible options raises issues about the latter's determinants and the role of social structure in circumscribing options.

Equally, temporality is not an explicit central feature of analysis, although it features in repeat plays in game theory where prolonged games may result in cooperation for mutual benefit. Theories of choice assume that future preferences are exogenous, stable, consistent, and precise, assumptions that draw the criticism that rational choice theory confirms or enacts the 'autonomy of the present' (Wagner 2000). Desired future states raise the relationship between interests and 'enlightened' self-interest, the logic of consequential choice, and the ability to anticipate the future and establish a set of preferences to deal with future outcomes. Preferences may be inconsistent, change over time, or be time-consequent in that actions taken in the present impact on preferences for the future. Some preferences may only be known in the light of experience. Some experiences change people and alter life chances.

In its defence, rational choice theory would argue that it is providing a normative model or an abstraction and is engaged in parsimonious theory-building that describes established patterns of behaviour rather than reflecting the 'real' or giving a realistic portrayal of behaviour. It offers a minimalist account of the human actor to explain aggregate patterns, where individuals act 'as if' they were engaged in rational choice behaviour.

Modern society is now so fully imbued with this concept of rational action and the rational individual that Elster (1986: 27) can move from a general discussion of rationality to this model without equivocation:

There are strong a priori grounds for assuming that people, by and large behave rationally. In our dealing with other people, we are compelled to treat them as, by and large, rational. Communication and discussion rest on the tacit premise that each interlocutor believes in the rationality of the others, since otherwise there would be no point to the exchange. To understand other people, we must assume that, by and large, they have consistent desires and beliefs and act consistently upon them. The alternative to this assumption is not irrationality, which can only be predicated on a broad background of rationality, but chaos.

The anthropomorphization of organizations

From the depiction of the purposeful individual, it is an easy, if inaccurate, step to impute the purposefulness of a number of individuals to a collectivity and assume, through reductionist reasoning, that this functions in the same manner, that is, that organization, group, and collective behaviour can be reduced to individual action and calculus. The organization becomes viewed as a purposeful agent, the 'individual decision-maker'. The organization is anthropomorphized.[3]

From this perspective, individual rational efforts are the foundation of collective organized action. Individuals have a common or collective interest in banding together to achieve certain collective goals or objectives, as greater efficiency can be achieved through collaboration and collective organization than individually, especially where coordinated through hierarchy and achieved through a division of labour. The organization is seen as an instrument or a means of realizing concrete expressions of interests. Early definitions of organizations reflect this perspective. Barnard's (1938: 4) definition was of 'formal organization [as] that kind of cooperation among men (sic) that is conscious, deliberate, purposeful'. For Selznick (1948), organization 'is the arrangement of personnel for facilitating the accomplishments of some agreed purpose through the allocation of functions and responsibilities'. For Eldridge and Crombie (1974: 17), 'a particular kind of social system, one which is purposeful and which is structured so as to facilitate the realization of purposes'. While for Mintzberg (1983), organizations are 'collective action in pursuit of a common purpose, a fancy way of saying that a bunch of people have come together under an identifiable label ... to produce some product or service'. From this, we move to March and Simon (1958: 4) for whom 'The high specificity of structure and coordination within organizations—as contrasted with the diffuse and variable relations among organizations and among unorganized individuals—marks off the individual organization as a sociological unit comparable in significance to the individual organism in biology'. And with the organization as a quasi-individual, the focus then becomes the noun 'organization', rather than the activity organizing.

Note that these broad definitions were not restricted to economic organization. Early organization theory has a broad interest that stimulates work on what constitutes an organization. On what grounds would one label corporations, prisons, schools, trade unions, political parties, and hospitals as organizations; but gangs, playgroups, religious groups, informal work groups, sports teams, not? Types of organizations are categorized in terms of their goals (Parsons 1956); functions (Katz and Kahn 1966)[4]; beneficiaries (Blau and Scott 1962)[5]; types of regulation that they rely on (Etzioni 1961)[6]; technologies (Woodward 1958)[7]; structures of authority (Ackoff 1970)[8]; and their configurations of work (Mintzberg 1983).[9] It is only Weber's later definition emphasizing the importance of issuing orders and being obeyed, that is, structured social relationships, that authority relationships are placed central to the definition.[10]

From a premise of deliberate intent and cooperation, the focus then becomes the mechanisms and techniques through which this can be secured. As one of the defining features of formal organization is that they are purposeful, oriented to the pursuit of relatively specific goals (as quasi–self-interested utility maximizing individuals), goals are presumed to be specific, clearly defined, and explicit. Organizations must be centrally coordinated for the pursuit of these, and there must be unambiguous criteria for selecting among activities to achieve predetermined goals with maximum efficiency. Organizations become presented as a single, unified rational decision-maker, purposive and intentional, with clear goals and identifiable preferences for outcomes.

Organizational goals are preference or utility functions that direct organizational behaviour. Not only do goals reflect rational interests, but they also support rational behaviour in organizations, guiding not only choice between alternative activities but also determining the design of organizational structures. Organizations are designed specifically to achieve goals, ends, or objectives, and this depends on structuring the organization as rationally as possible. Organized actions lead to predetermined goals. Certain structures and processes result in certain outcomes or performances. Maximizing these arrangements, specifying their means–end relationships, ensures that organizational efficiency is maximized. It is for this reason that Gouldner (1959) identifies a 'rational' model of organizations as implying a mechanical model of organizations, with its various elements or components separately modifiable or manipulable.

The assumption is also made that good decisions require clear goals and that improving the clarity of goals, making them unambiguous, improves the quality of decision-making. Clearly defined, specific goals provide the unambiguous criteria for selection among alternative means (strategies, structures, policies, positions, roles, etc.) to achieve specific goals. From these, rational decision-making entails an analysis of the alternatives and the choice of the most efficient option.

The organization is a calculated, rational instrument: its goals fixed and stable; its formal structure the translation of these goal into means, that is, activities; and its integration based on hierarchical authority. It informs the classical model of organizations associated with works of Taylor (1911), Fayol (1949), and Gulick and Urwick (1937). It also positions the 'disarray' of the informal.

The conception of the organization as a rational actor has much broader purport than as a historical quirk or anomaly. As Allmendinger and Hackman (1996) note, it underpins the individual/environment model of organization studies. Donaldson (1987) identifies the literature on 'organizational fit' as a continuation of rational decision-making. Adaptation assumes managerial rationality. Strategic choice and structural contingency emphasize managerial identification and adaptation to environmental constraints (Aldrich 1972; Aldrich and Pfeffer 1976; Child 1972). Equally, resource-dependency models, the competitive struggle for scarce resources to put to the service of its predetermined ends, continues this theme (Mindlin and Aldrich 1975).

The formal organization is the materialization of an instrumental rationality. Or not. For just as the model of rational action informs perceptions of organizational functioning, it also generates its antithesis, and opinion divides as to its relevance and accuracy. One strand of criticism points to organizational 'reality' in order to dismiss it. As Zey (1998: 38) notes, 'structural elements are often loosely linked to each other and to activities, rules are often violated, decisions are often unimplemented, or if implemented, have uncertain consequences, technologies are of problematic efficiency, and evaluation systems are subverted or rendered so vague as to provide little co-ordination.' Research highlights: multiple goals; diverse and ambiguous linkages between means and ends; different groups having different preferences and beliefs about appropriate choices and goals prompting negotiation and bargaining; the collective nature of an enterprise; ambiguous, unclear, and inconsistent preferences; the choice of means influencing ends; coalitions of agents with overlapping and distinct aims; ambiguous information; conflict over goals; decision situations that resemble organized anarchies; the garbage can processes of organizational choice; decisions remaining unimplemented; and solutions in search of problems (Cohen et al. 1972; Cyert and March 1963).

Bounded rationality

A second strand of criticism attempts to modify the concepts of rationality to accommodate elements of 'organizational reality'. Again, there is ambiguity as to whether this modification constitutes a theoretical abstraction or a realistic presentation of organizational behaviour.

Simon (1959) identified decision-making as the fundamental activity of organizations, proposing the decision premise as the unit of analysis for study. The modification that Simon made to rationality was that behaviour was intendedly rational. Rationality, as the pursuit of a specific goal or objective through both the decision and the action processes, is undertaken within constraints, including the bounds of information, the limitations on the processing of information, computational capability, problem solving, and the organization and utilization of memory. For Simon (1957: 79):

It is impossible for the behaviours of a single, isolated individual to reach a high degree of rationality. The number of alternatives he must explore is too great, the information he would need to evaluate them so vast that even an approximation to objective rationality is hard to conceive. Individual choice takes place in an environment of 'givens'—premises that are accepted by the subject as bases for his choice; and behaviour is adaptive only within the limits set by these 'givens'

Bounded rationality substitutes an omniscient rationality, recognizing the informational and computational limits of the latter. Intendedly, rational behaviour is behaviour within constraints.[11] By 'grounding' decision-making, Simon moves through the sequential properties of rationality detailing the ways in which people approximate classical rationality by moving iteratively through a search process. Rather than maximizing, what is engaged in is satisficing, decision procedures that are sensible given the constraints. 'Rationality in real life must involve something simpler than maximization of utility or profit' (Simon 1959/2002: 172). Subjects do not behave in a way predicted by straightforward application of utility theory.

The resemblance of decision-making to logical reasoning is only metaphorical because there are quite different rules in the two cases to determine what constitutes 'valid' premises and admissible modes of influence. The metaphor is useful because it leads us to take the individual decision premise as the unit of description, hence to deal with the whole interwoven fabric of influences that bear on a single decision but without being bound by the assumptions of rationality that limit the classical theory of choice.

(Simon 1959/2002: 183)

By viewing differences between perfect rationality and bounded rationality as the explicable consequences of constraints (March 1978/2002: 197), Simon thus obscures a distinction between normative and behavioural theories of choice. Broadening the definition of rationality also distinguishes between the objective environment in which the economic actor 'really' lives and that which he or she perceives and to which he or she responds (Simon 1959/2002: 169–70).

Simon's writings on bounded rationality have been understood to mean the computational and informational limitations on rationality. This is to limit its significance for the study of organizations. As Scott (1981) notes, bounded rationality is a concept that attempts to integrate both goal specificity (an economic concept) and formalization (a bureaucratic concept) within one concept (bounded rationality).

Viewing an organization as a system of decision-making individuals (Pugh 1966: 180) requires that the participants' decisions are restricted to the ends to which activity is directed. Organizational goals can be imprecise mechanisms for guiding actual behaviour. Organizations therefore need to simplify decision-making. A means–ends chain of hierarchically structured goals is perceived by Simon as a mechanism for translating broad organizational goals to lower levels in a hierarchy, thus: '(1) starting with the general goal to be achieved, (2) discovering a set of means, very generally specific, for accomplishing this goal, (3) taking each of the means, in turn, as a new subgoal and discovering a set of more detailed means for achieving it etc.' Each level acts as both a goal (for levels below) and a means (for levels above) to produce a hierarchy of goals. As Scott (1981: 74) explains:

Viewed from the bottom up, the rationality of individual decisions and activities can be evaluated only as they relate to higher-order decisions; each subgoal can be assessed only in terms of its consistency or congruency with more general goals. Viewed from the top down, the factoring of general purposes into specific subgoals which can then be assigned to organizational subunits (individuals or departments) enhances the possibility of rational behaviour by specifying value premises and hence simplifying the required decision at every level. From this perspective then, an organization's hierarchy can be viewed as a congealed set of means-ends chains promoting consistency of decisions and activities throughout the organization.

'Structure' is the means whereby organizations can achieve bounded rationality, for the rationality of structure is the means of ensuring the rationality of individuals. 'The organization permits problem subdivision, simplifies choices, channels information and restricts alternatives' (Scott 1981: 145). Individuals behave rationally because structure limits choice and circumscribes behaviour. Control requires a rational structure of restricted discretion and centralized decision-making. Other mechanisms that function this way include sequential attention to problems, the use of existing repertoires, stable expectations, etc. Control serves rationality; rationality serves control.

It is in this sense that Simon's concept of bounded rationality has more purchase for organization theory. It also owes more to the antecedents of the concept as originally formulated by Barnard, for whom bounded rationality refers to zones or 'arenas of relevance'. Barnard originally refers to those issues to which employees unquestioningly comply as the 'zone of indifference' (1938: 168–9). This later becomes in Simon's work the 'zone of acceptance' (1957: 12), and a potential avenue of exploration is lost as bounded rationality becomes synonymous with information processing and cognitive limitations (Douglas 1995; Scott 1981).[12] Focus then shifts to time costs involved in seeking information; the lack of access to full information; and stopping searches for alternatives when satisfactory alternatives are reached.

Behaviour is seen as intendedly rational, but only limitedly so (Simon 1957: xxiv). It introduces 'good enough' solutions that are the best that are attainable. Rationality is reaching a defensibly good position or decision by a defensible, rather than optimal, process. In this sense, it is a pragmatic and procedural norm. Organizations are the embodiment of a pragmatic, bounded rationality (March and Simon 1958; Simon 1959). Further modifications introduce the distinction between substantive rationality, the degree to which appropriate choices are made, and procedural rationality, which, because of the constraints of decision-making, the changes in membership of those involved, the complexity of the situation, etc., concentrates on the procedural aspect of decision-making.

Decision-making

'Decisions' and the impact of bounded rationality as computational and informational limitations have become something of a focus for those studying organizations. Reliance on salient information easily retrievable from memory; stereotypes and anchoring; judgements based on initial decisions; the personal assessment of risk; problems handled as they arise; sequential attention; the incompleteness of knowledge; the difficulties of anticipation; the role of memory and habit; the relevance of certain stimuli; issues of problem framing; problems of prediction and understanding uncertainty are all recognized as contributing to a bounded rationality (Zey 1998). Another work emphasizes the importance of decisions associated with a course of action rather than an isolated choice (Staw 1981).[13]

A later work by Brunsson (1985) differentiates between what he terms decision rationality and action rationality, identifying the cognitive, motivational, and committal aspects of decisions and illustrating how each informs behaviour. He argues that organizational decision-making tends to be irrational, and rational decision-making is a poor basis for action. Searching for alternatives, estimating consequences, and evaluating alternatives are likely to lead to uncertainty, inconsistency, and conflict, and thus reduce motivation and commitment. In effective decisions, few alternatives are analysed; only the positive consequences of actions are considered. Objectives are not formulated in advance.[14]

Decision-making is to be distinguished from decision theory and its variations, where the expected utility of an action can be ascertained by calculating probability of action and its utility. 'Rational choice involves two kinds of guesses . . . guesses about future consequences of current actions and guesses about future preferences for those consequences' (March 1978/2002: 196). Decisions are usually classed according to whether they are decisions of certainty, risk, or uncertainty. Decision theory under certainty refers to an optimal choice where there are a set of alternative actions, the certainty of outcomes of which are known, and the individual has ranked the outcomes of actions according to preference. In decision-making under risk, there is knowledge of the range of actions but their outcomes are only likely or probable. In decision-making under uncertainty, knowledge of the range of options is uncertain, that is, their probability is unknown, and therefore outcomes are unknown.

Simon (1990: 196) criticizes subjective expected utility theory for being 'a highly simplified representation of a tiny fragment of the real-world situation' depending 'much more on the adequacy of the approximating assumptions and data supporting them'. Certainly, Kahneman and Tversky (1990) illustrate how as a descriptive model of choice, utility theory is undermined by people's attitude to risk and chance (the certainty effect); whether issues are posed in term of gains or losses (the reflection effect); and whether choice is presented as being made up of a series of composite choices and whether these are presented as a whole or sequentially (the isolation effect). Their modification of decision-making under risk, prospect theory, distinguishes between the editing and evaluation phases of choice to capture these influences. The heuristics that people use to guide them in assessing probabilities in decision-making, especially the role of framing in decision choices, may lead to serious errors in assessment of predicting likely outcomes, and result in actions that are less than rational (Tversky and Kahneman 1974, 1990). Interestingly, advocates of decision theory always qualify its relevance in terms of whether situations are correctly specified and procedures correctly applied (e.g. March 1978).

While decision-making under conditions of uncertainty and ambiguity focuses on individual decision-making and the optimization of individual utilities, game theory, and the stream of research it fosters, focuses on competitive decision-making. Competitive decision situations are situations where one's actions are dependent on the actions of others, of which the Prisoner's Dilemma is the most well known (see Chapter 9). This requires that individuals identify all possible strategies available for both themselves and others. Game theory thus explicitly considers the actions of another. In this sense, it extends rational action to social action in that in Weber's (1978: 4) sense, action is social only insofar as it takes into account the behaviour of others and is 'thereby oriented in its course'.

BOX 2.1. THE PRISONERS DILEMMA: GAMING AND THE CRIMINAL JUSTICE SYSTEM

One of the major institutions of society is founded on a model of rational decision-making. It has as one of the major planks a belief in the efficacy of a rational cost–benefit calculus. 'Deterrence is at the heart of an effective criminal justice system' (McInnes 2004: 7). The criminal justice policy of deterrence presumes that an individual will refrain from crime if he or she is aware that he or she will be caught and punished. A policy of deterrent sentencing policy (the costs of crime outweigh its benefits) is also based on the same principle. And indeed, calculation permeates the criminal justice system at several stages. It is most evident in approaches by the accused to decisions as to whether to plead guilty or go to trial and rely on possible adjournments in court proceedings in the hope of getting off:

If you are customer focused,* to use the language, the criminal justice system should be run for the benefit of the victims of crime. It's not in anybody's interest that a case should wait for 2 years. By that time evidence is stale and memories have faded. It's in everybody's interest, except the accused. It's in the accused interests for it to go on as long as possible.

(Policy)

Thus is gaming introduced:

The ones that know the system, that have been through the system, really know how to play it. The minor cases, road traffic, are usually unproblematic. They usually play by the rules. Others, for example, drug addicts, they have been through the system before. They know the rules. They know how the game works. There is strong anecdotal information that if the accused turns up, and sees that all the witnesses are there, they plead straight away. (Police)

The easiest thing is if the client pleads not guilty and hopes that the witnesses won't turn up. Or that if he turns up on a day when the PFS has 40 cases, then he will agree to a lighter plea in return for not considering more serious offices. (PF)

'Solutions' focus on rebalancing the calculations that must be made:

There may be cases where there was a degree of hanging on, hoping that the Crown [PFS] does not get witnesses. Although now there is sentence discounting [sentence reduction based on early pleas], solicitors have to make their clients aware. When a Sheriff court can give a sentence of years that's a lot out of a young person's life. (Defence)

*When asked about the use of this term for the accused and the plaintiff, the response was: 'they are all customers now'.

The new rationality

A second strand of thought that informs an economic rationality comes from the discipline of economics. It should be noted that as a foundation concept, rationality comes late to economics (Zouboulakis 2001). Political economy originally signified the production and distribution of wealth. Economic rationality in the form of neoclassical economics only gains greater purchase following the marginalist revolution in economics and its focus on scarcity, competition, and diminishing marginal utility (Parsons 2003).

For Weber, 'rationality' is introduced into an economy with the need for a common calculus or 'coinage' for comparisons between disparate entities. The most rational comparator, for Weber, is money, whose value lies in its capacity to enhance calculation and exchange. With its use comes the enhanced formal rationality of economic production and exchange. Economic rationality is thus the degree of formal rationality of economic production organized principally using monetary exchange and rational accounting procedures (Weber 1978: 85)[15].

A large element of the discipline of economics has since evolved to focus on homo economicus. As Toulmin (1990: 125) notes, 'economics did not explore the causal tangle of motives or feelings behind real human choices.' This is left to economic history, economic sociology, and other branches of the discipline and social science more generally. For Coleman (1990), the basis of neoclassical economic theory is that of the rational actor for whom different actions or goods have a particular utility, prompting him or her to choose the action that will maximize utility. For Granovetter (1985), classical and neoclassical economics borrows from the utilitarian tradition involving individuals who choose those options that seem most likely to secure their largest net advantage. Part of this assumption is of 'rational, self-interested behaviour minimally affected by social relations. The model is the pursuit of self-interest by rational more or less atomized individuals' (Granovetter 1985/2002: 363).

Whether real or ideal, normative or descriptive, 'the self interested utility maximizer becomes the metric against which rationality is judged' (Archer and Tritter 2000a: 34). Classical economic thought assumes that rationality obtains when self-interest and the maximization of economic return is served. However, from the initial formulation of self-interest, as the driving force motivating behaviour of firms and consumers, is derived the extrapolation that there will be a collective benefit from individuals following their rational interests, the archetype of which is Smith's rational hand. As Wagner (2000: 67) notes, 'rational choice has "morphed" into utility, profit and wealth maximization.'

An earlier concept that informed economics is transaction. Transaction as a basic unit of analysis was originally advanced by Commons (1934), its premise being that in every relationship there is a transaction associated with costs related to the negotiation of the contract. Its later manifestation in Williamson gives rise to transaction costs economics and the analysis of the rise of hierarchy through market failures. This takes from Coase (1937) the idea of the inefficiencies of the market in conducting certain transactions, especially where there is asset-specific investment and incomplete contracts. The frequency of interaction; the uncertainty inherent in the transaction, in terms of the degree of monitoring and examination required; and whether the investments are transaction specific increase transaction costs, as does the problem of small numbers bargaining, uncertainty, bounded rationality, and opportunism (Williamson 1975). The inability to capture these factors in a market transaction or an *ex ante* incentive alignment prompts alternative forms of organizing, principally hierarchy, but also governance structures, ownership, vertical integration, forward integration, relational contracting enforced by trust and reputation, and operational design (Perrow 1979).

For economists, organizations are economically rational because they reduce the cost of transactions in circumstances where the market fails. (Williamson uses the term organization to refer to social arrangements where transactions take place, rather than confining it to hierarchies.) Economic exchange under hierarchical structures permits auditing, surveillance, and incentive structures to minimize opportunistic behaviour and stabilize interdependent team performance where individual contribution is hard to determine. Superior information processing and reduced transactional costs make organizations more economically rational.

The behavioural assumptions of transaction cost economics are designed to 'add realism' and to distinguish it from neoclassical economics. There is the recognition that agents are subject to bounded rationality. 'From the hyperrationality of economic man, organization man is endowed with less powerful analytic and data processing apparatus . . . but remains intendedly rational' (Williamson 1981/2002: 222). However, in this presentation, Williamson presents rational man as engaged in opportunism, 'self-interest with guile'. The calculating self is an enterprising self. 'Economic man is thus a more subtle and devious creature than the usual self-interest seeking assumption reveals' (Granovetter 1985/2002: 368).

A variation on the transactions framework is the Principal Agency problem. Premised on the separation of ownership and control that characterizes contemporary capitalism and asymmetrical access to knowledge and information that results, control devolves to the agent who acts purportedly in the interests of the principal. The problem for principals (shareholders) is to get agents to behave in a way that is consistent with the principals' interests. Again, the model of rational actors seeking to maximize their own self-interest or utility still predominates, as does the assumption of inherently opportunistic individual behaviour. Control or governance structures and economic incentives and disincentives are designed to align the agent with principals' interests. In the absence of the external controls of mergers, acquisitions, and divestitures to regulate behaviour, a series of internal controls of financial incentive programmes, performance evaluations, and audits are required to ensure that the divergent interests of the agent do not lead to losses for the principal.

In Jensen and Meckling's (1976) analysis of Principal Agency relationships, they propose to view the organization as a 'nexus of contracts'. They are viewed as a series of contracts in which exchanges are governed by competitive self-interest, with the maximization of individual self-interest. Given this, Jensen and Meckling (1976) and agency theorists generally stress the importance of performance contingent contracts. As monitoring contracts is costly, there is a need to write and monitor contracts to minimize violations (Perrow 1986).

The broader implications of this are to see social interaction as a form of economic transaction. The concept of transactions breaks loose from its moorings in economic exchange to become a metaphor for how one might characterize all social engagement, that is, one might depict *all* transactions in society as conforming to this model or, rather, all forms of social engagement are transactions, which may then be understood and structured as such.

Thus, we have the template for organizational structuring and for understanding organizational behaviour. Behaviour is goal directed with means adopted according to desired ends. Choice arises from preferences and expectations. Individuals are utility maximizing, engaging in a rational choice among alternative outcomes, their relative costs and benefits weighed. It is a model that informs expectancy theory (to the extent that certain types of behaviour will lead to instrumentally valued outcomes; actors will change their behaviour accordingly); goal theory (people undertake actions to achieve goals, e.g. goal setting, MBO, the pathgoal theory of leadership); and needs theory (behaviour is purposeful to fulfil needs, even though needs are not necessarily 'rational') (Pfeffer 1982). It is the foundation of the incentive system, the design and evaluation of which are the pre-eminent mechanisms for organizational control. Homo economicus, given the right incentive, can be engineered as an instrument (Mayntz 1964/2002: 90).

In addition to the standard criticisms that humans do not have clear utilities to maximize; nor much information; and do not understand cause and effect relations sufficiently, Perrow (1986) argues that the setting in which interactions or contracts occur is the most important factor in explaining behaviour. Where interactions are minimized, rewards are individualized, interdependence is minimal, and hierarchies are elongated, self-interested behaviour is promoted. Frequent and durable interactions based on cooperation among

---

BOX 2.2. THE PUBLIC SERVICE AGREEMENT FRAMEWORK: A 'NEXUS
OF CONTRACTS'?

The Public Service Agreement Framework (PSAF), introduced in 1998 by the UK
Government, outlines the rationale for targets. The PSAF represents 'an agreement
between the Government and the public...for the first time [it] set measurable
targets for the full range of the government's objectives for public expenditure
programmes' (PSAF: 2). The public is cast in quasi-principal terms, to which the
agent, the government, reports. As a contract with the public, PSAs explain 'what
departments plan to deliver in return for significant extra investment' (PSAF: 3). The
framework sets up a series of cascading relationships: between government and
departments; departments and agencies; and agencies and direct service providers.
Principal Agency relationships organize much of the CJS structure, governing relationships between the government and the prison service, court service, legal aid,
local authorities, criminal justice social work, and voluntary agencies. Targets are
ubiquitous. All organizations have their own performance measures with audits
monitoring agency or service performance.

The aim of targets is sixfold: 'to provide a clear public statement of what the
government is trying to achieve; a clear sense of direction to delivery agents; a focus
on delivering results from improved services; a basis for monitoring what is working
and what isn't; to ensure that good practice is spread and rewarded and poor
performance is tackled; accountability to the public through regular reports' (PSAF
2003: 3). They are seen as a means of ensuring consistent and efficient decision-
making through structured decision-making. They are Simon's cascading means–end
chains:

Targets are a way of making sure that people will focus their energy on the things which
you think generally are the priorities, otherwise everyone has got their own view about
what they should be doing   (PASC 2002–3: 8)

The Scottish Prison Service now has purchaser/provider performance contracts with each
establishment [prison]. The client is the Prison Service: 'this is what we bought and this
is what we are getting'. And the provider is the governor. The governor is essentially a
contract manager. There is a job contract with performance measures and performance
targets. If there is a problem with performance, this is handled through performance
appraisals or a performance review. There wouldn't be much change between a prison
warders job now and before, except that now he would know that what he did was tied
to a monetary outcome. Measures essentially ensure that what gets measured gets done.
Performance targets are designed to ensure that you don't get mavericks. If it ain't in
the performance measure, it ain't getting done. It has stopped a focus on what is not in
the performance measures. For example if a new circular comes round [about changing
practices], but it is not in the performance measures then it won't get done. The argument
is used that it's not in the performance contract. This had led to arguments that things
have become too bureaucratic. It doesn't stop innovation. It's just that the other things
have to get done on budget and then you can think about innovation.   (Prison Services)

---

individuals promote other-regarding behaviour. For Perrow (1986), authority and power relations in organizations set the conditions of self-interested
behaviour, and the rational agent needing an incentive to do anything becomes
a self-fulfilling prophecy. The social determinants of self-regarding behaviour
illustrate its non-essential nature.

BOX 2.3. INCENTIVIZING BEHAVIOUR

In addition to various government agencies, the CJS is dependent on independent defence agents, the 700 solicitors' firms paid through legal aid who represent the accused in approximately 80,000 summary criminal cases a year. Solicitors are paid a set fee for handling a case in the Sheriff Court. They do not get paid if the client has already pled guilty.

Two things that have to balance is the efficiency and effectiveness of justice and the rights of the accused. The issue is how do you influence incentives, how do you manage incentives to create the highest probability of certain behaviour? If these are not set up properly then they can stop the system working. The system has recently moved to a fixed payment system. It has made things more efficient. The solicitor is not paid separately for precognitions [taking statements from witnesses]. Previously he was paid separately for this. With the fixed payment regime, now this comes out of his fee. This affects behaviour. The whole business is one of incentive management. The question of what causes behaviours? Is the system operating in the way we want it to? Do we need to change behaviour, to change the way the system works?   (Policy)

In the case of solemn or High Court cases, the nature of incentives becomes a little more complicated:

Basically we want to get to a situation where people plead and then Counsel go on to the next case. Basically we want Counsel to do several things: to streamline and front load issues, to read the documentation and, where it is warranted, to proceed. There is an issue of how we pay Counsel. The issue of fees is central. We want them [Counsel] to take on cases and get them to plead. We don't want them in court to make money. Fees are paid for preparation, for documentation, consultation, notes, and the day in court. There is a basic fee. If it goes to trial there is another fee. If there is 500–600 page documentation then it is so much a page. Once beyond that, then there is a long trial fee. Fees can be positive disincentives. Some Counsel keep cases for a long time. We want them to look at a case and deal with it.   (Policy)

Suggested reforms are for fees to be 'front loaded', for Counsel to be paid for pretrial meetings where cases are discussed, and perhaps settled, prior to their going to court, rather than being reliant on court fees. However:

On the issue of pretrial meetings, you are really expected to be prepared enough to settle a case. But there is a lot of work in that. To settle a case you must be as familiar as to run a case. You have to be paid commensurably to do the work involved to achieve settlement. You need to be on top of the case. Its a lot more work than a standard 'just agreeing things'. But if you are going to front load in that way, and achieve that in some cases, then you need payment for that.   (Advocate)

Mayntz (1964) sees the 'nexus of contracts' presentation of organizations as the renaissance of the classical model influenced by mathematical games and decision theory. He terms it the 'new rational model'. While the technologies used to model these arrangements might have changed, the model of organization posited does not differ radically from Simon's suggested structure of hierarchically ordered 'means–ends chains' of cascading goals and objectives, allied to performance measurement and monitoring schemes.

Conclusions

This chapter has given a brief indication of some of the dimensions of an instrumental, economic rationality, indicating some of the facets of its development and assumptions. Some of its elements are relatively uncontentious: the assumption, for example, that human action is purposive and intentional, aimed at the achievement of ends or goals, or that the weighing of cost and benefits among different alternatives can indicate efficient or productive courses of action.

Others are more so. The privileging of an instrumental, economic form of reasoning to the exclusion of others, its presentation as a universal characterization of human action, constructs a very individualist, contractarian interpretation of the social world. An instrumental, economic rationality

---

BOX 2.4. ECONOMIC AWARENESS

An economic rationality stresses a cost–benefit calculus. This abstraction, however, does not directly address practical cost–benefit concerns which may be better termed economic awareness (Lave 1986). It is the latter that informs the recognition of, and acceptance of, the need for changes:

We do evaluations on court abstractions [appearances of police officers to give evidence in court]. We now have a court standby process where the police have half an hour's notice to attend. It was estimated that £1m was lost in waiting at court. We also found out that only 11% of those called to court ended up giving evidence. This has a massive impact on resources   (Police)

The police have no interest and no remit post-sentencing. But there are issues if the accused has failed to continue to pay a fine. So the police turn into a type of debt collection [agency]. The Court argues that it has no facility, no authority to go. But it could always appoint a third agency. It would save us over £1m a year   (Police)

There are constraints, however, as to where an economic calculation may be applied:

The cost is £1600–1700 per probation and community service order (CSOs), as compared with £31,000 for prison [estimated annual cost of imprisonment per person]. And CSOs have a success rate of 47% which compares favourably with other forms of disposal. Prison has a success rate of 45%. The [government] has only just taken on board these arguments about cost.   (Social Work)

It is very easy to abuse simplistic measures and because of this it is easy to justify not having measures. But if you have no measures, you don't know what you are doing with the resources that you have got. What the outcome is for the resources that have been put in. But what is society getting for spending this money on prosecuting this type of cases? A lawyer may answer that 'this is not my concern'. But they are getting a lot of resources that they need to justify. How effective is this if you don't know how much things are costing and the resources that are consumed in dealing with aspects of work?   (Sheriff)

The aggregate impact of targets from different sources which converge on particular organizations and individuals does not appear to be monitored. Neither, it appears, is the opportunity cost of setting and monitoring targets.   (PASC 2002–3: 31)

---

engenders a highly attenuated form of rational being. Homo economicus is atomized; engaged in the narrow utilitarian pursuit of self-interest; stripped of antecedent associations, history, and attachments; a rational being sovereign over his or her own choices whose preferences arise mysteriously. The individual is the disembedded, atomistic, individual sovereign artificer, Hollis's Adam (Hollis 1987).

As a model, it reflects very specific socio-historical configurations. Archer and Tritter (2000*b*) describe rational choice theory in particular as being the grand theory of high modernity, based as it is on the postulate of autonomy, the enactment of will and mastery (Wagner 2000). It also absorbs much of the ambiguity that surrounds the motifs of individuality, rationality, and freedom that underwrite it (Lukes 1973).

It is a mode of rationality that influences the cast of organizational analysis and its image of the organization as an extant object or tool for the securing of collective purpose. The same rationality informs its assumed antithesis, the political model of organizations, the contrast drawn between rational and political models of organization notwithstanding (Pettigrew 1973). The idea of the political model is of actors motivated by self-interest as they strive to acquire, manage, and control resources, be this finance, power, etc., and the political process as based on attainment of valued goals, guided by a rational calculus. This is an instrumental, economic rationality. Equally, some Marxist analyses, although identifying the centrality of economic domination and relations of production, argue that organization structures are rational solutions to the problem of control over labour. As Zysman (1994: 44) notes, 'the underlying logic of rational choice and institutional economists is similar to Marxists. Both define groups by their economic interests, ask what crucial economic relations are and how groups stand to gain advantage. Rational choice theorists and neo-marxists write stories whose core narrative is very similar.'

A calculated, instrumental economic rationality is forced to view everything, and everyone, as a means to an end. To treat someone as a means 'is to seek to make him or her an instrument of my purpose' (MacIntyre 1981: 23). Within such a position, moral judgements are the expression of preference, an expressive assertion. 'Reason is calculative, it can assess truths of fact and mathematical relations but nothing more. In the realm of practice therefore it can speak only of means. About ends it must be silent' (MacIntyre 1981: 50). *De gustibus non est disputandum.*

3 Bureaucratic rationality

As with an economic rationality, bureaucracy commonly features in the literature on organization studies. Not so the rationality that underpins it. Emphasis is on an organization or structure and yet it is the substratum of bureaucratic rationality that offers greater insights into organizing. That the focus remains bureaucracy is testament to the early, and largely inaccurate, translation of Weber's work and its influence on organization studies. Influenced by Parsons (1959), organization theory's incorporation of Weber is based on two misconceptions: a selective and a historical interpretation of bureaucracy; and a misinterpretation of the concept of the ideal type. Thus read, Weber's reception into English laid the foundations of an abstract organization theory; the commonly assumed view of bureaucracy as synonymous with organization; and a prescriptive theory of bureaucratic organizations as superior to other formal organizations. Subsequent work augments the first, sought to disprove the last, while remaining ambivalent over the second. Each misconception reflects a failure to adequately address the concept of rationality that underpins bureaucracy. This chapter considers the early work on bureaucracy before examining the foundations of a bureaucratic rationality.

Bureaucracy

Bureaucracy is identified by Weber (1978: 223) as 'the most rational known means of exercising authority over human beings' and as such capable of the 'highest degree of efficiency'. He makes the comparison between the technical superiority of bureaucracy, to that of the machine over non-mechanical modes of production. The choice in organizing administration is between 'bureaucracy' and 'dilettantism'.

The reception of Weber's work by management and organization scholars following the Second World War led to bureaucracy being read alongside texts on the classical model of organizations. Thus read, bureaucracy becomes synonymous with organization, with both description and prescription failing to distinguish the two (Mayntz 1964). Weber was read through Fayol's identification of the division of work, unity of command, and a scalar chain of line authority as principles of management (1949). Barnard's work (1938) specialization and unity of direction, and March and Simon's view (1958) that bureaucracy overcame the 'computational' limits of individual decision-making through the division of labour, reinforced this reasoning. Organizational borrowing from Weberian descriptions of bureaucracy, however, is quite selective. Hierarchical authority and task specialization are adopted wholescale as properties common to all organizations. Less so, rules defining activities and rule-governed behaviour, official spheres of competence, bureaucratic authority, and recruitment by contract based on skill. Vocational security, incremental salaries, and tenure are rarely adopted as essential components of organization. The latter, seen as characterizing mainly public administration, are in the main castigated as promoting inefficiencies and cautioned to be avoided.

Nor is it just classical texts that identify bureaucracy with organization. More recently, Di Maggio and Powell (1991: 63) state that bureaucracy is 'the rational spirit's organizational manifestation'. By far, the most serious consequence of the association of bureaucracy with organization is that bureaucracy is taken to be a mode of organization regardless of function, applicable, for example, to state, political parties, church, sect, and firm (Clegg 1994). In this way, the common properties of organizations, irrespective of function, may be highlighted. Any organization can be compared to any other. The substantive qualities of specific organizations become of less conceptual importance. This abstraction is an element of organization theory that continues apace. As Meyer (1994: 54) notes, 'one can discuss proper organization without much mentioning the actual substantive activities that organizations will do. An older world in which schools were managed by educators, hospitals by doctors, railroads by railroad men [sic] now receded into quaintness. All these things are now seen as organizations.'

From the understanding that bureaucratic organization is the embodiment of rationality, offering a 'machine' model of organizations, bureaucracy is transformed into a prescriptive model, identified with a particular form of organizational structure, and deemed to be more efficient than other forms of organization. Such descriptions prompt a stream of research into the administrative functioning of bureaucracy and the consequences of a bureaucratic organization for the achievement of organizational goals. Organization theory focuses on bureaucracies rather than a bureaucratic rationality.

Initial research questions bureaucracy as a monolithic representation of organization. It confronts but does not resolve the confusion as to whether bureaucracy should be treated as a structural type or as a variable, that is, whether something is or is not a bureaucracy or whether it is more or less bureaucratic. The Aston studies, although saturated with a Weberian vocabulary, cloud the issue with their stated aim of an 'empirically based multidimensional analysis of structural variables of organization based on conceptually distinct elements that go into Weber's formulation of bureaucracy' (Pugh et al. 1963, 1968/2002: 231). They identify different types of bureaucracies based on 'profile characteristics' of organizations, relating to the structuring of activities, concentration of authority, and line control of workflow[1]; identifying structure, specialization, standardization (of rules and procedures), formalization (of employment practices), centralization, and configuration (spans of control) as dimensions of bureaucracy.[2] They conclude that bureaucracy is not a unitary phenomena, but that organizations may be bureaucratic in a number of ways. Since then, Mintzberg has differentiated between machine and professional bureaucracies based on degrees of decentralization.[3] Current concerns, however, are with trying to identify the post-bureaucratic organization,[4] or 'soft bureaucracies' (Courpasson 2000).

A second stream of research considers whether bureaucracies are 'strictly rational and efficient'. Blau's study (1955) of an employment agency illustrates how central procedures for finding jobs are more productive when modified locally. Only where employees identify with the purposes of the organization as a whole and adapt their behaviour according to changing circumstances is there 'efficient' administration. Informal organization and local modifications are important features if bureaucratic organizations are to work. For Crozier (1964), the impersonality of rules and the centralization of decision-making meant there is an inability to learn from errors. The development of impersonal rules, the centralization of decisions, strata isolation (the isolation of specialized groups within bureaucracies), and group pressure on the individual reinforce a 'vicious circle'. The 'possibility of play' is opened up by the impossibility of impersonal rules being able to prescribe behaviour or delimit individuals in organizations. Centralization results in those being called upon to make decisions never having the first-hand knowledge of the problems they are called upon to solve; and those who know the problems not having the power to adjust procedures, innovate, or experiment. Nor are those who made decisions confronted by those affected by decisions. Crozier concludes that bureaucratic systems of organization are characterized by relatively stable 'vicious circles' arising from centralization and impersonality, with any variations being met by a greater elaboration of rules and further centralization. 'Dysfunctions' result in the reinforcement of position, rather than allowing greater autonomy, thus further reinforcing rigidity. His conclusion is that bureaucracies do not equate with rational efficiency. 'The advantages of rules transformed too readily into inflexibility and red tape; impersonality into indifference and insensitivity; hierarchy into a lack of responsibility and initiative; and officialdom into officialese' (Crozier 1964: 180).

Further studies question hierarchical authority and its failure to distinguish between hierarchical and technical competence and expertise. Identifying the conflict between professional and bureaucratic authority, Gouldner (1955) differentiates between authority based on incumbency in a legally defined office (obeying an order because it is an order) and authority based on technical competence (obeying an order because it is the best way of realizing a goal). Other studies focus on the 'environment' of bureaucratic structures, contrasting mechanistic with organic structures and their appropriateness for dealing with rapidly changing environments (Lawrence and Lorsch 1967; Pennings 1992).

More recent studies focus on whether 'bureaucratic' organizations operate on the principles of bureaucracy. Jackall's study (1988) of large-scale bureaucracies finds personalized authority; fealty, patronage, and vassalage; and the importance of social networks and interlocking commitment (allies, power cliques, protégés, etc.) all thriving. Heckscher's study (1995) of why people in bureaucracies obey again finds the 'non rational' predominating. In addition to personal dependence and paternalism offering protection and security, corporate loyalty and loyalty to a community of purpose or collective mission, an ethos, are important principles of behaviour. Loyalty is identified as a latent social identity in a rational bureaucracy (Gouldner 1955).

Bureaucracy and rationality

As Albrow (1970: 89) notes, there is a major distinction between bureaucracy as a 'rational organization' and an organization 'where men [sic] apply the criteria of rationality to their action'. Weber's understanding of rationality, however, is quite specific. Bureaucracy offers a *technical* superiority over other forms of organization. From 'a purely technical point of view', bureaucracy is 'formally' the most rational or technically superior form of organization (Weber 1978: 223). 'It is superior to any other form in precision, in stability, in stringency of its discipline and in its reliability.' A technical or formal rationality, however, does not equate with operational efficiency.[5] 'Ideally rational' cannot be equated with perfectly efficient as Weber's early translators assumed (Weiss 1983), just as a bureaucracy cannot be assumed to be an 'ideal type' organization.

Bureaucracy's superiority lies in its formality, and with this, its guarantee of calculability. Formality refers to calculability. Just as the formal rationality of economic action is the extent of quantitative calculation or accounting that is technically possible and applied (with money being the 'most perfect' means of economic calculation, and therefore providing a rational basis of uniform numerical statements), so rational bureaucracy is formally rational because it provides the calculability of means and procedures. Bureaucracy allows administration to be discharged precisely and unambiguously, and in doing so it 'makes possible a particularly high degree of calculability of results for heads of organizations and those acting in relation to it' (Weber 1978: 223). It excludes arbitrariness.

Weber's writing on bureaucracy must be placed in context. His work was not seriously taken up by management scholars and organization theorists until after the Second World War, almost half a century after it was written. Given this, and some of the vagaries of translation (the use of leadership for domination, e.g. Weiss 1983), it is not surprising that Weber's work is removed from his oeuvre and the concerns that sustain it.

The work on bureaucracy is located in a historical analysis of the function of political rule, a theoretical consideration of the nature of domination, and the claims to legitimacy of systems of domination. Weber identifies bureaucracy as formally the most rational mode of rule or domination in contrast to traditional and charismatic domination. The distinction and the superiority of the bureaucratic form resides, historically speaking, in its unique amount of predictability. Whereas traditional rule means independent fiefdoms threatening political independence, and charismatic domination is reliant on unstable followers, 'decision making according to fixed rules makes political domination calculable' (Derlien 1999: 67). Historically and comparatively speaking, neither traditional nor charismatic domination offers the predictability of a bureaucratic form of rule.

Rational legal authority is a continuous organization of official functions bound by rules.[6] Weber's identification of the characteristics of bureaucracy are thus related to propositions on the legitimacy of legal authority[7]; the structuring of legal authority systems[8]; and the characteristics of bureaucratic administration that administers authority based on rational legal principles[9] (Albrow 1970).

It is from this framework that Weber then goes on to consider legal authority and the employment of a bureaucratic administrative staff. Within a specified sphere of competence, an administrative organization has a sphere of obligations to perform. Obedience is owed to a legally established impersonal order based on the formal legality of the commands issued within the scope of the authority of the office. The effectiveness of a bureaucratic administrative system thus depends on the acceptance of intentionally established abstract rules, and the person occupying an office being subject to an impersonal order to which actions are orientated. The fundamental categories of rational legal authority include the principle of hierarchy, whereby each lower unit is under the control and supervision of a higher one; rules regulating conduct; an administrative staff separate from the ownership of the means of production and a separation of the official position from the incumbent; and that administrative acts, decisions, and rules are formulated and recorded in writing. 'The combination of written documents and a continuous organization of official functions constitutes the office' (Weber 1978: 378). Employment of a bureaucratic administrative staff is based on appointment, technical qualification, and contracts. There is a fixed salary, career system, and disciplinary procedure.

That which is to be avoided is arbitrariness as a distinction between bureaucracy and patrimony highlights. In the former, jurisdictional areas are clearly specified; there are regular activities and official duties, rather than these being at the behest of a patrimonial leader. The organization of offices follows the principle of hierarchy, rather than being diffuse and dependent on personal loyalties. An intentionally established system of abstract rules governs official decisions and actions. These are stable, exhaustive, and can be learnt, rather than being vague, ill-defined, and subject to whim. The means of production and administration belong to the office, rather than the ruler's personal household business being mixed with public business. Officials are selected on the basis of technical qualifications, appointed and salaried, rather than on a particularistic basis and operating through beneficiaries. Employment constitutes a career and there is protection from arbitrary dismissal. Incumbency is not at the behest of the pleasure of the leader. Predictability has advantages, as Derlien (1999) notes, both for the ruler and the ruled.[10]

Weber identifies bureaucracy as an irresistible force. Its superiority is secured through the provision of predictability and calculability. Because of this, bureaucracy transforms social action into 'rationally organized action'.[11] It promotes action in accordance with rational rules, while calculability is an important dimension of the 'capacity for purposive manipulation' (Weber 1978: 483). The technical superiority of a formal rationality ensures its success. 'Since bureaucracy has a "rational" character, with rules, means end calculus, and matter of factness predominating, its rise and expansion has everywhere had "revolutionary" results ... The march of bureaucracy accordingly destroyed structures of domination which were not rational in this sense of the term' (Weber 1978: 1002–3). The formality, unambiguity, and precision that provides the superiority of a bureaucratic administration is also a source of disquiet, hence Weber's reference to the iron cage of bureaucracy. Weber is well aware that bureaucratic domination has social consequences. His own writings recognize some of the potential dysfunctions, including its stifling of improvization, its inculcation of a ' "painstaking obedience", a "rational matter-of-factness", and the "personality type of the professional expert" ' (1978: 988). In words that resonate with Bauman's later analysis of the role of bureaucracy in the Holocaust (1989), Weber remarks that 'a rationally ordered officialdom continues to function smoothly after the enemy has occupied the territory; he merely needs to change the top officials ... bureaucracy as a precision instrument ... can put itself at the disposal of quite varied interests' (1978: 899–990). This is because a purely formal rationality is indifferent to substantive ends and values. Indeed greater the degree of formal rationality, the more an area becomes potentially vulnerable to criticism for substantive irrationality. This is the paradox of consequences. Formal rationality implies calculability, predictability, and stability. As Bittner (1965/2002: 79) notes, 'pure bureaucracy obtains when the principle of technical efficiency is given overriding priority above all other considerations.' It does not guarantee substantive rationality.

The response to uncertainty: Domination through knowledge

We can take from Weber's work a dominant theme that gives bureaucracy its rational character and exemplifies a bureaucratic rationality. Bureaucracy allows for the discharge of business according to 'calculable rules' (Weber 1978: 975). Predictability or calculability comes from something being known. To act rationally is to act on the basis of knowledge. A bureaucratic rationality is thus the operation of 'domination through knowledge' (1978: 225). Or more precisely, a bureaucratic rationality is that which allows things to become known: the construction of written documents and files; the identification of spheres of application; the construction and application of rules. It is this substrata that permits the bureaucratic form. It is perhaps for this reason that bureaucracy has been defined as 'the control of ideas over action realized in institutional form' (Swidler 1973: 41).

WRITING THE WORLD

As Weber identifies, one of the essential elements of bureaucracy is the existence of written documents or files. Seemingly insignificant, these taken-for-granted technologies provide the basic tools for domination through knowledge. As Bauman (1993: 8) notes of the ubiquity of forms, records, inventories, catalogues, questionnaires, etc., 'modern practice is not aimed at the conquest of foreign lands but at the filling of blank spots in the *compleat mappa mundi*'. One necessary dimension of their operation is the provision of a standardized vocabulary for encoding or 'writing the world'. This enforces a degree of precision and explicitness. At its very basis, 'writing the world', naming and classifying, is the process of giving the world structure. It depends on the identification and naming of objects and standardized definitions of entities such that they may be recognized as such across disparate times and places (Meyer 1983; Townley 1995). Such standardized definitions, however, do involve an element of loss. The 'success' of writing the world is secured by 'the neatness of divisions between classes; the precision of their definitional boundaries and the unambiguity with which objects may be allocated to classes' (Bauman 1993: 2). 'Writing the world' depends on spatio-temporal robustness that can 'carry' over times and between different locations. Indeed Bauman (1993) defines the power of the modern state as the power to define and make definitions stick.

The provision of standardized understandings of terms ensures organizational and social functioning. For Fayol, in the General Principles of Management, written records and files are crucial: 'an important part of the rationality of the system is that information is written down' (Pugh 1966/2002: 180). Cyert and March (1963) identify the operation of rules, standard operating procedures, task performance rules, records and reports, information handing rules, and plans as some of the many procedures that write the organization into existence. For Simon, bureaucracy is the outcome of bounded rationality 'the limits of human rationality helps us to understand why representation is important and how policy statements imply representations' (1991/2002: 58).

Written documents, however, do not have the stability or finality that may be assumed. Cyert and March (1963) talk of plans acting as a goal, a schedule, a theory, and as a precedent according to the circumstances of their use. Van Maanen and Pentland (1994) note how organizational records are not neutral, factual, or technical documents, but are 'self-conscious' and 'self-interested'. Keeping records mediates the front or public regions of an organization from the back or private regions. 'Documents turn a "this" into a "that" ' (1994: 81). The mediation of information especially through hierarchy can lead to the loss of 'reality' at the top of organizations, as they respond to organizational 'fictions'. As Mintzberg (1994: 54) notes, 'organizations can certainly define on paper what they chose to be goals and strategies. But what have the labels to do with real phenomena and working processes?' It is a fallacy that 'a phenomena has been captured because it is written down, labelled and put in a box, ideally represented by numbers'.

'Writing the world' finds extension in classification. Bauman (1993: 1) writes of classifying: 'it means first to postulate that the world exists of discrete and distinctive entities; then to postulate that each entity has a group of similar or adjacent activities within which it belongs; and then to make the postulated real by linking differential patterns of action to different classes of entities'. He notes, 'Modern mastery is the power to divide, classify and allocate' (Bauman 1993: 15). Its antithesis is ambivalence, the possibility of assigning an object or an event to more than one category. 'Modernity is an era of a particularly bitter and relentless war against ambivalence' (Bauman 1993: 3).

Categories and classifications are an inherent element of organizing work and supervising a division of labour. Assigning things, people, and actions

---

BOX 3.1. WRITING THE WORLD

Performance measures require a basic statement as to what is to be measured and what appropriate definitions are. The endemic problem of performance measures is, however, what is the definition of things and how do you apply the definition? Seemingly simple definitions and classifications can be problematic:

'Injury', for example, is defined in terms of medical treatment. A reportable injury [on staff and inmates] is an injury over 5 stitches. But now they don't use stitches. They use staples and glue. The definition hasn't changed, so that if there is an injury in one part of the country that uses stitches it may get reported as an assault, but if it's in another part of the country where they use glue and staples then it's not an assault. So the definition has not kept abreast of the medical advances.   (Prison Services)

There are two definitions of overcrowding [in prisons]. There is design capacity. This is based on cell size, and may be for one or two persons. Then there is accommodation according to contract. [X] prison has 1000 places in the contract, that is, it is agreed that they should be able to take this number of prisoners. Resources are allocated on this basis. When the HMIP makes comments on overcrowding he is using the design capacity definition.   (Prison Services)

Meetings with probation officers should be held within seven days, five working days, according to National Standards. But variable practice results in some offices understanding this as 'was seen', or 'was offered an appointment'. Then the person doesn't always keep the appointment   (Social work)

We used to record how much [police] time was spent in 'community safety', 'traffic' and 'crime management', 'public order', and 'call management' and 'support activities'. 'Support activities' usually refers to all those over inspector rank in management, IT, finance, and Chief Constables. We used to refer to this as 'overhead' until a Chief Constable objected.   (Police)

Once areas are constructed, bracketed off as an entity, there are difficulties of eradicating the bureaucracy surrounding them:

It is the Fiscals [PFS] decision as to whether a case will be prosecuted. Now the police have been given a certain discretion on minor cases. The PFS have given the police a list of minor offences where they will not give an official police report. This helps the PFS with their workload. They don't want minor cases taken through the court. And the police benefit because they do not have to complete reports. But the police want the credit with the figures, in that it has still taken up someone's time, and there is no credit for that. And the PFS still want to be given the figures. So it will have to be recorded to keep the figures. The figures may indicate that something has dropped by 10%. We still want some credit. You've solved a crime. The police have been involved. You want to get some credit.   (Police)

---

to categories is foundational for coordinating activity distributed in time and place. March and Simon identify categorizations as the basis of decision-making techniques in organizations. Jacoby (1995) and Clawson (1980) examine the role of bureaucracy in the evolution of industrial capitalism. Clawson (1980) portrays it as a 'structural necessity' of taking greater control of the labour process, and bureaucratic production as that where decisions are not made by those who do the work but by those who plan and direct the work process. Organizing and controlling production results in orders, specifications and directives, 'extensive record keeping' needed to reorganize and increase the division of labour. Classifications, however, also have to address 'common sense', what Bowker and Star (2000) refer to as 'socially comfortable classifications'.

Weber recognizes bureaucratization as an intensive and quantitative expansion in administrative tasks. He (1978: 987) writes, 'once fully established, bureaucracy is among those social structures which are the hardest to destroy.' The professional bureaucrat is 'a small cog in a ceaselessly moving mechanism', that is neither 'put into motion or arrested by him'. The tendency to expand is inherent in the process itself. As Bauman (1993: 3) notes, 'ambivalence is a side-product of the labour of classification and it calls for yet more classifying effort.'

DRAWING BOUNDARIES

A second element of bureaucratic rationality's domination through knowledge is the circumscribing of jurisdictional areas and spheres of competence: the act of drawing boundaries. For Weber this is restricted to the delineation of office or official jurisdictions, the formally structured and articulated juris-dictional areas that determine the distribution of authority. The drawing of boundaries, however, occurs in multifarious forms, sanctified by numerous tools, for example, briefs, mandates, job descriptions, and budgets. Seemingly well-established jurisdictions, however, may appear quite fungible on closer inspection. Equally, established boundaries and jurisdictional spheres often prompt a response to a perceived problem through the creation of a new jurisdictional area. Burns (1963) makes reference to a 'mechanistic jungle', the tendency to 'grow' branches of bureaucratic hierarchy, where the 'solution' to a problem is seen as bringing somebody new in, in a new department, job, or committee system.

Standardization, the agreed upon rules for the production of a textual or material object, imposes a classification system that allows for replication over distance, over time, and over heterogeneity. It ensures a regularity of defini-tions or objects from one sphere or location to another, from one context to another, eradicating the local through extending the boundaries for practices. Standards, codes, and procedures establish universalistic norms. They intro-duce a mechanism for differentiating between good and bad ways of organiz-ing actions or things, ensuring a degree of comparability. They may also act as boundary-spanning objects allowing one jurisdiction to communicate with another (Bowker and Star 2000).

BOX 3.2. DRAWING BOUNDARIES: THE CRIMINAL JUSTICE SYSTEM

What is encompassed by the criminal justice system (CJS) and the extent of its jurisdiction influences debates as to its performance, its problems, and its needs for reform. It also influences perceptions of the degree of control over factors measuring its 'success'. Although intuitively understood by those who practice in it, asked for definitions or precise boundaries, and the CJS becomes more nebulous:

Where would you set the boundaries? The CJS encompasses all the agencies and bodies that touch at all on criminal justice. It's as broad as that. A narrow definition would focus on the courts, the prosecution arm and the police. A broader definition would see a focus on social work and the prisons. A broader definition still would include health and housing as part of the strategy for something to be achieved. Equally, Community Safety or Safety in the Community programmes, Social Inclusion partnerships, parenting skills, community schools, might also be incorporated in the CJS under some definitions. Equally, within organizations that might be seen as central to the CJS, there are activities that are not seen as core to it. There are thus boundaries of activities within organizations.   (Policy)

The question is, what are you looking at it for? What are you looking for it to do? The definition of the CJS is the operation of all the agencies and processes involved in the detection and prosecution of crime, and the handling of witnesses, the accused and offenders, moving into how do you reduce offending happening, and how do you manage crime generally, and how do you get people out of the system. You can make it that broad. But then that question has to be what are you trying to do today?   (Policy)

The CJS is a rubbish bin for so many different problems. It's completely inadequate to call it a CJS. At the boundaries, at the extremes, are the health service, social work in all its forms. We're obliged to deal with all kinds of things we shouldn't have to deal with. If you looked at it in terms of what are the problems? What do we want to achieve? Then there should be an analysis in terms of health professionals and others, social work in all its guises, but they are just not there. We should be trying to deal with serious criminal cases through the criminal courts. That's why it is creaking as it does. We should be handling the prosecution of serious crime but we're obviously not. The CJS is terribly defined. Mental health is one of the main areas. How CJS attempts to deal with mental health is just wrong. It doesn't work. It shouldn't be here. It shouldn't be dealt with like this.   (Defence Agent)

BOX 3.3. STANDARDIZATION, HOMOGENIZATION, OR JUSTICE?

Standardization, particularly in sentencing, raises issues of the balance between the local and the national:

There are big variations in sentencing depending where you are. You can go to [X] where there are no stabbings, and the person will get the maximum possible sentence because it is a socially unacceptable crime. You can go to Glasgow and some Courts will give a fine. It is a much more 'accepted' crime. It happens every day. This raises interesting questions, because one response would be that crime X in [a largely rural area with a low crime level] is not the same as crime X in Glasgow, and therefore different sentencing patterns should reflect this. How standardized should sentencing be?   (anonymous)

Rationalization operates through standardized definitions and practices becoming accepted across time and space, as seen in the standardization of time (Thompson 1967); the standardization of practices through the standardization of architecture, daily routines, and practices of the early monasteries (Kieser 1987); the standardization of architecture (Guillen 1997); and the standardization of measures and measurement systems (Kula 1986).

FOLLOWING A RULE

The third element of bureaucratic rationality Weber identifies is the importance of rule-governed conduct. This he identifies as a means of distinguishing formal organizations from traditional organizations and informal groups. Rules and formal role systems define position, place, and action within an organization, reinforcing their calculability and predictability. For Weber, rules are rational insofar as their intention is to help the achievement of purposes (technical rules) or to realize values (norms). Their rationality applies to the *intention* in the design of a rule and to the *procedure* involved in the rule's application (Albrow 1970: 63). The expert application of rules is central to the formal rationality of bureaucracy. He writes that 'management of the office follows general rules which are more or less stable, more or less exhaustive, and which can be learned. Knowledge of the rules represents a special technical expertise which officials possess' (Weber 1978: 969). Following a rule provides discipline: 'The content of discipline is nothing but the consistently rationalized, methodically prepared and exact execution of the received order...in which the actor is unswervingly and exclusively set for carrying out the command...What is decisive for discipline is that the obedience of a plurality of men is rationally uniform' (Weber 1978: 1149).

The study of rule making and following has been an important feature of studies of organizations. One of the earliest examples of 'following a rule' is seen in the Rule of St Benedict in the early monastic system. Kieser (1987) also illustrates the function of rules in the promotion of discipline and rationalization of practice in his study of Benedictine monasteries. Gouldner (1954) took rules as the basis of bureaucracy or a bureaucratic system, noting the different ways in which they function according to context. On the basis of an analysis of the recognition and perceived usefulness of rules; who initiated them; whose values they legitimated and violated; explanations given for rule deviation; and the effect of rules on perceived status, Gouldner (1954) identified three different types of bureaucracy: mock, representative, and punishment centred.[12] His work demonstrates the use of general and impersonal rules to decrease the visibility of power relations. It anticipates Edwards's later identification of systematic rational–legal rules as an important dimension in the control of the labour process (1979). Merton's study (1940) of the 'bureaucratic personality' illustrates some of the dysfunctions of rule following, identifying such features as goal displacement where the aims of the organization become displaced through close adherence to rules; day-to-day routines taking on special emphasis; methodical performance leading to a rigidity and inability to adjust, 'trained inappropriateness'; the sanctification of rules as they become an end in themselves; depersonalization with the particularities of individual circumstance and case being ignored; and entrenched interests that focus more on those higher in the bureaucracy than on its clientele. What Merton (1940) describes is what he terms an over-internalization of rules, such that they become absolutes, no longer relative to a set of purposes.

While these early studies identify rule-governed behaviour as an important dimension of formally bureaucratic structures, more recent work focuses on rule making in less bureaucratically structured organizations. 'Post-bureaucratic' organizations, with their creation of shared meaning, are supposed to obviate the need both for principles of hierarchy and explicit rule-governed behaviour. Barker's work (1993), however, highlights how rule-based rational control becomes tighter in post-bureaucratic team-based organizations. He identifies the concept of concertive control for control that passes from management to workers, the latter collaborating to develop their own control, based on a negotiated consensus of how to shape behaviour according to a set of core values found in corporate vision statements. 'In a sense, concertive control reflects the adoption of a new substantive rationality, a new set of consensual values, by the organization and its members' (Barker 1993/2002: 183). This is achieved through rule generation that attempts to reflect the negotiated consensus about values. The locus of authority changes from a bureaucratic system and rational–legal constitutive rules to value consensus of members and a socially created generative rule system. Barker argues that such a system practically and conceptually transcends bureaucratic control to create concertively controlled self-managing teams. Deciding issues such as ground rules for good work, deciding who is to perform which tasks, overtime, hiring and firing, strong norms become enforced as rules which, through a process of stabilization and formalization, become rationalized and codified, to serve as a strong controlling force for the teams' actions (Barker 1993/2002: 191). 'Rational' rules are a necessary process whereby teams integrate new members. Roles and responsibilities become more objectified, tasks more specified. Normative rules become more and more rationalized, formulated into objective rules. There are complaints that 'rules were taking on their own rationality and legitimacy' (Barker 1993/2002: 201). Absolute faith is placed in the written record 'if we can just get this written down, everyone will know what to do'. Thus, for example, being five minutes late constitutes an 'occurrence', four occurrences lead to a warning, seven tardies (less than five minutes late) equal an occurrence. Barker (1993/2002: 207) concludes that concertive control works by 'blurring substantive and formal rationality into a "communal-rational" system', where concertive workers create communal value systems that eventually control actors through rational rules. Studies such as Barker's identify the importance of distinguishing bureaucratic ratio-nality from bureaucratic structures, for while structures and control pat-terns may vary, the underlying rationality of domination through knowledge remains vibrant.

Other writers have taken the rule motif as typifying organizations in gen-eral, conceptualizing organizations as rule-based systems. Cyert and March (1963), for example, analyse organizations from the perspective of the func-tioning of formal rules, decision rules, and standard operating procedures. 'Rules' are the 'rational' solution to repeated games. From this perspective, organizations are seen as a collection of rules, with behaviour being rule and identity based. They determine organization activities, authority rela-tions, connections among subunits, and decision-making structures. They are designed to make actions reliable and consistent, thus ensuring coordination and communication. They construct organization reality by depicting the way things happen or ought to happen, and are also the encoding of history, memories, experience, and the depositories of knowledge. Their durability is an important dimension of organizational continuity in the face of turnover. They enable individuals to make predictions or prophecies about how rule followers are likely to behave.

Rules, however, present inherent difficulties. Weber confines the 'ratio-nality' of rules to their intention or design and their procedure for appli-cation. Rules cannot be inherently 'rational' because of the ambiguity of their interpretation and the complication of translating generic rules into specific action as they 'encounter' specific situations. As each particular cir-cumstance has a number of different possible interpretations, a number of different rules may be evoked in a context. Rules are infinite in the sense of being open ended or applicable to an indefinitely large range of future applications. It is this ambiguity that leads to rule adaptation, creation, and revision (March, Schultz, and Zhou 2000). Rule application is the movement from the previously known (how to apply a rule) to new cases (does the rule apply in this circumstance?). This movement is guided by a perceived sense of sameness. The 'sameness' of a situation or object does not exist in advance. Classes of objects are not given. 'The problem of the next step is ineradicable' (Bloor 2002: 11). (Systems of) rules are thus troublesome for the element of discretion they allow, either because of their being too closely followed 'red tape' or because their indexicality allows too much freedom in application.

The early studies of bureaucracy illustrated problems with the indexical-ity of rules. Merton's work (1940) may be taken as an example of this, as organization members generalize the responses from one situation where rule application is appropriate to other situations where it is inappropriate, thus resulting in unanticipated and undesired consequences. Rules originally devised to achieve organizational goals assume a positive value independent of those goals. Crozier's work (1964) identifies cases in which rules, identified as dealing inadequately with a case, result not in their abandonment but rather, 'pressure to make it more complete, more precise and more binding' (Crozier 1964: 187). Organizations enter into a vicious circle of increasing ossification as each deviant behaviour is met with new rules, finally leading to a 'rigidity circle' and collapse in crisis. Blau (1955) illustrates how unplanned, deviating behaviour fills in the gaps in formal rules, adapts to unforeseen situations, innovates, and preserves the flexibility of the organization while maintaining the pretence that it is efficient to comply with formal rules.

An analysis of rules inevitably raises the issue of how they relate to social norms (shared understandings among members of a group) and conventions (stable solutions for coordination problems); tacit understandings, standard practice, and rules of thumb; and the extent to which they include routines, procedures, regulations, standards and conventions. That it is possible to separate formal rules from other 'rule-like' forms of social regulation is the foundation of Weber's distinguishing formal organizations from informal groups, and later becomes the distinguishing feature of the 'informal' organization (1978). The sharp distinction between formal rules and social conventions is problematic. As Wittgenstein demonstrates, rule following is about normativity (Bloor 2002). 'To follow a rule is to participate in an institution to adopt or conform to a custom or a convention' (Bloor 2002: 87). Through practice, a sense is achieved of what applications are appropriate and which are not. This identification of sameness is informed by socially educated perceptions, experience, training, etc. Rules are social institutions, customs, or conventions. It is the normative standards of a number of interacting rule followers that maintain a consensus by collectively monitoring, controlling, and sanctioning individual tendencies in interpretation. It is in this sense that following a rule is to follow a custom, convention, or institution. It is the consensus that makes norm appear 'objective'.

It is for these reasons that Bittner (1965/2002: 79–80, emphasis added) argues for an ethnography of rule following and interpretation, an ethnography of bureaucracy. He writes:

rational schemes appear as unrealistic normative idealizations only when one considers them literally i.e., without considering some tacit background assumptions that bureaucrats take for granted. Literal interpretations of formal schemes is not only inappropriate but strictly speaking impossible…tacit assumptions are not simply unspecified, but instead come to the fore only on occasions of actual reference to the formal scheme. Insofar as a term refers meaningfully to some determinate object it does so only in the context of actors making sense of it in consequential situations…*The standard itself and the correct way to use it therefore are part of the self-same order of action they purport to control*

Bittner (1965) identifies several uses of rules such as the 'gambit of compliance', where rules are invoked to clarify the meaning of actions retrospectively;

BOX 3.4. RULES AND DISCRETION

The identification of crime raises interesting issues of identification and indexicality. Note how the distinction is drawn between a 'domestic shoplifter' who lives in the area and a 'foreign shoplifter' who comes from outside. Although the action is the same, the 'crime' is not.

X jurisdiction has one of the largest shopping centres in Scotland. It also has one of the largest number of shop lifters. The two go together. X is the worst shop to steal from. You take it off the shelves and don't need to take it out of the door. You don't need a receipt to get a refund. There is a policy at the centre that any shoplifter will be prosecuted, because they don't want the reputation of its being the place to go. But there are differences between a domestic shoplifter and a foreign shoplifter, for example, from Glasgow. These [shoplifters from Glasgow] are not our criminals and this is not our crime. I know my needs. There [shoplifters from Glasgow] there is aggravation and intent. It's a different type of case. There are weird and wonderful edges to crime issues. For example, if there are frauds on business but there is no security in the store then a different approach is taken. There was a case where X had a policy of credit sales of £2000 goods, but they didn't do a credit check or ask for identification. People use false names and there is fraud. Essentially this is turning the police into debt collectors. It is not in the public interest to prosecute in this case because of store policy. But where there are security checks, we'll prosecute even though it's exactly the same crime   (anonymous)

There is a recognized ambit within which rules may be interpreted:

There are guidelines that PFS are supposed to follow, although there are always issues of discretion. On issues such as minor common law offences you use your discretion. For example on a shoplifting charge, a 45 year old woman, first offence, may be given a warning. A 16 year old male, second offence, may well be given a fine.   (PFS)

In certain areas there is no discretion at all:

The guidelines come from the Lord Advocate's [chief law officer] office. For example, public interest says that they must deal with cases that have racial aggravation, for example, aggression towards a shopkeeper. They will prosecute even if the shopkeeper is not bothered. The police have to report this and the PFS has to prosecute. This is in stone from the Lord Advocate.   (PFS)

---

the 'gambit of organizational acumen', finding in the rule the means for doing whatever needs to be done; and 'corroborative reference', when work cannot be appraised, the overall functional significance can be judged by invoking the formal scheme.

PREDICTABILITY

Weber's identification of the superiority of the bureaucratic form lay in its formal properties and the extent to which this aids predictability. Bureaucratic rationality is the means through which predictability is achieved. The impersonality of formally rational regulations is an essential element of ensuring constant, stable, and predictable results. Predictability provides the basis for longer term decision-making and security of action. It refers to the routines, procedures, roles, and rules that allow individuals to function or operate with a degree of certainty. Standardized elements, the ability to reassemble them, also provide the ability to act flexibly to contingencies, thus rendering the potentially unpredictable more predictable (Hasselbladh and Kallinikos 2000). Predictability does not imply the ability to know for certain every contingency.

Ritzer's work (1996) has picked up the theme of predictability and calculability as part of his analysis of Weber's rationalization thesis. He identifies four dimensions of this process: efficiency (optimum means to a given end); calculability (the use of quantification as an indicator of quality); predictability (as seen in standardization); and control (the substitution of non-human for human technology). He gives examples of their various manifestations, illustrating how calculability has invaded the seemingly insignificant (through precise measurement in cooking recipes) to major institutions, as for example, higher education (through grades, scores, rankings, and ratings); healthcare (with diagnostic-related groups); and politics (through the impact of opinion polls). Increasing order and standardization leads to

---

BOX 3.5. PREDICTABILITY?

The essence of a bureaucratic system is that it ensures predictability. This is not always possible:

But basically there are always more trials than courts can deal with. There are always going to be cases adjourned, whether this suits the accused or not. There are always going to be witnesses not turning up, on holiday, ill etcetera. You shouldn't underestimate the sheer difficulty of getting all these people with disparate interests together in one place at the same time. You have to have floating trials for if a case doesn't come off, so that you can use the court. You have fixed trials and floating trials. There are genuine situations for delays, witnesses take ill. But it's always the case where the potential is for more business than can be dealt with (Judge).

The system relies on some cases not taking place. So if umpteen cases, say 50, are set for a two week period. This is absurd. There is no way they are all going to be tried. You hope that some will plead guilty. A few go to trial.
Q: Is there a way round the problem?
A: I can't see one. (Defence Agent)

On trial courts you don't know in advance whether the case is a runner or delayed, until the last minute. Counsel are busy performing a juggling act day in and day out, of when cases finish and when the next one starts, so that there is no gap. You can't blame them. They are trying to earn a living. The legal aid fees are a fraction of what you can get for the civil court (Advocate).

It is impossible to predict which cases will not go ahead on the day of the trial in advance of the day of the trial and not easy to calculate how long the trial is likely to take.

(McInnes 2004: 192)

increasing predictability in travel (geographic replication in hotels and services; package tours); higher education (through textbooks and national curricula); and healthcare (standardized judgements). His focus is how all these elements combine to produce a predictable, standardized, homogenized, uniform engagement with the world, the MacDonaldization of commodities and experience.

Crozier (1964: 177) writes: 'in his analysis of bureaucratic rationality [Weber] identifies above all the predictability requirements and standardization of behaviour that provides the only way to meet them'. As Crozier notes, predictability is not just dependent on structured processes, it also requires the standardization of behaviour. A bureaucratic rationality must impact on behaviour. The technical efficiency of bureaucracies relies on the reliability of behaviour that it instills. It demands disciplined standardized behaviour in organizations. As Weber notes, bureaucratic rationalization 'first changes the material and social orders and through them the people...' (Weber 1978: 1116).

'WITHOUT REGARD FOR PERSONS'

A necessary prerequisite of domination through knowledge is 'impersonality'. Bureaucracy functions according to 'calculable rules' and as such must eliminate that which cannot be made calculable, namely, the individual, the personal, and the idiosyncratic. Calculable rules are 'without regard for persons'. 'Sine ira et studio, without hatred or passion, and hence without affection or enthusiasm. The dominant norms are concepts of straightforward duty without regard to personal considerations' (Weber 1978: 225). Weber writes:

homo politicus, as well as homo economicus, performs his duty best when he acts without regard to the person in question, sine ira et studio, without hate and without love, without personal predilection and therefore without grace, but sheerly in accordance with the impersonal duty imposed by his calling, and not as a result of any concrete personal relationships. He discharges his responsibility best if he acts as closely as possible in accordance with the rational regulations of the modern power system. (Weber 1978: 600)

Bureaucracy aims to develop the most efficient methods for achieving its goals by depersonalizing the whole administrative process. However, the nature of the impersonality that bureaucratic rationality introduces is ambiguous. A bureaucratic impartiality, one rule for all, relies on a formalistic impersonality. This stresses the importance of formality in relationships, the engagement with another regardless of personal feelings, an impersonal objectivity, and a reliance on formalized rules and procedures. Impersonality introduces a formal equality of treatment. 'The dominant norms are concepts of straightforward duty without regard to personal considerations. Everyone is subject to formal equality of treatment, that is everyone is in the same empirical situation' (Weber 1978: 225). Formal role systems and rule-bound behaviour uncouple the individual and the office. (The essence of Weber's definition of organization lies in the formal authority between positions and its continuity despite the turnover of personnel. Organizations are not an aggregate of individuals, but of roles and patterns as the result of an interdependence of roles.) The functioning of bureaucracy in this way depends on an ability of individuals to separate out or suspend personal elements that have no bearing on a role. Bureaucracy thus has implications for the construction of the individual who successfully functions in them. There is the individual qua individual and individual qua role agent (Kallinikos 2005).

Some interpretations of an impersonal formalism conceive this as a form of dehumanization (Brubaker 1984), interpreting it as the elimination of love, hatred, and all emotional elements, the invocation of the private expressive and the public instrumental (Ferguson 1984). Weber does say that 'bureaucracy develops more perfectly, the more it is dehumanized, the more completely it succeeds in eliminating everything which escapes calculation' (Weber 1978: 975). However, rather than depersonalization being seen as the strict suppression of the emotional, the personal, and the sexual, for du Gay (2000) it is rather an emphasis on the strict adherence to procedure, a commitment to the purpose of the office, independent of the personal moral properties of others. The norms of impersonality are adherence to due process and an ethos of responsibility ensuring fairness and probity. And, it has to be said, predictability and reliability. These elements also give bureaucracy an ethos of vocation. The ethos is to set aside the private, emotional, political, moral, regional, or other commitments both of oneself but also of those with whom one is dealing, unless this is explicitly allowed for informal regulation. It is to be without regard for person. It is this to which du Gay (2000) refers. Rather than portray bureaucracy as a one sided 'instrumental rationality', du Gay (2000) emphasizes the ethos of bureaucratic office, identifying a substantive ethical domain which guards against corruption and the improper exercise of personal patronage. A bureaucratic ethos is free of arbitrary action and discretion. Because authority resides in principles, rather than personalities and tradition, impersonality limits authority and the improper exercise of personal patronage, based on religion, political beliefs, economic status, etc.

Impartiality, the dutiful application of process, however, depersonalizes the structure of power and authority, denying the interests that inform its construction. Equally, following standardized rules and procedures in a quasi-mechanical manner, without regard for purposes and effects, ignores the individual circumstance of the 'other', and thus may contravene concepts of fairness or justice that might pervade. It is for these reasons that Arendt (1967) identifies the impersonality of bureaucratic systems as 'rule by nobody'. Authority rests not with a person, but within the system.

Impersonality is the appeal to a disembedded persona. Bureaucratic rationality continues to construct the disembedded concept of the rational subject. The impersonality of bureaucratic rationality, however, ultimately faces the difficulties of indexicality and its reliance on social conventions or mores. Indeed as Weber (1978: 979) identifies, 'In principle a system of rationally debatable "reasons" stands behind every act of bureaucratic administration'. Equally, as Weber notes, an ethos is based on a substantive justice and is 'oriented to some concrete instance or person'. This conflicts with the 'formalism and rule bound, cool matter of factness of bureaucratic administration' (1978: 980). Non-formalistic criteria ultimately sustain formal criteria.

Conclusions

This discussion strongly distinguishes between the bureaucratic form and a bureaucratic rationality that underpins it. Bureaucratic rationality is identified as domination through knowledge, or that which allows things to be known. It is the mundane, seemingly insignificant acts of semantics, drawing definitional boundaries, rules, procedures, codes, protocols, writing the world in formalized terms that enables it to be known, become predictable, and be acted upon. As such, bureaucratic rationality is the underlabourer allowing bureaucratic structures to function. And it is this bureaucratic rationality that persists, if not more so, when the organizational form identified as bureaucracy undergoes many changes. As the formal structures of bureaucracy, career, formal hierarchy, etc. change, to be replaced by portfolio careers and project teams, bureaucratic rationality persists. It is a form of disembedded rationality, 'without regard for person', the attempt to introduce a disengaged 'view from nowhere', the impartial overview of how organizing should be structured and individuals handled. It is because it aims at a universal level that its focus is on attributes of 'process' rather than outcome. This can lead to what Weber terms the paradox of consequences, whereby the increasing attempts at more rationally formal systems prompts a high level of substantive irrationality.

4 Technocratic rationality

The definition of rational action identifies three elements: action is consequent upon a desire or belief, action is caused by this desire or belief, and action is caused in the intended way. Rational action is thus not only consequent on an agent's beliefs and desires but also relies on the causal efficacy of the action. As a reason is a rational cause of action, for action to be reasonable, it must be causally efficacious. The link between actions and consequences indicates that some actions are more rational than others.[1] Causality is thus inextricably linked to rationality. Rational action presumes beliefs and knowledge about cause and effect, that is, knowledge of means–ends relationships. The link between rationality, knowledge, and causality introduces the third aspect of a disembedded rationality, that which speaks to the concept of causality embedded in rational action. Where ends are uncontentious and means well defined, that is, cause–effect or means–end relationships are well understood, rational action is the adoption of technically rational means or solutions to achieve desired ends. Where ends are not well defined and well understood, or means are not apparent, technically rational action is not possible. Most organizational issues involve either a degree of contention over ends or means are not well defined. Hence the reference to a technocratic rationality. Technocratic denotes the application of technical means to areas as if cause and effect relationships are well established and technically rational action is possible. Technocratic rationality is the presumption or fabrication of means–end relationships. This chapter outlines how the technical has been portrayed in organization studies and the ease of its transformation into the technocratic.

Technology and organization

Organization is derived from the Greek *organon* meaning 'tool'. Dawson (1996: 53) notes how at the core of organization is a 'transformation process', 'the acquisition of inputs of natural, human, financial and fabricated resources', and their transformation into 'the production and distribution of outputs of goods and services'. In this sense, an organization is a 'technology' that allows inputs to become translated or converted into out-puts. Technology, and its affiliates technical, technique, technocratic, derives from *techne*, meaning technical knowledge or know-how.[2] Technologies are the manifestation or materialization of coordinated means–ends relations; the mechanism whereby means–ends relations become, or are made, manifest. In this sense, 'technologies' is the shorthand term for coordinated action and knowledge for the achievement of goals. Organizations are the institu-tionalization of inferences of causality and means–end relationships.[3] They are the mechanism through which means become ends. Perrow (1967) pro-posed that as technology or the work done in organizations is their defining characteristic, this may be used as the basis for their comparative analysis. In which case, 'variations within one type of organization may be such that some schools are like prisons, some prisons like churches, some churches like factories, some factories like universities and so on' (Perrow 1967/2002: 207).[4]

Very narrowly defined, technology has been associated with the 'hard-ware' of machinery, apparatus, physical objects, and artefacts. A broader view emphasizes the organizational dimension, relationships structured by and through the production system, the skills and knowledge that result, and thus locates studies of equipment and machinery within the skill, knowl-edge, expertise, and know-how that encompass them, considering not only the 'hardware' but also the 'software' of production. Classical research into technical systems and work organization has been concerned to identify and characterize types of technology (Thompson 1967); the impact of technology on social organization [the Tavistock School and socio-technical systems (Trist and Bamforth 1951)]; the impact of technology on worker responses to work (e.g. Blauner 1964 on alienation); the impact of technology on the pattern of organization and structure of management (e.g. Woodward 1958); and general patterns of technology and work organization operational in labour control (Braverman 1974). More recent research has addressed the impact of new electronic and computer technologies.

Debates in these studies have straddled the technical/social divide, fore-grounding one or the other in discussions of degrees of technological deter-minism and the ability of those who engage with technology to modify its designs and effects. They emphasize technology's association with the reduc-tion of uncertainty and the enhancement of predictability, its promise of more orderly and predictable qualities in a production process and of predictability and controllability of the labour process. Technology offers the prospect of transforming voluntary and subjective action into a 'more ordered and objec-tive texture of programmed rules and procedures' and the translation of com-plex socially organized activity into an 'objective' workflow and operations (Scarbrough and Corbett 1992: 18). Underlying these, however, is the recog-nition that technology absorbs its structure from substantive and historically situated factors. There is no pretence at technology following unvarying rules of logic and method.

Technology as technique

Technology all too often connotes machines, the hardware or software of physical pieces of machinery, physical objects, and artefacts. A broader view of technology emphasizes technologies of representation: knowledge acting as a form of tool, as seen in technical procedures, forms, plans for work flow, and technical systems. These too act as technologies of transformation. This broader definition sees technology as technique: knowledge objectified. It stems from the work of Ellul (1964) for whom the mechanical or machine was too restrictive a view of technology. For Ellul (1964), the machine is only a small dimension of technique and not the most important one.

Technique is the 'immediate technical operation carried out in accordance with a certain method in order to attain a particular end' (Ellul 1964: 19). Most organizing entails the operation or application of a certain technique or techniques. What Ellul refers to are technologies or instruments for the formulation and accumulation of knowledge: methods of observation, techniques of registration, procedures for investigation or research, the techniques of quantification, calculation, and control. It is manifest in IQ tests classifying students; opinion polls judging political climates; cost–benefit analysis in health; audits of practice, and can be identified in every discipline. Although each displays their own specialized version, instruments 'migrate' across areas and between disciplines (Hoskin and Macve 1986). Ellul (1964) sees technique as a 'bridge' between reality and abstract man (sic). He writes that it achieves 'in the domain of the abstract what the machine did in the domain of labour' (Ellul 1964: 5). Technique is intimately linked to reason. 'Technique is the translation into action of man's concern to master things by means of reason, to account for what is subconscious … make clear and precise the outlines of nature, take hold of chaos and put order into it' (Ellul 1964: 43).

Technique relies on a form of representation or modelling. For Hacking (1983), this process is grounded in human beings being 'representers' or 'depicters', that is, they construct external and public representations in an attempt to represent the world. This may include models, pictures, theories, calculations, etc. The organization chart, for example, is the representation of the organization as a simplified means–end chain, with 'inputs marching inevitably along through procedures to benefits' (Meyer 1983: 235). Pie charts, organization charts, etc. are all representations, instruments, or techniques that permit one arena to be 're-presented' in another.

Techniques act as 'technologies of translation', designed to be independent of the location and the individuals whom they represent or report. Functioning in this way, they facilitate long-distance control (Latour 1999; Law 1986). To exercise power over events removed in time and space requires that events be 'inscribed' so that they may be transported to decision centres. A 'centre of calculation' requires 'immutable mobiles' which re-presents that which is distant in a single plane, making it 'visible, cognizable, amenable to deliberation and decision' (Latour 1988). Inscriptions represent and re-present that which they relay through standardized forms, records, graphs, tables, figures, etc. They are a 'literary' basis that may be disseminated through a variety of different sites, and, as such, representations must be mobile, stable (rather than immutable), presentable, readable, and combinable with one another (Latour 1988). Through their action, disparate areas become connected through a complex relay of inscription and calculation, permitting the centre to act as a centre, ensuring that those who are distant from events and actions can maintain a degree of control over them. Representations speak 'as sole representatives. They take the place of the original situation, summarizing and replacing' (Latour 1999: 24).

Inscriptions are thus constitutive. They render visible, inscribe homogeneity, and standardize. As Ellul notes of technique, it 'creates' that which it describes. Techniques are not passive observing instruments but are productive of phenomena under investigation. They establish classifications of people. 'Consumers', for example, are constructed through 'statistical networks of questionnaires and pollsters' (Latour 1987). As such, representations are productive or 'performative'. They operate as agents, actants in Latour's terms, having the ability to produce an effect or an impact, transforming or modifying others.

As we saw in Chapter 3, standardization of definitions is an important aspect of disciplining social meanings. It secures categories and in doing so is the foundation of data. It ensures that the local is replicable across time and space and facilitates coordination between locations (Porter 1995). The standardization of categories of things and people also makes things easier to count and through this become the object of quantification (Hacking 1982*b*). Locales can be aggregated, compared, the subject of, and subject to, calculation, measuring scales, and the construction of the norm or the standard. Although technique in itself is not reducible to numbers, for Ellul (1964: 132), technique is a process of transforming the qualitative into the quantitative. It 'compels the qualitative to become quantitative'. Although categories constructed for statistical representation claim a transparent relationship to the object represented, the recording of what exists, this disguises the productive role of statistics and its role in organizing material.[5] Calculability is one step further in the desire for predictability and enhancing means–end rationality. It offers the prospect of something being exact and unambiguous. Costing, budgeting, cost–benefit analyses, risk assessment, censuses, samples, etc. are powerful not because of their accurate representation but because of their numerical representation (Porter 1995). Numbers acquire objectivity from their stability, their ability to be transported in time and space.

These are so familiar to us that the fabrication and representation of technique is forgotten. Everyone 'is able to go from form to content, from pie chart to what is charted, from statistics to market forces, from bookkeeping to profit' (Latour 1987: 259). A lot of representations are 'black boxed', taken for granted, normal, their assumptions and conventions remaining unexplored. There is a seamless move from concept-formation, to scale construction, to data collection rather than recognizing that the measuring instrument constitutes the measured object. Standardization, however, not only relies on standardized instruments but also relies on the uniformity of observation and recording practice: the 'standardization' of people (Porter 1995). Techniques of observation, recording, and interpretation are part of a discipline, with disciplining effects. The 'making of social actors' accompanies the making of facts and gives a particular community a disciplinary objectivity.

With the creation of a physical form, either as a material technology or as a bureaucratic form, there is the association with an 'objective' form of knowledge. The faithfulness of representation lies not in its 'correspondence' to the world, although it is often taken for this, but in its ability to transport something through a variety of circumstances.[6] In practice, representation loses information. There is reduction, a compression of data. The locality and the particular is lost. With reduction, however, things are also gained: comparability, standardization, calculation, and the 'big picture', the ability to oversee and control. As Latour (1999: 49) notes, invention and discovery are simultaneous.

The claims to objectivity, however, carry a number of effects (Daston 1992). Because techniques are 'objective', they can claim independence from the conditions of their production and the circumstances of their use or application. They may thus be used in diverse and disparate contexts. As the objective claims independence from particular historical and cultural dimensions, and independence of the perspectives of particular individuals, it becomes 'a view from nowhere' (Nagel 1989). In essence, however, the objective privileges the universal over the local. It invests power in techniques not in people. The 'objective' not only delineates the observer and the observed, but it also introduces hierarchy: the hierarchy of the active recording subject and the relatively passive recorded object.

Representation is the harbinger of intervention (Hacking 1983). Representations, surveys, opinion polls, league tables, etc. are not merely mechanisms that are brought in to aid decisions. They also mobilize issues (Latour 1999).

BOX 4.1. MEASURES AND SCIENTIFIC PEDAGOGY

Scientific knowledge comes with its own vocabulary:

PASC provides a glossary of inputs, outputs, outcomes, performance indicators, management information, performance measures, targets, league tables, PSAs, standards, and benchmark (2002–3: 5).

There is a strong pedagogic role involved in getting people to use measures, as is reflected in this comment on making an argument for funding for Community Safety projects. But also note how this is undermined at the end, recognizing the impact different forms of 'data' can have:

We want them to focus on top line strategies and outcomes and performance indicators. These have to be measurable and statistically based or founded. I would like them to demonstrate trends. I would like them to use statistics and community based information and to put this in context, for example, in comparators that are made, statements on: 'per 1000 population evidence shows that there is this problem in this area', 'this is the reason this housing estate has been chosen versus other housing estates'. One area that they have fallen down on is on assessing their performance and evidencing their needs. Previously it had been the case of 'this village should have this'. We want them to be more targeted. Now that they are more comfortable at performance measures we can ask them to focus on specific projects that can be evidenced and supported, for example, 'this is why this area is chosen', in relation to statistical material, for example, Scots average, comparable area. No doubt the Community Safety Partnership will offer up anecdotal information also. Some of this can be very powerful. More powerful than the numbers   (Policy)

The move to 'objective' quantitative measures is problematic for some:

There is a real resentment of the quantitative nature of them, especially in community policing. In community policing there is a lot of liaison, communication, consultation. People get very frustrated with the measures.   (Police)

Some of the Community Safety Partnerships did inter-generational work. They held events based on what kids do and what adults did as kids. This was sent out to Schools and Old People's Homes. How do you evaluate this? It is easy enough to indicate the number of kids attended, people through the door. But issues whether this translates into outcomes, decreased vandalism, community happiness . . . [tails off]   (Police)

They create that which is to be recorded and measured and, with this, create the possibility of new interventions, behaviours, and forms of being. Fear of crime, return on investment, market share, and examination results become new 'object domains' to which there must be a response.

There are two distinct issues at play here (Hacking 1983). There is representation. And there is what affects us and what we can affect. The two are often confused. As Mintzberg (1994: 66) notes in relation to strategic planning, representation prompts the assumption that because a phenomena has been 'captured', because it has been 'written down, labelled and put in a box on a piece of paper, ideally represented by numbers', that action will take place. He continues: 'to engage in planning is not necessarily to plan; nor does strategic planning lead to strategic thinking' (1994: 117).

Management as science

To understand technology as technique is to broaden understanding of the role that 'technology' plays in organizing and the coordination functions of organization. The legitimacy of technique lies in its appeal to objectivity and calculability. Through this, technique claims the mantle of disinterested science.[7] It guarantees the sacrosanct virtues of truth and objectivity, and offers a mode of knowledge analytically distinct from values (Poovey 1993). As the paradigm for knowledge, it reflects its origins in, and takes on the function of, Enlightenment, where scientific knowledge is seen as the 'crowning achievement of human reason' (Hacking 1983: 1).[8]

The Enlightenment legacy is of science as the means of accessing and acquiring 'true' or accredited knowledge and thus enabling individuals to decide social and political ideas using their own reason. The representation of scientific practice as the operation of reason, the rational procedure for correctly discerning the nature of things, sets up a correspondence relationship between science (reason) and reality (truth), and between truth and rationality. Reason or rationality becomes 'the application of scientific or true rules to particular cases' (Brown 1992: 69). Empirically verifiable and deductive knowledge is to be the pre-eminent form of knowledge, thus engendering debates within the philosophy of science relating to the role of evidence, foundationalism, method, verification, falsification, the 'rational' justification of scientific knowledge, and what is established 'truth'. Rather than being *one* form of knowledge, science is taken to be *the* theory of knowledge, having exclusive validity. Nor is science simply associated with rationality; it becomes associated with introducing greater or *more* rationality into debate. Science becomes the highest level of an objective rationality (Trigg 1993). An act is rational if it is in accord with 'the cannons of logic and procedures of science' (Trigg 1993: 6).

As the neutral disclosure of the real, scientific, and technical knowledge provides solutions that override 'interests' and 'politics'. Political controversy thus becomes a matter of argument and fact to be decided by 'rational' methods and the 'one best way'. The one best way is not a relative concept, that which is best in comparison to other means. 'The choice is less and less a subjective one among several means … It is really a question of finding the best means in the absolute sense' (Ellul 1964: 21). This has several potential effects. It helps foster thinking that all problems have technical solutions and are, in principle, controllable. It implicitly devalues modes of thinking and acting that cannot lay claim to the status of scientific or technical rationality. It brings with it the distinction between the expert and the lay person. The specialist chooses the means and demonstrates the superiority of the chosen means and in doing so, 'forms a closed fraternity with their own esoteric vocabulary' (Merton in Ellul 1964: xi). Through these features, science and technology have been associated with rationalization: the 'disenchantment' of the world and the enhancement of rational control over social and natural processes. Displacing magical and religious views of the world, they promote the 'view of the world as causal mechanisms that in principle can be mastered by technical means and calculations' (Brubaker 1984: 31).

Management also lays claims to this mantle of a disinterested science,[9] although the extent to which it is legitimate to do so is contested (Marsden and Townley 1996). As Brown (1992: 68) notes, 'most writers on organization have either accepted the authority of science as unproblematic or have rejected such a claim as imperialistic, as a form of unacceptable scientism'. Notwithstanding debates as to whether management 'is' a science; may lay claims to being a science; or proceeds according to scientific principles, the underpinnings and assumptions of science are ubiquitous. The analysis of management is suffused with scientific imagery (Brown 1992). The image of the factory or workplace as laboratory has a long pedigree, perhaps reaching its apogee with Taylor and scientific management. The initiative of the workforce, its 'hardwork, goodwill and ingenuity' would be 'obtained with absolute regularity' rather than on a haphazard basis if 'the deliberate gathering of the great mass of traditional knowledge' were recorded, tabulated, and 'reduced to laws, rules and mathematical formulae' (Taylor 1911/1982: 125). Science was designed to replace the 'old rule of thumb knowledge' of the workforce kept in the latter's heads, to make a permanent or complete record. The codification of unclassified knowledge and the formulation of laws, rules, and formulae is the first principle of scientific management. The three other principles involve the scientific selection and progressive development of the workforce; the bringing of science and scientifically selected and trained workmen together; and the division of work between workmen and management. It was recognized that this would require a 'mental revolution' and individuals would have to 'change their ways in accordance with science' (1911/1982: 146). For Taylor, the legitimate authority for managers to assert control stems from the application of 'scientific' and impartial principles of efficiency. Work is 'rationalized' through making the connection between means and ends, success and failure, transparent. 'With the help of suitable methods of measurement, the optimum profitability of the individual worker is calculated like that of any material means of production' (Weber 1978: 1156). What is involved in the process, however, as Zuboff notes (1988: 56), is the transfer of knowledge 'from one quality of knowing to another', from a knowing that is 'sentient, embedded and experience-based' to one that is 'explicit, subject to rational analysis and perpetual reformulation'. Through this, management thus becomes the legitimate holder of explicit knowledge and takes on the rational planning role.

The scientific metaphor informs the mechanical view of organizations, organizations as machines to which scientific principles or laws may be applied, 'organizations as a structure of manipulable parts each of which is separately modifiable with a view to enhancing the efficiency of the whole' (Gouldner 1959: 405). A mechanical view of organizations is of their being instruments for task accomplishment, multiple parts designed in such a way that they mesh neatly into one another. Note also that the rational, mechanical model of organizations assumes that means and ends are connected regardless of the type of organization that is being considered.

The mechanical metaphor is discarded, when from the 1950s, 'systems' begins to enter management thinking, and from the 1960s, dominate.[10] This new vocabulary colonized previous analyses. Systems approaches focus on how 'inputs' from an 'environment' are incorporated into an internally ordered system. Based on sensing, monitoring, and scanning significant aspects of the environment, and the ability to relate these to operating norms and detect deviations from norms, there is then the possibility of initiating corrective action. As Hill (1988: 53) notes, however, 'a system involves an ordered relationship between ordered parts'. Defining a process as a technical system entails its reduction to discrete, identifiable components, the interrelationship of which may then be assembled into a predictable and formally controllable system. Task interdependencies and workflow become identified as discrete interlocking systems susceptible to formal analysis and alignment.

Systems engineering and systems analysis eagerly applied a scientific rationality to a wide variety of organizations. 'The logic of science offered a way of comprehending and creating systems of technical action ... systems should smoothly interconnect and inefficient or dislocating components within systems should be eliminated' (Jackson 2000: 32). One of the implications of systems is its association with, or assumption of, design. With this comes prescriptions for intervention and redesign, often in the absence of the experience of those who operate within a perceived 'system'. The inefficient components of a technological system lie not so much in technical arrangements as 'in the human labour that connects them' (Hill 1988: 50 quoted in Scarbrough and Corbett 1992: 79).

The systems approach reaches it apogee in cybernetics which emphasizes the importance of self-regulating behaviour, error detection, and automatic correction. The model is one of monitoring change and initiating the appropriate response. The image is that of flows of inputs, throughputs, outputs, and feedback, susceptible to linear programming, operations research, and systems analysis. If possible, organizations are not only to use cybernetics but also to become self-regulating cybernetic systems themselves where self-regulatory devices and feedback controls, that is, programmed decision-making in a system, make managerial intervention superfluous. Impersonal control models substitute for the personal exercise of authority. 'In such systems, the need to use power would indicate an organizational deficiency, i.e., behaviour is not sufficiently goal-oriented to do what had to be done automatically' (Mayntz 1964/2002: 112–13).

BOX 4.2. A CRIMINAL JUSTICE 'SYSTEM'?

The term Criminal Justice System is used frequently, but although a common term, it has different referents. Each has implications for how the CJS should be managed, may be measured, and the nature of interventions that can be made. One understanding of CJS is *as an interlinked activity*, the recognition that the operation of each area impacts on others:

An unhappy police officer is when they are writing warrants and police reports. What this means is that behaviour unconsciously impacts counter-productively on the behaviour of the system. The police have a clear up rate target. Because this is their driver, it has outcomes on the quality of the evidence gathered [in police reports], and how they present the information gets overlooked, naturally so. But then low quality, iffy reports are sent to the PFS. The number of 'no proceedings' goes up and the police get annoyed. This is an example of the two targets fighting each other. You need quality input because of its impact at later stages [in the prosecution process].   (PFS)

The PFS handing out warrants on a Friday night merely clogs up more cases for [the prisons] over the weekend when there are fewer staff. This is one of the symptoms of the system. People are thinking of, are only aware of, their own issues. They are not recognizing other folk's needs and priorities.   (Court services)

A lot of court cases are adjourned because of late Social Work reports. There was a case of Social Work in one office each having their own cases. So that when they were off their reports for court did not get done. Even when they were ill. The argument for Social Work having their own cases is that with recidivist offenders [reoffenders] it builds up a relationship between them and the Social Worker. But there is a production line in PFS and social work.   (Policy)

System thus becomes a shorthand term to denote a series of interlinked activities:

The issue is how do individual organisations interact and the extent to which they understand their impact on what others do. Certainly there is an impact of one area on another, exacerbated through the lack of knowledge of the system. There is a real lack of knowledge on the impact of procedures on working elsewhere.   (Policy)

There is a process. You can't be blind. Your actions impact on other agencies. You need to see it as a continuum and as part of a process.   (PFS)

From the recognition of interlinked activity, it is all too easy to construct the metaphor 'system' as a quasi-mechanical operation, *as a mechanical artefact*:

This tension runs through the entire system. All parts of the system have to work together if it is to work as a system. What is really called for is system definition and understanding. Within that the first objective would be shared understanding of the operations of the system and the outputs from the system, and an understanding of the relationship between the outputs and the outcomes.   (Policy)

The intention is to remove where the system rubs. If you do this then the system can become a system.   (Policy)

It comes down to processes and systems thinking in a management processing approach. What it needs is a structured systems thinking approach, until we do this, we will still be here in 10 years time. It's very exasperating.   (Policy)

(cont.)

BOX 4.2. (*continued*)

With this metaphor comes the need to create a 'system':

There are not may feedback loops in CJS. For example in rubbish collection. There are many stages in the system of rubbish collection, from the individual sorting rubbish, tying up bags, putting it outside, rubbish being collected, enough collection trucks etcetera. There is visible 'proof' of the systems results. If rubbish isn't collected there's rubbish on the streets and people complain. In CJS there are not such feedback systems, there is not such instant feedback of information, if it isn't working. You need internal pressures through targets because there are no external pressures. Because there are no external pressures in the system. Another problem with CJS is the extent to which you can rely on those who participate in the system. In health for example the patient wants to cooperate. Customers [in CJS] don't want to be recipient of the service. You try and introduce incentives, as for example, the sentence discount. But there is not the same sense of urgency as there would be in health. The accused doesn't want to cooperate. There is no urgency from there. Generally victims and witnesses are reluctant. They are frightened of the situation. There is not the urgency if summonses or citations don't materialise. People don't realise, until you get to the situation where people don't arrive at Court. The accused is not going to be chasing the system as in health. They would rather it were forgotten.   (Policy)

If there was a clarity as to what the CJS was to achieve, what it was there for as a system, then some parts could see where they fitted in.   (Policy)

To the extent that a system exists, it exists through the circulation of documentation that ensures that the processes of charge, prosecution, trial, sentence, appeal, and punishment may be secured. A 'system' is literally constructed through the circulation of files. It is *a flow of documentation*:

Look at a flow chart, the routes taken by cases in this, some are more complex than others. There are some simple cases. These would probably be dealt with by fixed penalties. But others go through the court process. A shop lifter usually has drugs, and will be a case of breach of the peace. The police will caution and charge. But certain charges will result in 'no pros'. Or the PFS will roll up charges or will add others. So you are progressing different types of report from the original charge. Its not one production process. Cases go from the first court hearing to the PFS to Courts and then back to PFS.   (Policy)

Whether the dominant motif is mechanical or cybernetic, management profits from science and technology being perceived as a problem-solving mechanism. Barnes and Edge (1982: 246) note how modern decision-making has spawned a succession of 'scientific' techniques 'having explicitly scientific pretensions'. It lays claims to theories, models, formalisms, and methods. Certainly, management abounds with acronyms: PERT, CPM, IDP, PPBS, MBO, and ZBB. 'Science' masters the world. But only, as Latour (1999: 29) reminds us, if the world comes 'in the form of two dimensional, superposable, combinable inscriptions'. The ubiquitous 'two-by-two' diagrams of management textbooks come to mind.

Management as a science, the repository of technical expertise, induces or inculcates a certain cognitive style, that of problem-solving and the problem solver. As Heydebrand (1979: 45) notes, this follows a certain predictive path: the identification of an antecedent, indeterminate situation (perceived as 'uncertain, unsettled, disturbed, doubtful, troubled, ambiguous, confused, obscure' and characterized by conflicting tendencies); the institution of the problem, that is, defining the situation as problematic and in need of problem-solving; the formulation of hypotheses through 'fact-finding' and discovery; subjecting these to reasoning and observation; finalizing a 'theory' that explains the problems and points to a solution. It is the transformation of an indeterminate situation into a definite one. From this framework, the organization as a problem-facing or problem-solving phenomena is embraced (Cyert and March 1963; Thompson 1967). Organizations as systems that 'solve' problems stress how efficiently information is dealt with, how decisions are made in an uncertain environment, and how information is processed. Solutions focus on information processing, input processes and output sequences, and hierarchies of information and knowledge. Information processing is a problem-solving activity, often to the neglect of the creation of information and knowledge (Nonaka 1994). Management as a science, and a cognitive style of problem-solving, places an emphasis on management as a causal agent. It is, for example, central to the management of change. The effective management of stasis, although in many respects far more important, does not carry the same cachet. Not only is management the causal agent, but it also becomes the necessary causal agent (Townley 2002a).

The form of knowledge that has been institutionalized as the foundation of management focuses on what Mintzberg (1994) terms a formal rationality with its emphasis on decomposition, articulation, and reductionism. It emphasizes analysis, detachment, partitioning of the whole into means–end relations, aggregation, and an emphasis on 'hard data'. It is an approach that is heavily influenced by a classical Newtonian concept of science and antecendent causality (Cohen 1994). Mintzberg details half a century of increasingly rationalistic approaches to management in the private sector, a process that is paralleled in the public (Carter et al. 1992). 'Strategic planning' was at one point identified as the route to effective management. Associated with being rational, systematic, and efficient, its virtue, as Wildavsky (quoted in Mintzberg 1994: 19) notes, is that it 'embodies universal norms of rational choice'. It is assumed to offer what Mintzberg terms the two solitudes of planning, performance control and action planning. It is for these reasons that planning 'is not defended for what it accomplishes but for what it symbolizes rationality. Key words appear over and over ... systematic rather than random, efficient rather than wasteful, coordinated rather than helter-skelter, consistent rather than contradictory, rational rather than unreasonable' (Wildavsky quoted in Mintzberg 1994: 189).

The dominance of a technical rationality in management education, the concern of management with technique, has been recognized (Grey 2005).

'Managerial problems' come to be understood as the discovery and application of a proper technology, its equipment, fact, means, and measurable effectiveness. Legitimacy and expertise becomes the mastery of formal methods rather than long experience:

With the rise of business schools, consulting firms and a great deal of professional and scientific development, the world is now blessed with general theories of organizations in the abstract . . . a world wide discourse now instructs on the conduct of organization. This produces a great expansion of management. It also standardizes this management across sectors and countries so that theories of proper leadership or organizational culture or financial accounting can be discussed increasingly consensually between a Korean manufacturer and a British education administrator.   (Meyer 1994: 53)

It is, as MacIntyre (1981) notes, the perpetuation of management as the 'morally neutral technician'.

Technocratic administration?

Understood as being the means employed to achieve ends to which action is oriented, techniques vary in their degree of rationality.[11] Weber identifies techniques 'for every conceivable type of action' (Weber 1978: 66), to be found in action as varied as prayer, administration, or love making. The highest level of rationality for Weber is technical rationality, founded on scientific knowledge, calculability, and predictability. Technical or formal rationality is informed by logic, calculation, and scientific knowledge and is dependent on being expressed in numerical, calculable terms. Logical and mathematically related propositions, for Weber, are immediately or unambiguously intelligible.

'Technical rationality' is 'instrumental problem-solving made rigorous by the application of scientific theory and technique' (Schon 2000: 21). Disagreement about means can be resolved 'by reference to facts concerning possible means, their relevant consequences, and the methods for comparing them with respect to the chosen ends of action' (Schon 2000: 33–4). However, as Weber reminds us, 'technical' concerns arise only where the end is accepted beyond question and the means to it involve 'purely technical consideration' (Weber 1978: 66). The presence of a 'technical question' means that there are doubts only over the choice of rational means to an end. It is specialized or scientific knowledge applied to a firmly bounded issue or problem. 'Science' thus can only be decisive under two conditions. First, in cases where there is an unambiguous end; second, where there is an unambiguous way of comparing means for achieving ends. However, as Weber notes, only a narrowly defined class of problems involving no conflict over ends or values have technically rational solutions. Most problems involve clashes about values or ends and as such are not solvable in an 'objectively' rational manner.

BOX 4.3. CAUSAL RELATIONSHIPS?

There is no clear agreement as to precisely what the 'problem' is to which overarching measures are seen as the solution. There is a general recognition of the 'need to work together more effectively in a joined up way':

The operation of the system will have an impact. If the system is working in an optimum fashion, if the system works efficiently and effectively, there will be an impact on crime levels and reoffending. For example, youngsters, who are the main group that goes through the system, if things are dragged out, this will only make things worse. If they go through the system quickly things may help. If you want the system to be more effective then there must be a close relationship between actions and consequences. You do not want this to fall behind. If you can achieve the certainty of detection, and the certainty of speed of disposal then there's an impact on crime.   (Policy)

There is little confidence, however, that overarching measures are the way to proceed:

Rather than setting an overall through target for all cases it might be better to focus on known problems areas, areas that are identified as problem areas. Perhaps our objectives should be to iron out the kinks, as for example those not appearing in court and court adjournments.   (Policy)

The transition from technical rationality, where the application of technical criteria is appropriate, to its application in areas not capable of technical resolution is signified by the term technocratic rationality. This is manifest where social and political problems become likened to technical problems, prompting the thinking that not only do these require technical solutions but also that all such problems *have* technical solutions.[12] It presupposes that 'human problems', like technical ones, 'have a solution that experts given sufficient data and authority can discover and execute' (Kuisel quoted in Porter 1995: 146). A technocratic rationality offers the illusion of 'scientific' objectivity, 'one best way', understood and decided by experts, and guaranteed by the impersonal knowledge of the objective and the 'real'. A technocratic approach to problem-solving and technical expertise offers neutrality, efficiency, and depersonalization. 'Politics' can be avoided or reduced when there is agreement on 'technical' issues, as rationality resides in, and is assured through the tools, techniques, and systems that provide calculation. Technique is the 'neutral' mechanism or instrument that aids in the provision of solutions to problems transposed into 'scientifically' manageable and rationally resolvable ones. It is independent of the passion and interests that usually cloud political debate. A technocratic rationality offers the prospect of technical solutions for being possible difficult problems

The tendency to convert value issues into a technical discussion, whereby technical expertise 'determines the conceptualization of political problems, the language in which they are expressed, and the institutional forms by which decisions are reached' (Barnes and Edge 1982: 244), has been identified as a form of 'scientism', the attempt to colonize territory through scientific language, techniques, approaches, models, and metaphors. The parameters of choice are dictated by technical imperatives not political ones. Politics becomes the contention between rival techniques. Authority is based on expertise and credentials.

A technocratic rationality is manifest in the appeal to the increasingly quantitative in decision- and policymaking. Measures play a particularly privileged role as positivistic science encourages the view that things cannot be known or indeed managed until they are measured (Hacking 1990). Hacking (1982) talks of the 'avalanche of numbers', the political arithmetic of numerical representation acting to construct an 'imagined community', in a world conceived in increasingly quantitative forms. Rose (1999) also makes reference to the 'political sociology of numbers' in his analysis of how numbers are an intrinsic mechanism for conferring legitimacy on political authority. Not only is there the increased promise of predictability through calculability, but there is also an increasing number of areas to which calculability is applied.

Numbers play a particular role in technique and constitute a particular form of representation.[13] Debates on the functioning of quantification reflect its ambiguity. On the one hand, it may provide transparency, the basis for discussion, debate, and contestation and thus the process of 'holding to account'. Their use prompts a number of questions concerning the politics of accuracy (is this a correct measure?); adequacy (do they reflect that which they are taken to represent?); their use and abuse (how are they used, for what purpose?); and ethics (should these measures be used in this context?) (Rose 1999). They stimulate debates as to 'what to measure, how to measure it, how often to measure it and how to present and interpret the results' (Rose 1999: 198). Because of this, Porter (1992: 28) sees quantification as the counterpart to representative democracy, associating quantification with democratization and empowerment. Quantification is a means of communication, providing a common vocabulary or language, for arguments to be played out. It plays this role because the rules for manipulating numbers are widely shared. Quantification is designed to minimize arbitrariness.[14]

As publicly available 'political intelligence', quantification enables individuals and groups to communicate with one another, subvert rank and power, act as a means of reducing unchecked power, and avoid the suspicion of the personal and the arbitrary. For Porter (1992: 29), it is the 'impersonality' of numbers that ensures their authority rather than any claims to 'truth'. Making issues explicit through illustrating the calculations that have been made allows for the possibility of agreement. There is thus the potential for disinterest. In addition, quantified techniques, algorithms, etc. offer uniformity and administrative convenience, may serve as a substitute for ad hoc decision-making, and lessen the burden of personal responsibility. Quantification is thus a 'neutral, objective language, a basis for minimizing arbitrariness' (Porter 1992: 32).[15]

As Hacking (1983) reminds us, however, it is important to distinguish reasons for measuring from the function of measurement. One of the advantages of quantification for Porter is that it imposes 'constraints on the issues that can be raised and what can be properly said about them' (Porter 1995: 32). It is this latter element, the constraints on debate, which raises contrary concerns about the role of the quantification in 'political' decisions. A less-benign view than Porter's sees it as the technicization of politics. The language of quantification, although a highly structured and impersonal one, may sacrifice other meanings. Cost–benefit analysis, for example, is a convention for reaching recommendations. It offers a highly structured and impersonal template for exchange of information and negotiation of outcome. It is not neutral, however. To measure is to isolate certain features of the 'object' measured. Certain vocabularies and ways of structuring debate are facilitated by such techniques. Through the reduction of complexity, important dimensions become lost to debate. Others lose legitimacy. Moral and ethical arguments are difficult to feature in representative form. Debates focus on that which is certain rather than that which is appropriate.

Although there are conventions that determine the manipulation of numbers, decisions as to what to measure, how to measure, when to measure, how to present and interpret results are not neutral decisions. Measures and quantification construct choices. They are a particular form of representation and there are an array of judgement decisions and disputes that go into measuring or devising a scale that are obscured or hidden. The boundaries of the problem, the alternatives, and what is regarded as appropriate all influence what is considered to be 'data' and 'facts' and technical knowledge. While many debates may be about technical questions and in certain circumstances increased knowledge may separate facts from values or clarify technical constraints, often debates involve political choices about competing social values (Nelkin 1984).

These concerns were recognized by Ellul whose understanding of technique is broader than the individual technique itself. Technique is not only the 'means' but also the 'ensemble of means' (Ellul 1964: 19). As an ensemble of means, technique displays an autonomy manifest in the increasing search for greater efficiency and the constant improvement of technical means. 'Automatism' is where a technique 'determines' an outcome, displacing human judgement. If the technique is not exactly adapted to the end, the end is usually modified rather than the technique. Technique gradually transforms means into ends. As the product of specialization, it not only hinders mutual understanding but also, 'having ruptured the relations between man and man, proceeds to rebuild the bridge which links them' (Ellul 1964: 132). It can also inform all areas of life, 'for technique nothing is sacred, there is no mystery, no

---

BOX 4.4. 'ACCURATE' MEASURES?

Targets should 'meet SMART criteria, i.e., Specific, Measurable, Achievable, Relevant and Timed' (PSAF 2003: 3).

One of the rationales for a performance measurement system is the attempt to remove 'politics' by introducing robust measures that give an indication of progress and do not mislead. Measures support an 'evidence-based' approach to policy and focus on outcomes:

The objectives of the Justice ministry are to make people safer and feel safer (measured by the reduction of serious crime, increased drug seizures, and reduced fear of crime); a fair and more efficient justice system that commands confidence of customers and public (including court case completion); and a reduction in offending and the provision of more effective non-custodial penalties. (Scottish Executive 2002)

Devising the 'right' measures, however, confronts the vexed question of how events, activities, and practices taking place over space and time may be represented in a manner that can be taken to be an accurate account. For example:

Reoffending rates

Someone comes who is an alcoholic, unemployed, poor housing, poor socio-economic circumstances, prison provides a stable environment. But then they are released and go back to the same environment. (Prison services)

But the issue is how do you measure effectiveness? Is effectiveness going through the Community Service Order? If someone is later reconvicted but for a lesser offence, this could still count as successful. (Social work)

It has taken years for people to get to the stage where they offend. There are expectations of quick returns. There are over exaggerated views of what programmes could or might provide, and the expectations of quick change, after people have been treated and living in a particular way for 15 to 20 years. The main thing is that people have got to want to change. (Voluntary agency)

Drug measures

What do you measure? The value of drug seizures is influenced by price on the market. If you use the weight of drug seizures, this does not indicate overall supply on the market. It's difficult to see how you would estimate this. Drug supply depends on a whole range of issues outwith individual police force control, the nature of harvests, the activities by other police forces, the logistics of supply. (Policy)

Reduced crime

The aim of the CJS is to reduce crime? NO. It can help to contribute to the reduction of crime, along with education and health. It's OK to think about the outcomes as a Minister. This would be low crime, public confidence. But don't have executive agencies thinking about outcomes. They don't deliver on outcomes. They can help towards them. (Policy)

Fear of crime

No matter how many police we put out on the beat there are so many other factors that have an impact. How do people get fear of crime? It's their own experience. The experience of family and friends. Local media reports. National media reports. The Crime

BOX 4.4. (*continued*)

survey asks you how you feel about going out in the streets in the dark and in the High Street in the day. As soon as you mention the dark there is fear of crime. Also if there was no fear of crime? Would that be a good thing?   (Police)

The police are reluctant to have this as an indictor. But if people are petrified, if they are afraid to go out and there is crime in the street. It has to be tackled. Who is going to tackle it? If it is not the CJS?   (Sheriff)

Public confidence and satisfaction in CJS

People have such artificial expectations of the legal process. There are problems of false expectations. The finding is that if the individual feels badly treated, either through a non-guilty verdict or a perceived low penalty, then it doesn't matter how helpful or how good the various agencies were. It's as though we hadn't bothered. If the view of [an agency] was positive and the overall view of CJS was negative then the experience of the whole system is negative. The positive feelings don't last very long.   (Voluntary agency)

If there is no confidence then people don't report a crime. If there is a bad experience people will be much less willing to be a witness in the future. We need to understand this. It is not a matter of public duty. It doesn't work like this now. They would be much more likely to look the other way.   (Sheriff)

Case completion

All police reports have to be in in 28 days. Caution and charge minutes [starts] a case. It gives details on the computer, a record, the offence, details, evidence, culprits etcetera. So [now there are] skeleton pending cases. So everything is held and detailed on this, because this does not get the clock running. This causes delays before there is caution and charge. But the clock may be running in the big cases. There may be big delays. Drugs cases take longer. You have to wait for forensics in drug cases. You may need this as corroboration or evidence before you can take a case forward.   (anonymous)

In working on the targets on the length of time taken to get to court, there is a 28 day period for the police to report to the PFS. Why 28? Why not 30, 15. Why pick 28? Why not that they should be done as soon as possible? The measure of 28 days doesn't give you anything. It doesn't give you percentages of over and under, not how far over, not 80% are done within 30 days. It doesn't tell you 90% are naturally completed in 60 days, and that this is the best people do under the circumstances. These measures are set. We don't know why. Management circles always use averages, and then they try and manage the average. Map users use UCL, upper control limit. The average doesn't tell you very much. The upper control limit tells you the normal process, which is that the normal range is between 1 and 118 days. Some go higher, but this is an indication of things going horribly wrong. These figures tell you that unless you change the system, this is the only way that you are going to get the UCL to reduce.   (anonymous)

---

taboo' (Ellul 1964: 142). In this, Ellul surfaces a number of concerns relating to the role of technique: the transformation of tools as guides to analysis, informing debate, to their becoming a universal standard of rationality; the internalization of a mechanical objectivity or impersonal decision rules that replaces or displaces other forms of judgement; the substitution of a technology or technique for enlightened reflection.

Just as bureaucracy signifies rule of the office, so technocracy conjures up the rule of techne, rule exercised through the use of technical knowledge, expert power, and problem-solving. Technical rationality, however, is restricted to a limited number of cases or issues. The failure to recognize this can result in the technical becoming a source of domination as it elides into the technocratic. It is a phenomena that is identified by others under different names and within different theoretical or explanatory systems: as scientism or the belief in science per se, not as one form of knowledge but as exclusive knowledge (Habermas 1971)[16]; as performativity, the best possible input/output equation, failing to realize that all formal systems have internal limitations (Lyotard 1984); and as technocracy or a technocratic administration, the combination of scientific–technical knowledge and technique in the pursuit of efficiency, productivity, and cost-effectiveness (Burris 1993; Heydebrand 1979).[17] It is a concern expressed by Habermas (1971), as the distinction between the technical (the efficient and calculated pursuit of goals) and the practical (a generalized reflection on what goals should be chosen) becomes eliminated in a technocratic consciousness. Not only is there, in this process, an 'instrumentalization of things', but there is also an 'instrumentalization of man' (Marcuse 1964: 159). Its effects are evident from the cost–benefit analysis used in the Pinto case (Corbett 1994) to its operation in the Holocaust (Bauman 1989).[18]

Which science?

Although claimed as universalistic, the science that has informed a technocratic rationality is a specific reading of classical Newtonian science (Cohen 1994). Newtonian models of science rely on certain meta-assumptions: analysis, detachment or subject/object separation, objectivity, and linear progression in cause and effect relations. Analysis presumes that the whole is the sum of its parts and that a reduction of elements to their component parts will allow for synthesis. Detachment presumes an objective reality to be known, independent of the knower, and knowable through observation and recording what is out there, the objectivity of 'accurate and reliable' information.

The Enlightenment's mechanistic aspiration was of human action regulated by social laws, open to ideas of mastery and control and appropriate ways to manipulate it. That this Newtonian model was transferred to human actions reflects the heavy borrowing from physics to human behaviour that occurred in the seventeenth and eighteenth centuries and continued into the nineteenth century (Cohen 1994; Klamer and Leonard 1994; MacIntyre 1981; Mirowski 1994a). Adam Smith, for example, borrowed from Newton's physics and Hume intended to do for moral philosophy what Newton had done for natural philosophy. In doing so, the mechanical element of Newton's work, the assumption of a mechanical form of causality, causality as unidirectional, antecedent conditions or efficient causes, and causal relationships independent of time, was heavily exaggerated.[19]

Management also reflects this model. The focus on the rational and the purposively intentional (reflected in concepts of strategic management); the mechanistic and reductionist (vision, mission, goals, objectives, measures, targets, etc.); adaptation (to environments); predictability achieved through monitoring and negative feedback; the importance of equilibrium and stability; the assumption of a change in variable x leading to a specified change in variable y; the decontextualized ideal of the universal model (abstract management systems); and the role of the leader/elite in promoting change are all reflective of a particular 'Newtonian' concept of science (Fox Keller 1985). Taking rationality to imply the construction of coordinated means–end relationships has inevitable implications for when such means–ends relationships do not materialize, or when their implicit

---

BOX 4.5. WHICH SCIENCE?

The sense of the CJS as a complex non-linear system can be seen from the following accounts of two interventions designed to 'solve' problems in one area of the 'system'. The first is an initiative to introduce private firms to transport those in prison to court, to save police time:

CJSW relied on links to the police computer to see which cases were to arrive in court, who was coming to court, who they would have to report on. With the introduction of the private contractor these links were lost. This caused major problems. There is an effect on the whole criminal justice system, the courts, the police, the PFS. The failure to produce Social Work Reports means setting up another remand court, it means going for a warrant, because the individual probably won't come, this means more work for the police, and the setting up of a custody court. All this mushrooms from a Social Work report not being on time. Everyone is affected. The Sheriff, the Court, Social Work. (Court services)

The second is an initiative to move to fixed fees for solicitors taking on a case, designed to cap legal aid costs, simplify procedures and stop solicitors charging for taking large numbers of statements from witnesses:

With the legal aid move to fixed fees a lot of firms stopped taking on trainees. They didn't know whether they would be able to afford them. This fed into the university and people stopped taking criminal law. But firms do not turn away any cases. You have however many cases. The knock on effect of legal aid changes is that there is a small number of criminal lawyers with the same number of cases. (Defence agent)

The problem with performance measures is there's an assumption of linearity. There is an assumption that you have an ability to achieve these targets. It is not like throwing a pebble into a pond and then using physics to predict the waves. It's like letting lose a live bird, you don't know where it's going to go. (Social work)

linearity does not hold. It is this linear model of antecedent causality and assumptions of a unique or well-defined cause that gives rise to analyses in terms of 'unintended' consequences, rather than the latter being seen as the direct consequence of interventions brought about as the universal meets the particular (Kerr 1995).[20]

The implications of 'new science' and developments broadly labelled complexity theory question the assumptions of Newtonian science in several important respects. It stresses the importance of complex, non-linear systems, where coherent and patterned structures can emerge from the dynamics of the system, without conscious intention or design[21]; where micro-level interactions can lead to macro-level patterns[22]; and small-scale interaction can have large consequences due to amplification and positive feedback.[23] Complex interplays between actions and outcomes indicate that there are problems of predictability and planning, certainly the impossibility of long-term predictions. The difficulties of measuring the conditions of the system accurately also points to the difficulties of reducing uncertainty and instability. The inability of predicting long-term outcomes points to the problem of distinguishing between strategic and tactical decisions. It indicates the importance of experimentation, the ability to remain open to changes, flexibility, the importance of the holographic image of the organization with each unit having an overall picture, as well as the importance of the redundancy of parts and functions (Marion 1999; Stacey 2000; Waldrop 1992).

Management as practice

One antidote to management as a technocratic science comes from the social studies of science. These illustrate how science and the generation of scientific knowledge may be better understood as a social practice (Pickering 1992). As McCarl Nielsen (1990) notes, 'a close analysis of what scientists do, as opposed to what they say they do' shows that 'the scientific method is less distinguishable from other ways of knowing'. The embedded nature of the production of scientific knowledge is now readily acknowledged in this literature (Hacking 1992; Pickering 1992). Knowledge or meaning is intersubjective, negotiated, and collective. Science is a social practice; 'cognitive' processes of scientific enquiry are themselves social (Bloor 1991; Longino 2002). This practice becomes black-boxed in the presentation of science. The array of judgement decisions, the disputes that go into measuring and devising a scale, are rendered invisible, and with this incontestable. The importance of the analysis of science as practice is that it illustrates how practices, techniques, and 'science' reflect the assumptions of place and time, the intellectual, technical, institutional, and organizational factors that shape knowledge claims.[24] What the social studies of technology and science illustrate are the processes and practices of stabilization behind 'facts' such that they acquire their facticity (Knorr Cetina 1981; Pickering 1992). Hacking (1992), for example, details the processes that underpin the transformation of data ('uninterpreted inscriptions'), as it makes its way through data assessment, data reduction, data analysis to interpretation, as decisions are made answering questions as to what is treated as representation, by whom, and for what. For Latour (1987), it is networks, associations, alliance, and enrolment that constitute the foundation of knowledge, of which science is but one form. The formation and durability of networks is key to understanding science as it is this that tests and forges the epistemological characteristics of knowledge claims. Knowledge is objective if it is shared and enduring: the greater the agreement among measurers, the greater the 'objectivity' of the measure.[25]

What is true for science is equally true for any claims for 'science' in management. Neither is the transparent reflection or representation of the 'real'. It is not a correspondence theory of truth that determines objectivity, but a coherence theory of thought, action, and practice (Hacking 1992). Instruments of observation, be these microscopes, bureaucratic forms, balance sheets, the explanatory grid, or balanced scorecard, require training in order to see what is there (Barley 1986; Hacking 1992). 'Seeing objectively' requires practice. There is a pedagogic role in the application and use of any technique (Oakes et al. 1998). Hence the caveat that is usually found with the recommendation for techniques in management, 'when properly applied and with sufficient amount of time to make them really effective' (Taylor 1911/1982: 124).

Conclusions

Science and technique establish a hierarchy of knowledge. They privilege a disembedded disembodied knowledge in relation to the 'subjective', the 'personal', the qualitative, and the ad hoc. The self is disembedded to the point of its disappearance, in the sense that 'facts', science, or technique determines that something should be done in a particular way. Along with the economic and bureaucratic, the technocratic is another form of exemplifying Nagel's (1986) 'view from nowhere'. It is to claim the impersonal and the universal. A technical or technocratic rationality, however, defines issues in terms of 'problem-solving'. This is to the neglect of problem-setting: 'the process by which we define the decision to be made, the ends to be achieved, the means which may be chosen' (Schon 2000: 40). As Schon (2000: 40) notes:

problems do not present themselves to practitioners as givens. They must be constructed from the materials of problematic situations which are puzzling, troubling and uncertain. In order to convert a problematic situation into a problem, a practitioner must do a certain kind of work. He [sic] must make sense of an uncertain situation that initially makes no sense. Problem setting is a process in which...we name the things to which we will attend and frame the context in which we will attend to them...It is the work of naming and framing that creates the conditions necessary to the exercise of technical expertise

This is necessarily an embedded process to which we next turn.

Part II
Embedded Rationality

Introduction

A disembedded rationality is founded on reason as universal and impartial, removed from local circumstance. Rationalism's supremacy from the Enlightenment period onwards is, however, sustained through the suppression of its soft underbelly, an embedded rationality.[1] Constructed in opposition to tradition, authority, experience, and anything that speaks of context, specificity, or history, the equation of the rational with abstract analysis and universal laws has come under periodic assault in a variety of ways. It is evidenced in rejection of language as the transparent presentation of the 'real'; rejection of an external objective reality accessible in an unmediated way to the omnipotent knower; rejection of foundationalism, that is, the transcendence of the knowing subject or the object of knowledge; a critique of an individualist, essentialist concept of human nature; and a critique of an epistemology that sees knowledge as an individual project. Moreover, there has been a rejection of the universal, transcendent nature of reason.

The work of Kuhn (1962) and his critique of a disembedded rationality in science are particularly influential in this respect. Kuhn introduced the view that there is no knowledge outside a frame of reference. There is no objective, universal knowledge to which the rational pursuit of truth can aspire that is not dependent on prior theoretical assumptions and perspective. That knowledge proceeds from a perspective denies the transcendent position: knowledge or theory is always 'embedded'. Communities share paradigms. Paradigms 'close off' certain foundationalist assumptions that then become the background knowledge from which enquiry may begin. Each paradigm has a discrete set of conceptual, theoretical, and methodological assumptions. Data and observations are theory laden; theories are paradigm laden; and paradigms are culture laden (McCarl Nielsen 1990). Rationality or rational procedures alone cannot decide scientific ideas.

Within organization studies, Kuhn's work was taken up in the 'paradigm wars' (Pfeffer 1993; Van Maanen 1991a; see Clegg 2002b, vol. 8) where discussions were fought to an impasse. A more productive entrée into this debate comes from Hacking's (1983: 2) assessment of Kuhn as having 'unintentionally inspired a crisis of rationality'. Broaching issues in these terms poses debate in terms of whether something is rational or not, not whether it is 'true' or not. This allows for the possibility of alternative positions to be seen as an extension of rationality rather than being embroiled in a valorization of the 'truth' of one paradigm 'against' another.

The crisis in rationality was brought to the fore in discussions of the work of the anthropologist Evans-Pritchard (1976) and his work with the Azande and their belief in witchcraft (Tambiah 1990; Wilson 1970).[2] The question was raised: what should be the response to beliefs that appear 'irrational'?.[3]

In particular, how may one account for the 'unreason' of witchcraft? Is belief in it as rational as Western belief in science? On what grounds is it equally as rational? It is a debate that raises issues of translation between cultures or 'paradigms', commensurability, and relativism; whether it is possible for one 'culture' to understand another; whether understanding implies that there are some shared processes of intelligibility and reasoning (rationality) between the two different cultures; and if standards of rationality do not coincide, on what grounds can we understand, or make intelligible, that which is different (MacIntyre 1970; Winch 1970)?

Lukes identifies five possible responses to the 'witchcraft' problem: to treat irrational beliefs as symbolic; to apply 'objective' universal standards of what constitutes rational beliefs, from which one position would be judged irrational; to test positions against certain criteria of rationality in terms of thought and use of evidence; to emphasize fundamental differences between 'modern' and 'primitive' beliefs recognizing that both might be 'rational' although not specifying how; or to interpret 'irrational' beliefs as rational and 'seek contextually given criteria according to which they appear rational' (Lukes 1967: 255). In the latter, rationality may only be judged in relation to a 'way of life', that is, irrational beliefs will be interpreted as rational 'in the light of the criteria of rationality to be discovered in the culture in which they occur' (Lukes 1967: 258). In other words, 'rules of reasoning are bequeathed by culture' (Polanyi 1983: 48). Lukes (1967) dismisses the first response on the grounds that to treat beliefs as 'symbolic' is to deny the issue of rationality. It is no longer perceived as relevant to debate. The other positions raise the universalist/relativist conundrum.

A universalist position would argue for one form of rationality based on rules of logic and inference. Cultures can be mutually understood or be rational to each other because they have foundational assumptions on truth and inference, coherence, and rational interdependence of beliefs (Hollis 1970; Lukes 1970). These determine a core group of beliefs or experiences and act as 'bridgeheads' through which translations or comparisons with one's own culture may be judged (Hollis 1970).[4] As there is some measure of comparison and commensurability, there must then be some measure of common rationality, and some criteria on which to base some form of a universalist position of rationality. In the strongest statement of this position, it may be possible to make judgements of some cultures, belief systems, etc. being more 'rational' than others.

A 'contextual rationality', on the other hand, identifies actions which, within a context, are reasonable within that context (Lukes 1970). Rationality is thus context dependent rather than an absolute concept (MacIntyre 1970). This position is informed by what Davidson (1980) refers to as a principle of interpretive charity, that is, actions must be judged against some measure of rationality or else they could not be deemed explicable. What appears irrational might, when its context is understood, appear rational, thus raising the question as to whether there are alternative or different standards of rationality (Lukes 1967). A contextual rationality holds that there are different styles of reasoning, each of which must be judged according to its own principles (Winch 1970). Under a contextual perspective, rationality cannot be judged by rigid principles. Logical conventions are defined through institutional usage and are therefore not context free. There is no 'really' rational. Rational norms must be sociologically explained (Bloor 1991). Thus, there are no good and bad reasons, but there is reasoning appropriate to whatever is under discussion; and styles of thinking bring their own body of knowledge. In other words, there are webs of beliefs that sustain the belief that something is a good reason. For MacIntyre (1970), raising the question of whether something is rational or not presupposes criteria of rationality that are impossible to weigh independently of the existing norms of rationality. Understanding requires comprehension within its own regime. From this perspective, rationality is more akin to Wittgenstein's language games or forms of life. Understanding can only be within its own frame of reference. It is a relativist position.[5]

The essence of a contextual rationality is that rationality is embedded in the context in which it occurs and acquires meaning in reference to that context.[6] Hence the reference here to an embedded rationality. As the converse of an abstract, decontextualized rationality, an embedded rationality concomitantly denies the depiction of the separate, disembedded, autonomous self. 'The ideal of impartiality requires constructing the ideal of a self abstracted from the context of any real persons: the deontological self is not committed to any particular ends, has no particular history, is a member of no communities ... [it is] a fictional self in a fictional situation of reasoning' (Young 1987: 60).[7] An embedded rationality entails an embedded self. 'Reason is the contingent achievement of [the] linguistically socialized' (Benhabib 1992: 6). The individual lives within a specific geographic, temporal, socio-economic context, and as such has a history, an identity, a gender, and a race. Connections embed this self within a social context of relationships and obligations.

An embedded self critiques the epistemology and methodology that informs the scientific assumptions that individuals are interchangeable as knowers and that value-neutral objectivity and impartiality characterize legitimate enquiry. The contrast that is being drawn is between 'a world directly experienced from oneself as centre' and 'a world organized in the abstracted conceptual mode, external to the local and particular places of one's ... existence' (Smith 1987: 84).[8] It is the latter that is deemed to be the guarantor of 'scientific objectivity'. An embedded self critiques the knower as an abstract, socially anonymous entity and claims them as a historical social identity. Circumstances of birth, family, linguistic, cultural, and gender identity are important dimensions of the individual who reasons. Positions shape and constrain what is known and structure understanding (Harding 1991).[9] It denies that authority is secured through the elimination of any knowledge of the speaker and defends experience and socially situated 'truths' as a (not 'the') source of knowledge. The context of discovery is as important as the context of justification for a fuller account of the context of that which is claimed as knowledge or a right position (Harding 1991). Knowledge as partial, perspectival, and necessarily limited recognizes that there are other perspectives on the world. There is not a singular, exclusive, or privileged access. Recognizing that knowledge proceeds from some perspective requires not that 'bias' is eliminated, but that it is used. Location becomes an important source of understanding. 'Strong objectivity' requires a critical evaluation of the social situation of knowledge claims (Harding 1991). It is a recognition and consideration of the partiality that impartiality claims. 'Objectivity' requires taking 'subjectivity' into account (Code 1993: 32; Harding 1991). It is, in Haraway's (1991) terms, the only way that one becomes answerable for what one sees. Positioning implies responsibility. Unlocatable knowledge claims are for Haraway (1991) necessarily irresponsible. 'Partial, locatable, critical knowledges' open the way for 'sustained, rational' enquiry (Haraway 1991: 191). Location, positioning, and situating are the 'condition of being heard to make rational knowledge claims' (Haraway 1991: 195). 'Rational knowledge is a process of ongoing critical interpretation among "fields" of interpreters and decoders. Rational knowledge is power-sensitive conversation' (Haraway 1991: 196).[10]

But, if reason is contextualized, does this mean that all positions are 'reasonable'? Is rationality only 'what the majority says it means' (Nicholson 1999: 121)?[11] That there is no 'correct' concept of rationality implies that there is no neutral place to stand, no external vantage point to judge what is rational. Something being context dependent, however, does not collapse into an 'anything goes' relativism whereby there are no standards for assessing the reasonableness of a position. It is not social or communicative breakdown (Nicholson 1999). Haraway (1991) notes that ' "Relativism is a way of being nowhere and claiming to be everywhere", but absolutism is a way of being everywhere while pretending to be nowhere, and neither one in its starkest articulation will do ... knowledge is always relative to (i.e. a perspective on, a standpoint in) specifiable circumstances' (quoted in Code 1993: 40). Denial of a single objective truth does not deny the multiplicity of truths that guide the particular and the contingent.

From an embedded rationality, principles of rationality are considered in relation to particular communities. Rationality is embedded. It is to be accountably rational, that is, reasonable to others.[12] Three embedded rationalities are identified in organization studies: the institutional, the contextual, and the situational. Each challenges a fundamental dimension of rational action in its disembedded form: its claims to universalism; its assumptions of a fully conscious awareness of reasons for actions; and its temporal assumptions that reasons precede action. Institutional rationality takes issue with the principle of universalism. It identifies different value spheres: political, religious, aesthetic, economic, etc. Each different sphere has a different foundational rationality informing what constitutes rational action within it. A contextual rationality takes the issue with the explicitly conscious dimension of rationality and highlights the importance of background knowledge in framing rational understanding. This is the foundation of being able to function in a community, be this, work, occupational, or epistemic group. A situational rationality takes issue with the temporal assumptions of a rationality, the assumption that rationality precedes action, and argues that rationality is constructed as action is ongoing or after action has occurred. Each rationality also differs in terms of their scale of reference (Strathearn 1995). Scale emphasizes different magnitudes of time and space coordinates. The institutional, contextual, and situational differ in terms of their scope of time–space dimensions, from the historically grounded (institutional) to the immediate and localized (situational). Through these different coordinates of scale and the challenges that each poses to rational action, each constitutes different dimensions of an embedded rationality.

5 Institutional rationality

The first embedded mode of reasoning to be examined is institutional rationality. Its significance lies in its critique of a universalistic concept of rationality. Interrogating the fiction of the disembedded individual, it recognizes that, as Simon noted (1957: 102), 'the rational individual is, and must be, an organized and institutionalized individual'. An institutional rationality acknowledges that there are different spheres of society reflected in the major institutions that organize social life (government, law, the family, religion, etc.), and that of these each has its own inherent or immanent logic. The individual is thus embedded in different institutional modes of reasoning. This chapter outlines the extent to which this institutional rationality has been recognized in organization theory.

The rationalization of value spheres

The starting point comes from Weber's writings on rationalization. Rationalization is part of the disenchantment (or 'demagification') of the world, the transformation of an uncontrollable and unintelligible world into one that may be understood and open to prediction.[1] There has been a tendency to reduce rationalization to the institutionalization of a purposive rational action, and indeed Weber (1978: 30) writes, 'one of the most important aspects of the process of "rationalization" of action is the substitution for the unthinking acceptance of ancient custom, of deliberate adaptation to situations in terms of self interest.'[2] This, however, does not exhaust the concept. Rationalization is a general process that encompasses the expansion of empirical knowledge and the enhancement of technically rational control over natural and social processes (Brubaker 1984; Kalberg 1980; Lash and Whimster 1987; Ray and Reed 1994). It includes the systematization of ideas, the intellectualization of realms of knowledge, and the enhancement of specialized knowledge.[3] Socially, this is manifest in processes as diverse as the institutionalization of science in universities and art in theatres and museums, the development of harmonious music, the use of linear perspective in painting, scientific jurisprudence, and formal law. Weber cautions against viewing rationalization as a unilinear, monolithic process.[4] For Weber, rationalization takes varied forms and directions. It is also characterized by deep internal tensions and contradictions as a multiplicity of rationalization processes conflict and coalesce (Brubaker 1984; Kalberg 1980; Lash and Whimster 1987).

One dimension of the processes of rationalization is the growing differentiation between separate spheres of existence, in particular the social differentiation, and relative autonomy of law, religion, economy, and polity. Thus, the development of modern science, the emergence of the modern state, a formalistic legal system, and an administrative bureaucratic structure are all manifestations of the process of rationalization. They all contribute to a calculable external environment. Each institutional sphere has a developmental history of its own, further reinforcing their differentiation.

As rationalization differentiates society into different spheres of activity or value, 'institutional spheres', there is an increased elaboration of what Weber terms value spheres, each with their own immanent logics. Human life is partitioned into a variety of independently functioning domains. Weber specifically identifies the religious, economic, political, cultural, aesthetic, erotic, and intellectual (Weber 1948: 323–59). With the increased autonomy of these value spheres comes increased conflict between them, with each value sphere displaying a separate and inner logic informing social action.

Value spheres, law, economy, religion, education, etc. become increasingly autonomous and incommensurable in three distinct senses. Conduct within the sphere takes place according to its own laws (causal autonomy); each sphere has its own inherent dignity or intrinsic value (axiological autonomy); and each generates its own norms and obligations (normative autonomy) (Brubaker 1984). Value spheres exist independently of the individuals who participate in them. Thus, individuals confront them as a given, independent of their personal value orientations.[5] The social world is thus comprised of a plurality of value spheres, each with their own inner logics and autonomous norms. 'Truth', 'justice', 'efficiency', 'beauty', 'authenticity', and other abstract ideas become central in informing the values of these different spheres, with each sphere developing or refining their central values in further elaborations. What constitutes rational action within the spheres involves 'regimes of truth', the criteria, norms, and procedures that inform what constitutes 'true' propositions in a given case (Hindess 1987). Each has different patterns of action and ways of life that are defended as 'rational'. There are thus multiple rationalities.

The incompatibility of these abstract standards leads to tensions among rationalized spheres of life.[6] Their enhanced autonomy intensifies antagonisms and sharpens the clash of value spheres (Lash and Whimster 1987). As a result, social life involves irreconcilable value conflicts. One consequence of this is that the modern self moves from sphere to sphere compartmentalizing its attitude. Acting or being a competent agent within a particular value sphere requires an adherence to its dominant axiological and normative prescriptions, orientating conduct to ultimate values, be these political, religious, intellectual, cultural, aesthetic, or erotic.[7] The rationalization of value spheres leads to the multifaceted rationality of modern life. Many different patterns of action and ways of life may be 'rational'.

The import of Weber's work lies in understanding the institutional nature of rationality. What is 'rational' depends on the institutional organization of society. The rationality of an action is thus conferred by its location within a broader institutional logic and the framework of knowledge and belief that sustains this. As Albrow (1987: 171) explains,

> the uncertainties and complexities which would attach to individual purposive action (due to unpredictability) are replaced by institutionalized expectations of behaviour that are stabilized over time, projects and people...The actions in which people engage then become part of the wider system and their rationality is attributed...in their relation to the durable and consistent set of normative expectations.

The institution of reason

Rationalization is the process by which spheres become distinct, giving rise to the 'art world' or 'political world'. Each is defined by a distinctive style of thought. The 'rationality' that informs action and behaviour in these spheres is an institutional rationality.

'Institutions' have been identified with the 'great institutions' of church, government, law, private property, and the family, that is, the fundamental political, social, and legal entities that establish the basis of social organization. Additionally, 'institutions' also include a wide variety of things that may become institutionalized, in the sense of taken-for-granted, valorized ideas and practices that have the appearance of stable entities, be this, the rules of a game, ceremony or ritual, the system of queuing, stopping for traffic lights, etc. Minimally, an institution is a convention and arises 'when all parties have a common interest in there being a rule to insure coordination, none has a conflicting interest, and none will deviate lest the desired coordination is lost' (Douglas 1987: 46). As Douglas notes, however, 'the entrenching of an institution is essentially an intellectual process as much as an economic and political one...To acquire legitimacy, every kind of institution founds its rightness in reason and in nature' (Douglas 1987: 45). She gives as an example 'justice'. She writes, 'the most profound decisions about justice are not made by individuals as such, but by individuals thinking within and on behalf of institutions' (Douglas 1987: 111). Choosing rationally involves choosing among social institutions. 'When individuals disagree on elementary justice, their most insoluble conflict is between institutions based on incompatible principles. The more severe the conflict, the more useful to understand the institutions that are doing most of the thinking' (Douglas 1987: 125). In other words, the concept of rationality is embedded in institutional life. There is an institutionalized set of rational principles.

Within organization studies, Stinchcombe (1990) develops Weber's concept of rationality linked to institutional rules in his analysis of what he terms the 'institution of reason'. He identifies 'reason' as 'norms governing a body of thought recognized as authoritative in a culture, so that reason is characteristic of science, of law, or of accounting practice . . . a socially established method of calculating what should be authoritative in a particular case' (Stinchcombe 1990: 289). He gives as an example legal reasoning. This includes the application of precedent, reasoning from precedent, following principles of discovery, etc. These are 'principles of reasoning' acceptable within a discipline, a 'generative grammar' of judgements. 'People agree that they are participating in a science, they agree that a particular set of norms of reasoning will be taken as authoritative, unless and until that body of norms of reasoning is improved by the application of more general and high ranking principles of reasoning' (Stinchcombe 1990: 292).

The foundation of an institutionalized reason is a body of practitioners who know and are able to practise the system of reasoning. Where practitioners are formally educated rather than through an apprenticeship, there is a greater institutionalization of reason as practices are systematized into paradigms of reasoning and learning that is not dependent on the immediate work context. The 'institution of reason' is a 'pervasive logic', embedded within historically developed practices that inform individuals within that sphere as to what it is they should do. Stinchcombe (1990) identifies five characteristics that are indicative of the institutionalization of reason: practitioners are trained in schools where knowledge and practice are rationalized; different practitioners or experts are able to come to the same judgements in cases; reasons can be given to justify decisions to persuade other experts; there is a process for 'disinterestedness' whereby individual interests are excluded; and the criteria for information collection before judgement in practice is socially established.[8] This bears some similarities to, but is not synonymous with, the professions, although Stinchcombe (1990) does not deny that institutionalized reason works for the advantage of its practitioners. The professions and other occupational groups may coalesce around an institutional rationality and use it in claims for occupational autonomy. 'Medicine and law try to create monopolies for people officially certified as practitioners of reason in their field . . . Institutions of reason . . . depend as little as they can on the altruism of their members' (Stinchcombe 1990: 295). It is important, however, to differentiate between the 'politics of the profession', guided by a rational interest in preserving autonomy, and an institutional rationality. There may be an appeal

---

BOX 5.1. INSTITUTIONAL RATIONALITY

An institutional rationality informs how individuals within the CJS see their role:

Defence agents play an active and important role in the whole system. If the defence agents are doing their job properly then the courts work better. You are trying to encourage, when there's overwhelming evidence, clients to plead guilty, when the evidence is obvious. This is the defence agents' role, especially now when early pleas are encouraged by sentence discounts. It's my job to tell them that, and to encourage them not to wait to see the whites of the witnesses' eyes which used to be the situation before. The Sheriff court can deal with 5 year sentences. You are talking about years of your life, not months. So an early plea can make a big difference, especially if you're dealing with someone of a relatively young age. Also the role of the defence agent is to avoid trials, if the evidence doesn't support a trial. And the defence agent has a part, has a role in bringing information that will influence the sentence. You try and get a reduced sentence for the client.   (Defence agent)

Basically I see my role, the role of the defence, is testing the crown case. The role is to make sure that the evidence is good enough to justify a conviction. When you're facing pleas of guilty, the defence role is to understand, get information on what happened. The Crown usually presents a black and white case. There are no shades of grey. Equally if you initially listen to a client, there are no shades of grey. Our job is to restore the shades of grey, which is always the case, and communicate this to the court. Your role, responsibility, is to minimize the damage to the client, to reduce a prison sentence, within limits.   (Defence agent)

The overriding responsibility is to the court, not misleading the court in terms of information. The relationship with the court is built on trust. Thereafter the responsibility is to the client. But there is also commitment to one's colleagues and to one's self. Not misleading the PFS and other officers of the court.   (Defence agent)

Although guided by abstract 'regimes of truth' such as the administration of justice, this does not mean that there are not variations within this interpretation:

I suspect that some Sheriffs apply the law in an academic way. [In my view] the purpose of Criminal Justice is that it should allow people to fulfill useful lives, without being subject to crime and to the fear of crime. It provides a structure in which people can go about and lead their lives.   (Sheriff)

This institutional rationality underpins resistance to the CJS as an integrated system, with fears that overarching measures from charge to disposal herald a new fledgling institution as something distinct from the operation of the CJS with its constituent, independent agencies and bodies:

Some people don't accept the concept of a system. Clearly there are connections between areas. But those within the system would say that there are very good reasons for a separation within the parts. The essential outcome is that the guilty are convicted, and the innocent are not convicted. Separations exist to avoid abuses, corruption, systemic and individual and political interference. There are elements of independence, between judges, prosecutors and Chief constables. It is absolutely crucial that they are independent.

(Advocate)

(*cont.*)

BOX 5.1. (*continued*)

There are actually two customers of the Criminal Justice System. The victims and the accused. The accused has the same rights as the victims. But all the focus is on the victims. (Policy)

There is no overall view of the Criminal Justice System that we are supposed to be affecting crime levels, reducing crime and reoffending. The focus is not to deliver the Executive's [government's] targets (Judge)

This institutional rationality informs practices within the CJS:

Summary cases should be dealt with summarily. This is known by the Sheriffs, so that now they are asking if something comes before them 'why is this case 6 months old?' It's increasingly difficult for a defence to argue that they are not to be prepared, or that a client has not contacted them. The Sheriff is not willing to accept that. That sort of guide is used by Sheriffs who are policing their courts and cases properly. But if either side has a good reason, for example if the defence has not had a list of witnesses on time or not had police statements, you can still hear the phrase 'in the interests of justice', in the context of their willing to grant adjournments. 'In the interests of justice' is one phrase that is still frequently used. (Defence agent)

And raises concerns over the use of measures:

[overarching targets for case completion] There are speed and quality issues. There is need to speed up the process, reduce the time between committing the offence and the consequence of the action. But there is real concern that speed and quality do not get taken as synonymous. There is a real danger and real worry with the notion that efficiency just equals speed. There is an issue of quality. Sometimes you really need the time. There is a real worry over this. (PFS)

This was to the chagrin of those who viewed the role of overarching measures as a mechanism to introduce a much more directed or targeted system:

People have such a parochial, insular approach. 'This is not what we do'. They do not have much understanding of it against the entire process. They have to see thing as being much bigger than their area and they need to subsume their needs against the system as a whole. You need to balance independence of the agencies with a greater clarity of what the system should achieve. (anonymous)

---

to the latter (the 'sacred') in pursuit of the former (the 'profane'), and there may be serious conflict between various occupational groups as to who may lay claim to interpret and preserve the latter. But the two are not synonymous.

Institutionalized reasoning not only exists as a (partially) rationalized body of reasoning, but it must also be applicable to particular cases. This requires that a skilled practitioner not only makes a judgement in a particular case but is also able to offer an explanation of the reasoning used in the judgement that can be judged by other skilled practitioners as valid. 'This social institutionalization of reproducibility criteria provides a mechanism for ensuring discipline in the application of the paradigm' (Stinchcombe 1990: 298). There are thus distinct styles of reasoning allied to institutional spheres. Toulmin et al. (1979) describe these as fields of argument, each having their own form of claims, grounds, warrants, backing, modal qualifiers, and possible rebuttals.[9]

The 'function' of such institutional reasoning is that it provides social predictability, rather than its being 'the most rational method for the calculation for individuals' (Stinchcombe 1990: 294). 'Rationalized institutions, the embodiment of reason in social life', improve the rationality of individuals through regularizing expectations and reducing uncertainty (Stinchcombe 1990: 313). Institutions are thus organizers of information, a theme later picked up by Williamson's institutional economics. 'Institutions of reason' render social life more predictable (Stinchcombe 1990: 315).

Institutional theory and rationalized myths

Within the study of 'organizations', as opposed to the 'sociology of organizations', institutions are generally part of an 'external' environment. The acknowledgement that organizations are deeply embedded in institutional environments arose relatively late in response to the model of organizations as being relatively autonomous entities. Institutional theory, often understood as an extension of open systems theory, is a broadening of the understanding of organizational 'environment' and an analytic focus on the social and political elements that influence organizational behaviour and action (Scott 1995). Early institutionalizers, for example Selznick (1949), were concerned to locate important factors for organizational change in the political and cultural environment. Selznick (1949) emphasizes the importance of values and norms of the broader environment influencing organizations, with such established values giving an organization its identity.

Institutional thinking, however, goes further than this. It argues that the 'visible structures and routines that make up organizations are a direct reflection and effect of the rules and structures that are built into wider environments' (Scott and Meyer 1994: 36). In other words, organizations reflect patterns or templates established by wider institutional forces. Rather than organizational rationality reflecting concern for efficiency and productivity, the concern within organizations is with that which is 'rational' as determined by a wider institutional environment. Thus, institutional theory differs from the earlier open systems approach with the recognition that organizations are immersed in their environments rather than just interacting with them. An institutionalized environment is 'internal' to an organization. For Meyer and Rowan (1977/2002: 277), 'norms of rationality are not simply general values but exist in more specific and powerful ways in rules, understandings and meanings that are attached to institutionalized social structures'. Not only this, but organizations themselves are also institutionalized forms. 'Organizational forms are standardized through the effortless evolution of commonsense understandings about how to organize' (DiMaggio 1991: 268).

Institutionalism in organization theory focuses on a 'finite slice of sociology's institutional cornucopia' (DiMaggio and Powell 1991: 9).[10] It stresses the importance of the institutional environment in influencing the structure and activities of organizations and the role of the institutional environment in providing legitimacy and legitimating structures. Organizations display institutionalized practices. Organization forms and practices become institutionalized over time, the taken-for-granted ways of doing things that become sedimented to the extent that their initial rationale is forgotten.

Meyer and Rowan (1977/2002: 275) argue 'one of the central problems of organization theory is to describe the conditions that give rise to rationalized formal structure' and account for why 'rational formal structure is assumed to be the most effective way to coordinate and control complex relational networks'.[11] The institutional approach argues that prevailing rationalized concepts of organization, work practices, and procedures are institutionalized in society, and organizations incorporate these legitimated practices and procedures rather than adopting practices and procedures on efficiency grounds. It is for this reason that organizations are similar (the original rational for Meyer and Rowan being an explanation as to why organizations do not differ more than they do). For Meyer and Rowan (1977), formal organizational structure is the embodiment of the rationalized myth of formal rationality. Organization 'structure' (the codification of what takes place in an activity domain, such that this account and no other prevails) provides a rational account. It is built upon and legitimated as, and builds upon and legitimates, a rational myth. In this, Meyer and Rowan (1977) see organizations as 'dramatic enactments of rationalized myths'.

Rationalized myths are important for the survival and legitimacy of organizations. Organizations must incorporate legitimated practices and procedures to increase their legitimacy and survival prospects independent of the immediate efficacy of their application. As institutional myths increase, so organizations expand their formal structures and practices to become isomorphic with them. Techniques may become 'myths' binding on organizations, as for example, accounting procedures and formalized personnel selection. These are requisite rational procedures, the absence of which is indicative of negligence.[12] Their incorporation avoids claims of illegitimacy. 'The modern world favours collective actors that can demonstrate or at least reasonably claim a capacity for reliable performance and can account rationally for their actions' (Hannan and Freeman 1984/2002: 159).

Rationalized myths are especially important in organizations that have ambiguous technologies, that is, uncertain means–end relationships, and where outputs are ambiguous and difficult to appraise, for example, schools, prisons, and hospitals. In these circumstances, organizations are more susceptible to conforming to institutional rules that promote trust and confidence in outputs. Equally, such organizations also become much more susceptible to fads and fashions in organizational practice. Pressures for accountability are particularly strong when organizations produce symbolic products, when substantial risks exist, or they are highly political.[13]

While institutionalized techniques or practices may function as powerful myths, they may conflict sharply with efficiency criteria. As Meyer and Scott (1992: 212) note, 'the legitimating celebration of rationality in principle (the essence of formal structures), is best sustained by a certain inattention to fact.' Writing on education characterized by 'human inputs' that are 'highly and unpredictably variable', 'technologies of instruction nonexistent or variable in nature and consequence', and 'outputs unpredictable and uncertain in measurement', all of which is generally understood in the field, they advise that any attempt to introduce highly rational systems 'requires a good deal of sustained ignorance' (Meyer 1992: 220). Efficiency and technical demands may conflict with institutional demands in organizations whose success depends on isomorphism. Because institutional rules are highly generalized, there are different sources for the ceremonial rules with which there should be conformity. This introduces potential inconsistencies and conflict. In order to accommodate rationalized structures, organizations are forced to adopt various strategies such as rigid conformity; resistance or rejection, often with high costs; ceremonial conformity and formal compliance; loose coupling (the buffering of formal structures from technical activities); concealment; and 'shadow rationalizations' (reporting institutional definitions rather than organization 'realities').

The homogeneity of organizational forms and practices further rationalize the field. Expanding on Meyer and Rowan's (1977) initial question of why organizations appear similar, DiMaggio and Powell (1991: 64) identify the state and the professions as 'the great rationalizers of the second half of the 20th century'. They identify three sources of institutional isomorphism, that is, the homogeneity of practices and arrangements found. Coercive isomorphism stems from resource dependence, particularly funding relationships, although also political legitimacy, and can be identified in the State pressing for certain types of practice to be adopted. Mimetic isomorphism results from imitation and is reflected in standardized responses to uncertainty as organizations follow other organizations. Benchmarking, for example, is an institutionalized form of this practice. Normative isomorphism sees the influence of trained professionals introducing practices seen as being inherent to 'normal' practice. Dependence on a single source for resources, transactions with state agencies, ambiguous goals, and an uncertain relationship between means and ends in the delivery of goals are factors that heighten the tendency to isomorphism.

Research in the field is stimulated by a range of questions such as where organizational templates come from; why organizations of the same type, for example, hospitals, schools, resemble each other even though they may be geographically disparate; to what extent behaviour is 'rational' or reflects conventions, routines, and habits, that is, reflects shared meanings that have a broader social legitimacy; and how to explain the diffusion of practices and structures through organizations in a particular organizational field. Studies of homogenization and mimeticism focus on processes that influence the perceptions of situations and perceived similarities; the imitator's self-identity and conception of the others' identity, thus influencing mimeticism; studies of diffusion and dissemination either 'into' a population or 'within' a population, with a focus on practices (the 'objects' of diffusion) or the networks or channels through which diffusion is spread (the 'infrastructure'); the extent to which imitating organizations are passive adopters or in picking up an idea are able to translate it into something that fits their own context (as for example in the work of Strang, Lounsbury, and Tolbert). Analyses reinforce the view of change or resistance as emanating from a few rational actors or groups, an ideological individualism if not a methodological one is prevalent. Unlike Weber's emphasis on the clash of value spheres, neo-institutionalism places an emphasis on the stability of organizational arrangements, with limited attention to change and conflict.

Institutional theorists are credited with directing attention to the importance of the symbolic aspects of organizations and environments. In arguing that organizations are isomorphic with environmental rules and adopt 'rational' systems not for efficiency but for 'symbolic' purposes, neo-institutionalism continues the problematic distinction between the technical and the institutional or 'social'.[14] The rational is contrasted with the 'symbolic'. The distinction is in danger of supporting the view that institutional structures are 'irrational' because of their failure to conform to 'rational' efficiency requirements. As Lukes (1967) argues, to treat beliefs as 'symbolic' is to deny the issue of rationality; rationality is no longer perceived as relevant to debate. Equally, institutions are portrayed as embodying collective norms and values. They are the taken-for-granted, agreed set of rules that carry meaning for, and inform, the interaction of actors. In each case, they are open to depiction as 'non-rational' forces that constrain 'rational' actions. The two have been posed as contrasting 'non-rational' versus 'rational' behaviour, 'rule following' rather than 'decision-making' (Scott 1995).[15]

Although institutional theory, particularly its view of social action as highly structured by institutionalized rules, does much to counter a model of organization as an autonomous rational entity, it still carries traces of this,

---

BOX 5.2. PERFORMANCE MEASURES AS RATIONALIZED MYTHS

The political context, to which performance measures are both a response and a contributing cause, reflect broader challenges to the logic of good faith. Institutions that were previously taken for granted now have if not their legitimacy then their effectiveness questioned. There is a move from the logic of appropriateness to the logic of consequentiality, a demand for 'evidence', objective outcomes and means–end causality. Demands for legitimacy are now posed in epistemological terms: 'how does one know?'

You have standards, but does this improve quality? How do you ensure quality? How do you make an argument to Treasury for more money for salaries, more money for buildings if you can't show evidence? What have we learnt? There have been huge increases in funding, but how do we know that this makes a difference?   (Politician)

A number of rationalized myths inform the rationale for performance measures in government: the importance of government being able to 'deliver' outcomes; the role of performance measures as an indicator of responsible and accountable government; and the capacity of performance measures to improve outcomes. Each generates political pressure for demonstrated change and results:

Government wants to meet targets because it wants to demonstrate that things have changed. It's the climate for government. They want to deliver. They want to be seen to deliver. They have to be seen to be delivering. There is too much control. They have to be seen to be in control. They fear the consequence of not being in control. This is very much the political climate of the time.   (Policy)

The government is driven by the need for initiatives. It has to be seen to do something. The political agenda dictates what we do. There are so many initiatives around. There's initiative after initiative. England and Wales is run ragged with political imperatives. This is pendulum politics. So much emerges from that. People have had enough of change. They do not want to see another initiative.   (Policy)

The First Minister [leader of the government] once made a speech about doing less better. This has since shifted to doing more. I wish we were able to persuade him, that doing less better was the foundation of sound government.   (Policy)

Institutional isomorphism is also influential:

There had been an exercise in England and Wales. Scotland was well aware of that. Also we were aware of significant developments that had been taking part in Northern Ireland. There was a growing feeling that we needed a closer look at the Scottish system. It is not a case of England and Wales are doing it and therefore we have to. Obviously we look at what things or how things are developing down south. We obviously keep a close eye on what's happening down there, primarily to see if it's going to be useful.   (Policy)

Although measures are now recognized as institutionalized practice:

Everyone now accepts that it is something that we have to do. People now tend to have been recruited into the performance measurement culture.   (Voluntary organization)

Systems purists say that targets are bad, the work of the devil, with an ideal world we wouldn't have these, but we have to have them. But give us measures that are more meaningful.   (Police)

(cont.)

BOX 5.2. (*continued*)

There has to be something that lets us know how we're doing. How we're going. How things are working. You've got to have something that people can work towards. And targets have been around so long. They are presumed to be motivational and to guide people to do what's desirable, to achieve what they're aiming for.   (Court services)

Political pressure is seen as influencing the adoption of specific measures:

The politicians are so target driven. There is an issue of 'direction of travel' versus targets. You can have a direction of travel X, and Y is an indicator of this. But there has been a move away from direction of travel to targets.   (Policy)

[On reducing the re-offending rate being set as a target] There are political problems. They must do something. Sixty percent of offenders are sent to prison, fifty eight percent of those who go to prison, re-offend. But there are no comparative figures given in relation to other countries. It is political rather than looking for evidence. Figures are plucked out of the air. Ideally you should talk in terms of the reconviction rather than the re-offending rate. But this is not as politically appealing. The reason why it is in there is because it is a good political headline. It's a soundbite. It looks good for politicians. I'm not sure how the measure was arrived at or why it was included. It has a soundbite element to it. It is introduced because there is an election in a few months time.   (Social work)

[reduced crime figures] Ministers need good news stories for an election. Performance measures all depends on political issues. We know what the hot potatoes are. But we need to tell them, you can't have, for example, a 10% reduction in housebreaking every year.   (Police)

The CJS is not 'isomorphic' with private industry where measures are less contentious:

It is difficult to get overall measures of success. In private industry there are bottom line measures for example, changes in share price, net profit, or turnover. Nobody disagrees with these.   (Policy)

---

particularly a view of organizations as entities with boundaries and an external environment. Thus, there is still the sense of institutionalizing or rationalizing pressures emanating from the 'outside'. It is an analysis infused with the concepts of hierarchy and boundaries. Institutional theory is a little unclear, for example, about how practices acquire legitimacy.[16] In some readings, it is the evaluative expectations of others that induce organizations to adopt practices. Other interpretations give greater weight to shared beliefs and the acceptance of practices as being 'the way things are done'. The confusion arises from the various meanings of institutions. 'Institution' is variously understood as that which becomes institutionalized; is the taken for granted; is synonymous with the social norms and values of a situation, or with 'cultural rules' or general belief systems.

Institutional theory is best understood as operating at the level of the organizational field, a 'level' between the major institutions of social life and organizations. Organizational fields provide structures within which specific organizations operate and are defined by DiMaggio and Powell

(1991: 65) (somewhat tautologically as Friedland and Alford 1991 note) as 'those organizations that, in the aggregate, constitute a recognized area of institutional life: key suppliers, resource and product consumers, regulatory agencies, and other organizations that produce similar services or products'. It is the mutual awareness among participants of the field that they are involved in a common enterprise, increased interaction among organizations, and interorganizational patterns of coalition that define their existence. Field boundaries heavily influence the choice of organizations to emulate and how practices are diffused. Fields also limit the extent to which institutional environments are perceived as pluralistic with multiple legitimate rationalities.

Institutional logics

While neo-institutional theory identifies the role of 'rationalized myths' that prevail, the concept of 'institutional rationality' has not really been incorporated into its accounts. Although Scott (1995: 140) states that 'institutional rules invent rationality, defining who the actors are and determining the logics that guide their actions', offering modes of reasoning, and shared understandings of reality, he does not proffer an analysis in terms of institutional logics or institutional rationality. He refers rather to institutions incorporating representational, constitutive, and normative rules (Scott 1995). Representational rules give an understanding of the world, how it works, and the means by which claims are validated and challenged. Constitutive rules define the nature of actors and their capacity for action (actors of type X do actions of type X). Normative rules elaborate this, giving appropriate actions, roles, routines, and scripts for actors and prescriptions for behaviour. Institutional logics, or institutional rules to use Meyer et al.'s terms, define actors within a particular sphere and legitimate certain types of action. 'The terminology is one of duties and roles rather than anticipatory decision making . . . to describe behaviour as driven by rules is to see action as a matching of behaviour with a position or situation. The criterion is appropriateness rather than consequential optimality' (March 1981: 221). The logic of appropriateness informs an organizational identity, focus, and purpose, and provides criteria of accountability (March 1981). Founded on 'obligation, identity, duty and rules', it provides answers to 'what kind of situation is this? what kind of person am I? what is appropriate for a person such as I in a situation such as this?' It is introduced as an 'alternative decision logic' to the consequentialist logic of intendedly rational decision-making, with the latter's assumptions of calculated and consequential action based on the pursuit of interests and future consequences.

It is Friedland and Alford (1991) who identify the role of institutional logic in institutional theory. They identify several institutional domains or institutional orders each with its own logic of action, that is, a set of practices and interpretations that constitute its organizing principles. 'Each of the most important institutional orders…has a central logic—a set of material practices and symbolic constructions—which constitutes its organizing principles and which is available to organizations and individuals to elaborate' (Friedland and Alford 1991: 248). They identify the central institutions of Western societies as capitalism (accumulation and commodification of human activity); the State (regulation by legal and bureaucratic hierarchies); democracy (the extension of popular control over decisions); family (unconditional loyalty and support); and religion and science ('truth', albeit acquired through different means). They state that 'institutions are symbolic systems which have non-observable, absolute, transrational referents and observable social relations which concretize them' (1991: 249). Examples would be private property concretized through ownership; democracy concretized through voting; and 'God' through prayer. Behaviour only makes sense in relation to this broader system.

Multiple institutional logics provide alternative meanings which are played out in debates as to whether education, health, and prisons should be public or private; who controls the regulation of production and reproduction; the relative boundaries of citizenship in economic organizations, etc. Positions are temporarily established in an ongoing battle over 'legitimate' boundaries. These institutional logics may be played out in major political debates, but are also evident when practices associated with one logic are introduced into practices associated with another, as for example, payment by results with its resonance of a market logic is introduced into arenas characterized by collegial concerns of equity of outcome.

While institutional logics are very general rationales that inform behaviour in particular spheres, their level of purchase at more disaggregate levels may be more limited. They may be supplemented, for example, by Whitley's (1992) 'business recipes', the institutional arrangements that shape economic activities that come to dominate business behaviour in different societies. Thus, within the single economic logic that shapes market behaviour, there are other differentiated rationales that construct the rules of the market and successful behaviour within this. Whitley illustrates the variation that can occur between the nature of market organizations that set up different business recipes that vary according to national financial and labour market institutions. Rationalities at the national level influence the configuration of organizations, work structuring and coordination, and qualification and career systems (Maurice et al. 1980). Institutional theory has also analysed how technology and market relations are not disembedded but develop in communities that have local roots (Uzzi 1997). In a comparative analysis of France, Germany, and the

UK, Sorge (1991) illustrates how features of the work context such as work interaction, the design of jobs, recruitment practices, education and training patterns, and industrial relations practices reflect the institutional norms that structure them. These in turn influence issues such as flexibility and cooperation, the autonomy of the workforce and supervision patterns, qualification, and career systems.

Although economic markets place a premium on rationality, the economic embeddedness literature makes reference to the importance of market activity embedded in institutional contexts (Langlois 1986; Smelser and Swedburg 1994; Swedberg 2003). Zysman (1994/2002: 31), for example, makes the point that 'all economic exchange takes place within institutions and groups. Markets do not exist or operate apart from the rules and institutions that establish them and structure how buying, selling and the organization of production takes place'. There are therefore, he concludes, multiple market capitalisms and different market logics (Hall and Soskice 2001). National institutional structures set national political economy, predictable patterns of policy and strategy, and national institutions, routines, and logics lead to a distinct capacity to address sets of tasks. He argues that there are national institutional roots of growth trajectories and technological development. 'The social context, the particular character of market institution in a specific society, sets the nature of the 'rational' problem ... the optic through which a problem is defined and a solution perceived varies with a community' (Zysman 1994/2002: 45).

Rationality institutionalized?

Although not developing the concept of institutional rationality, interestingly, institutional theory highlights the institutionalization of rationality. Meyer and Rowan (1977/2002: 279) write that 'once institutionalized, rationality becomes a myth with explosive organizing potential'. 'Rationality' has become a dominant myth for organizational change and reform. Structures and practices not designed to enhance 'unity, hierarchy, coordination, purposefulness or efficient action' do not have legitimacy. The rational model carries enormous weight to the extent that it is difficult to argue against. As Brunsson and Olson (1997: 67) remark, it is difficult for management to argue seemingly in favour of its antithesis: 'conflicts, inconsistencies, hypocrisy and poor control'. Even where 'rational' models raise difficulties for practice, the rational model is reaffirmed. It is practice that is considered problematic.

As Sahlin-Anderson (1996: 78) comments, what spreads are not experiences or practices per se, 'what are imitated are rationalizations ... standardized models and presentation of such practices'. Diffusion is influenced by reproducibility; the perishability or durability of the representation; the ease of its communication and comprehensibility (Czarniawska and Sevon 1996; Latour 1987). This depends on rationalization, objectification, and the extent to which it is possible to 'materialize' an object through rendering ideas solid and durable. This includes the extent to which forms of actorhood, that is, patterns of action and actors are transmissible; the development and specification of abstract categories and causal accounts of their efficacy; the simplified and generalized nature of organizational practices and structures; and a general ahistorical analysis that reinforces the sense of the universal applicability of principles such that they are more easily appropriated (Sevon 1996). Rationalization as diffusion is a process of typifying contexts or situations. Through this, it becomes possible to compare oneself with others and engage in mimetic action (Abell 1992). General models free up the possibilities for 'identifying' similarities. As Meyer (1992) notes, the development of disembodied or standardized organization theory, independent of sector, country, and history, means that as 'organizations', schools and hospitals are now open to the same prescriptions as car manufacturers. The template from which copying is 'reasonable' is greatly extended, not only between organizations but also internationally. This is the engine of rationalization: an increased rationalization, through simplification and abstraction, leading to increased rationalization in the homogeneity of organizational form and practice. Although this is not to deny that there will be learning by adaptation from the diffusion that results.

Institutional 'rationality'?

There has been much debate about the significance of institutional theory for rational models of organizations (Abell 1992). DiMaggio and Powell (1991: 8) claim that 'new institutionalism in organization theory and sociology comprises a rejection of the rational-actor models...units of analysis cannot be reduced to aggregations or direct consequences of individuals attributes or motives'. Selznick (1996), however, argues that 'new institutionalism' is the reconception of formal structures as 'thickly' institutionalized, 'rational-choice assumptions are loosened to allow for political and symbolic depictions of action' (Meyer 1994: 15). Selznick (1996) thus sees in institutional theory the opportunity to overcome the 'apparent' conflict between rational choice and institutional models.

Debate essentially focuses on two areas: the extent to which following wider norms and values is understood to be rational and the extent to which individual interests are institutionally determined. The question is how taken-for-granted the taken for grantedness of institutions is. In some interpretations of institutional theory, institutional rules are assumed to be socially determinant: 'Actors enact rather than act' (Abell 1992: 6). To what extent do institutions provide the 'context' for action, to what extent do they structure it, that is, they are deterministic? It is also a question of definitions of rationality, whether rationality lies in neoclassical definitions of utility maximizing or is constrained by gauging social roles and rules. Is action guided by institutional rationality, rational or not? To what extent does acting in line with an awareness of one's social role and what is appropriate behaviour in the circumstances, rather than following the cannons of self-interest, constitute rational behaviour?

The question is explicitly addressed by Stinchcombe (1990) in his comparison of the 'institutions of reason' and 'rationality'. Within 'institutions of reason', action that is rational from the individual's point of view, that is, is in their personal interest, would be irrelevant or would detract from the credibility of institutional reasoning. Indeed, the declaration of conflicts of interest is indicative of an institutionalized reason. The 'rationality' that is involved for the individual in an institutional rationality is that they should be 'rational on behalf of others or on behalf of a value, rather than on behalf of one's own utilities or purpose' (Stinchcombe 1990: 302). Thus, in an example of such an 'institution of reason', such as the military, it becomes 'rational' for individuals to go to war. Translating the vocabulary, rationality on behalf of others or values ('justice', 'aesthetics', 'truth') may be thought of as the 'utility function of the institution'. 'Practitioners are supposed to act in their institutional roles as rational actors trying to maximize the institutional utility function as if it were their own' (Stinchcombe 1990: 303). Institutions of reason function by controlling and limiting the individual rationality of individual practitioners.

Such reasoning although distinct from the rationality assumptions of rational choice theory with its assumptions of individualism, optimality of outcomes, and self-interest is not to argue that it is not rational per se, nor that it is an unreflective process. Decisions still have to be made as to what the situation is and what form of behaviour is appropriate. Actors must still identify what is 'appropriate' in the circumstances, interpret the meaning of the situation, and which rules are applicable. Although not 'rational' in terms of utility maximizing, the individual does not act according to maximizing self-interest, it is not the slavish following of a script. Behaviour is still evaluated on the criteria of reasonableness, that individuals act reasonably in the circumstances and are able to proffer 'reasonable' reasons for a course of action. Hence the reference to institutional rationality as the application of rationality within an institutional context. An institutional rationality delimits the framework within which modes of reasoning operate, but rationality is fully operative thereafter. It provides the legitimating language that enables and constrains actors to effect their motives. Stinchcombe (1990: 306) writes, 'The more the rational faculty of people adapting to a situation is governed by an institutionalized definition of what utility function ought to be maximized, the more we have to deal with "reason" than "rationality".' It is the historical evolution of an institutionalized reason, what Stinchcombe (1990) calls an 'institutional wisdom', 'a rationality at a deeper level than is routinely understood consciously by practitioners', that ensures that individuals 'behave more rationally than they would do unaided by rational faculties' (Stinchcombe 1990: 307). Institutional rationality is the improvement of rationality through the institutionalization of reason.

Conclusions

To say that all organizations are institutionalized organizations, that is, they reflect an institutional rationale may not be saying a great deal, in that it does not have a lot of purchase at explaining variation at more disaggregate levels. The significance of an institutional rationality, however, lies in its critique of a universalistic concept of rationality. In recognizing different spheres each with their own rationalities, it recognizes that what is rational in one sphere would not be rational in another. In doing so, it also allows for the importance of history with the recognition that 'past experience is encapsulated in an institution's rules so that it acts as a guide to what to expect from the future' (Douglas 1987: 48). It thus broadens the concept of rationality to encompass different modes of reasoning. Within such a conception, as Langlois (1986) recognizes, the division between rule-oriented and interest-driven behaviour in conceptions of rationality is much less firm. Where it is recognized that institutions construct the concept of the actor and his or her interests and their capacity to pursue these, then it must be equally accepted that the concept of the 'rational actor' and 'rational action' reflects institutional constraints. Institutions 'set limits on the very nature of rationality... Rationality as well as the appropriate contexts of its use are learned' (Friedland and Alford 1991: 251). It is to recognize that interests themselves are institutionally determined, confining rational choice to those circumstances where institutional systems validate individual social actors and private interests acting as such (Scott 1995). As Douglas notes (1987: 98), 'The high triumph of institutional thinking is to make the institutions completely invisible.'

6 Contextual rationality

One of the features of an embedded rationality is that it recognizes the importance of the contextually determined nature of rationality. Rationality is context dependent; something is rational only in 'relation to' or 'because of'. While an institutional rationality recognizes that the rationality of action is informed by the institutionally grounded, historically evolved, value sphere in which it takes place, contextual rationality identifies a more limited scale of reference. Context has various synonyms: background, circumstance, situation, framework, milieu, perspective, and environment. These, however, do not indicate 'containers' of rational action. Rather the metaphor should be that of an image where the eye cannot take in every element in detail of a picture at once, but must foreground some elements of the image at some points, foregrounding others later. All elements constitute the 'picture', none are a container for the others. As such, a contextual rationality obviates two other elements of rational action: that it must be fully conscious and, in being so, causally efficacious. A contextual rationality recognizes that rational action does not need to be fully aware of the reasons for action, nor does it have to be fully informed of the causal efficacy of action for it to constitute a rational thing to do. Both elements may be left to the 'context' in which the action takes place to gain their significance as rational action. This chapter outlines how contextual rationality has been handled in organization studies and illustrates how context is integral to the functioning of rationality.

Hidden from reason: A Romantic legacy

Contextual rationality has been taken up in the organization studies literature as 'culture'. The Enlightenment legacy is of a separation between reason and culture (Gellner 1992). Reason, an individual practice rather than a cultural tradition, provides access to truth. Culture, rooted in the unconscious and in traditions, is antithetical to rational thought. More particularly, the reason/culture division reflects the division between romanticism and neoclassicism or a mechanical rationalism (Gellner 1992). Romanticism was born in reaction to the rationalist dominance of the eighteenth century. It stemmed from the belief that not all areas of experience can be open to reason, and was a denial of the neoclassical belief in the latter's supremacy. Underlying an understanding of culture is of its being 'hidden' from, or unknown to, reason.

Just as culture is seen as the enemy of reason in this broader context, so has culture been taken as the antithesis of the 'rational' model of organizations. Martin and Frost (1996: 615) note, 'we were originally drawn to culture as an emancipatory way of approaching organizational phenomena, and as a metaphor for revitalizing organizing theory.' It offers an 'other than' to a dominant rationalistic concept of organizations. Smircich (1983/2002: 160) writes, 'for practitioners it provides a less rationalistic way of understanding their organizational worlds, one closer to their lived experience.' For Linstead and Grafton-Small (1992/2002: 230), 'the cultural orientation would restore emotion, expression and sensitivity to the cold world of rational-technical organizational analysis'. 'Culture', or organizations as cultural phenomena, was thus introduced in opposition to rationalistic approaches. The division between culture and reason still holds. Alvesson (2003: 6), for example, writes that even diverse studies of culture agree on several assumptions about cultural phenomena that they are 'holistic, intersubjective and emotional rather than strictly rational and analytical'. The antithesis between 'cultural' and 'rational' models also reflects the growing development of, and antagonism between, philosophies of social science heralded by 'paradigm wars'. 'Culture' represents the 'soft' or 'subjective' side of organizations, accessible through 'qualitative' research methods, informed by interpretivist or constructivist theory.

The formal organization was taken to be the structural expression of the rational (Selznick 1949). Through coordination, delegation, control, and 'interchangeable individuals', the formal structure can become an instrument of rational action. However, 'as we inspect formal structure we begin to see that it never succeeds in conquering the non rational dimension of organizational behaviour' (Selznick 1949/2002: 51). The Human Relations School identified elements of 'culture' in informal work groups having their own work standards and ethos. The potential for harnessing this informal system for productive effort has influenced a stream of writing on organizational culture thereafter. In an early piece, Lewin and colleagues (1939) introduced the term 'organizational climate' to argue that an organizational 'context' of collective attitudes, feelings, and social processes are influential in how an organization functions. Climate is taken to be the values and attitudes that are held by those within the organization, that is, it is the widely shared perception of the organization's attributes. 'Organizational climate' or 'group norms' were descriptors before 'culture' became more generally adopted (Schein 1994). The former now represents the 'surface' manifestations of the deeper entity of 'culture'. By the 1970s and 1980s, drawing from the field of anthropology, an understanding of the 'informal organization' was transformed into a wholesale study of 'organizational culture'.[1] It was encouraged by changing economic circumstances of the success of Japanese production in the 1980s and the move to more decentralized 'post-bureaucratic' organizations requiring a degree of coherence and self-identification. Debate became entangled, either to criticize or defend, prescriptions for a 'strong culture' (Deal and Kennedy 1982).

Having dismissed the classic rationalist school of organization studies, culture appears as the explanation for why individuals engage in coordinated action, recognizing that structure alone (roles, relationships, and rules that define these) is an inadequate mechanism for coordination and control (Dawson 1996). Culture is invoked as a means of explaining degrees of stability in organizational behaviour (Schein 1991). This focuses a stream of research on structure and culture: whether 'culture' is a 'byproduct' of production systems, pay structures, etc. or is relatively independent of this; how changes in structure, personnel, and financial control systems may have a strong impact on the 'culture' of an organization; the relationship between structural and cultural change; and whether changes in behaviour in response to structural changes are sufficient by themselves to effect 'lasting change' or whether this must also be accompanied by a change in 'values'. Earlier understandings of the role of structure, in particular organizational roles, prompt a broader interpretive understanding. Thus, Simon (1997: 278) states that in assigning an individual to a role, 'it specifies the particular values, facts, and alternatives upon which decisions in the organization are to be based'. Rationality in this sense is rational role-playing.

Precisely, what culture involves is vague. Culture 'is what we have done around here' (Weick 1995: 189)[2]; incorporating beliefs, ideologies, language, ritual, and myth (Pettigrew 1979); organizational glue (Martin 1992); and basic assumptions (Schein 1991). It captures meaning, values, and actions; is a guideline for behaviour; reflects shared values and internalized norms; includes the role of traditions, stories, and symbols and their impact on beliefs, values, and meanings. Its study includes policies, informal rules, norms, stories, rituals, jargon, symbols, dress codes, and jokes.[3] 'Ideational' perspectives consider values, cognitions, and symbolism; more materialist interpretations, formal procedures, task design, payment systems, etc. for what they display or manifest of the 'culture' of the organization. It fosters an analysis of different organizational cultures.[4] There are attempts at providing a lexicon of cultural forms, as for example, language, symbols, narratives, and practices (Trice and Beyer 1984); rituals, stories and scripts, jargon, and humour (Martin 1992). For Alvesson (2003), who prefers to refer to 'the culture concept in organization studies', there is no agreed meaning of culture, even in anthropology, from where studies of organizations borrowed.

Generally, depictions of culture highlight four dimensions or characteristics:

Culture as values: A dimension that 'culture' addresses or encompasses to counter the apparent inadequacies of rationalistic models is that of 'values'. 'The term "culture" in organizational analysis refers to "shared values and beliefs"' (Dawson 1996: 141). Organizational culture is 'values in action' (Anthony 1999: 3) as opposed to espoused values, and is revealed in the 'behaviour, policies, and practices' of the organization and its members. The emphasis on values in culture varies. For some, 'values' are central. For others, values are less important than other manifestations of culture (Alvesson 2003). Values or value structures are deeply held beliefs or norms that inform behaviour. While rationalistic models focus on 'means'; values inform the ends to which means are directed. In this sense, they inform purpose and the sense of right and wrong. They are an attempt to create an element of the 'sacred' in work, a moral involvement (Ray 1986). Values also encompass the 'irrational'. They are not easily rationally defended and are reinforced through ceremonies, rites, rituals, myths, and histories. Values, however, remain at a fairly general level of abstraction. How concretely these translate into informing the specifics of action of particular groups is difficult to ascertain, as is how values embodied in organizational policies and practices relate to the range of other experiences to which an individual, living in multiple worlds, is open.

Culture as shared: Not only does culture encompass values and beliefs, but it is also the 'shared' nature of these values and beliefs that characterize it. It is the understanding of sharedness that informs Schein's (1991: 247) definition of culture as

> a pattern of shared basic assumptions, invented, discovered, or developed by a given group, as it learns to cope with its problems of external adaptation and internal integration, that has worked well enough to be considered valid and therefore, is to be taught to new members of the group as the correct way to perceive, think, and feel in relation to those problems.

Or of culture as 'a set of meanings to be shared by all members of the organization which will define what is good and bad, right and wrong, and what are the appropriate ways for members of the organization to think and behave' (Watson 1994: 112). Alvesson (2003: 1), for example, writes, 'how people in a company think, feel, value and act are guided by ideas, meanings and beliefs of a cultural (socially shared) nature.' Thus, culture, reflecting its intellectual heritage in Durkheimian views of organic solidarity in contrast to a contractual rationality, ushers in an understanding of individuals bound together by a 'glue' expressed in shared beliefs or ideology, norms, rituals, values, language, and symbols. Barnard (1938) identifies a key management role as promoting social integration; developing a sense of common purpose and cooperative relationships; and shaping and managing shared values (Starkey 1992). Ouchi's (1980) 'clans', relatively unified cultures able to establish enculturation of members, are a form of organic solidarity held together by common values and beliefs. The assumption of culture as shared understanding raises questions as to whether 'shared' presumes 'consensus', that is, organizations as well-integrated social mechanisms. Schein, for example, writes, 'sharing or consensus is core to the definition' (1991: 248). The integrationist or 'strong cultures' perspective supports this 'homogeneity and harmony' perspective of organization-wide consensus, internal consistency, and clarity over shared values (Martin 1992).[5]

Culture as hidden: The romantic legacy of 'hidden from view' imbues concepts of culture. It informs the metaphor of 'background' or 'depth', that which is unknown or unfathomable to the individual. The model is of a cultural 'manifestation' of a 'cultural essence'. Thus, Schein (1991: 144) notes, 'the core concept remains implicit and often undefined, while its manifestations such as rites, rituals, and organizational stories, symbolic manifestations of the "deeper" phenomena, occupy centre stage and become the de facto definition of culture'. Culture as a hidden dimension 'stresses the deep values and basic assumptions of organizations—unconscious or half-conscious beliefs and ideals about objectives, relationships to the external world, and the internal relations that underlie behavioural norms and other "artefacts" ' (Alvesson 2003: 51). It functions in the unconscious: 'culture is best understood as referring to deep-level, partly conscious sets of meanings, ideas, and symbolism' (Alvesson 2003: 14). This is why a focus on 'values' alone is inadequate. 'To analyze why members behave the way they do, we often look for the values that govern behaviour.' Espoused values 'focus on what people say is the reason for their behaviour, what they ideally would like those reasons to be, and what are often rationalizations for their behaviour. Yet the underlying reasons for their behaviour remain concealed or unconscious' (Schein 1984: 3). The unconscious or deep-seated guides behaviour, 'culture emerges from history, is rooted in practice, sustained by structures and becomes habitual—and therefore unconscious and unthinking—as the result of routines of repeated behaviour' (Anthony 1999: 98). 'Hidden' also carries with it implicit assumptions of 'hidden powers': 'Cultures are anchored in the organizational collective and exercise influence without the direct involvement of particular key actors' (Alvesson 2003: 51).

Culture as symbolic: Associated with the hidden dimensions of culture is the role of the symbolic, literally that which stands in the place of something else, as a representation of it. For Alvesson (2003: 5), culture concentrates on 'meaning anchored and transmitted in a symbolic form'. A symbol is rich in meaning, 'condensing a number of meanings into a particular form' (Alvesson 2004: 319). Pondy describes a symbol as 'a sign which denotes something much greater than itself, and which calls for the association of certain conscious or unconscious ideas, in order for it to be endowed with its full meaning and significance...Symbols are signs which express much more than their intrinsic content; they are significations which embody and represent some wider pattern of meaning' (quoted in Anthony 1999: 44). Alvesson (2003: 15) suggests using 'symbol' 'as a conceptual tool for making sense of the hidden or latent meanings of an object'. Actions are undertaken because they have symbolic value and are an important element of organized and organizing activity. For example, Feldman and March's (1981) study of information as symbol, examining the meaning and use of information in organizational settings shows how information is often not required for facts or to aid decision-making but is used for reasons of security and legitimation. Its symbolic role is valued more than its 'rational' purpose, or becomes its rational purpose. This use reflects the symbolic nature of 'rationality'. The symbolic is the antithesis of the rational in that it directly contradicts the direct causal assumptions that inform concepts of rationality. If reason is associated with purpose and its systematic realization, then culture and the symbolic are the enemies of reason (Anthony 1999: 92). The symbolic is not causally efficacious in that it is not action based on 'cause–effect' thinking. It does not directly produce effect, but is undertaken for what it represents (which may of course prompt effects).

Culture is variously understood as values, meanings, and symbols; it may be hidden, unconscious, shared, or common. It covers a broad range of phenomena and extends over a variety of groups and subgroups. It is an approach that can include industrial cultures and subcultures, organizational culture, occupational culture, and, more recently, communities of practice. It is because culture seems to encompass so many things that Anthony (1999: 98) comments 'it is surprising that a concept so vague and vaporous has commanded managerial attention'.[6] It has commanded attention because this 'cloudy concept' is reason's 'other'. Certainly, the claims that are made for its role— 'Culture acts a perception filter, affects the interpretation of information, its moral and ethical standards, provides rules, norms and heuristics for action, and influences how power and authority are wielded in reaching decisions regarding what actions to pursue' (Brown 1995: 197 quoted in Alvesson 2003: 78)—owes more to the poverty of the rational than to being a meaningful statement of a useful concept. Culture is that which is relegated so that reason as individual, conscious, and causal can be secured and maintained. Because it is rationality's 'other', 'culture' acts as a receptacle for everything that is not 'rational'. And as a receptacle, and as the antithesis of the rational, it is not much of a remove for 'culture' to be depicted either as a constraint on the rational or relegated to the 'merely symbolic' (Anthony 1999). The complex interplay of the rationality of culture and the cultural nature of reason is shielded by a deferred binary opposition.

Rationality versus community

Another strand in culture literature focuses on the community or group. The community as an alternative to an economic rationality is a theme that has dominated social theorizing. Weber and others have contrasted the 'rational' with the traditional or communal. It forms the basis, although with different nomenclature and within different theoretical frameworks, of the work of Comte, Weber, Durkheim, Tonnies, and Marx. For Weber, there is the contrast between the traditional or communal and the associative or organizational aspects of the modern economy. It is reflected in the transition from 'gemeinshaft' to 'gesellshaft' or the contrast between organic with mechanical.

The association of culture with community is with that which is relatively settled, where there are identifiable values, beliefs, and actions into which newcomers are acculturated. Anthony's (1999: 29) definition is suitably expansive on this: 'Cultures develop in communities which are distinctive from their neighbours and are held together by patterns of economic and social cooperation reinforced by custom, language, tradition, history, and networks of moral interdependence and reciprocity. As these are established and sedimented over time they lead to customary understandings and obligations [and] patterns of expectation.'

Extrapolated to organizations, the culture as community motif raises a number of questions: whether a culture is something an organization 'has' (a critical variable) or 'is' (a root metaphor) (Smircich 1983)[7]; whether culture is an entity or process; and at what 'level' it operates, that is, where one may draw boundaries.[8] The organization as the boundary of a culture implies that organizations are mini-societies which, apart from organizations that act as total institutions, is denied by most observers. If organizations are the 'containers' of cultures, this then raises the problem of how boundaries are drawn, around what units, and what the causal relationship between cultures and units is. Thus, for Schein (1991: 247), 'If one cannot define the group, then one cannot define the culture of that group'. Schein identifies a group as having a common history, experience, and a relatively stable membership, rather than a common behaviour or attitude.[9] The identification of a culture with a group is, however, potentially problematic, as the signifiers of the group tend to determine that which is identified as its shared culture.

Culture as 'commonality': One of the dimensions of culture is that which is held in common, the commonality of thought and action that creates the 'community'. It is this commonality of thought and action that defines the boundaries of a 'community'. The 'shared, fundamental (though often implicit) assumptions about why events happen as they do and how people are to act in different situations' (Bartunek 1984: 355). This has been taken up in the concept of 'interpretive communities' (Fish 1980), speech communities (Barley 1983), provinces of meaning (Schutz 1962), and 'frames of reference' (Goffman 1969). These capture the way in which members of a collective are drawn together by a common framework that provides a common under-standing of issues, a common language or set of conceptual categories, not however, a consensus. This 'socially shared orientation to social reality' is the product of social interaction and negotiation. It is taken for granted, only partly verbalized, to the extent of being regarded as 'natural'.

The approaches to 'commonality', however, tend to downgrade another dimension of community, that of its being a continuing coordinated activity (Geertz 1973). Relatively cohesive systems of meanings, such that patterns may be discerned and picked upon, provide the basis for coordination. If there is insufficient coherence within a particular set of ideas, then there is greater room for ambiguity and conflict, thus coordination may not be secured. Con-tinuing organized or coordinated activity requires a common interpretation of situations so that interaction can take place without constant interpretation and re-interpretation of meanings. Things must be placed 'into context' for organized and cooperative work to function. 'Through the development of shared meanings for events, objects, words and people, organization members achieve a sense of commonalty of experience that facilitates their coordinated action' (Smircich 1983/2002: 165). It is the importance of coordinated action that characterizes the communities identified in the literature on workplaces and organizations.

Workplace culture: Inherent to the concept of a workplace culture is its inti-mate connection to the way in which a job is performed. As Alvesson (2003) notes, job content, work organization, skill levels, and the social interactions structured by work organization are important dimensions influencing how a work 'culture' emerges and functions. Roy's (1959) study of Banana time, for example, illustrates how one group of machine operators keeps from 'going nuts' in a situation of monotonous work activity through a common under-standing of the work and its meaning. A common meaning informs coffee time, peach time, banana time, window time, coke time, and lunch time, and its themes, kidding themes, serious, 'professor' chatter. Roy (1959/2002: 218) writes, 'As I began to develop familiarity with the communication system, the disconnected became connected, the nonsense made sense, the obscure became clear, and the silly actually funny'. Its disintegration on 'Black Friday' led to boredom and fatigue. Collinson's (1988) analysis of humour reveals a workplace culture that informs behaviour and identity, providing the foundation for differentiation, dignity, freedom, and autonomy. It is a workplace culture that is ultimately defensive and superficial, maintaining an ongoing resistance, but failing to provide a response to factory closures.

Industrial subcultures: Writing in the early 1970s, Turner identifies the role of industrial subcultures as 'similarities of behaviour' across industrial organizations. It is 'a distinctive set of meanings shared by a group of people whose forms of behaviour differ to some extent from those of the wider society' (Turner 1973: 67). The industrial subculture is segmented from the individuals' home and leisure, and thus physically contained. It is broad enough to encompass different industries and different companies, and is distinguishable from 'micro-cultures' limited to departments or work groups found in organizations, each having their own 'normative patterns, perceptions and values'. It is also broad enough to encompass companies, trade unions, management, and supervisory groups that belong to the same industry, even though there are differences between these groups; and encompasses plants, occupations, organizations, and industries. Thus, coal mining or steel making constitutes industrial subcultures. It is thus an 'ensemble' of those 'participating in one world' (Turner 1973: 71). These industrial subcultures inhabit a different 'context of meaning' than, for example, academics, civil servants, and the clergy. As Turner (1986) later acknowledges, implicit within his analysis are very strong class divides, rarely dealt with by the literature on culture.

Turner's emphasis is very much on shared meanings that sustain an industrial subculture, a 'commonly held fabric of meanings' expressed in the daily life of the industry (Turner 1973: 74). Socialization into institutionalized patterns of behaviour preserve this distinctive set of meanings, ensuring 'common motives, common reaction patterns and common perceptual habits'. Shared meanings, demonstrated (and developed) in communication and exchanges, constitute membership of a subculture. 'Naming processes', a special coda and acquired sets of social definitions 'which are not acknowledged in this way in the wider society', are a means of identifying and understanding an industrial subculture.[10] Although industrial subcultures provide different 'contexts of meaning' in industrial organizations, they are 'minor variations' of a dominant culture (Turner 1986: 110).

Occupational community: Van Maanen and Barley reject the confines of organizational boundaries in their identification of an occupation as denoting a distinct community.[11] An occupational community is 'marked by distinctive work cultures promoting self control and collective autonomy for the membership' (Van Maanen and Barley 1984: 291). To be a member of an occupational community is to 'know the cognitive, social and moral contours' of the occupation. This includes its knowledge, practice, and values which, for some occupations, may be transmitted from generation to generation.

Occupational communities are bounded work cultures determined through self-identification, or a 'consciousness of kind', seen in individuals who consider themselves as engaged in the same sort of work; identify with their work; share 'a set of values, norms, and perspectives that apply to, but extend beyond, work related matters'; where relationships between work and leisure are blurred. The occupational value system shapes both work perspective and self concept. 'Members of occupational communities claim a distinctive and valued social identity, share a common perspective toward the mission and practices of the occupation, and take part in a sort of interactive fellowship that transcends the workplace' (Van Maanen and Barley 1984: 347).

An important element of an occupational community is autonomy, the ability of the membership of the group to determine how labour is organized: to specify the knowledge, skills, and orientation as to how work is performed; its content and conduct, including the quality of products and services provided; and how, and by whom, work is to be evaluated and assessed. It is a form of work that is 'socially constructed and validated in practice by members of an occupation' (Van Maanen and Barley 1984: 294). Membership of a group judge 'the appropriateness of one another's actions and reactions'; proper and improper work behaviour; and ensure that practices, vocabularies, values, and identities are transmitted to new members of the community (Van Maanen and Barley 1984: 303). 'External' standards, work definitions, and assessment procedures are threats to this autonomy. Occupational communities, however, vary greatly according to whether, and how, they are able to enforce such autonomy.[12] Those that are more able to lay claim to an institutional rationality, especially where this is supported by the State such as with law ('the service of justice') or medicine ('curing the sick'), are more able to maintain autonomy than are others, indeed an institutional rationality is a large element of the claim to autonomy. Autonomy is sought and secured through strategies of professionalization and unionization.

For Van Maanen and Barley (1984), the relationship between occupational communities and employing organizations varies according to the degree of autonomy that may be maintained and is reflected in whether the organization provides the locale for the occupation or is heteronomous, that is, organization and occupation are not co-extensive. In the latter, occupational cultures may reside with organizational cultures in varying degrees of harmony or conflict. The distinction between an occupational community and an organizational culture is that in the latter, identities and culture remain within the confines of the employing organization. Their existence is dependent on the organization and is organizationally specific. As such, these elements are not central to identity and meaning outside work. An occupational community draws on sources of legitimacy outside of the work organization.[13]

An important element of Van Maanen and Barley's (1984) description is the importance of a social identity that is attached to an occupation, identities that are quite central to a self-image. This sense of identity communicates both a sense of being a part of a group and a sense of being different from others. Equally important is the existence of a system of codes, or a specific language, through which members of a community communicate with one another about work. It is through these codes that an individual is able to construct meaningful interpretations.

Communities of practice: The communities of practice (CoP) literature stems from an interest in learning and knowledge acquisition, and sees organized activity as a form of knowledge system. It combines both the sense of 'community' and the immediacy of practice (see Chapter 7). 'Practice' provides coherence for a community, and participation, an important dimension of learning, facilitates learning processes, and through this establishes boundaries.[14] A community of practice is a collectively developed understanding of the nature and the identity of the community to which its members are held accountable, sustained through norms and relationships of mutuality and a shared repertoire of communal resources, language routines, artefacts, tools, and stories. Those who are involved in a particular 'community' understand the limits or boundaries of the community. It focuses on the practices of communities, defined as social configurations engaged in enterprises, the latter being very broadly understood including families, education, and those engaged in cultural activities (Wenger 2003). Communities of practice define competences and establish identities that sustain the practices of the enterprise. As part of learning to function in a community, individuals 'acquire that particular community's subjective viewpoint and learn to speak its language' (Brown and Duguid 1991: 48).[15] Wenger (2003: 47) states that 'Communities of practice are the prime context in which we can work out common sense through mutual engagement'.

Within the work context, communities of practice differ from earlier designations such as teams and work groups in that they are not canonically bounded entities, but are more fluid and interpenetrate, often crossing organizational boundaries and remaining unacknowledged by the organization. Although having a different emphasis, it has resonances with studies of organizational and workplace 'cultures'.[16] 'Practice' achieves shared meaning and covers many of the features of organizations identified in the earlier culture literature.[17] Equally, a community of practice is reflective of a division of labour that creates work groups.[18]

What differentiates a 'community' from 'culture' is its focus on ensuring the social coordination of activities,[19] be this work group task, practice, occupational practice, or industrial product. The coordination of action sustains the common interpretive framework of behaviour and action

---

BOX 6.1. OCCUPATIONAL AND ORGANIZATIONAL IDENTITIES

The CJS is sustained by strong organizational, agency, and professional identities (self-identified and sensed by others):

We are very task oriented. The police has always been a very 'can do' culture in no matter what it is, we will do it. The police are best as crisis managers. It's more a can do attitude. This is in stark contrast to the Advocates and the PFS.   (Police)

There are two kinds of Sheriff. There are the sheriffs who were solicitors and have been in private practice. They have managed staff, dealt with budgets, and worked in teams, worked in a business. They have come into contact with clients off the street. They are street wise and they understand some of the difficulties. The Sheriffs who have been advocates, with an advocacy background, do not have this background. They work as individuals. They do not have a business background. Nor do they have a solicitor background. They are not as streetwise as a solicitor. But they are more thorough with a case. X [a sheriff with an advocate background] would probably be seen as fussy. Basically he's more attentive to detail. He is more thorough. He spends more time with the cases. That's his training. His training is precision and attention to detail. He could take longer to get through things. Basically he's involved in a massive risk assessment and prepares for things that might go wrong. He has back up situations as part of his training. The others are more action learning. If you are scheduling him [the advocate background] for a two week jury sitting, you know that the trial will last two weeks. The others [solicitor backgrounds] would probably not. If you know that you have a case that is going to run then you know he [the advocate background] is going to snooker my programme for weeks. I would probably not schedule him.   (Court services)

Lawyers think in terms of litigation for handling problems. They can't help it. It's their nature... training. They would litigate things, no one else would dream of   (Policy)

This is not to argue that there are not hierarchies within occupations:

There is a big difference of interest between the Appeal court judge and the ordinary judge in the street.   (Judge)

But there is still a view that criminal cases are below the salt. The hot shots do civil cases.

(Judge)

---

that ensures that actions can be performed: 'organized patterns of thought with accompanying understanding of what constitutes adequate knowledge and legitimate activity' (Smircich 1983/2002: 163). A commonality of actions needs a commonality of interpretation, a community. Background assumptions are necessary to ensure ongoing activity, to be shared sufficiently to provide a sense of community. The focus of 'community' acts as a type of epistemic community (Polanyi 1983; Knorr Cetina 1999),[20] based on the 'principle of mutual control', and informs and controls the styles of reasoning that operate within the community and from this the production of knowledge that results (Polanyi 1983: 72). This mediated consensus allows members of the community to be members of a community.[21] In this sense, rationality and community are mutually sustaining.

Culture as competence: Rendering rational

What these various depictions present is the importance of being able to function within a collective. It is to recognize that 'culture' 'consists in whatever it is one has to know or believe in order to operate in a manner acceptable to its members' (Geertz 1994: 218). 'Culture' enables individuals to function in a rational manner in the context in which they find themselves. It is a matter of knowing and displaying competencies defined by a social community. To do otherwise is to render an individual being labelled, at the very least, as incompetent, of not displaying the competence required of a knowledgeable individual, or, at worst, if behaviour is so out of context, as irrational. Context is the non-explicit, or taken-for-granted dimension of, and for, rational behaviour. It is that which renders behaviour rational. Contextual rationality refers to the competences that must be displayed in order for action to be deemed reasonable. Behaviour is rational because it is competent. Being competent thus involves learning how to speak, act, understand, and function in ways that are recognizably intelligible and rational. Its accomplishment indicates that the non-explicit knowledge required to function reasonably, to display reasonable behaviour, has been absorbed. It is learning how to be and behave in context and being 'able to articulate contextually appropriate accounts' (Barley 1983: 114).

Although much of what is learnt are implicit, unexamined assumptions, the 'tacit' knowledge of a community, because this consists of socially established structures of meaning, it is, in Geertz's words, 'public' (Geertz 1994: 219).[22] The competences displayed in being part of a community are public. They are able to be learned as part of socialization into a group and the means by which competence is judged by other members. Such competence (technical and social) may not be fully explicable. It has both explicit or declarative knowledge and implicit or tacit skill or know-how. The explicit or declarative are those reasons that are presented for public evaluation, to be accepted or rejected. The criterion of evaluation is akin to plausibility, or an inherent persuasiveness in order to judge whether the individual is a responsible epistemic agent. Although the implicit or tacit is that which practitioners are unwilling or unable to describe, it too is public in that it is able to be demonstrated and in being able to be demonstrated, it may be communicated. As Pettigrew (1979/2002: 144) recognizes in an early piece, 'culture is the system of such publicly and collectively accepted meaning operating for a given group at a given time'.

The shared rules and definitions that are embedded in a culture underpin the rationality of action. A contextual rationality provides the lens through which actions are viewed, the perceptual building block through which experience is organized, and through which things are made sense of, rendered sensible or reasonable. It allows individuals to make sense of events, to render them

---

BOX 6.2. A 'PERFORMANCE CULTURE'?

One of the aims of performance measures is to change culture:

Targets can be an important symbol of the need to change, helping to transform cultures.

(PASC 2003: 9)

The introduction of performance measures has had an impact on some agencies:

In the past people paid lip service to performance measures. Police officers thought performance measures were for 'tecky' people. Police managers, now they know it's their responsibility, they need to know what's happened...happening. The change in forces has been immense. The change in culture. The only barrier is from the older members of the force. They do not appreciate the changes as much as the new recruits. Now support staff are much more valued.   (Police)

The [prison] governor previously was basically a fiefdom, in charge of a £25 m budget, between 300–1400 inmates, and 600–1000 staff. They were 'commanders'. It was a very hierarchical top down organization. They have now moved from commanders to contract managers. You can imagine some of the difficulties in this in terms of response, with people who were 'commanders' now being asked to report to essentially middle managers about performance. We now evidence what we do and are focused on what we do. Previously it would be the case that governors could say 'we hear what you're saying but this is our pet project', and they would go ahead with their pet project. It could be accreditation programmes one year, sanitation the next. You could get new managers coming in with their schemes, and staff would pay no attention, 'we've heard it all before' element. Now there is a performance contract and it focuses on evidence. It is broadly welcomed. It focuses on basics. It is a new culture. It's a matter of culturally changing the managing role, so its not one of the troops. So that they make sure that these things are done.   (Prison service)

'The key objective [of performance measures] is to develop and nourish a performance culture within public services' (PSAC 2003: 30). Allied to this are calls that emphasize the need to 'manage' the system:

If you are looking for a joined up approach, you really need to tackle the issue of Sheriffs. For example, when defence asks for an adjournment because they do not have a police statement, Sheriffs have not asked the PFS or police why not. And in 45% of cases they are adjourned because the defence is not prepared. The Sheriffs have to request 'why aren't they prepared?' The Sheriffs need to operate on this. For a PFS, it depends on which individual is on the bench whether you need to be prepared or not. With some you know you need to be prepared. With others you know there is no point being prepared because they will grant adjournments. But this is a difficult issue to control.   (PFS)

The senior judicial official officer is the Sheriff Principal who has statutory responsibility for the efficient and timely disposal of cases. In the past the Sheriff Principals have not been managerial. But there is a management role, a management issue. There is a management role to direct. Some Sheriff Principals are pushing this. But there is not a line management relationship between Sheriff Principals and Sheriffs...You have to be careful when you talk of 'management' of CJS because there are concerns with the independence of the system. The Sheriff Principal has a substantial managerial role. It is a source of frustration that this role has not been recognised. But the Sheriff Principals are not known for their management background and knowledge. There has to be an interest in getting things done.   (Policy)

BOX 6.2. (*continued*)

There is a confusion of judicial independence and issues of accountability and transparency that we are all held to. Some of the more managerially minded Sheriff Principals can see the management issue with the Sheriffs, and would like to deal with it. But it's a very sensitive issue. (Policy)

Overarching measures are to give the Sheriffs and the Sheriff Principals an idea of how things work. To ask the question, 'how is it working?' For example, there may be some measures on the type of criminal legal case that these should generally not take longer than X days. The concern was that if there were targets set for the court that this would impinge on judicial freedom and affect judges. That setting measures would impact on judicial independence. (Policy)

This has to balance an institutional rationality:

There is a perception of a lack of control in the conduct of the actual cases. The length of cases are determined by the prolixity of the counsel. This is inefficient and wasteful. But judges are too feart. The judges are frightened. There is a lack of confidence, a lack of confidence that they will be backed up by the Appeal Court. There is a fear of being seen to do an injustice. There have been reforms on the management of the cases. But not on the conduct of the trial. There is a fear of preventing justice being done. (Judge)

rational and thereby capable of action. The rationality of social engagement is only understood or appreciated in its breakdown, as witnessed in Garfinkel's studies of students acting as boarders at home, or friends asking questions as if strangers. As Chan (2003: 316) notes, 'breaking the expectations would mean that it was no longer possible to define meanings and actions as rationally understood and shared...encounters would become senseless.'

Rationality operates through a system of understandings, 'templates' of behaviour, patterned over time and through experience, constituting a collective understanding that is accessed and operated by members of a collective. It is akin to a language. It is the ability to discern and correctly utilize a repertoire appropriate to a context. It does not imply a consensus of values, shared understanding, or homogeneity. It denotes competence not agreement. It is important, as Alvesson (2003: 2) notes, for 'acting wisely', not just being able to do the 'right' things, but being able to develop or embellish action, informed by an understanding of how this would be suitable.

Rationality thus is not located within the individual. It does not reflect cognitive aptitude, but is the property of the community. By participating in the community, a contextual rationality is strengthened as the individual reflects on acceptable, successful, and unsuccessful engagement. A community has its own standards of rationality and acceptability, maintained and secured though an ongoing process of criticism and debate. There must be sufficient room for criticism, questioning, and argument where the community responds to challenges, thereby reinforcing or slightly moderating practice and, through this, slowly changing background assumptions. Through the principle of mutual control, every member of the community is considered to be capable of contributing to this dialogue. Where background assumptions are so taken-for-granted, however, challenge to them may be understood as a form of 'heresy' (Longino 2002).

Culture has been deemed unreasonable. It has been depicted as the antithesis of reason. Reference to a contextual rationality makes the 'reasonable' element of culture accessible. It denotes the contextual understanding of actions shared by a group or collectivity. Context not as a 'setting' or a 'backdrop' to action and understanding, but an integral part of it. It gives action and understanding its viability.[23]

Rationality as thick description?
A narrative rationality

Geertz (1994: 220) says of culture that it 'is not a power, something to which social events, behaviours, institutions or processes can be casually attributed; it is a context, something within which they can be intelligibly—that is, thickly—described'. Description constitutes explanation. Thick description also highlights the importance of stories and narratives as a way of understanding what is rational.[24]

In organizations, stories and narratives function as a 'key part of members sense-making' allowing them to 'supplement individual memories with institutional memory'. Stories are an important part of socialization. They function as a means of defining characters and scripting actions (Boje 1995). They discipline conceptual constructions and perceptual themes, interpreting and framing organizations and characters. Orr's (1990) work, for example, illustrates the way in which stories are used to provide new accounts of how work should be conducted. Stories add both to personal competence, through the sense-making activities that are engaged in as the story unfolds, and to collective knowledge by becoming part of the repertoire of those in the field. They function as a means of 'common law', a means to interpret new circumstances in the light of accumulated thinking and 'wisdom' on a topic. They are an important element of being able to get the job done, facilitating knowledge creation, and constructing shared understandings. The collaboration and exchange of ideas through shared narratives and 'war stories' elaborate shared meanings that help the organization adapt and transform (Brown and Duguid 1991; Nonaka 1994/2002: 244). While some stories may be 'unique' to a community and very much related to the exercise of practice, other stories are common to a range of organizations, although told 'uniquely' about one.

Martin et al. (1983), for example, identify several stories that revolve around the themes of equality and inequality, security and insecurity, and control and lack of control, that are a feature of all organizations.

For Weick (2001), in addition to being important for reminding people of values and providing guidelines for activities, 'Stories are important, not just because they coordinate, but also because they register, summarize, and allow reconstruction of scenarios that are too complex for logical linear summaries to preserve'. They hold the potential to 'enhance requisite variety among human actors', and that is why for Weick (2001: 341), 'high reliability systems may handicap themselves when they become preoccupied with traditional rationality and fail to recognize the power of narrative rationality'. He gives an example of the *Challenger* disaster where arguments about the pros and cons of launch between NASA and Morton Thiokol were conducted in linear, sequential fashion: 'If somewhere in those discussions, someone had said, "That reminds me of a story", a different rationality might have been applied and a different set of implications might have been drawn' (Weick 2001: 342).

As Mumby (2004: 245) notes, 'narratives are not just stories told within social contexts.' They constitute context. They function as important sense-making activities. They are a process by which people learn to function and gain competence. Narratives 'work'. They organize attention, indicate what is important and why. They allow understandings of what constitutes competence, success and failure, and authorized action, that which may be said and done in the context in question. An important element of narratives, is not only learning the story but also knowing the appropriate occasions for telling them, to whom and by whom. They are a means through which 'culture' is transmitted, as a 'quintessential form of customary knowledge' (Riley 1991: 220).

For individuals, it is a way of linking the general to the individual, allowing the individual not only to locate their place within a broader field but also to link the validity of the narrative to their own experience. There is a validation process with narratives and stories, although a different validation process from 'expert' technocratic knowledge. Not all constructions offered as stories are accepted as such. Not all interpretations and constructions of events are valid or believable. As Gabriel (2004: 73) notes, 'facts are recalcitrant.' Fischer (1987) links narrative to the production and understandings of 'good reasons'. 'Rationality is determined by the nature of persons as narrative beings— their inherent awareness of "narrative probability", what constitutes a coherent story and their constant habit of testing "narrative fidelity", whether or not the stories they experience ring true with the stories they know to be true in their lives' (Fischer 1987: 5 quoted in Riley 1991: 221). As such, narrative privileges inductive reasoning. For Fischer, narrative is located in a logic of 'good reasons'.

BOX 6.3. RATIONALITY AS 'THICK DESCRIPTION'?

All agencies and professions recognize the importance of the role of stories and 'thick description' as a means of learning roles and acquiring occupational or professional knowledge:

Generally as a profession we talk to each other an awful lot. There is a lot of dialogue with others, with other colleagues. With others you have your funny stories; with colleagues you go into the details of the cases. We bore each other with the minute details of cases. It's a quid pro quo, you bore them with details and then you listen to them as they bore you. You have detailed conversations with colleagues. It's also a small world. Some of my friends are now Sheriffs and you talk about cases with them. A solicitor is going out with a PF and you talk about cases. It's a way of learning.   (Defence agent)

And people like talking about work. The worst night out is to get the Scottish Courts and the Police together. All they talk about is work, although maybe the Rangers' [football] match. But its never boring working in the area. People have a genuine interest in their work.

There are also a smallish number of judges out on the circuit. Information gets out as to what happened in which case. And consistency in sentencing arises through this. They are aware of what's happening in the High Court. Sentencing is clear in many cases. The exceptional cases are the non custodial and the discretionary life sentences. You want to be careful you are not completely out of orbit on these things. You see what other judges do in other cases. But no two cases can be the same. No two people are the same. For example there can be a drugs courier, with a couple of convictions and a Drug Treatment programme may be useful. In other cases, there may not be the circumstances and the background, a Drug Treatment is not going to work. Culpable homicide may range from a deferred sentence to life imprisonment. It depends on the circumstances. There may be a fight, someone falls, hits their head and dies. This is different from where there is a knife attack which has a degree of premeditation.   (Judge)

Conclusion: Rational communities?

If you are talking with, giving orders to, or planning for making use of a man who is living in a world or feels he is living in a world, of which you are ignorant, whose existence you do not suspect, is there any ground for thinking that what is logical and reasonable to you will be so to him? If you do not know his axioms, it is probable that your axioms will not be his, and besides, he cannot in general be persuaded by reason but only by an appeal to his sentiments. How shall you appeal to sentiments that you do not know?   (Henderson and Mayo 1936/2002: 312)

The argument that culture is context which enables rationality to function raises two disputed and interrelated questions: whether all activity sanctioned by a collectivity might be seen as rational action and whether there is the possibility of communication and understanding between cultures, and if so, how? How is it possible to communicate between cultures if standards of rationality or intelligibility are different? It is the debate which, as we have seen, is at the heart of discussions on an embedded rationality. The same debate has exercised, although in very different terms, much organization studies thinking and management practice. To clothe these debates in terms such as culture obscures the centrality and importance of the rationality that informs practice. Recognizing the importance of a contextual rationality allows for debate to be engaged as to whether there are any core principles that cover differing communities and whether there is the possibility in principle of rational engagement. At the very least, it removes the hierarchy that is implicit in the romantic legacy of 'hidden from reason' and the claimed superiority that accompanies these debates in practice, the supposed supremacy of reason or 'rational' approaches or solutions and the easy dismissal of that which is unwelcome as 'cultural'. The recognition that both are examples of a contextual rationality, and that both are 'reasonable' as such, a reflection of the context-dependence that sustains them, not only casts debates in a different light but also requires, in the absence of the direct operation of power, a more 'reasoned' position be adopted by those caught up in such disputes.

7 Situational rationality

A situational rationality takes issue with the temporal dimension of rational action, the assumption that behaviour is foresightful and that rationality occurs in advance of action. A situational rationality recognizes that action is retrospectively rational. It is the product of action, occurring either concurrently or after, rather than before, action. This is not, however, to assume an *ex post facto*, retrospective rationalization of events. The second facet of a situational rationality is, as its name implies, the importance of its 'situatedness', the situated nature of social action. Rationality is an ongoing accomplishment, achieved through interaction with people and objects in a particular time and setting. A situational rationality is the temporally and spatially located sequential and interactional rationality of daily life. This chapter traces the various dimensions of a situational rationality and how they inform our understanding of organizational action.

A presumption of logic

A situational rationality focuses on the 'common sense' concept of rationality identified by Schutz (1962). For Schutz, rationality based on an assessment of means, ends, and secondary results does not describe actions within the common sense experiences of everyday life in the social world.[1] A means–end rationality reflects a specific model of the world made by social scientists. He writes:

These models of actors are not human beings living within their biographical situation in the social world of everyday life … they do not have any biography or any history, and the situation into which they are placed is not a situation defined by them but defined by their creator, the social scientist. He has created these puppets or homunculi to manipulate them for his purposes … The homunculus was not born, he does not grow up, and he will not die. He has no hopes and no fears; he does not know anxiety as the chief motive of all his deeds … the homunculus is invested with a system of relevances originating in the scientific problem of his constructor and not in the particular biographically determined situation of an actor within the world … In such a simplified model of the social world pure rational acts, rational choices from rational motives are possible because all the difficulties encumbering the real actor in the everyday life-world have been eliminated. Thus the concept of rationality in the strict sense already defined does not refer to actions within the common-sense experiences of everyday life in the social world; it is the expression of a particular type of construct or certain specific models of the social world made by the social scientists for certain specific methodological purposes.   (Schutz 1962: 41–2)

A means–end rationality is a function of a 'conceptual scheme' or 'intellectual shorthand' where 'subjective' elements are deemed irrelevant. 'We have to distinguish between rational constructs of models of human actions on the one hand, and constructs of models of rational human actions on the other' (Schutz 1962: 44). The postulate of rationality makes the rational actions or reactions of homunculi possible. But this is distinct from the rational course of action of an actor in the social life-world.

In situations, encounters, and 'everyday life', there is, in Weick's terms, 'the presumption of logic', an assumption that these are rational. A presumption of logic is where a person 'presumes in advance that the event will have made sense' (Weick 2001: 392). This is an a priori. Actions are taken as evidence of rational action. Rationality is ascribed to action. Action and events have a rationality within them that has to be identified and sustained. The competent participant, drawing on the immediate situation, then 'supplies' the meaning that renders the action rational. 'Having made this presumption, the person then tries to make the event sensible as it unfolds, postpones premature judgements on whether it makes sense or not, and thereby makes his or her own contribution toward inventing a sensible, complete experience' (Weick 2001: 392). It is a style of thinking that goes from the particular to the particular, not from the particular to the general.

With the presumption that people tend to be rational within situational contexts, the immediate social context shapes what is perceived to be rational at a given moment. Actions are *made* rational by their situational nature. This argument follows that of Garfinkel (1967: 33) who rejects the prevailing view that the rational properties of practical activities may be adequately described 'using a rule or a standard obtained outside actual settings within which such properties are recognized, used, produced, and talked about'. It is the immediate connection with socially organized practical action, the practical contexts of social interaction, that allows for the interpretation and understanding of actions. 'The rational structure of social actions is internal to the practical context(s) within which they are produced, recognized and understood' (Bogen 1999: 7).

Local order thus has its own internal logic. This is discovered 'from within'. As Boden notes (1994: 40), 'rationality is through and through an enacted affair.' It is managed *in situ*. The understandings and accounts of reasoned and reasonable activities develop for social agents over the course of action. In this respect, Boden appropriates the concept of bounded rationality, seeing rationality as an interactionally bounded phenomenon. Local interpretations then become the foundation of a retrospective and prospective sense-making, as they are made to mesh with both earlier actions and future projects.

Local rationalities necessarily inform organizations to the extent that Boden argues organizational rationality is a local rationality: 'actions taken in organizations and ... their overall effectiveness, efficiency, and success depend utterly on local understandings and local rationality' (Boden 1994: 20). Her work illustrates the 'local logic' of organizational rationality, how the unfolding of a collective collaboration structures practical action. Local rationalities devise what the appropriate means might be to achieve a particular end. The temporal coordination of joint activities, the 'what nextness' of work tasks, and the ability to identify and act upon knowledge of the work environment creates and sustains an organizational rationality. Through the ability of working through rules, regulations, and procedures worked out on the spot, deciding which are relevant to use in which circumstances, creates a local logic that sustains the organization so that it looks rational, efficient, and correct. Organizations rely on this, the situations of action, the purpose at hand, in order to function and make the organization work. It is this local ingenuity that, for Boden (1994), 'creates' 'rational' organizations.

Although local logic is built out of a cooperative competence and is thus a local phenomenon, local rationalities cannot function entirely on their own. Local actions must not only make sense to their participants but also be seen as reasonable in organizations, or be judged 'irrational' according to some externalized notion of rationality. 'Immediate reasoning' must be linked to 'relevant institutional rationalities' which in organizations requires that they are efficient, adaptive, and accountable (Boden 1994: 22). 'The spatio-temporally intense logic of everyday rationalities' must fit, or be made to fit in with broader organizational rationalities of how things should work, and other work practices that constitute the whole.

The rationality of situated action

Rationality as applied to everyday experience, a situational rationality, is premised on knowledgeable agents, active and competent participants and collaborators, interactively constituting a shared world. This situational rationality relates to the 'need for social actors to create and maintain intersubjectively binding narrative structures that are constitutive of the social relations in which they are implicated' (Smith 1987: 56). It recognizes the embedded nature of social actions and their collaborative and co-productive quality. The rationality of situated action has its own vocabulary of motives (Wright Mills

1940).[2] Situational rationality has certain foundational assumptions: locality; retrospection; precariousness; the ongoing nature of its construction; and its practical verification.

Locality: Schutz (1962) emphasizes the importance of 'position', the biographically determined situation of understanding. Things are rendered intelligible through one's place in the world; the personal coordinates of time, space, and biography. Action is thus always situated in an immediate social context and in the 'quiddity of local historical processes' (Smith 1987: 123). It takes place in particular, concrete circumstances. It is these 'mundane circumstances' that influence the mundane reasoner and mundane reasons (Pollner 1987). This immediate context influences action in two respects. 'Situatedness' is based on interaction. Through indexicality, the specific, local, and the contingent give action its significance. Local interactional work produces intelligibility *in situ* (Suchman 1987: 69). It is the specific context that allows individuals to produce mutual intelligibility. 'Meaning is constituted in the interplay of people and objects under the concrete conditions of a particular setting' (Boden 1994: 35). As Bittner (1965) recognizes, all accounts 'all manner of describing, analyzing, questioning, criticizing, believing, doubting, idealizing, schematizing, denigrating, and so on, are unavoidably and irremediably tied to the social settings that occasion them or within which they are situated'. Second, this shared experience may then provide the foundation for shared understanding: 'Although people may not share meaning, they do share experience. This shared experience may be made sensible in retrospect by equivalent meanings, but seldom by similar meanings...So if people share anything, what they share are actions, activities, moments of conversation, and joint tasks' (Weick 1995: 188).

Retrospection: In Schutz's (1962) analysis of rational action, he distinguishes between action, act, and behaviour, a distinction that is important for how he understands meaning. Action is an ongoing process, devised in advance and based on a preconceived project. An act is the outcome of the process, an accomplished action. Meaning results from an interpretation of past experience.

As long as I live in my acts, directed towards the objects of these acts, the acts do not have any meaning. They become meaningful if I grasp them as well-circumscribed experiences of the past and, therefore, in retrospection. Only experiences which can be recollected beyond their actuality and which can be questioned about their constitution are, therefore, subjectively meaningful.

'Perceived but not apperceived' experiences, 'undetachable from surrounding experiences', are neither 'delineated nor recollected' as 'subjectively meaningful experiences' (Schutz 1962: 210–11). Meaning is the consequence of a 'reflective attitude' to one's acting. It is to 'stop and think'. 'I may live either in the ongoing process of my acting, directed towards its object' or 'step out of the ongoing flux and look by a reflexive glance at the acts performed in previous processes of acting' (Schutz 1962: 214). Meaning therefore is retrospective. 'Retrospective constructions are the principal means by which we catch hold of situated action and reason about it' (Suchman 1987: 39).

Precariousness: The precariousness of a situational rationality stems from the intersubjective nature of the world and the problems that this poses (Schutz 1962). Because one cannot directly know the 'other', knowledge has to rely on what Schutz refers to as typifications (socially derived 'typical' patterns of motives and ends, attitudes and personalities) and the 'idealization of the interchangeability of standpoints or reciprocity of perspectives' (i.e. that one can put oneself in the others' place and understand them).

We come, therefore, to the conclusion that 'rational action' on the common-sense level is always action within an unquestioned and undetermined frame of constructs of typicalities of the setting, the motives, the means and the ends, the courses of action and personalities involved and taken for granted. They are, however, not merely taken for granted by the actor but also supposed as being taken for granted by the fellow-man.   (Schutz 1962: 33)

Common sense involves a set of generalizations, abstractions, etc., only certain elements of which are paid attention to in order to function. The 'so-called concrete facts of common-sense perceptions are not so concrete as it seems' (Schutz 1962: 3). To believe that they are is the fallacy of misplaced concreteness. Objectivity is achieved rather than given. 'Mundane reason' (Pollner 1987) assumes the existence of a world 'out there', 'public' and 'objective'. It sees objects, events, and processes as pre-given and 'real'. It thus expects encounters and experiences to be objectively 'real', rather than accomplished or achieved, and it works on this presupposition. The formal expectation of objectivity and the simultaneous interpretive practice, through which this appearance of objectivity is achieved, is the paradox of everyday interaction and the source of its precariousness. Meaning is temporary and fragile and has to be repeatedly accomplished or enacted in everyday encounters (Garfinkel 1967; Weick 1995). It is this inherent indeterminacy of action that participants in interaction stabilize. People grant one another a version of 'practical ethics' (Garfinkel 1967) which discourages individuals from 'calling one another to account for failure to treat the impossible tests of the objectivity assumption' (Molotch and Boden 1985: 313). Each grants the other the right to trade on implicativeness in portraying reality. 'Mundane reasoners exercise an unwitting ingenuity in their capacity to preserve mundane reason from incipient threats' (Pollner 1987: 127).

Ongoing co-production: Precariousness requires the 'on going concerting of activities' (Smith 1987: 125), the ongoing nature of making situations sensible. Because they are ongoing, there is no finality to the making of meaning.

As Smith (1987: 90) notes, 'the order, coherence, rationality and sense of social situations and relations are an active work.' Sense-making and meaning construction are practical and social accomplishments. They also involve co-production. Interaction and sense-making are an ensemble work.

> The coordering or concerting of actual activities by actual individuals is continually being worked out in the course of working together, competing with one another, conversing, and all the other ways in which people co-act. People work together in concrete actual situations...Our everyday world of practical activities continually confirms for us and others a shared world of objects and people. (Smith 1987: 124)

Rationality and meaning are an emergent property of this ongoing action. The ongoing organization of practices 'continually and routinely reaffirms a world in common' (Smith 1987: 125). 'Order arises in and is accomplished by the actual practices of actual individuals, including their practices of reasoning, interpreting, rendering what has happened accountable' (Smith 1987: 175). It is through ongoing activity that 'organization' is achieved as an emergent property of interaction (Suchman 1987: 179).

Practical verification: What has been identified are various dimensions of *in situ* reasoning. Throughout is reference to practical reasoning, that is, the reasoning that is required as part of the successful accomplishment of everyday activities, to get things done (Schutz 1962). This is the temporality of practice. It necessarily involves the attempts to make things work in real time. It is reasoning applied to people's 'practical activities, practical circumstances and practical actions' (Garfinkel 1967), the 'actualities of what people do on a day to day basis under definite conditions and in definite situations' (Smith 1987: 166). Suchman (1987) points to the importance of the immediate context or 'situation' of conduct, the 'practical situations of choice', that profoundly influence practical action. Actions must be practically rational. They must be rationally adequate for all practical purposes (Garfinkel 1967: 8 cited in Molotch and Boden 1985/2002: 331).[3] 'We speak from the known-in-practice ongoing concerting of actual activities' (Smith 1987: 189). In this context, plausibility becomes the criteria for evaluation. The meaning of 'objects' such as plans and documents are largely influenced by the circumstances in which they are invoked and the context of their use. It is 'common sense reasoning' that 'determines' their sense, deployment, and meaning, and their use in the organization of actors and actions. Practices are known, understood, and produced in a particular way because they *work* (Boden 1994). It is thus their practical efficacy that ensures their rationality, not the other way round. There is thus a concrete or specific test of rationality. 'Practical' however is based on what people 'know', not on whether what they 'know' is true (Hindess 1987: 102).

Situated knowledge

Following Schutz, Garfinkel (1960) distinguishes between the 'attitude of daily life' and the interests of scientific theorizing, and is critical that the rational actions of daily life have been given a residual status. Although everyday life does not function according to the rigours of scientific rationalities, he identifies rational action as 'the ability of a person in conducting his everyday affairs to calculate, to project alternative plans of action, to select before the actual fall of events the conditions under which he will follow one plan or another, to give priority in a selection of means to their technical efficacy and the rest' (Garfinkel 1960: 82). Rationality, for Garfinkel, designates types of behaviour, 'the rationalities', and he sees all elements of the rationalities occurring in everyday life, including categorizing and comparing; the search for means; analysis of alternatives and consequences; the concern for timing and predictability; following rules of procedure; and the exercise of choice and its grounds. The difference between the attitude of everyday life and scientific theorizing is that in the former:

The ability of a person to act 'rationally' ... depends upon the fact that the person must be able literally to take for granted ... a vast array of features of the social order. In order to treat rationally the 1/10th of his situation that, like an iceberg, appears above the water, he must be able to treat the 9/10th that lies below as an unquestioned and, even more interestingly, as an unquestionable background of matters that are demonstrably relevant to his calculation, but which appear without being noticed.

(Garfinkel 1960: 82)[4]

From this perspective, as Bittner (1965: 79) notes, 'it is not possible to have any rational construction of reality that does not rest on some such tacit assumptions', a taken-for-granted body of background information that provides a tacit foundation of all that is explicitly known. This is an individual's 'stock of knowledge at hand' made up of 'typifications' of the common sense world that constitute the 'social reality', the self-evident, and the 'rational'. It is the 'foundation for all deliberative considerations without itself being deliberately considered. While its content can be raised to the level of analysis, this typically does not occur ... information enters into the commonplace and practical orientation to reality which members of society regard as "natural" when attending to their daily affairs' (Bittner 1965: 79). It is 'everyday common sense'. It is manifest in several guises.

Everyday knowledge: From Schutz (1962), everyday knowledge is based on an intersubjective stock of knowledge 'handed down' and learnt from experience. It is based on likelihood and typical sequences, rather than certainty or probability. It is the 'taken-for-granted' 'common sense world' of everyday life which is only questioned when there is a serious disruption. Garfinkel's (1967) understanding also is of rationality as being constructed through everyday interaction, which then become constitutive of institutionalized common understandings, to the extent that it is only through the modifications of everyday interactions that these institutionalized understandings will change (Garfinkel 1964/2002: 259).

'*Common sense*': 'Common sense knowledge ... is institutionalized knowledge of the real world' (Garfinkel 1964/2002: 245). 'Common sense knowledge' of everyday life portrays a real society. It is knowledge 'known in common with others'.[5] (But, as Bernstein 1978 notes, common sense knowledge is both socially performed and socially distributed. It differs among individuals, groups, and classes.) The taken-for-granted, sedimented experience of the group, its 'common sense', acts as an unexamined foundation of beliefs and action. It may have 'stood the test of time' and therefore comes to be taken as given. This, however, is only 'until further notice' (Schutz 1962: 74).

Geertz (1983: 75) makes the argument for understanding common sense as a 'relatively organized body of considered thought, rather than just what anyone clothed and in his right mind knows'. It comes from reflection on experience rather than being the mere reporting of an unmediated or unreflective experience, and thus distinguishes between the 'mere matter of fact apprehension of reality' and 'down to earth, colloquial wisdom, judgements or assessments'. Common sense assumes a degree of judicious, intelligent, perceptive engagement with the problem at hand. For Geertz (1983: 76), it is historically constructed and as such 'subject to historically defined standards of judgement'. As a cultural system often disputed and not highly integrated, it has, nonetheless, a value and validity. He describes it as 'one of the oldest suburbs of human culture' (Geertz 1983: 77),[6] and sees it as 'the truth claims of colloquial reason' (Geertz 1983: 78), the properties of which are 'naturalness', 'practicalness', 'thinness', 'immethodicalness', and 'accessibleness'.[7] 'Common sense represents matters ... as inherent in the situation, intrinsic aspects of reality, the way things go' (Geertz 1983: 85). As such, it is capable of being uncovered. 'Common sense seems to us what is left over when all the more articulated sorts of symbol systems have exhausted their tasks, what remains of reason when its more sophisticated achievements are all set aside' (Geertz 1983: 92).

Recognition of the 'everyday' and 'common sense' has a broad political significance. Both refer to 'the world where people are located as they live, located bodily ... It is the organization of their known world' (Smith 1987: 91). For Smith (1987), the everyday world is a 'point of entry' to understand the institutional relations that determine everyday worlds and their local organization. Individuals 'always start from themselves. Their relations are the relations of their real life'. In her presentation of everyday life as problematic, Smith (1987) does not focus on 'meaning', 'interpretation', and 'common understandings' but focuses on the concrete relations with which people engage as part of their daily lives. Her focus is on the knower in the everyday world from which their knowing originates and emphasizes the importance of studying

---

BOX 7.1. SITUATED KNOWLEDGE

A situational rationality addresses the 'what nextness' of work, focusing on making activities within an organization work. Easy, shorthand terms, for example, the 'court scheduling' or the 'use of postal citations', hide complex work operations and much local knowledge:

On postal citations [to appear at court] the legislation says you have to use recorded delivery. If you use recorded delivery you try and get it delivered on Saturday. Otherwise the postie goes, and if they're out, then leaves a note. But most people know that recorded delivery is something they don't want to know. If the address is wrong or it is not delivered, it has to be hand delivered. This is done by the LDO [letter delivery officer], ex police officers. They know the areas, they may know the people. They have access to intelligence and historical data bases. If you want the figures to be higher [for court appearances], then you might have to do them all through the LDO. But the police don't want that impact on their budget.   (Police)

[on allocating prison accommodation] There are also issues that you can't put some people together [thus impacting on violent assaults and influencing performance measures]. If a prisoner has enemies, and another prisoner has other enemies, in cases of seven different people, each with different enemies, it makes accommodation decisions difficult.

(Prison services)

You need quite skilled clerks. They need internal local knowledge to be alert to things. There is a huge learning curve involved in all this. This really shows the importance of the continuity of personnel. But the problem is having experienced staff. The emphasis was on relief work and part time workers but this has made more work because there is not the tacit knowledge that allows you to pick up on issues. Decisions have been made on employment, casualisation of the workforce. This was introduced on the grounds of cutting down costs. But the issue is how do you measure costs? The Fiscal at X have to deal with a lot of temps, they are constantly retraining temps.   (Court services)

There used to be a police officer in the court who would write down all the disposals [court decisions]. Writing down disposals is sometimes [now] of poor quality and you need knowledge of the business to pick up when things are entered wrongly. You can't rely on temps to pick this up because they don't have the knowledge to understand something. For example, if there is a mistake on registering bail conditions, you might end up making a false arrest. If the disposal is entered incorrectly then the [arrest] warrant is in doubt. And the police get it in the neck.   (Police)

Often this knowledge is ascribed to 'common sense':

We used to have a training centre. This used to deal with basic legal procedures. But there was nothing on programming. This was seen as plain common sense. The only guidance you have on [court] scheduling are targets...the programme ought to be devised to achieve targets. Programming is basically getting a handle on things and common sense. You reckon that 7 trials are an optimum load. The whole thing is based on risk management. Everyone is involved in risk management. You work on the probability that not all the cases will go on. 7 is a reasonable number. Of 7 cases, 2 will go ahead. Of the 5 of the 7 cases that may not run, they are adjourned because the witnesses do not turn up or they [the accused] pled earlier. It's not because they have all pled guilty. So you end up with fewer or less cases. You always work on this basis. You do over book the diary. You accept the risk. If it doesn't work, if other cases don't collapse, the impact is quite high. On the day, you manage it on the day. We won't know until it's actually

BOX 7.1. (*continued*)

in the courts how many of the cases will go. The PFS know some cases won't go on. Or someone says give us time to plead, and they don't plead and you've lost an hour and a half. What you are dealing with is calculated risks. It is folk knowledge, although this is backed up by statistical evidence. But it is local folk knowledge over decades of fine tuning of a programme. It is not always right. It may not happen in aggregate in one day. You are trying to optimise court time and resources and the demands of business. You always set more business than can be dealt with on one day. There is no way round this. You want to reduce the number of witnesses turning up unnecessarily, and make sure the building is not chock a block.   (Court services)

One initiative was for this situated knowledge to be traced to get a full understanding of the 'system'.

Basically the intention is to process or 'map the system' from arrest to disposal to see where the pinch points are. A lot of data has to be manually collected, literally following what happens to a piece of paper.   (Policy)

The assumption is that you give the police report straight to the PFS, but it goes to the report checker, and to the typist, and to the record department for previous cases. For a caution and charge it has to be entered on the criminal records data base. They need it in case the accused applies for a job. They enter the details. If the charges are changed by the PFS then it has to reenter criminal records to be changed. We need to know how things work in detail.   (Police)

A common complaint was that management did not understand the nature of this situated knowledge:

Its common sense because we're steeped in it, we work with it. This is part of the known world. But this is not true further up. Management doesn't know the process, the minutiae of the work. They don't understand it. They are brainwashed that management means that they don't need to know about the work. Management sees their role as to influence policies and procedures, not in terms of helping people do their work properly.

(anonymous)

the activities of individuals that produce social order within the context in which they live: the practical activities of real people engaged in concrete situations. As Garfinkel (1964/2002: 260) notes, 'the production and recognition of reasonable, realistic and analyzable actions is not the monopoly of philosophers and professional sociologists. Members of a society are concerned as a matter of course and necessarily with these matters both as features and for the socially managed production of their everyday affairs.' This is not to pose the everyday world as an object of study divorced from broader social and economic relations, as it is often taken to be. Nor is it to take the everyday as a self-contained object of enquiry. The everyday world cannot be known or understood entirely within its own scope, given that it is organized by relations that are not fully apparent within it (Smith 1987: 92). But the question then becomes 'how does it happen that their relations assume an independent existence over and against them?' (Smith 1987: 141).

Situated studies

As Silverman notes, the focus on situational rationalities has been influential in organization studies in several respects: early studies of informal organizations; the emphasis on 'common sense thought'; the emphasis on the intersubjective nature of social life; the recognition of social order being a 'negotiated order'; and an emphasis on language (Bittner 1967; Dalton 1959; Strauss et al. 1963; Sudnow 1965).[8] It is most often found in ethnographies that can illustrate the intricacy and sophistication of this rationality.

ETHNOGRAPHIES

Ethnography 'is the craft of place' (Geertz 1983: 167). It is the recording of the *in situ* production and reproduction of social life. A term devised by Garfinkel (1968) ethnomethodology refers to the methodology deployed by members of society to achieve this. It grants status to common sense reasoning. Garfinkel writes that the term captures the sense of 'common sense knowledge': ' "Ethno" seemed to refer, somehow or other, to the availability, to a member, of common-sense knowledge of his society, common-sense knowledge of the "whatever" '. Garfinkel's concern was to counter the 'cultural dope' presentation of the individual's ability to evoke cultural understanding. His concern was 'how society gets put together ... how it gets done' (Garfinkel 1964/2002: 235). Where Schutz takes the intersubjective world as a given, ethnomethodologists see this as 'contingently accomplished by members' situated practices'. The stability of the social world was not the consequence of a shared body of meanings, or the reading of a script, but the ability to find coherence in situations and actions. Ethnomethodology aims to recognize individuals as 'the competent practitioners of their everyday worlds' (Smith 1987: 125). Its focus is *in situ* rationality, the structures of everyday life that make organizations and social life happen, and to uncover the work that is done with others to prove social competence and the rationality of action. It is to recognize 'the genius of mundane reason and mundane reasoners' 'in the construction of "rational", intelligible or "accountable" action' (Pollner 1987: xii).

Its purpose is to explicate the known-in-common and the taken-for-granted by treating as problematic the actual methods whereby members of a society make the social structures of everyday activities possible. Schutz's stranger seeks to make sense of this.

'For background expectancies to come into view one must either be a stranger to the "life as usual" character of everyday scenes or become estranged from them' (Garfinkel 1964/2002: 235). For Garfinkel, this is achieved by interrupting the 'natural facts of life' and the 'taken-for-granted'. 'Procedurally it is my preference to start with familiar scenes and ask what can be done to make trouble.' This is exemplified in the various 'experiments' of 'What do you mean?' (questioning every statement in a conversation); 'boarders' (offspring acting as though they are boarders in their home); and 'hidden motives' (assuming hidden motives on the part of those with whom they communicate). Garfinkel illustrates how the socially managed production of the everyday has to be actively worked at: the unnoticed background of common understandings; where understandings are disputed, people work to make these situations 'rational'; that sense is not decided unless there is knowledge of biography, the purpose of the speaker, circumstances of the utterance, previous conversations, and relationships. The focus of ethnomethodology then is to illustrate 'the highly ordered and orderly reasonableness of everyday action' (Boden 1994: viii) or the 'extraordinary organization of the ordinary' (Pollner 1987: xvii). It is also to recognize the contingent in everyday practices.

Ethnomethodology explicates the 'orderliness' of how individuals experience everyday life. It also recognizes the individual as an expert practitioner of the constitutive work essential for the successful accomplishment of everyday activities. Competence is reflected in an individual's ability to achieve that which would be considered normal and reasonable. 'The fundamental facticity of the social world' is the practical accomplishment of social actors (Boden 1994). As Pollner (1987: ix) notes, 'one of ethnomethodology's contributions to the understanding of social life is its capacity to produce a deep wonder about what is often regarded as obvious, given or natural.' It reveals 'the richly layered skills, assumptions and practices through which the most commonplace ... activities and experiences are constructed'. From this perspective, rationality is an ongoing accomplishment.

Applied to organization, it is a process to 'uncover and explicate the ways in which people in particular work settings come to understand, account for and take action and otherwise manage their day-to-day situation' (Van Maanen 1979/2002: 360). Questions of 'how' things get done are more significant than questions of 'what': organization or organizing rather than organizations.

The importance of an ethnomethodological study of organizations is identified by Bittner (1965: 80), who, drawing on Schutz, critiqued Weber's work for an 'idealized reconstruction of organizations' that:

failed to explore the underlying commonsense presuppositions ... the meaning and warrant of the inventory of properties of bureaucracy embedded in the attitude of everyday life and in socially sanctioned commonsense typifications ... Plucked from its native ground, i.e., the world of common sense, the concept of rational organization, and the schematic determinations that are subsumed under it are devoid of information of how its terms relate to the facts. Without knowing the structure of this relationship of reference, the meaning of the concept and its terms cannot be determined

By not considering the tacit background assumptions 'that bureaucrats take for granted', rational schemes appear 'unrealistic normative idealizations'. The 'literal interpretations of formal schemes is not only inappropriate but strictly speaking impossible'. Tacit assumptions only come to the fore in the use of the formal scheme. It is this element that Suchman (1987) portrays in her analysis of the use of planning. It is 'common sense reasoning' that 'determines' their sense, that is, the ways in which plans and documents are read, understood, used, and exchanged, that constitute them. 'The meaning and import of the formal schemes must remain undetermined unless the circumstances and procedures of its actual use by actors is fully investigated' (Bittner 1965/2002: 78). This requires the study of 'how the terms of discourse are assigned to real objects and events by normally competent persons in ordinary situations'; 'how certain objects and events meet, or are made to meet, the specifications contained in the scheme'; and 'the ways in which the scheme can be invoked for information, direction, justification' (Bittner 1965/2002: 81). In other words, the rational construction of objects and events, and their rationality, is only apparent when they are invoked. In a comment prescient of Cohen et al.'s (1972) garbage can description, he notes, 'if one views a rational organizational scheme without information about what it is ostensibly meant to be, then it emerges as a generalized formula to which all sorts of problems can be brought for solution' (Bittner 1965/2002: 82).

The classics of the early ethnomethodological studies of work are found in the work of Bittner (1967), Sudnow (1965), Emerson (1973), and Strauss et al. (1963). Each illustrates how situated activities have their own rationality, sense, and meaning that is accomplished and sustained through ongoing action.

Bittner's (1967) study of police of Skid Row illustrates how an ingrained situational rationality is used to maintain order in an environment different from usual policing activities, where the lack of social structures, the importance of the 'here and now' to those who live there, exploitation, and lack of trust render it quite dangerous. Rather than 'enforcing the law', the priorities become forestalling the possibilities of violence and protecting those who live there from predators. A particularized knowledge of people and place informs action. Intervention is determined by exigency, the nature of the incident, and the context and background of the situation. Strict culpability or considerations of 'merit' or 'desert' are secondary considerations. Action is ordered by the 'occasion of the moment'. 'Just as the past is seen … as having only the most attenuated relevance to the present, so the future implications of present situations are … generally devoid of prospective coherence … That which is not within the grasp of momentary control is outside of practical social reality' (Bittner 1967/1973: 332). Strict rational legal definitions of ownership, stealing, and swindling do not apply in the context. The patrolmen apply their own situational understanding of what counts as rational behaviour, using a richly particularized knowledge, secondary consideration of strict culpability, and the exigencies of the situation. The importance and value of the officer's knowledge and judgement are viewed as a form of craftsmanship. Violating this through harsh, indiscriminate, or personally motivated actions are condemned.

Emerson's (1973) work illustrates how much effort is required to sustain 'definitions' of the context in which people are placed and how 'reality' is embodied in routines and reaffirmed in social interaction. In her analysis of a gynaecological examination, she illustrates how there are dominant definitions and counter themes: the tension between the medical and the sexual; the impersonal and the intimate; the 'detached', matter-of-fact, and the emotional; the technical and the personal, the balance of which must be established to ensure that the interaction is successfully concluded. Her analysis demonstrates how definitions of reality are inherently precarious and how the internal contradictory definitions of reality found in most situations must be handled through good judgement. 'Sustaining a sense of the solidness of a reality composed of multiple contradictory definitions takes unremitting effort' (Emerson 1973: 370).

In a similar vein, Strauss et al. (1963) illustrate how a hospital is characterized by a 'negotiated order' and the role of interacting individuals who attempt to define situations constrained by prior interactions that have become institutionalized. While the hospital has an overall institutional rationality of 'making patients better', this is understood by each group, doctors, nurses, patients, etc. in different ways that has to be negotiated among them. Meanings established between groups who worked together for periods of time are disrupted on regrouping, causing new understandings to be negotiated. Continuously negotiated orders of organizing are the feature of everyday activities (and sometimes formally encapsulated in rules or decisions), until these cease to be maintained through a common understanding.

SENSE-MAKING

Where ethnography deals with the taken-for-granted, sense-making is the making sense of 'an uncertain situation that initially makes no sense' (Weick 1995: 9). Sense-making also extends the temporal dimension of rational action by emphasizing the retrospective nature of what is understood. Weick puts forward sense-making as a counterpoint to decision-making and rational models of organizations. 'Efforts to maintain the illusion that organizations are rational and orderly in the interests of legitimacy are costly and futile. They consume enormous energy and undermine self-acceptance when managers hold themselves to standards of prescience that are unattainable . . . In the last

---

BOX 7.2. HOMO ECONOMICUS?

The following is an excerpt from a defence agent speaking about the clients he deals with, 'typical' summary criminal cases. The emphasis throughout is on the situational rationality that dictates their lives:

Most of these people live a very chaotic lifestyle. There are a lot of assumptions made about the person and how they should . . . do behave. There are other things that are the most important things in their lives. [I'm] talking about people with drug and alcohol problems. Occasionally the delays are deliberate. People adopt an ostrich approach to letters. Those that have some knowledge of the system will try and delay things as much as possible, but it's more a reflection of an ostrich approach. Sometimes when they get the citation [to appear in court] they fill it in themselves on the hope that it will go away. There are issues such as many changes of address and a chaotic life style. Citations don't get received. They may find themselves arrested on four warrants. Some are charged so frequently that they don't know which citation is which. It's just not their life. If we were charged we would get representation, answer letters. But not them. They lose the citation. They won't remember which is which. In these cases we try and get them bail or a reduced sentence and start legal aid. Those who know that delays work to their advantage sometimes leave it to the last minute. They usually know that the outcome will be a prison sentence. They fear a prison sentence so they put it off for as long as possible. This counts as a victory for them. But usually it's [the delay] because there's something more important in their lives, something has come up.

The situational is counterposed to the institutionalized patterns that inform a 'way of life' that also influences their lives:

Most of the clients are repeat business. And also by word of mouth. Occasionally you get people off the street. But some of the clients are second and third generation. The criminal fraternity of X [a city] are sufficiently small in numbers and there are connections between many of them. That's why word of mouth works so well. You see a relatively limited spectrum of human activity but there are interesting dynamics involved. You see different generations and so you see the generational impact. When you see Social Work Reports you see environmental conditions and the impact of this on their life. Very occasionally there's a chance of things happening, but this happens relatively rarely. Mainly its repeat clientele. It's rewarding if there's a young offender, where there's a good outcome that changes the course of a life. Basically we try and limit the continuing damage that people seem determined to do to themselves. Some clients do the same things over and over again. You can get them out twice on bail and then they go and get arrested for the same thing. So you say to them: 'do this again and there's nothing I can do'. It's rewarding occasionally when you bump into someone. You see someone married with kids or they've gone to college, but this happens rarely. Some of them reach, hit, an age limit where they give up the stupid things. They have family responsibilities, although it's not certain for how long, so the same amount of money cannot go on drugs and alcohol. It has to go on other things.

---

analysis, organizing is about fallible people who keep going' (Weick 2001: xi). As with ethnography, sense-making emphasizes the importance of ongoing accomplishment as individuals attempt to create order and make retrospective sense of situations in which they find themselves: the 'processes through which they attempt to make situations rationally accountable to themselves and others' (Weick 2001: 11).[9]

Weick's mantra in sense-making, 'how do I know what I mean until I see what I say', points to the importance of retrospective sense-making.[10] He takes the latter from Schutz's position that individuals only understand an experience through reflection, as a discrete segment, after it has been 'isolated' from the ongoing flow of experience. 'Meaning' is the consequence of an act of attention, but this must always be on that which has occurred. There may be relatively short time spans between act and reflection, but the situation or circumstance of the action *and its recollection* heavily influence the meaning that is attached to it. As Weick (1995: 29) notes, 'the feeling of order, clarity and rationality is an important goal of sense-making, which means that once this feeling is achieved further retrospective processing stops.' Reasoning is thus provisional, plausible, subject to revision, swift, and directed towards the continuation of the interrupted activity.

Sense-making reverses the usual understanding of actions following beliefs. Rather there is a retrospective and reflexive component as actions stimulate beliefs. Actors and actions 'enact' sensible environments. People act and, in doing so, create that which is then taken to be 'given'. The stimuli 'action' prompts the process of bracketing and punctuating that is part of sense-making activity. It is this which is meant by enactment. Weick (1995: 134) writes, 'sensemaking starts with actions rather than beliefs. Oddly enough, this seemingly irrational inversion of the recipe think-then-act results in the eminently rational recipe, seeing is believing.' It is also important to note that Weick sees sense-making as an active process, rather than a passive process of interpretation. Unlike interpretation, sense-making is the process of identifying cues from an ongoing flow of experience; their construction and bracketing as cues; and their interpretation and possible revision in the light of subsequent action. It involves placing events, stimuli, and 'things' into some kind of framework whereby they become intelligible. This process is recognized in Weick's (1995: 9) description of problem-solving:

although problem solving is a necessary condition for technical problem solving, it is not in itself a technical problem. When we set the problem, we select what we will treat as the 'things' of the situation, we set the boundaries of our attention to it, and we impose upon it a coherence which allows us to say what is wrong and in what directions the situation needs to be changed. Problem setting is a process in which, interactively, we name the things to which we will attend and frame the context in which we will attend to them.

Again, sense-making is most noticeable when expectations are disconfirmed or disrupted. The complete activity of sense-making involves several aspects. It is based on people experiencing an interruption, or something unexpected occurs; beginning to act (enactment); retrospectively noticing meaningful cues; interpreting these cues in the light of individual or collective identity, which helps them discover (retrospect) what is occurring (ongoing), what needs to be explained (plausibility), and what should be done next (identity enhancement); and use these plausible meanings in subsequent enactment (Weick 1995: 17). It is a boundary drawing activity in response to unpredictability and ambiguity.[11] What may begin as a momentary, expedient understanding may then, if judged plausible and 'reasonable', become more solidified into established ways of seeing. In an analysis that has some parallels with actor network theory, Weick then illustrates how that which is bracketed can take on a degree of facticity; how the socially constructed becomes the externally specified: turning, in Weick's terms, 'nominalists into realists'. In his analysis of Battered Child Syndrome (BCS) (Weick 1995), he illustrates how a discrepant set of cues recognized in retrospect become plausibly interpreted. These interpretations are then objectified and are taken up by other contacts and adopted in networks. This knowledge then becomes part of an established identity or reputation or, equally, is disrupted as strongly established identities deny its possibility.[12] In the USA, BCS was first suggested in 1946 by a paediatric radiologist. Through a discrepant set of cues from X-rays that did not fit explanations; retrospective thinking over previous experience; plausible speculation about explanations; publications that provided an object for others to notice, the 'sensible' slowly became stronger. Through social contacts and networks, BCS became an object of perception about which identities and reputations were constructed.

PRACTICE-BASED STUDIES

'Practices' is a deeply elusive concept, used in a variety of contexts, with a number of provenances. It also has a large number of 'family' terms including tacit knowledge (Polanyi 1983), 'knowing how' as opposed to 'knowing that' (Ryle 1949), 'tradition' (MacIntyre 1988), and practices (Rorty 1980). Each incorporates the understanding of knowledge as irremediably 'local'. It may perhaps be understood as a 'stream of conduct' (Munro 1999). Generally, an emphasis on practice illustrates how the interaction between individuals, activities, artefacts, and context captures the enacted, relational, and emergent features of social activity. It illustrates the 'situated production of understanding', the role of artefacts and sites to define issues, talk through them, construct stories around them, and 'resolve' them through an articulation that becomes socially embedded (Brown and Duguid 1991). It is seen in

Reflection-in-practice: Schön's interest is in the 'epistemology of practice', the 'kind of knowing in which competent practitioners engage' (Schön 2000: viii). He is particularly concerned with the practice of the professions, which he sees as characterized by complexity and uncertainty. For Schön, practice involves 'knowing-in-action'. When there is something troubling or puzzling, the individual is forced to reflect upon this 'knowing-in-action', the action and its outcomes, in the 'action-present'. 'Reflection-in-action' is often prompted by the mismatch that can occur between patterns of knowledge, and practice and features of the situation in which the practice takes place. 'In order to convert a problematic situation to a problem, a practitioner must do a certain kind of work. He [sic] must make sense of an uncertain situation that initially makes no sense' (Schön 2000: 40). In words that echo Weick, he writes, 'Problem setting is a process in which . . . we name the things to which we will attend and frame the context in which we will attend to them' (Schön 2000: 40). His concept of 'reflection-in-action' refers to the capacity for, or ability to, reflect in the midst of action on deeply held knowledge that is often the taken-for-granted element of practice, 'knowing-in-practice'. While 'reflecting-in-action', 'thinking about doing something while doing it', involves 'thinking on one's feet' and 'learning by doing'; 'reflection-in-practice', is a deeper reflection on practice. 'Reflection-in-practice' is the reflection on 'reflection-in-action'. Interestingly, Schön makes the point that while managers sometimes 'reflect-in-action', they rarely reflect on this 'reflection-in-action': 'because awareness of one's intuitive thinking usually grows out of practice in articulating it to others, managers have little access to their own reflection-in-action' (Schön 2000: 243). As a result, 'reflection-in-action' becomes sedimented and remains unchallenged, protected by a system of organizational games and norms that prevent organizational learning.[13]

Organization as practice: Recent practice-based analyses of organizations have also emphasized the 'ongoing' nature of organizing (Jarzabkowski 2005; Nicolini et al. 2003; Schatzki et al. 2001). The emphasis is on ongoing practices of action and interaction and the importance of participation in interaction, engagement in practice, and becoming a member of a collectivity and how these function to sustain the 'logics of action' that inform practices. 'Practice-thinking connotes a world in which activities and knowing always have a specific "where" and "when": they are always "situated" . . . competent action always happens within a materially, historically and socioeconomically defined horizon, a "context" that far from being pre-given emerges as a result of the conditions put in place by the practices themselves' (Nicolini et al. 2003: 27). Distinguished from earlier ethnomethodological studies, although often following this method, the breadth of focus is generally much broader, encompassing the human and non-human, linguistic and technological artefacts, repertoires and routines, and communities and systems.

The emphasis is on practice or what people actually do: 'Only by considering the concrete totality of interconnected activities that engender socially productive activities can one grasp the meaning of human action' (Nicolini et al. 2003: 8). Emphasis is thus very much on activity, action, acting on and in; the situational and emergent; sense-making or ongoing construction

of meaning; trial and error; and the contingent in socially constituted practice. 'Situated actors in situated work practices and in local interpretations
of...meaning' (Gherardi and Nicolini 2002: 220). Also emphasized is the
importance of spatio-temporal location. 'The term "situated" indicates that
knowledge and its subjects and objects must be understood as produced
together within a temporally, geographically or relationally situated practice.'
Locality in time and space also emphasize their 'ephemeral, provisional and
emergent nature' (Nicolini et al. 2003: 23), the importance of the precarious, the partial, disruption, disturbance, and inconsistency that characterize
practices. Again the emphasis is on organization, order and stability as the
outcome of effort. Indeed, the emphasis of this approach is 'to explain how
the durability of orderings is achieved in practice, how facts become such,
how order is performed, how things are put in place and stay that way'
(Nicolini et al. 2003: 18). Although practices may become institutionalized,
this requires continual enactment and reproduction, through which variation
and change occurs. Because of this, the approach has been portrayed as a 'valid
alternative to the image of the rational organization' (Suchman 2003: 201).
This is not to imply that there is a unified approach to the study of practice.
Several theoretical traditions inform studies: an interpretive framework, social
learning, activity theory, and the sociology of translation or actor network
theory.

Situated learning: Learning is a special type of social practice or a feature
of a practice. Lave and Wenger stress that situated learning is more than
'learning *in situ*' and 'learning by doing'. Although incorporating a location in
time and space and meaning being dependent on an immediate social setting,
for Lave and Wenger (1991), 'situated' takes on a boarder meaning, of being
relational, negotiated, focused, or purposeful, involving the comprehensive
involvement of the whole person, such that individual, activity, and knowledge
about the world are mutually constitutive. Learning is thus not 'situated' in
practice but integral to practice.[14] An important element of situated learning
is the construction of identities. Because identity is the relation between an
individual, place, and participation in a community or collective, 'Learning
implies becoming a different person with respect to the possibilities enabled
by these systems of relations' (Lave and Wenger 1991: 53). It is the gradual
construction of an identity and learning to talk within a practice (rather than
about it), that allows one to become part of a community. Situated learning thus emphasizes participation and social engagement in which learning
takes place (Lave and Wenger 1991). It is thus the increasing participation in
communities of practice. Brown and Duguid's (1991) analysis of evolution of
communities of practice emphasizes the situational context of the way people
work and their attempts to solve practical problems, contributing to links
between individuals who can provide useful information, developing into an
exchange of information within evolving communities.

BOX 7.3. PERFORMANCE MEASURES: THE TEST OF PRACTICE

The importance of situated knowledge and a situational rationality means that performance measures must confront the ultimate test of relevance that comes from the 'reality' of the context. Performance measures that cannot speak to the immediate context of 'keeping the show on the road' are not seen as relevant:

[on reducing court processing times] When I started, 76% of cases were within the 20 week range. When we got the 85%, it was 'yeah, we've done it'. There is an element of pride, but basically the reality is this is a 24 hour cycle. The main issue is, is the daily issue of 'will there be enough clerks? Is somebody going to phone in sick? Are there going to be enough Sheriffs?' On Monday we were two [Sheriffs] short and there was no part-time sheriff. You do the juggling but people get caught out. [A central department]s got us a Sheriff for two hours and this was just enough. That's not saying that you don't feel good when you reach a target but that you are too caught up managing meteorites that crash through the ceiling. (Court services)

[on a voluntary agency looking after the victims of crime] The bulk of the service deliverers are volunteers. They see themselves as there to help. They don't see the relevance or point of some of the record keeping, especially if it's high volume. The volunteers record the time spent with an individual, when they were seen, what their circumstances were, what the main issues were, what was recommended or suggested, when they will visit again. But we have difficulties getting hold of ethnic monitoring data. People hate asking this and hate being asked. They also have to ask how many people are in the household. This gets information on how many people were affected by the offence. But there are very few circumstances where this information would be naturally recorded or asked. It is a political measure. You can see why it's important from a political point of view. There is an issue of measures for the agency and measures for others. You know that if performance measures are not useful at the front line, then you are not going to capture the right information. There is also the issue of buy in especially with volunteers. Performance measures cause more work. There is an opportunity cost involved. There is an issue of why are we using all these people to collect information and input data when they could be doing something useful. (Voluntary agency)

There has to be something that lets us know how we're doing. How we're going. How things are working. But a target doesn't tell you why you didn't meet it, why you exceeded it, if you could have exceeded it. Targets can't be a tool for improvement. They do not tell you what's falling by the wayside to meet the target and what's being manipulated in the background. The measures go through things on the surface. They don't tell you what's going on. They get measured because they can. (Police)

Greatest scepticism was expressed by front-line staff on overarching aims and targets. Targets and measures were not seen as a beneficial way of achieving the organization's objectives. Complaints were raised about bureaucratic impediments both to achieving objectives and to what was seen as being the focus of the agency. There was also a fear of a huge proliferation of targets and measures (Normand 2003). For front-line staff, much more useful are experiments with the co-location of personnel from different agencies, regular joint meetings between areas to discuss common problems, task-based problem-solving, and training beyond the immediate prerequisites of the job so that individuals can understand the implications of their work for others.

Conclusions

A situational rationality initially drew its rationale from writing keen to distinguish it from a scientific rationality (Garfinkel 1960; Schutz 1962). It emphasizes the spatially and temporally located nature of rational action, its *in situ* specificity. In this, it proposes a form of 'retrospective' rationality, rationality as simultaneous to, or following, action, and thus is contrasted with disembedded understandings of rational action which deal mainly with a 'prospective' rationality.[15] A situational rationality recognizes that organizing is an activity of becoming, and thus recognizes the ongoing constructed nature of organization. It also has implications for positions that must be adopted in trying to ascertain the rationality of the situation. 'In trying to understand reasons ... the interpreter is forced to relinquish any claim to an extramundane position, and to assume, at least virtually, the mundane status of the layperson' (Smith 1987: 184). The embedded self in this context not only needs to be aware of the institutional and contextual rationalities that inform action but must also be 'concretely' embedded in the situation in order to understand it.

Part III
The 'Other' of Reason

Introduction

Discussion so far has considered disembedded rationality and challenges made to this by an embedded understanding of rationality. Both concepts, however, neglect the physical nature of an embodied rationality, to which we now turn. Disembedded implies disembodied and sustains itself through the exclusion of any corporeal substance to the rational cogito. It denies the finite and embodied. And although the embedded recognizes the self in relation with others as the social grounding of reason, the physical reality of the body is not acknowledged. The denial of the embodied is the consequence of rationality being known through its relation to the 'other'. 'The other of reason is nature, the human body, fantasy, desire, the feelings or better: all this, in so far as reason has not been able to appropriate it . . . it is the aesthetic, body centred experiences of a decentred subjectivity that function as the placeholders for the other of reason' (quoted in Habermas 1992: 306).

This 'other' of reason has many familiars. It is manifest in many forms, only to be dismissed as 'irrational'. For Weber, the 'irrational' is the supernatural and magic, the 'enchanted' which remains outside of 'rational' explanation, the province of the incomprehensible.[1] Through the 'rationalization' of the world, its gradual 'disenchantment', the supernatural becomes demarcated from 'nature'. In contrast to the supernatural, nature can be understood, and if not altogether tamed, is the subject of universal laws. Reason's relationship to nature is ambivalent. While giving access to nature, reason's sovereignty remains intact; as part of nature, however, it loses its authority to stand outside and above it. The body is the most pertinent reminder of 'nature' and reason's history has largely been in oppositional relation to it. The body, 'nature', and its associated realms have remained antithetical to reason. The animal or the bodily were automatically associated with the inferior (Homiak 2002). Aristotle viewed menial labour as detracting from engaging in rational activity, even to the extent of excluding those whose work is associated with the body and bodily functions. Women, 'the symbolic embodiment of pollution arising from birth and death' (Schott 2002), also become excluded from reason's activity.

This mind/body division is given stark prominence in the work of Descartes. From this came the twin beliefs of reasoning as a type of restricted activity, 'pure thought', and the association of the body with the non-rational. With its dependence on (unreliable) senses and its potential to corruptibility, particularly through the passions, the body cannot be the source of 'true knowledge'. The latter is the province of reason, the disembodied cogito. Previous contrasts now amplified into stark polarizations. The divided soul inherited from classical thought, between the higher, intellectual, and the lower, or sensation, was replaced with a mind/body dichotomy. Reason was associated with the mind; passion with the body. Passion, sense, and imagination were intrusions from the body. Reason was thus vulnerable to corruption; the body had to be subject to the mind.

Within the scientific tradition and rationalism, the dominance of 'pure' reason or logic gained supremacy over empiricism with its reliance on directly observing, recording, and monitoring the world. Where the latter does gain legitimacy, it must be guided by the strict protocol of scientific method to ensure that the weaknesses the body is heir to do not contaminate that which is observed by the senses. Empiricism sought not to deny the importance of sensory experience but to ensure its reliability, and this was to be achieved through detachment rather than 'sympathy' (Atherton 2002). The debate was engaged between Cartesian rationalism and Baconian empiricism and between Bacon and Paracelsus (Fox Keller 1985; Noble 1992). It was the beginning of modern science. Modern science 'disenchants' the world, 'nature' is constructed as being calculable, manipulable, and amenable to causal laws or mechanisms.[2]

Subsequent debate in philosophy and the natural sciences took up the mind/body dichotomy, reinforcing the dualism and sustaining philosophical debate on immanence and transcendence. It gave rise to a disembodied agency and a transcendental mind and with this the possibility of objective truth, knowledge accessible to the mind only through reason, and independent of those who know. The body was associated with the animal, the carnal, the loss of control, all of which had to be tamed by reason. The civilizing process defined the individual in opposition to the animal and the natural, with the gradual dispatch of 'natural functions' to enclosed and private spaces (Elias 1978). Reason derived its unity by eliminating desire, affectivity, the erotic, and the body's sensuous engagement with the world. Thought processes that do not aspire to strict method, 'right reasoning', the 'disciplined imagination', or are the product of the untrained mind such as imagination and intuition, are also left to the province of the body.

Rationality's dependence on the mind/body split reinforced further binary divisions that inscribe theorizing: reason/passion, logos/eros, science/nature, culture/nature, objective/subjective, science/art, rational/irrational, exclusion/inclusion, formal/informal, self/other, and conscious/tacit. The public/private split inaugurated with the Enlightenment and further reinforced by the development of industrial capitalism, instituted the public domain of work and the market and the private domain of the family. Each binary division privileges the former over the latter and each further constructs the primary male/female dichotomy.

Since the seventeenth century, the body has been taken to be the defining element of the foundation of difference (Laqueur 1987). As Shilling (1993: 156) notes, 'with the bodily functions which people shared increasingly hidden from view, the manners and dispositions which separated individuals could increasingly be taken as markers of their value and self-identity.' With the body as a marker of difference comes the recognition that the body is always concretely 'sexed', or sexually coded (Grosz 1993). Binary divisions served to construct the creation of women in relation to a particular image. It is, as Lloyd (1995) notes, the construction of femininity through exclusion. Logos is the masculine, active, intellectual; eros the feminine principle of emotion and relatedness. Maleness is active and determinate; femaleness associated with a passive and indeterminate nature. Because of their body, women's rationality is not only different but also deficient. Reason as attainment saw an exclusion or transcending of the feminine that was built into the ideals of reason (Lloyd 1995). The female became associated with the non-rational, the disorderly, and the unknowable.

Feminist critique has privileged the importance of the body if only to critique some of the essentialist, ahistorical, and biological determinist arguments that justify such binary divisions. By illustrating how the body functions as a surface of social inscription, a conduit between a lived interior and a socio-political exterior, there is the recognition of the body as the site of discursive practices and its rejection as the source of foundationalism (Scott 1992). This highlights the importance of the social community within which the body becomes and learns to be a self. This is not just restricted to an embedded identity, of history, ethnicity, class, and social network. An embodied identity recognizes that specificity is necessarily grounded in the embodied reality of physicality. It is the lived, embodied, corporeal experience of being in the world that functions to give access to knowledge of the world. It is only through an embodied self that a self, others, and the world can be known: 'the perceiving mind is an incarnated mind' (Merleau-Ponty quoted in Dale 2001: 57). An embodied rationality recognizes the physical reality of the embedded and embodied subject. The recognition of the corporeality of the body is that rationality and the knowledge that it informs cannot be divorced from the individual who reasons. Responsibility, morality, and politics are also embodied, as the aphorism 'where I stand depends on where I sit' testifies. Not only this, but also gender-sex is a crucial grid 'through which the self develops an embodied identity, a certain mode of being in one's body and of living the body. The self becomes an I in that it appropriates from the human community a mode of psychically, socially and symbolically experiencing its bodily identity' (Benhabib 1987: 80).

From this, feminist theory has been keen to identify how a sexed corporeality impacts on 'relations between knower and objects known and on the forms, methods and criteria of assessment governing knowledges' (Grosz 1993: 188; Hanen 1987). It emphasizes the importance of examining the role of the body 'as the unacknowledged condition of the dominant term, reason' (Grosz 1993: 195). From Augustine's claims that 'the mind has no sex',[3] rationality had been discussed in gender-neutral terms. Although rationality presents itself as universal and impartial, this impartiality is, in Benhabib's (1987: 81) terms, substitutionalist; it identifies 'the experiences of a specific group of subjects as the paradigmatic case of humans as such'. Feminist critique identifies the androcentric ideals of masculinity underpinning ideals of rationality. In particular, it notes the phallocratic assumptions of language and the neglect of relatedness and connectedness in the liberal self's privileging of rationality, autonomy, and individuation. ' "Rationality" requires as a condition of its existence the simultaneous creation of the realm of the personal, the emotional, the sexual, the "irrational" . . . Masculine rationality is constructed in opposition to the feminine, as a denial of the feminine, but does not exist without it' (Pringle 1989/2001: 1270).

As rationality has historically been understood as a separation from the body, recognition of the importance of the embodied deepens areas open to enquiry and permits the identification of further dimensions of rationality. It recognizes the status of non-articulate knowledge and that the spectrum of knowledge ranges from the articulate to the unspoken. The embodied nature of knowledge recognizes, from Aristotle, that although the formal may be the 'proper' object of knowledge, it is grasped in the particular and the sensible. All the senses, not just vision, but touch, smell, hearing, and taste can access that which is to be known.[4]

These dimensions of rationality have been largely neglected in organization studies and management. The organization had been defined in terms of its rationality, the 'structure of roles, activities and interrelationships in an explicit and unified way' (Meyer 1992: 264). Just as the rationality of the subject has been disrupted by the passions, 'interacting impulses that . . . perturb the workings of . . . reason' (Hobbes cited in O'Connor 1999/2002: 347), so the informal aspects of organizations are the province of the 'logic of sentiments' disrupting the formal and rational (Roethlisberger and Dickson 1939). The 'non-rational' is the consequence of the definition of formal organization. Informed by a mechanistic image of organizations, where the irrational has been equated with the unpredictable, the human has also been equated with the irrational. Management is epitomized by its claims to rationality and reflects the privileging of consciousness and the values of a disembedded rationality. It is a 'cognitive' enterprise, a goal-oriented, problem-solving, decision-making function. It structures individuals and activities. Within management texts, irrationality stands as the modern equivalent of the false or heretical, the sinful or the wicked (Barry and Hardin 1982: 368). Even where this is ostensibly denied: 'all that stuff you have been dismissing for so long as the intractable, irrational, intuitive, informal organization, can be managed' (Peters and Waterman quoted in Willmott 1993/2002: 274), management and a particular depiction of rationality mutually reinforce one another.

An embodied rationality explores the 'other' dimensions of rationality and their necessary role in organizing. In keeping with the 'other of reason' as 'the human body', 'fantasy, desire', and 'the feelings', three dimensions are explored: the role of the body and the means through which it accesses knowledge of the world; the emotions and the insights that they have for rational understanding; and finally, the 'irrational' subconscious, illustrating how accessing this can shed light on the rationality of actions. All reclaim the embodied as the other important dimension of rationality.

8 Embodied rationality

The subject is not only situated, embedded, within a specific context but is also a corporeal, embodied subject. An embodied rationality recognizes that rationality and the knowledge that it informs cannot be divorced from the physical reality of the individual who reasons. An embodied rationality encompasses three dimensions: the body, the emotions, and the 'irrational' unconscious. Their locus is the body. Each introduces a different avenue through which an event or circumstance may be rendered rational or reasonable. This chapter outlines the role of each and their place in organization studies.

The body

The body has traditionally been understood as natural or presocial. But the body is inextricably social in its deportment,[1] bearing, adornment, presentation, and the experience of its sensations. Bodies have been invested with a wide range of meanings. Absent its birth and death, there is no 'natural' body.[2] It is for this reason that Foucault (1984b: 87–8 quoted in Dale 2001: 73) writes, 'nothing in man—not even his body—is sufficiently stable to serve as the basis for self-recognition or understanding other men [sic].' Douglas's (1970) work illustrates the relationship between the physical body and the social body and how conceptualizations of one inform the other. Goffman (1969) demonstrates how the management of the body is a central component in the presentation of the self in social encounters and interactions. Foucault (1977a) details the links between the micro-physics of the body and bio-power. Turner's (1984) work focuses on the regulation and reproduction of populations and the restraint and representation of bodies. Bourdieu (1984) identifies the role of physical capital (profoundly influenced by social class) and the symbolic value the body can acquire and carry.[3] Bourdieu also identifies habitus, predisposed ways of relating to familiar and new situations located within the body, revealed in bodily gestures and 'techniques of the body' including ways of walking, talking, eating, etc. (Shilling 1993). Elias's (1978) work provides a history of society's construction of the body, illustrating its 'rationalization' and progressive differentiation, and the increased division between drives and consciousness. Strategic thinking takes over from spontaneous action; drives and passions become internalized. The socialization of the body leads to its increased control through the 'rational' mind, with the 'self-control' of rational thought. 'The body, emotions and physical expressions are themselves formed by civilizing processes' (Shilling 1993: 166). Individuals come to see themselves as increasingly separate and detached from others. Individualization parallels civilization.[4] All reinforce the Aristotelian observation 'I am my body; my body is social' (MacIntyre 1981: 172).

The role of the body has had an ambiguous position in management and organization theory. It remains an absent presence. The neglect of the body, or more accurately the failure to explicitly articulate it, has led to an emphasis on the intellectualization of organizational life (decision-making, strategic thinking, etc.): knowledge and reason are the product of an (active) mind, the body, its vehicle or container (Dale 2001). Despite a very cerebral presentation of rationality in the classical model of the rational organization, however, the biological metaphor is quite ubiquitous. The organization is a bounded entity with a structure and subunits fulfilling different organizational functions or needs.[5] The anthropomorphization of organizations sees it go through the 'life cycle' of birth, youth, maturity, decline, and death. Individuals become 'members' of an organization to follow overall direction from 'headquarters'. Open systems theory[6] theorizes organizational responses to environmental challenges,[7] environmental fit, adaptation,[8] and survival.[9] Evolution, natural selection, and environmental adaptation inform contingency theory and population ecology. Current concerns of organizational wellness, delayering and 'lean/mean' organizations, reflect other elements of the biological metaphor.

Another strand of research has focused on the body in organizations. Taylor heralded an interest in the most efficient movement of the body for organizational productivity, while Taylorism provided the justification for the organizational manifestation of the mind/body split, the physical separation of work and human beings, and with this a separation of 'worker rationality' and 'management rationality' (Beynon 1975). The production of 'docile bodies' has been central to control of the labour process: basically 'how to get the human body to remain in one place, pay attention and perform consistently over a fixed period of time' (Zuboff 1988: 33). The disciplining of bodies was only partially achieved after workers were brought together under one roof as a 'body' of workers (Marglin 1974). Taylorism emphasized uniformity, codification, and standardization and helped create the 'moving, managed and disciplined body', its subjugation to strict routine (Shilling 1993: 22). The initial concern of the Hawthorne studies was the physiological concerns that might hamper productive activity with the study of fatigue, ergonomics, and temperature, before focusing on the social nature of work, and the complex social relationships outside work that influence behaviour. Then, as now, organizational and industrial conflict rests on the detailed performance of the body and the degree of discipline to which it might be subject.

BOX 8.1. THE EVIDENCE OF THE SENSES

The following was the reply when a defence solicitor was asked about the criteria for successful performance. Note the importance of sensing in accessing and assessing information:

One, does the client come back? Will the client still talk to you after he's been sent down to prison. And when he's released, will he come back and see you. Does the client recognise you've done what you can. They are not the best judges of performance, but they still are judges of performance to some degree. And are we still in business? Two, having the ear of the court is a performance measure. So much of the job depends on your credibility with the court. At the beginning the Sheriffs don't know you. But after a time you get to the point where they take something from you because they know that you do not say somethings unless there's a basis for it. For example you can say to them that something has been checked, or question if something has been checked, and they will follow this up. Or Sheriffs will allow a line of cross examination, questions, interventions, and submissions. I have seen cases where the Sheriff will intervene and make comments on the defence agent to the client, even to the extent of recommending they get another. This is quite an important measure. If you do not have the ear of the court, you do a bad job for the clients, or you do a worse job.   (Defence agent)

The body, 'seeing is believing', provides a lot of information on work and what can and cannot work:

The PFS have had a new computer system installed. This was supposed to create efficiencies. Jobs have been lost. But the staff efficiencies have not been achieved. So the people are missing. But there are still emails, callers and phones. But the people aren't there. People do not appreciate the difficulties unless they see it from their own eyes.   (PFS)

You get the sense of national objectives but you also need more local ones. It's a matter of common sense. For example you could have a national [crime reduction] target of housebreaking. This wouldn't make much sense in X [place]. People wouldn't thank you for it. But drink related offending and violence is a big issues. At some point you have to relate to what people see. You need to have a focus that is meaningful. You need a local face on this.   (Sheriff)

Generally I say to trainees, if you think something is wrong then there is something wrong. Go with your instinct, if you think something is wrong, chances are there is.

(Defence agent)

But if you have a close interface relationship with the Fiscals service. The thing is the interface relationship. Then you can say 'lets be flexible and make things work'.

(Court services)

A lot of functioning of the CJS depends on tacit knowledge:

[knowledge of court scheduling] It's intuitive really. Its built up over experience and working with the system. This is all rule of thumb. You just know from experience these figures are the number of days needed. There's no optimum number. You have crude figures in your head on each of these issues. A lot of it is tacit knowledge. You learn from that.   (Court services)

All you have on a case, how you handle a case, is knowledge and experience.   (Advocate)

The ambivalence towards the body, using it as a major metaphor for understanding organizations and yet because of the understanding of rationality, denying its relevance, has led to several lamentable lacunae, only recently remedied (Hassard et al. 2000). The silence on sex reflected the suppression of emotion generally and the fear of a (female) sexuality disruptive to (male) rationality (Burrell 1984). The body in organizations is now recognizably gendered (Gherardi 2003; Calas and Smircich 1996). Organizations are no longer seemingly 'inhabited by a breed of strange, asexual eunuch figures' (Hearn and Parkin 1987: 387).[10] The recognition of corporeality, however, is an important dimension of being rational and accessing knowledge.

Embodied thinking and knowledge

'Embodiment is not *about* bodies, it is *from* bodies' (Williams and Bendelow 1998: xviii).[11] There is an integral connection between embodiment or bodily experience and knowledge: the corporeal informs awareness and vice versa. The body sees, hears, touches, smells (produces and can detect odour), and tastes (likewise), all senses which contribute to knowledge of the world. It is this 'common sense' that feeds our 'rational' assessment. 'Common sense' originally referred to the five 'common' senses (sight, touch, hearing, smell, taste). In medieval thought, the brain was divided into three hierarchical areas. The first (and lowest) contained the five senses; the second received the report and summary of these senses and was informed by 'fancy' and memory; which were then passed on to the highest faculty of reason (third), itself composed of two elements: understanding ('wit') and the will. Reason was thus brought to bear on all the elements with which the mind had furnished it (Tillyard 1960). The modern era has undermined this 'common sense' through its emphasis on the visual as the window of the mind.[12]

The embodied nature of knowledge and thought raises the complex relation between thinking, knowing, and doing: an embodied knowledge versus abstract knowledge. It is a discussion that has a long pedigree in the philosophical literature. Dewey (1929) identifies two forms of knowledge: 'knowing how', that stems from habit and intuition, and 'knowing about' with its implications of reflection and conscious appreciation. Ryle (1949) distinguishes between 'knowing how' and 'knowing that'. In anthropology, Geertz (1973) draws the distinction between 'knowledge about' and 'knowledge of'. Thinking and doing are often through of as antithetical, the former paralysing the latter through infinite regress, thus losing the spontaneity of the moment.

The connections between thinking and doing have been given greatest expression by Polanyi (1983) in his discussion of tacit knowledge. Tacit knowledge stems from the precept 'we know more than we can tell' (Polanyi 1983: 4). 'All thought contains components of which we are subsidiarily aware in the focal content of our thinking, and that all thought dwells in its subsidiaries, as if they were parts of our body' (Polanyi 1983: x). Polanyi identifies the 'proximal' and the 'distal' as elements of tacit knowing. The proximal are the particulars of an entity which, when integrated, form a coherent whole.[13] The example he gives is how we are able to recognize a face in a crowd. Although unable to describe all the features of physiognomy that we know (the proximal), because we attend to them in relation to our knowledge of the face (the distal), we are able to recognize it. The proximal element informs the distal. Things are known, not in themselves, but only in relation to that which is attended to.[14] Rather than being aware of things in themselves, we attend to them in relation to something else.[15] We need to be aware of the particulars (the proximal) in order to grasp the whole (the distal), but undue attention to the particulars can make us lose sight of the whole.[16]

The body is central to tacit knowing. 'By elucidating the way our bodily processes participate in our perceptions we will throw light on the bodily roots of all thought, including man's highest creative powers. Our body is the ultimate instrument of all our external knowledge, whether intellectual or practical' (Polanyi 1983: 15). 'Indwelling' is the foundation of knowledge. The example given is of a blind man holding a stick to find his way. After a while, the stick is no longer felt as part of the hand, it becomes an extension of the body as it operates as a means to know the world. 'We incorporate it in our body, or extend our body to include it' (Polanyi 1983: 16). As we become familiar with something, an object or a scientific theory, we interiorize it, and attend to things using it. 'True' knowledge comes in its application, in our ability to use it. Tacit knowledge is thus an indispensable part of all knowledge, including explicit knowledge. While explicit or codified knowledge is that which is transmittable in formal systematic language, tacit knowledge, indwelling in the human mind and body, is hard to formalize and communicate. Attempts at trying to ignore or eliminate the tacit are not possible: 'the process of formalizing all knowledge to the exclusion of any tacit knowledge is self-defeating...True knowledge of a theory can be established only after it has been interiorized and extensively used to interpret experience' (Polanyi 1983: 20–1). It is our tacit foreknowledge that also allows us to recognize a 'solution' to a problem. 'Interiorized particulars', not yet identified as forming a comprehensive entity, help us follow a 'hunch'.[17] The quality of tacit knowledge is influenced by the variety of individual experience and 'knowledge of experience', the latter involving its absorption as a bodily experience. Thus, the body is thus fundamental to our knowledge of the world. 'Because our body is involved in the perception of objects, it participates thereby in our knowing of all other things outside. Moreover, we keep expanding our body into the world, by assimilating to it sets of particulars which we integrate into reasonable entities' (Polanyi 1983: 29).[18]

The role of the corporeal has had some recognition in organization studies. Barnard (1995), for example, contrasts logical and non-logical thought processes. Although the latter are distinct from logical thought processes, they are not illogical. The distinction is between conscious reasoning, thought processes capable of being expressed in words or by symbols, and intuitive processes, the latter known through immediate action, judgement, or decision. 'The sources of these non-logical processes lie in physiological conditions or factors' and are picked up without conscious effort (Barnard 1995/2002: 281). 'Some of it is so unexplainable that we call it intuition. A great deal of it passes under the name of 'good judgement'. Some of it is called 'inspiration' and occasionally it is the 'stroke of genius'. But most of it is called 'sense', 'good sense', or 'common sense', judgement or the 'bright idea' (Barnard 1995/2002: 283). While there is a bias against them, non-logical or intuitive mental processes are important in situations where strictly logical thinking is not apt, where 'good judgement', 'inspiration', or 'hunches', focus 'perhaps unconsciously, accumulated knowledge and experience on the problem at hand, during the time available, in order to arrive at what seems the sensible decision' (Barnard 1995/2002: 280). It is particularly manifest by those in high-pressure trading, sales, politics, and executives. On writing about being able to assess a balance sheet within minutes Barnard (1995/2002: 284) writes: 'Facts' do not lie in the numbers on the page but 'in the part filled out by the mind out of years of experience and technical knowledge. This makes out of a set of figures something to which then reason can usefully be applied.'

Barnard is against the exclusive use of either logical or non-logical thinking, arguing that too much of one inhibits the other, and that neither alone is sufficient. The two are reflected in most type of thinking and are influenced by the purpose of reasoning, whether this is directed at ascertaining the truth (which might be more dependent on following rules and tests), determining a course of action (which may be more speculative in terms of the balance of activities), or persuading, where there is the need to use reason but also to 'sense' what is required. It is also influenced by the degree of speed required and the nature of the material, whether this is precise information, hybrid information (of poor quality or of a limited extent), or speculative (based on impressions and probabilities). 'The real usefulness of genuine logical reasoning, the training in it that goes with education, all the pseudo logic of rationalization, are all causes of the false emphasis on the importance of reasoning. The harm lies in the consequent deprecation of non logical mental processes more than in the misuse of reason' (Barnard 1995/2002: 283).

For Simon (1997), intuition is not considered different from 'logical' thinking, 'we do not need to postulate two problem-solving styles'. 'Intuition, judgement, creativity are basically expressions of capabilities for recognition and responses based upon experience and knowledge' (Simon 1997: 129). Expert knowledge is based on recognition of patterns previously encountered and is usually characterized by speed and effectiveness. Without this, reasoning has to rely on systematic, logical processes. For Simon, intuitive or judgemental reasoning is not irrational, but largely logical reasoning in a more speeded form. He cautions, however, 'We must not confuse the "nonrational" decisions of the experts—the decisions that derive from expert intuition and judgement—with the irrational decisions that stressful emotions may produce' (Simon 1997: 139).

The embodied nature of knowledge is noted by Schein (1994/2002: 211) who observes that on entering an organization one is cognizant of the 'smell and feel of the place, and its emotional intensity', a recognition that led to his analysis of organizational climate. It is reported by Garfinkel's (1967) students on their 'experiments' into disrupting the taken-for-granted elements of social coordination. There is physical relief when life as usual resumes. It is recognized by the fieldworker who 'knows what he knows, not only because he's been there … but because "in his bones" he feels the worth of his final analysis' (Jick 1979/2002: 74). The role of hunch is well documented in self-reports of managerial or professional behaviour: the doctor who follows intuition that a diagnosis is necrotizing fasciitis (1,000 cases per year) rather than cellulitis (3 million a year), incurring the potential wrath and ridicule of superiors and colleagues. Comparing his decision-making with the technical rationality offered by decision trees, he concludes 'determining the relative desirability of outcomes seemed impossible … my decision tree looked more like a bush' (Gawande 2001: 306). Or that of a firefighter suddenly calling for his team to abandon the building after the flames had apparently been put out. Immediately after they had done so, the floor of the building collapsed. The fire had actually been elsewhere, the knowledge of which the firefighter had been intuitively responding to, although its explicit recognition surfaced only after several hours of in-depth interviews (Klein 1998). Martin's (2002) analysis of the senses, especially smell, illustrates the embodied knowledge of the researcher in accessing organization practice.

Just as the body is the site of tacit knowledge that Polanyi identifies, it is necessarily the site of learning. Knowledge is lodged in sentience. It forms part of what Zuboff (1988) refers to as 'action-centered' skill, based on acting-on objects, and equipment. It comes from sentience (of physical clues); action dependence (developed through physical performance); context-dependence; and personalism (the felt link between the knower and the known). Learning, remembering, and acting are physically experienced and located. The body is knowledgeable. Knowledge is inscribed in 'hands, fingertips, wrists, feet, nose, eyes, ears, skin, muscles, shoulders, arms, and legs' (Zuboff 1988: 40). The role of the body in knowing is recognized in an intuitive feel for what should be done, the 'rule of thumb'. Because it is situated, learning is analogical rather than procedural and analytic. It is robust knowledge in that it is available to be reactivated even after a period of time. This knowledge is 'know-how', derived and reflected in action. It is also highly dependent on an oral culture. In Zuboff's (1988) example, with the advent of new technology, operatives can no longer rely on embodied knowledge of production processes. Technical knowledge supersedes action-based knowledge. Intuition is no longer relevant. 'What counts' is understanding the production process. 'Absorption, immediacy and organic responsiveness are superseded by distance, coolness, and remoteness' (Zuboff 1988: 75).

Weick also acknowledges that sense-making is not only conscious but also unconscious or tacit. In addition to constructing the 'sensible', agents also act to construct the 'sensable'. Weick's (1993) study of Mann Gulch gives an indication of how deeply held and indwelling images of 'organization' can be, and what may happen when these are disrupted. The importance of the body as a source of understanding, particularly body language and facial expression, is highlighted in its absence. The *Challenger* disaster and disagreement over the decision to launch was hampered by the absence of face-to-face meetings to discuss qualms (Weick 2001). Weick (2001) gives the example of the importance of 'hands-on' experience as the foundation of requisite knowledge in order to sense when there are potential problems that may evolve into crises, as for example, at Bhopal (Weick 2001). Weick and Roberts (1993) make reference to 'heedful interrelating', where interaction and coordination can lead to the ability to 'read the intentions' of another.

Schön's (2000) 'knowing-in-practice' reflects tacit knowledge displayed by practitioners in the exercise of their practice. Knowing in action is the know-how that is in the action; the spontaneous actions, recognitions, and judgements that characterize work in practice. Prompted by pleasant or unwanted surprises the proximal becomes distal, in Polanyi's terms, and the action, its outcomes, and its intuitive underpinnings become reflection-in-action. 'Surprise' requires the individual to review what is done and think about things in a different way. To reflect-in-action, to be a 'researcher in the practice', is reflection on intuitive knowing (Schön 2000: 68). 'When someone reflects while in action, he becomes a researcher. He is not dependent on categories of established theory and technique but constructs a new theory of the unique case' (Schön 2000: 68).

Current writing on organizational knowledge and knowledge management make much use of the concept of tacit knowledge (Tsoukas 2005). Baumard (1999: 75) takes as his premise 'the impossibility of dissociating our acting body (practice) from our thinking subject (learning)'. There are various recommendations or analyses based on the relationship and possible translation between implicit and explicit forms of knowledge. Baumard (1999), for example, wishes to distinguish between intentional tacit knowledge and automatic tacit knowledge.

In keeping with the individualized view of the body, its role in collective social coordination and organization of activity has received less attention. The work of Hindmarsch and Pilnick (2007) indicates how inter-corporeal knowing functions as an important dimension of team activity. Activities have to be coordinated *in situ* and in real time. Learning is achieved through interaction, with informal and tacit practices, important elements of effective organization. The physical coordination of social activity is a dimension of embodied skill. Likewise, 'habit'. Habit is usually dismissed as the unconscious, reflexive response of physiological prompts, inferior to the conscious intentions of informed agency and therefore less worthy of study. It is viewed as an unreflective action, a 'fixed, mechanical reaction to particular stimuli...devoid of meaning from the actor's point of view' (Camic 1992: 191).[19] Reflecting Weber's identification of traditional (habit) and affectual social action as non-rational action, habit is restricted to actions that are 'unmotivated', not guided by means–end relations or a reflective process. Weber sees habit as 'an unreflective set disposition to engage in actions that have long been practiced' (Camic 1992: 202). Although a social action structuring relationships and social organization, ingrained habit or traditional action is dismissed as a form of meaningfully oriented action.

Habit is a durable or generalized disposition that informs action over a long period of time, 'a more or less self-actuating disposition or tendency to engage in a previously adopted or acquired form of action' (Camic 1992: 190). From an understanding of habit as being integral to an individual's functioning as a social being, during the nineteenth century, it came to refer to elementary activities that had no pertinence to understanding social engagement. Reflecting the impact of the physiological literature and the medicalized understandings of the body, habit became associated with the reflexes and reflexive action (Camic 1992). It was the opposite of conscious reflection, associated with 'inner' responses prompted spontaneously, or psychologized as an 'attitude', or a tendency of action (Camic 1992). In its collective sense or meaning, as distinct from an individualistic or psychologized meaning, habit reflects social regularities or 'custom', and as such is an important form of meaningful social action. Durkheim, for example, calls habits 'the real forces that govern us' (quoted in Camic 1992: 197). It is an internalized habituated action and way of being, a disposition or tendency to act in a previously acquired form of acting, frequently practised, a rule of conduct reflecting 'habits of acting and thinking in common' (Camic 1992: 199). These may then be transformed into moral norms.[20]

Within the organizational literature, habit is linked with routinization. Routine or habituated action is a form of organizational or institutional memory (Nelson and Winter 1982). Organizations 'remember' by doing. The metaphor is that of the body. Memory is an embodied process. Routines function as synapses, becoming strengthened through practice. Routines, habits, or practices inscribe, and are inscribed by, contextual and institutional rationality.

The emotions

As Hopfl and Linstead (1993) inform us, 'emotion' is etymologically a relatively recent term. From the Greeks to the eighteenth century, 'passion' was the more usual, derived from the Latin meaning to bear, suffer, support, or undergo (Hopfl and Linstead 1993). Emotion comes from the Latin, *exmovere*, to move away and the French, *emouvoir*, to stir up, and gives the definition of emotion as 'any agitation or disturbance of mind, feeling or passion: any vehement or excited mental state' (*OED*). These different etymologies give a sense of the associations of passion and emotion and their derivation reflects a historical evolution in thinking about the relative role of what Plato identified as the two human motivations: the passions and reason. Although the balance or role between the two has varied, generally, passions and emotions are to be controlled by reason. Debate turns on how this may be achieved.

There has been a tradition of thought that has expunged emotions from reason, seeing the two as opposites and oppositional: a disembodied rationality and 'irrational' emotions. Emotions pervert or disrupt reason. They threaten the calm mastery or 'self-possession' required for dispassionate, impartial assessment. The relationship between rationality and emotions, however, has never been categorical (Williams 2000). For the Greeks and medieval philosophers, emotion was not to be totally suppressed, it was to be appropriately channelled by reason. In Plato's *Phaedrus*, reason was a charioteer; emotions, the horses he guided. Emotions were regarded as important components of human experience. Of concern was excessive emotion or passions (Scheff 1992). For medieval philosophy, pride, envy, and greed were the major passions that were at odds with the dictates of reason. Stemming from St. Augustine, medieval philosophy had identified lust or unrestrained passion as one of the principle sins. With a weak and sinful body, rationality was in danger of being undermined by the uncontrollable passions of lust for money and possessions, a lust for power, and sexual lust. The virtues, duty, felicity, etc. would battle the vices for the soul of man. Passion in this sense was destructive. The role of reason in curbing it, doubtful.

Descartes's placing of reason at the centre of identity displaces emotions. Allied with the body, emotions are corruptible or mutable because the body is corruptible. It decays. Because they are corruptible, emotions can 'corrupt' reason. Although emotions may be regulated by reason, they cannot be entirely controlled by it. Descartes argues that because emotions are what the body does to the individual, the individual cannot be held responsible for them (Barbalet 1998).

Where moral philosophy and religious precept could not adequately curtail the passions, other alternatives were recommended. These included coercion or repression. 'Unruly' passions were to be repressed. Passions, however, may also be harnessed rather than repressed and, through this, transformed from being disruptive into being productive. Reflecting an understanding that owes more to the ideas of alchemy that were influential at the time, the destructive passions of 'ferocity', 'avarice', and 'ambition' might be transformed into the virtues of 'defence', 'commerce', and 'politics': private vices transformed into public benefits (Hirschman 1977).[21] A third thread of dealing with unruly passions was to counter or pit one passion against another, such that one would neutralize the other. Reflecting a later Newtonian physics, passions could not be restrained unless opposed, or counterpoised, by stronger passions. The love of pleasure might be countered by the love of gain, the love of luxury preferred over the love of sloth, for example.

The model of countervailing passions reflects the Humean position that 'it is the passions and not reason that moves us to action' (MacIntyre 1981: 46). Reason has a limited role as an adjudicator. Passion directs the will, and reason serves passion: 'Reason is, and ought only to be the slave of passion'. Reason becomes a mechanism for choosing which passion to follow to secure happiness. Countervailing passions, 'interests', act as a system of checks and balances, the mechanism whereby unruly passions might be checked. Attention shifts as to which passions require taming and those that might operate in this role. Passions still retain their association with being disruptive; interests are the means by which individual and general social benefits are to be secured. 'Interests' allows for an element of reflection.[22] Interest reflects self-love. It is a 'countervailing' passion, tempered by reason, to give direction to it. Reasonable, deliberate self-love, 'interest', would be sufficient to counter the passions. Wilfulness and passionate excesses could be curbed. The emergence of interest allowed for predictability over the unpredictable, erratic fluctuations of 'passionate' behaviour. Under the 'countervailing passions' thesis, calm passions in fact constitute reason (Hirschman 1977).

The controls over emotions are part of the civilizing process (Elias 1978). The corollary of the body being civilized is that its passions are also circumscribed: 'the autonomous individual self-controls ... such as "rational thought" or "moral conscience" now interpose themselves more sternly than ever before between spontaneous and emotional impulses, on the one hand, and the skeletal muscles, on the other, preventing the former ... directly determining the latter (i.e. action) without the permission of these control mechanisms' (Elias 1978: 257 quoted in Williams 1998: 753).[23]

By the eighteenth century, the passions are no longer viewed as the potentially destructive force of the seventeenth century. From the seventeenth

century opposition between interests and passions, the eighteenth century saw
the distinction between 'benign' and 'malign' passions, or calm and violent
passions. Calm passions or natural affections include benevolence and gen-
erosity; wild passions, or unnatural affections, are those of inhumanity and
envy. Distinctions are made between moderate and immoderate affections.
Whereas avarice would be an immoderate affection, a desire for wealth is
its moderate counterpart. The latter reflects calculation and rationality. The
evolution of interests and its association with a rational will, rising above
passion, develops the view that interests might be guided solely by reason.
Thus, reason is an instrument, its role to determine where interests lie. From
a countervailing passion to counter destructive passions, interest, informed
through a calculative reason, has now emerged as the dominant human motivation: 'the rational pursuit of interests' (Hirschman 1977).

Reinforced by developments in scientific thought, reason becomes more
associated with a purely instrumental faculty, the ability to draw valid inferences or argument. The division between nature and a moral order becomes
more defined, leading to a necessary realignment in the conceptualization
of emotion. Emotions are organically based in the body and are increasingly separate from rationality. They become more non-rational or irrational,
something the individual was prone to, or suffered from. True knowledge,
accessed through sense perception, can only be secured by methods that
neutralize emotions, passions, bias, and values. The invention of conventions
and methods for the elimination of the idiosyncratic secures the route to an
objective nature, a discernible reality accessible to reason. The conflict between
the 'head' and the 'heart' displays the contradiction.

Emotions in organizations

The historical evolution of thinking on the emotions has several consequences.
Because emotions are experienced 'within' the body, they are thought to be
private and mysterious. Because of the difficulty in their accessibility and
understanding, and their potential to disrupt, they are a threat to order. Both
carry over into the study of organizations.

They leave their traces on rational choice theory. Although an instrumental rationality is taken to be the universal mode of decision-making,
its premise is one of established preferences or ends. The question of how
these are chosen is avoided: *de gustibus non est disputandum*. For Archer
(2000: 37), rational choice has been 'excising emotion from desire, such
that the remaining preferences could be drawn into the ambit of rational
choice'. Desire, that which is 'internal', unobservable, and unmeasurable has

through a number of methods become transmuted and 'objectified' into revealed preferences and choice. As with wild passions earlier, strong emotions should be excised from beliefs. Beliefs should be demonstrable and rationally grounded. 'Irrational desires' should be purged from preferences. 'If people very strongly desire what they cannot get, they will be unhappy; such desires, therefore are irrational. A rational desire is one which is optimally adjusted to a feasible set' (Elster quoted in Archer 2000: 40). For some, this leads to the distinction between explicit preferences which may be tainted, and true preferences, as they would be without being tainted. But as Archer (2000) argues, the ends are not rationally chosen. 'Passion' dictates preferences and priorities, and it is this 'substantive irrationality' that underpins the rational choice model (Archer 2000: 36). For Williams (1998: 748), there is an 'irrational passion for dispassionate rationality', 'rationality itself is a "passionately" held belief or cherished ideal: one which is, in large part, "irrational" or "unreasonable"'. Despite the various efforts to transmute passions into interests, 'soft' (i.e. reasonable) passions, or pleasures (from utilitarianism), passion remains the foundation of rational decision-making. Denying the emotional foundation of rationality would 'grant supreme importance to impartial cognitive rationality, [this] can only be achieved at the cost of lacking anything one wants to be rational *about*' (Elster 1985*b*: 402, emphasis in original).

The historical legacy of the writings on the passions vis-à-vis rationality has been incorporated into modern organization studies, primarily through the work of Weber. Bureaucracy is a perfectly rational form because it is *sine ira et studio*. 'Bureaucracy develops more perfectly the more it is dehumanized, the more completely it succeeds in eliminating from official business love, hatred and all purely personal, irrational and emotional elements which escape calculation' (Weber 1978: 975). Weber identifies different 'sources' of irrationality: the 'emotional'; 'values' and more broadly, the 'enchanted'. Rationality excludes reference to emotions. Affectivity, although one of Weber's four types of social action alongside longstanding habits, is dismissed for being non-rational.

At its simplest level, irrationality for Weber is the lack of calculability (Weber 1978: 152). Rational action is 'integrated as to ends and means and governed by principles and rules' (Weber 1978: 549). A rationalist is one who rationally systematizes their own conduct and one who rejects the ethically irrational and aesthetic, or that which is dependent on emotional reactions to the world (Weber 1978: 544). It is for these reasons that bureaucratic authority is rational, because it can be bound by intellectually analysable rules. Its antithesis, charismatic authority, is 'specifically irrational' because it is 'foreign to all rules' (Weber 1978: 244).[24]

Weber's conception of rationality and rational action, however, is not as absolute as is implied, for, as he notes, 'absolute depersonalization is contrary to all elementary forms of human relationships' (1978: 637). Albrow (1997) argues that it is the translation of 'impersonal' that has caused confusion in understanding Weber's work. In German, impersonal is that of attending to the matter in hand, being business-like. Good doctors, for example, are 'sachlich', but not impersonal. Du Gay (2000: 213) critiques the suggestion that 'the establishment of bureaucratic organization privileges "instrumental rationality" and with this the simultaneous repression and marginalization of the other, the personal, the sexual, the emotional etc.', reinforcing the separations of work and life, reason and emotion, and pleasure and duty. For Du Gay, the impersonal is a reference to setting aside non-bureaucratic forms of patronage, 'personally motivated favour and valuation' (Du Gay 2000: 220; Weber 1978: 973). The rational does not admit the personal, but does not exclude emotion or personal relations, as long as these do not lead to the violation of formal procedures or corruption. Albrow (1992/2002: 382) also argues that Weber does allow for emotions in bureaucracy but only insofar as they become an intrinsic part of its working. Devotion, for example, where it is 'oriented towards a purpose, a common cause, a rationally intended goal, not a person as such' (Weber 1978: 1150). With regard to the relative standing between reason and emotions, Weber states that where ' "ethos" postulates a substantive justice oriented to some concrete instance or person' when this collides with 'formalism and rule-bound cool matter of factness of bureaucratic administration, emotions must . . . reflect what reason demands' (Weber 1978: 980).

Reflecting the Weberian and classical legacy, the study of emotions, like the body, has been rather marked by its absence. As Albrow notes, 'the real difficulty for those schooled in rationalistic organization theory is that organizations have no body, and feelings are intrinsically associated with corporeal existence' (1992/2002: 389). Emotion has been downplayed in favour of the 'rational' elements of problem-solving, decision-making, and strategy. The formal organization of interchangeable individuals needs to remove individual fealty or sentiment. Attempts at trying to accommodate this deficiency make reference to 'emotional man' as the counterpart of the 'rational' organizational actor (Flam 1990). Flam argues that the rational model functions as a form of emotion management. 'Formal organizations can be analyzed as a set of legal-rational rules for emotion management and substitute for authentic feelings'. Organizations produce 'tempered, restrained, disciplined but solidified and permanent emotions in place of unpredictable and wavering and often boundless feelings' (Flam 1990/2002: 367). Prescribed emotions, associated with organizational goals and corporate image, replace proscribed emotions, that is, obstacles to achieving goals and those inappropriate in terms of corporate image. Mumby and Putnam (1992) advocate a bounded emotionality as a counterweight to the bounded rationality of organizational decision-making. Bounded is an intersubjective concept, as opposed to a cognitive limitation, and is part of engaging responsibly in a community. Bounded emotionality is an 'alternative mode of organizing in which nurturance, caring, community supportiveness, and interrelatedness are fused with individual responsibility to shape organizational experiences' (Mumby and Putnam 1992: 474).

Where emotion has been considered, it has tended to be sanitized and scientized: 'affect' in contrast to 'cognition'. Emotion becomes theorized as physiological sensation (understood as having an affect or feeling) and a cognitive component (the latter interpreting or identifying the former). The separation of rationality and emotions stimulates a number of questions, including the impact of emotions on 'rational' activities such as decision-making; whether emotions may be chosen; whether emotions are rational; the relationship between cognition and emotion; and the cognitive antecedents and consequences of emotions (Elster 1985b; Williams 2000). Their understanding and role is compounded by sharp divisions between biology and sociology, prompting debates as to whether we smile because we are happy or whether we are happy because we smile.

Emotions become the province of 'mood', 'affect', or 'morale' to be probed through questionnaires on belonging and attachment, commitment and satisfaction; or in the most recent incarnation of this form of dealing with feelings, emotional intelligence. The psychologizing of emotions has led to accusations of organizations peopled by the 'emotionally anorexic' (Fineman 1993, 1996). Job satisfaction is discussed absent references to 'enthusiasm, pleasure, pride, happiness, delight' (Fineman 1996: 545). Emotions and the roles they play are heavily circumscribed by the constraints of the theory or hypothesis that constructs and investigates them. 'The feelings of being organized, doing work and organizing are hard to detect' (Fineman 1993: 10).

The role of emotions as a resource is highlighted in Hochschild's (1983) distinction between emotional work (feelings that are suppressed as part of the necessary or acceptable accomplishment of work) and emotional labour (the production of 'feelings' as part of the employment contract); and surface (where real emotions are disguised) and deep (altering what is felt) acting. Her work illustrates how flight attendants faced with 'unreasonable' emotions are obliged to make them 'reasonable', for example, imagining an 'irate' (a passenger who is irate) as having recently been bereaved. Emotional 'excess' is thus rendered understandable and excusable. It is the rationalization of feelings, 'like the rationalization of any other kind of human capacity in Taylorized manufacturing' (Albrow 1997: 112). There has also been the attribution of emotions to organizations, for example, the 'greedy organization', organizations that demand complete loyalty from members in the attempt to become the sole basis of an individual's social identity.

In addition to the study of the commodification of emotions and emotion management, studies now consider the emotions involved in work especially in caring roles; and how emotions are managed and self-managed to the extent of being exploited; and the role of emotional spaces. Emotions are identified in terms of emotional dimensions and emotion traits. An emotional culture has framing rules (ascribing the emotional meaning of situations); feeling rules (these control the range, duration, and intensity of emotions); display rules (how emotion is to be shown); and interaction rules (the use of emotion in interaction) (Rafaeli 2004). Burrell (1992) identifies various responses to pleasure (incorporating joy, love, joussiance, and play) and its role in relation to work: its incorporation, as organizations try and introduce programmes that further pleasure and 'unlock' creativity; as an alternative 'escape route' to the demands of work; and re-eroticization 'the attempt to reintroduce serious polymorphic emotions into human organization' (Burrell 1992: 79).

The relative neglect of explicit analyses of emotions is surprising, given that 'feelings are one of the principal sources of sense-making that people use in organizations' (Clegg 2002*b*: xviii). As Albrow (1992/2002: 390) comments: 'Can anyone doubt that organizations are emotional cauldrons?' Certainly, there are cogent emotions that inform behaviour including fear, resentment, vengefulness, shame, and supreme confidence (Barbalet 1998). Fineman (1996: 543) identifies 'the gripes, the anger, the anxiety, the frustrations; the glee, the joys, the tedium; the embarrassments and the despair' as part of the emotional panoply of organizational life. Certainly, as Brunsson (1989) argues, one would welcome an analysis of organizations if terms such as 'sin', 'hypocrisy', and moral responsibility were integral to them.

Earlier researchers identified the importance of emotions. Elias (1978) emphasizes the importance of 'shame' and factors that affect the threshold of feeling shame. 'No less a characteristic of the civilizing process is the peculiar moulding that we call "shame" and "repugnance" or "embarrassment"' (Elias 1978: 292 quoted in Scheff 1992: 111). Fear of physical attack is replaced by fear of shame and embarrassment. Goffman (1956) understands embarrassment as the disparity between self-identity (how individuals see themselves as a competent member of society) and social identity (how others see them). He illustrates how embarrassment is an important element of orderly behaviour; the fear of embarrassment, an important element of sustaining organization. Fineman (1996) identifies embarrassment, along with shame and guilt, as central to organizational order and control, prompted as they are by how an individual is judged. Jackall (1988) portrays a vivid depiction of fear in his presentation of managers. Anxiety is prevalent, prompted by a fear of failed career progression or loss of employment. Informal 'rules of the game' emerge to make these fears more manageable and to ameliorate some of the unpredictability of events. But given the operation of the organizations examined, none of these emotions could be regarded as irrational.

BOX 8.2. THE ROLE OF EMOTIONS

Emotional responses are an important part of understanding change:

Fear of embarrassment

This [agencies] working together is less the influence of the National Criminal Justice Board. It is the recognition that they are accountable to the Lord Advocate [chief law officer] and the Minister of Justice, and so if something comes up there in terms of adverse publicity, there is the need to be accountable.   (Policy)

Pride

Ego is a huge element in it as well. Although in about 75% of cases, the solicitors' presence makes no difference. But the longer you do it the more you think the outcome is because of you. If a case goes well or goes badly you think it's down to you. There's a large ego element. There's a large personal element as well. When you're giving a speech to the jury especially in the High Court, you convince yourself. If not, you can't convince them. So you take it personally if the decision goes against.   (Defence agent)

Empathy

Sometimes you require advanced notice on peculiarities of a particular case. For example, the disabled or child witnesses. For example, there is a case on Thursday for a deferred sentence. The complainer wants to come to court. This is a dangerous driving case where the individual ended up in a wheelchair. He wants to come to court. He wants to see justice. We had put the case in one court, but we needed to put it in another court, so that we can get the complainer access to the lift. This kind of information is essential. Who knows what the sentence will be? It's a very emotive issue. But we don't want to look like idiots, when quite rightly, we don't want the guy to be angry at that [lack of access to the lift]. It does not help the situation. It does not resolve the emotional issues, but you don't need to add to this.   (Court services)

Sympathy

For example, the Children's Panel held referrals every Friday. These deal with [child] custody, contact, residence and other disputes. I added another court on Thursday. This was the case where we had a number of families waiting, and child welfare hearings are a very emotive issue. It's highly emotionally charged. They are at each others throats, without hanging around waiting for a hearing. So we went to two days to spread it out more . . . This allows us to spread cases and try and clear the waiting. The solicitors weren't happy.   (Court services)

Apathy

The argument now is that if you don't have targets, the police would not get the reports in. There is a blanket assumption that all employees are lazy and you have to have targets. But if this is done long enough, that's the behaviour that you are going to get if you take away targets.   (Police)

Emotions are also the means through which individuals sense their own difficulties:

(cont.)

BOX 8.2. (*continued*)

Stress

You take an emotional cudgeling and you move onto the next case. Most people deal with issues in the work. You get have to be thick skinned. But one punch after the other. At certain levels it's difficult to get away from it. (A High Court Judge on hearing murder and other serious crime trials)

Certainly, the avoidance of embarrassment is one of the key unwritten codes of political parties and government. Flam (1990: 228 quoted in Albrow 1997: 107) identifies the 'feeling rule' of British Government:

This rule states that the ridicule which the parliamentary opposition tries to heap upon the government at every opportunity is to be incessantly avoided. And, indeed, the constant fear of embarrassment accounts for most of the workload of the British ministers, their staff and the Treasury staff, cooperation between ministers and staff, conflict between Cabinet ministers, and, finally, the type of information released up or across the government hierarchy and to the media.

As Albrow (1997: 107) notes, 'how many theories of organization can accommodate embarrassment?' The study of emotions comes almost as an additional component to conventional studies of organizations. It is not an embodied understanding of organizations.

Trust has been described as a 'social' emotion because of its role in coordinated interaction and social functioning. It prompts debates as to whether or not it is a 'rational' emotion. For Luhmann (1979), it cannot be, because knowledge of whether to trust someone is based on future action, that is, after the decision to trust or not has been taken. However, in terms of ensuring meaningful outcomes can be achieved, trust is 'rational'. There are proxies that help manage concerns over trust such as category-based trust (membership of an organizational or social category), role-based trust (occupying a role), rule-based trust (awareness of rules that structure appropriate behaviour) that dictate degrees of trust and the prudence of such behaviour (Kramer 2003). What these debates point to is the distinction drawn by Williamson (1993) between calculative trust, the individual decision-making process in a new encounter, and societal trust, which operates through the institutional environment.

Emotions straddle the individual and the social. Although they are experienced as 'internal' embodied experiences ('feelings'), their recognition, display, and understanding is irretrievably social ('emotions') (Fineman 1996). They are relational, borne in, and generated through relationships between and among individuals and the social context of that relationship. As Williams (2000) notes, emotions should be seen as socially constituted, rather than

socially constructed. 'Emotion is not merely personal individual and introspective or inner, but social, political and moral' (Barbalet 1998: 58). Emotions play an important role in ethical development, informing conduct and
understanding of social position. Inappropriate emotional behaviour will
offend 'because there is an "ought" clause in the language game of emotion'
(Crossley 1998: 20).

Rational emotions?

For Barbalet (1998), there are three positions that may be identified in the
relationship between emotions and rationality: that the two are opposed
(conventional); that emotions support rationality (critical); and that emotions
and rationality are continuous, the two sides of the same coin (radical). The
conventional approach relies on the broader culture/nature dualism, whereby
emotions or passions are seen as natural, spontaneous, and compulsive, and
are to be controlled or modified as a part of social engagement. The critical
perspective 'holds that reason and emotion are not necessarily opposed but
clearly different faculties...their differences allow each to serve in a division
of labour in which their distinct capacities contribute to a unified outcome'
(Barbalet 1998: 38). In this division of labour, emotions provide salience
or direct attention where a variety of factors demand attention or where
there are ambiguous or competing goals.[25] The radical perspective holds that
emotions play a significant part in reasoning (Williams 2000). One strand of
this argument stems from the work of William James for whom rationality
is a feeling. It is the absence of the felt need to explain, justify, or account
for something because of its self-evidence, and an 'absence of any feeling
of irrationality' (quoted in Barbalet 1998: 45). James goes further in identifying the emotional foundations of reason, arguing that rationality satisfies
a need for order, and the need for organizing or intellectual frameworks
(Barbalet 1998).

The other strand is that emotions themselves are 'reasonable'. They must be
'appropriate' to social and cultural conventions to be labelled as such. Emotions 'strike us as either appropriate or inappropriate, rational or irrational,
that we find them perfectly intelligible when we encounter them in others, that
we explain this in terms of reasons rather than causes, and that we hold people
responsible for them, just as we do for any other of their actions' (Crossley
1998: 30). A failure to respond with a predictable emotional response, to feel
outrage when faced with gross injustice, to be afraid when faced with danger,
etc. is deemed 'irrational' and requires explanation. Emotions are 'embodied, purposive, meaningful responses to situations' (Williams and Bendelow

1998: xviii).[26] The absence of emotion can be as disruptive as too much emotion.

Emotions are 'reasonable' in that they guide reason. Bodily feeling generates an image than can serve as a warning to a potentially negative or positive outcome, restricting future choice as certain options are discounted based on past experience. Emotions give 'salience, direction and purpose' to reasoning. As Williams (2000: 66) notes, 'emotion, on this reading, is no mere adjunct to cognitive processes...it is woven into the very fabric of our reasoning.' It would also imply that not only are emotions integral to the choice of ends, but they are also fashion means. Reason and emotion are mutually constitutive (Jaggar 1989). Both necessarily give an insight into our being in the world.

'We have expectations about reasonable and appropriate emotional responses to certain types of situation and we make judgements about the appropriateness and reasonableness of such responses...we expect to be able to argue people out of their emotions, particularly if those emotions are deemed either inappropriate or unreasonable' (Crossley 1998: 19).[27] Because emotions may be argued over as to whether they are appropriate or reasonable, Crossley (1998) identifies them as an important element of a communicative rationality. 'Emotions...form part of a mutually meaningful, intersubjective interworld and they are accountable' (Crossley 1998: 20). They raise validity claims and are rational or irrational.

A person who makes an emotional appeal effectively appeals to what he or she imagines will be the response of the other person to a specific situation or image, which, in turn, he or she believes is a reasonable and justified response, calling upon the other to act in a way which would justifiably follow from that response. The appeal is to the court of common sentiment...It is an appeal to common sense. All argument must appeal to what is commonly held to be true—to the assumptions of the lifeworld.

(Crossley 1998: 31)

Emotions emphasize the embodied mode of being in the world, a corporeal engagement with it. They do more than this. Emotions 'play a positive role in the constitution of the social world qua intersubjectively meaningful interworld, in addition to being constituted within that world' (Crossley 1998: 21). An embodied understanding emphasizes that our acknowledgement of emotions is not solely to incorporate an analysis of emotions into an overall perspective. It is not merely to write *about* emotions. Emotions are a necessary and important component of our knowledge of (being in) the world. Like light, emotions 'enable us to see (or make sense) but [are] not necessarily seen' (Crossley 1998: 26). An 'active, emotionally expressive body' (Williams and Bendelow 1998) stresses the importance of a reflexive assessment of the self in relation to the world in terms of location, actions, value, perceptions, and emotional responses to it.

The 'irrational' unconscious

The final bastion of the embodied lies in the analysis offered of the unconscious.[28] Whereas rationality is considered as that which is conscious: the irrational refers to that which is unconscious, often seen as being non-rational, irrational, or preconscious data. It is that which is buried deep within, and which may only be discerned through its manifestations in tiny details, small clues, the trivial, the inexplicable, and the 'irrational'. The 'irrational' unconscious is based on the premise that people have unconscious wishes or desires, in large part laid in infancy and early childhood, which not only set patterns for subsequent encounters but also form a place of retreat when an individual feels threatened, or when faced with ambiguous situations that arouse anxiety. Desires may be unconscious or repressed, open only to the cognition of unconscious processes. A psychoanalytical approach is an attempt to try and unravel some of these seemingly 'irrational' behaviours. Its basis is that the experiences of the child (following Freud) or the infant (following Klein) are the foundation for understanding adult behaviour. The intensity of experiences from this period, especially of pleasure and pain, can flood the emotions, so much so that they are relegated to the unconscious to appear later as the 'unthought known' (Bollas 1987),[29] that which is known at some level but which has not been put into words, whose manifestations appear as 'irrational'. Thus, responses in adult life to new situations will be based not just on the 'reality' of the new situation but also, in part, on an internal repertoire of responses based on earlier experiences. Shared and projected emotions, especially in hierarchical relationships, provide the dynamics of the enfolding organizational relationship.

Freud identifies the role of the id, ego, and super ego (or ego ideal) as operating in this process of mediation between the individual and the 'outside' world. His view is of behaviour as largely biologically driven, the drives of sex and aggression (life and death instincts), with the need to if not resolve, then reduce, these instinctual tensions. The id for Freud is 'irrational' (Diamond 1993), its 'motivations' dictated by the pleasure principle.[30] Its dictates are mediated by the ego, the 'reality principle' that portrays the external world. The ego is 'rational'. In terms of the relationship between the two, he continues Plato's image of the horse (id) and the rider (ego). The ego is constrained by the superego. This acts as censor, judge, and conscience. The distance between the demands of the superego and the actions of the ego are experienced as guilt. The ego ideal is an idealized image of the self. The extent to which this differs from one's actual self-image dictates the degree of the individual's self-esteem. (The higher the incongruity, the lower the esteem). The ego's position balancing contradictory demands between id and superego, and the external world leads to both anxieties and necessary defences against this anxiety.

Anxiety is in response to a (un)perceived danger, a rational response in a psychic reality, but not in an 'objective' sense.

Klein's object relations theory, the foundation of a relational perspective on psychoanalysis, has largely replaced such an instinctive view, but the basic model of anxiety and defence remains. Klein too recognizes the role of the ego (the manager of the psyche), libido (or life force), and morbido (or death instinct). For Klein, the primal relationship that influences all future relationships is the relationship with the mother's breast, the first 'object' the child comes into contact with, which is the source of satisfaction and pleasure or frustration and anger. It is this experience that provides the foundation for the 'good breast' and the 'bad breast'; and 'splitting', the projection of the bad breast outwards, and the introjection of the 'good breast' inwards. It is the resolution of these two different impulses, with the recognition that the good breast and the bad breast are in fact the same object, that is, the foundation for successful integration and the basis of future relationships (de Board 1990).

Ego defences in the face of anxiety include rationalization; splitting (the separation of things into two separate structures, all 'bad' (persecutory) or all 'good' (idealizing)); projection (unpleasant feelings are expelled and are projected or transferred onto an external world); introjection (the incorporation or internalization of elements of the external world as part of the individual ego); regression (a return to earlier modes or forms of relationships); repression (turning away from or resistance; keeping something at a distance from the conscious); reversal (taking an impulse as its opposite); transference (unconscious projections about one relationship being 'transferred' onto another relationship); and sublimation (displacement of a basic instinct into a higher form, usually gratification into work). None of these are mutually exclusive (Diamond 1993).

The unconscious is the foundation from which everything else emerges. 'Psychic reality' rather than 'objective reality' is the focus, with access to the former giving a more successful evaluation of the latter. Access to the unconscious comes through the surface manifestations of the unconscious, identified through dreams, associations, and transference. In an organizational context, the focus is on the interrelational through an analysis of patterns of relationships, and perceptions of experience. For Gabriel (1999), the unconscious is manifest in organizational stories and myths, rituals, humour,[31] architectures, and artefacts. For Diamond (1993: 33), the unconscious dimension of organizations is reflected in suppressed incidents, repeated errors, denial of reality, unsolved problems, avoided conflicts, ritualistic defences and routines,[32] and demoralized personnel. Diamond (1993: 35) identifies these elements, 'the unexamined, undiscussed, avoided and denied issues', as part of the preconscious, the consequence of suppression. This is to be distinguished from the unconscious, the result of repression. But this is not to posit an organizational psyche or unconscious, rather an unconscious life of organizations.

Psychoanalytic and psychodynamic approaches to organizational behaviour illustrate a deeper rationality that can inform seemingly irrational responses and acts, as unconscious fears, anxieties and desires are played out in their surface manifestations. Diamond (1993: ix) says that their purpose is to 'transcend the technical rational approach to the study of behaviour in organizations by isolating and then analyzing the nonrational side of administrative behaviour'. Psychoanalytical approaches to the study of organizations take the organization as being shaped by the unconscious concerns of its members. The focus is the deeper motives of actions. Unconscious 'frames' influence the way in which things are perceived and how they are read: primitive anxieties of dread of the unknown, or early personal traumas lead to protective defence mechanisms,[33] or through transference, repressed emotions of anger, guilt, anxiety, libido, etc. become displaced onto different objects. The dynamics of shared and projected emotions can result in institutionalized forms of oppression, in which individuals may act as collaborators.

The links between individual unconscious motivations and the organizational level, that is, recognized individual responses becoming established as patterns, is problematic. The application of psychoanalytic theory to the organization argues that, as a human creation, the organization will inevitably reflect human attributes, including unconscious ones. Structure, rules, and regulations can reflect unconscious drives and anxieties. There is dispute over the causal mechanism of 'irrational' behaviour in organizations, whether the direction of travel is from the organization to the individual or the individual to the organization. This is influenced by the definition of organization. Where it is used loosely as a collection of individuals, the source of dysfunction is located in the anxieties of the individual which then reflects on the operation of the collective, usually the group. Alternatively, if organization is used as 'an interconnected system of roles (positions) with explicit or implicit mutual accountabilities and authorities' (Jacques 1995: 343), this can cause anxieties for the individual. Jacques (1995: 346), however, cautions against using 'technical psychoanalytical concepts as organizational metaphors disguised in scientific clothing. It strengthens obfuscation' (Amado 1995).[34]

Certainly, studies of 'irrational' behaviour in organizations do not require psychoanalytical explanations. Jackall's (1988) work, for example, illustrates how unconstrained or absolute power operates as a source of much of what is 'irrational'. Many organizational studies illustrate the operation of megalomania, tyranny, and contempt in managerial actions, from early studies of how Geneen (1984) operated in ITT to more contemporary manifestations of the arrogance of executive action at Enron (Levine 2005). However, a psychodynamic approach would argue, as Diamond (1993: 57) notes, that 'institutionally supported authoritarian and totalitarian acts are organizational, psychosocial and political phenomenon...these forms of systematic oppression would not exist without group consensus (or collusion) about a set of unconscious feelings that support specific values, norms, ideas, or actions' (Diamond 1993: 57). He argues, 'Ultimately...it is the nonrational and unconscious dynamics of human relations at work that influence members' interpretations of their roles and tasks in the organization' (Diamond 1993: 89). Thus, psychoanalytic analyses are offered of training, the maintenance of organizational boundaries, psychodynamics and resistance to change, corruption, and organizational failure (as seen for example in the pages of *Human Relations*).

The failure to recognize the individual role and to view organizational systems as 'separate entities, detached from their decisions and actions' would from this perspective be to deny an important element of the reasons for seemingly irrational behaviour (Diamond 1993: 31). 'Organizational members' tendencies to blame structural and normative constraints for their problems without also acknowledging how their actions, thoughts and feeling reinforce and perpetuate such limits are counterproductive and ultimately, ineffective' (Diamond 1993: 158). It merely induces feelings of helplessness and powerlessness. Until individuals gain insight into, and an expanded awareness of, problematic patterns, errors will be repeated, problems remain unsolved, conflicts avoided, and general demoralization ensue. 'Conflicts in organizations are often repressed and unconsciously sustained in a latent social structure; denied and unresolved, they drain psychic and physical energy from staff who invest in managing around them' (Diamond 1993: 159). In this reading, the dark shadow of the 'irrational' is only rendered 'rational', or safe, if the deep unhidden is brought to visibility and consciousness.

Inevitably, perhaps the focus tends to be at the managerial and executive level, the levels assumed to be the more influential in organizations. The superego may be reflected in the externalized forms of authority and hierarchy. The executive becomes the ego, balancing internal and external demands. Organizational practice may display many of the forms of the neurotic organization (Kets de Vries and Miller 1984), where neurotic fantasies of key decision-makers, paranoid, compulsive, dramatic, depressive, or schizoid, influence strategy, structure, and culture. A range of characters may walk the organizational stage: the narcissistic, obsessive, conformist, heroic individualist, civic individualist, and occasionally, the mature.[35] Different personality types, narcissistic, perfectionist, and arrogant vindictive, can demand different behaviours from staff, namely, grandiosity and admiration[36]; exacting standards; winning regardless of cost. Self-effacing types may tirelessly do the work; the resigned want to be left alone; and intentional looked for shared responsibility (Diamond 1993: 65). People use elements of organizations as a source of potential omnipotence; to enhance self-esteem; exercise the 'legitimate' expression of aggression; or occasionally as a source of play or imagination

(Diamond 1993: 37). The suppression of emotions and the demands of being 'rational' may prompt work groups to engage in suppression, denial, splitting, projections, all of which 'distort cognition and reflective thinking' (Diamond 1993: 138).

As the individual is structured as having an unconscious, psychoanalysis, individual psychodynamics, and group dynamics become the foundation of understanding unconscious psychic processes and their impact on organizational functioning. Psychoanalysis has perhaps been most influential in the analysis of group dynamics. Psychology identifies the role of group norms and the strong pressures to conform, to the extent of distorting one's own judgement, even when not part of the group (Asch 1951). The Tavistock school understands group dynamics as mobilizing powerful forces, to the extent that defence mechanisms, anxiety, and identification can overwhelm the group and seriously disrupt task-directed work (Bion 1961).[37] Early work by Bion (1961) identifies the relational nature of behaviour where individual and group behaviour is equally reinforcing, with the 'rational' functioning of the group being affected by the unconscious 'irrational' feelings of individuals. Bion (1961) identifies three basic assumptions that may be held by groups, where members of the groups act 'as if' they hold the same basic assumption. Individual members contribute to this largely unconsciously, dependent on primitive feelings of dependency, aggression, and hope. The basic assumptions a group may adopt are dependency (dependency on an idealized, omnipotent, and omniscient 'leader', such that other members behave as if they are inadequate[38]); pairing (where the pairing of two individuals will lead to the birth of a messiah that will satisfy group needs and resolve difficulties[39]); fight/flight (where the focus is on one issue to the exclusion of all others confronted as 'the enemy', or suppressed and denied[40]). Working 'rationally', work groups develop personal and interpersonal skills in order to cooperate and function effectively as a group. However, where a group functions as a basic assumption group, such feelings interfere with the work task, as energy is dissipated in the anxieties that preoccupy the group.

Further work in the dynamics of groups is seen in Lewin's (1947) model for unfreezing, moving, and freezing as a way of initiating change in groups.[41] Again this is based on the assumption that groups have properties of their own, independent of the properties of individual members. This also forms the foundation of T group training where the blind (behaviour unknown to the self) and hidden (behaviour unknown to others) could be explored to bring self-knowledge and learning, thereby enhancing group functioning.[42] Although the unconscious (unknown to self and others) is not the subject of examination, in practice, it is difficult for this to remain an unexplored area.

Actors' anxieties and fears can result in 'organizational irrationality' in terms of the successful accomplishment of tasks. Menzies's (1970) study of nurses illustrates how the anxieties of death, attachment, and sexuality encountered as part of hospital work prompt defence mechanisms in structure, culture, and the organization of work. Examples include systems that separate the nurse and patient as much as possible through rotas, technical language, ritualized tasks, and routines; the splitting of responsibilities; and definitions of 'good nursing' that police these boundaries. These practices develop over time 'as the result of collusive interaction and agreement, often unconscious, between members of the organization as to what form it will take' (Menzies 1970: 10, quoted in de Board 1990: 142). The social defence mechanisms that are enshrined in these practices become part of an 'external reality'. However, this only serves to increase anxiety and leads to dysfunctions in terms of patient care. Similar examples are also seen in Miller's (1993) study of life in residential homes.

Psychoanalytical analyses can also be adopted on a broader scale. Miller (1993: 290–1), for example, offers the following psychoanalytic analysis of the operation of alienation within capitalist employment relations:

> Alienation remains as valid a description of the work experience of many employees as it was one hundred years ago; if anything it is magnified by the greater size of employing organizations. The individual feels forced to do something that gives him no satisfaction by someone else who has coercive powers and steals most of the fruits of his labour...At the rational level employees could give a clear and accurate account of the way in which their company worked; the market for their products; the relation between costs, prices, profits and investment...The coercive hold that the organization has over the individual...is that is satisfies his dependent needs and his infantile greed, though it does so indirectly by offering him the pseudo-autonomy of the consumer role...The individual's rage and his wishes—not always unconscious—to destroy the organization have to be split off and suppressed or repressed...this can lead to the formation of a compliant 'pseudo self' or 'false self'...split off from this and repressed is a private self...the creative potential; but it is held incommunicado, locked in an unconscious world of infantile omnipotent fantasy. By means of this splitting, any questioning of the institutional roles that the false self enacts, almost ritually, is inhibited.

The premise of psychoanalysis places a high premium on reason, making the irrational 'rational', known, and understandable, if not predictable. Knowledge of unconscious dimensions can bring to light reasons for actions. Gaining insight into reasons for actions and behaviour is held to be the foundation for the potential change of that behaviour. In this sense, bringing the reasons for 'irrational' behaviour to light is sufficient in itself. The therapeutic form of psychoanalytical theory is a form of action research. Its premise is a willingness to take responsibility for action and to work through the process. The focus is not on the past but to realize how interactional patterns in the present are limited, with this as the basis for changing behaviour. The sufficiency of the action lies in the process of bringing something to reason, restoring something to reason from unreason.

It is by these mechanisms that the 'irrational' becomes the province of the rational, 'a monologue of reason about madness', as Foucault (1967: xiii) says of psychiatry. In *The Paradoxes of Rationality*, Davidson (1990) cites Freud's work, the Plato principle that no intentional action is internally irrational. As Davidson (1990: 451) notes, however, 'psychoanalytic theory extends the reach of teleological or reason explanation by discovering motives, wishes, and intentions that were not recognized before . . . Freud has greatly increased the number and variety of phenomena that can be viewed as rational.' It certainly extends the range of phenomena that may be subject to 'reason explanations'.

Although premised on the operation of the 'irrational' and the unconscious, the model that is proffered in psychoanalytical theory bears a remarkable similarity to the rational man model (for some equally as 'irrational') of an economic rationality. The premise of both is the individual acting for the satisfaction of (unconscious) needs and in defence against costs (pain). This is not far removed from the utilitarian model of maximizing happiness and minimizing pain.[43] Within the psychoanalytic model, the basic needs and anxieties are not properly understood, nor are their sources. But equally, within economic rationality, *de gustibus non est disputandum*. In terms of an analysis of the operation of rationality, it appears that we have come full circle.

Conclusions

This chapter has presented the role of the body, emotions, and the 'irrational' and their role in making the organization rational. Although presented as the 'other of reason', their role is crucial in the functioning of reason. The body senses a range of cues and information that allows for the successful negotiation of social encounters. It internalizes and absorbs knowledge through which the accomplishment of tasks may be achieved. Feelings interpret information, while their physical expression in emotions ensures that the information feelings convey are communicated to others. Thus is an arena rendered sensable and sensible. The irrational again operates as a source of cues. Its outward manifestations give indications of that which requires attention, and that which should be reasoned with, for functioning to take place. In all these respects, the 'other of reason' makes the rational, reasonable.

Part IV
Conclusions

9 Collective rationality

Thus far, we have discussed the various dimensions of disembedded, embedded, and embodied rationality, all of which contribute in various ways to the means through which organizing and organization is facilitated. But what of the collective coordination of action? What is reason's role in this? How do we collectively organize and how does rationality function in coordinating collective action? Some embedded forms of rationality consider aspects of coordination, but these are facilitated by the assumptions of a shared understanding or a commonality of purpose, identity, task, or group. But where this is not presupposed, what of reason then? How does reason function to secure coordinated active purpose? Is there a means of securing a collective rationality? What is its role? And how does it function?

Collective rationality is rational cooperation guided by collective reasoning: 'a cooperative effort, involving linguistic exchange, to answer a question or solve a problem confronting a group' (McMahon 2001: 105). As the provision of justified argument or reasons as to why a course of action is preferable to another, it is thus distinct from discussion or conversation. Debate concerning collective rationality reflects the divergent disciplinary backgrounds that influence its discussion. Each trajectory influences the way debate is focused, the concepts used (collective action, collective reasoning, and communicative rationality) and how agreement may be achieved within a collective unit where there are disparate aims, interests, and objectives.

Two meanings of the concept of 'collective rationality' may be distinguished (Barry and Hardin 1982). The first is a collective decision, where 'collective rationality' records a form of group process to arrive at a decision. This may not reflect anything other than an aggregation of individual decisions (collective action). In the second, 'collective rationality' is a position or decision made by a collective entity. The 'rationality' reflects the position of a *collective* and is indicative of its collective agreement, however temporary (collective reasoning). At essence, both collective action and collective reasoning are debates about a collective good. Collective action, however, takes as its starting point the supremacy of the individual and from this, considers the issues involved in securing, among a group of individuals, a 'common good'. Collective reasoning, on the other hand, takes the collective entity, 'society', as given, and engages with how a collectively agreed, reasonable, or rational solution to common problems may be achieved.

Collective action

The collective action debate starts from the centrality of the individual. From a position of methodological individualism or utility maximization (although the two are often bed fellows), the perspective of a collective or collectivity raises a number of issues. Given the assumption that individual actions are motivated by self-interest, how might one explain collective action? Under what circumstances would a rationally maximizing individual join in inter-dependent or collective action? How may a collectivity, for example, a government, organization, arrive at decisions that reflect the desires of its constituents or members? And given the actions of a collective unit, or actions undertaken on its behalf, to what extent may these be characterized as reflecting a 'collective rationality'? Is the latter an aggregate concept of individual rationality or does it denote something distinct?

One debate centres on whether collective rational action can be assumed from individual rational action, that is, whether, because a rational individual will act in a certain manner in a certain situation, then a group of rational people with the same interests, being equally rational, will adopt a common action on the same basis. Olson (1971) is critical of the concept of collective rationality where it is presumed that because members of a group are rational, the group is collectively rational. He terms this the 'fallacy of composition', the assumption that knowledge about how individuals will act individually leads to knowledge of how a group will act. 'One who wishes to understand how a group succeeds in cooperative action for collective benefit can no longer merely assume that the group's success is rationally motivated in the sense that individual actions can be rationally motivated' (Barry and Hardin 1982: 42). He specifically questions the presumption that a group with common interests will work together to pursue those common interests. Acting rationally independently is not the same as acting rationally interdependently. Collectively rational action as interdependent rational action is always qualified in terms of 'an agreed way of acting is rational only if it leads to an outcome which is optimal so far as the parties to the agreement are concerned' (Gauthier 1982: 96).

If rational action at the individual level is inconsistent with definitions of rationality at the collective level, however, this raises definitional problems. It raises the possibility of there being two forms of rational action, individual and collective. For these reasons, the term 'collective rationality' is largely absent from the lexicon of these debates. Preference instead is for 'collective action'. Taylor's (1987) definition of a 'collective rationality', as the 'capacity of social system or collective decision making mechanisms to bring individual preferences into line with broad notions of individual rationality', is in line with the understanding of collective action.

The premise of the rational actor's maximization of expected utility raises questions of how to account for the behaviour of a collection of actors. Reflecting specific disciplinary backgrounds, the 'problem of collective action' is addressed in a number of forms: the Prisoner's Dilemma, the Tragedy of the Commons, the Free Rider problem, and Arrow's 'impossibility theorem'. Each raises the problematic relationship between individual actions and collective consequences.

In game theory, the Prisoner's Dilemma illustrates how the consequences of each individual pursuing their own interests results in an outcome that each regards as worse than if they had acted differently. X and Y are held on suspicion of a crime. If X confesses, Y gets twenty years and X gets one year. If Y confesses, X gets twenty years and Y, one. If neither X nor Y confess, they serve two years each for a minor offence. If both confess, they each serve ten years. It is rational self-interest to confess (and thus serve one year). However, if they both confess, this leads to the irrational consequence of rational self-interest (ten years each). The game illustrates the distinction between an individual and an interdependent rationality, in that the outcome of defection (confessing) is individually rational, but collectively deficient in that, had the players cooperated (not confessed), each player would be better off than if each defects (confesses). The individual interest is not to cooperate, to follow self-interest; the collective benefit would be if each cooperated. 'Rational egoists are unlikely to succeed in cooperating to promote their common interests' (Taylor 1987: 3).

The 'collective action problem' is exemplified in the Tragedy of the Commons (Hardin 1968), where individually owned animal stock graze common land. The individual interest is to follow the self-interest of grazing more stock. Individual rational action by each member of the group, however, leads to serious consequences for all. The common land becomes depleted and unable to sustain grazing. The collective benefit would be to take collective action which would prevent serious long-term consequences. Common action, however, opens up the Free Rider problem, whereby individuals benefit from the collective actions of others without contributing themselves to the action. This is particularly the case in large groups where individual contribution is less perceptible (Olson 1971). The cost of the individual's contribution is weighed against the benefit provided. (Excluded from consideration are altruistic, expressive, and intrinsic motivations.[1]) As the former usually outweighs the latter, there is little incentive to contribute. This is especially seen in relation to public goods, where goods are indivisible (consumption does not reduce the amount to others) and non-excludable (those which are impossible or prohibitively costly to exclude others from consuming it).

For some, these outcomes are expressed as a paradox, in that individual rationality fails to 'deliver' collective rationality, thus indicating that the two forms of rationality are distinct (Barry and Hardin 1982; Coleman 1990). Rapoport's (1982) discussion of the Prisoner's Dilemma sees the game as presenting the choice between an individual and a collective rationality. While each does better through following an individual rationality, both do collectively better following a collective rationality. He argues that this points to two conceptions of rationality.

[In the] prisoner's dilemma two concepts of 'rationality' compete for attention, namely individual rationality which prescribes to each player a course of action most advantageous to him under the circumstances, and collective rationality, which prescribes a course of action to both players simultaneously...if both act in accordance with collective rationality, then each player is better off than he would have been had each acted in accordance with individual rationality. (Rapoport 1982: 72)

McMahon (2001) also introduces a 'collective rationality' dimension to the Free Rider problem. While it is rational for the individual not to cooperate because they will obtain benefits of others' efforts in a public good, should everyone not cooperate then each loses through the failure of a mutually beneficial cooperative scheme. A way of accommodating this is to assess the costs and benefits of cooperation *and* non-cooperation (McMahon 2001). An individual rationality would assume that where there is sufficient cooperation to ensure that a scheme goes ahead, contribution or participation would not be rational. A collective rationality would participate, given an assurance that others will also be contributing, because the costs would be minimum compared to the loss of the outcome or benefits. Choosing not to participate is less preferable than the loss of a mutually beneficial cooperative scheme. The 'universal' that is appealed to here is for the agent to ask a 'free rider' question of 'What would happen if everyone did that?' (McMahon 2001: 28).[2]

The issue of collective action is made more complex where there is interaction over time. The most interesting collective action problems are generally dynamic rather than static in nature. With the introduction of the temporal dimension in repeated games, the iterated play of the Prisoner's Dilemma, cooperative behaviour can evolve over plays, as previous cooperative behaviour builds expectations of future cooperative behaviour (Rapoport 1982). An interesting aspect of this is that it is learnt behaviour. It is built up over time and dependent on the others behaviour. Rapoport (1982: 79) concludes that a reliance on an individual rationality in many conflict situations 'is a trap', with many important conflicts being more accurately presented as non-zero sum games.

The relationship between individual rational action and its consequences for a collective is ambiguous. For some, the superiority of individual decision-making for collective benefit is exemplified in the workings of the market; the logic of collective action reflected in the efficiency of market exchange. However, rationality at an individual level does not necessarily result in rationality at a 'system' level, an 'irrationality' has all too frequently been handled by reference to the term 'unintended consequences', rather than the more accurate description of Merton's (1936) latent consequences.[3] Given interdependence, pursuit of individual interests can lead to inferior results for all, a consequence that leads to the argument that rather than the premise of action being the independent actor, the individual acts as a component of an 'interdependent acting unit', a different entity entirely, and analysis should be premised on such.

Collective action and the 'collective good'

The issue remains nonetheless of how, what is the best method, to ascertain a collective position? What methods of decision-making are there such that a common position may be achieved that does not infringe individual positions to a large degree? Collective action poses the issue in terms of aggregation. 'Since a collectivity is, in Hobbes's terms, an artificial and not a natural person, it can have decisions attributed to it only via some rules for aggregating individual expressions of preference' (Barry and Hardin 1982: 377). Arrow's (1992) general possibility theorem, commonly known as Arrow's impossibility theory, however, indicates that three people or more with two alternatives would not be able to achieve a solution where everyone's preferences could be reflected.[4] In these circumstances, any method for aggregating preferences leads to 'inconsistent collective preference ordering' for individuals.

Because of the premise of individual maximization and, following from this, the need for some form of aggregation, the utilitarian solution of a public good as the greatest good for the greatest number, presents itself. The compromise is for majority voting, despite the strategic manipulation of voting intentions that is sometimes a consequence. Collective action thus is an aggregation of a multiplicity of individual actors and their actions. The aggregative view of public good is validated by having given equal consideration to the interests of each. The public good is ensured through having treated everyone equally. Under this prescription where politics may be public in nature, it is instrumental in purpose (Elster 1998).

The concept of a public good based on some notion of 'better for society' is rendered problematic within this framework. Preferences held in common are not collective preferences for the collective good. However, where 'calculation of what is best for oneself is felt to be unambivalently "rational"', then acting in a collective interest is either 'irrational' or, more commonly, behaviour that is 'moral', and as such, out of the purview of rational action. 'Doing what is for the common good evokes the idea of "sacrificing" one's individual interest' (Rapoport 1982: 73). For some, the 'solution' is to recognize that optimization rather than maximization is the best way to accommodate both: 'if it be agreed that morality must be rational, or at least not anti-rational, and that morality involves some restraint in the pursuit of one's wants and desires, then agreed optimization is the only candidate' (Gauthier 1982: 68). The rational man must recognize that he must participate in mutually beneficial agreements.

Collective reasoning

Collective reasoning explicitly rejects collective rationality as a process of optimizing independent individual decision-making or the aggregation of preferences. Its focus rather is deliberative democracy, a collective deliberation, with the aim of achieving free, uncoerced and reasoned agreement among equals.[5] Thus, deliberative democracy emphasizes a commitment to public reasoning as a means of resolving issues involving equality among participants to the debate, both in participating and decision-making; a willingness to listen and a preparedness to accommodate and alter opinion; a commitment to trying to find a rationally motivated decision that is acceptable to those involved in deliberation; and a commitment to decisions arrived at through such a process.[6] It is not consensus or unanimity, but the recognition of the need to reach some agreed way of progressing (Benhabib 1992). Discussion focuses on participatory decision-making procedures: conditions under which there is a willingness and ability to express reasons and openly consider those of others; individual and institutional criteria that must be adopted for this to apply in practice; and the nature of the institutional and procedural mechanisms chosen for the decision-making process, being aware that procedural mechanisms may strengthen some positions and weaken others.

Given existing inequities, debates focuses not only on the opportunity to participate but also the ability to participate; not merely equal access, but the equal opportunity of access at agenda-setting and decision-making stages (Knight and Johnson 1997). The distinction between formal and substantive equality is highlighted in Sen's (1987) concept of capability equality and recognizes the importance of having the material resources and capacity to engage in deliberation, with safeguards against 'political impoverishment', especially where a minority faces a dominant group (Bohman 1997; Young 1997). The legitimacy of decisions that are taken stems from their public deliberation and agreement, that is, that they are the product of free and reasoned argument among equals, where not only individuals are equal, but their reasons are also given equal consideration (Cohen 1997a). Practical discourse must therefore ensure that no one is excluded; all are equal partners; and all positions are equally respected. What is required is the institutionalization of procedures and mechanisms that can ensure a rationally shaped 'public opinion' (Chambers 1996).

One issue of debate is whether decisions consequent on 'fair' procedures are by themselves sufficient guarantee of the 'reasonableness' of outcomes. Is procedure alone sufficient to ensure an acceptable or reasonable outcome or do substantive, independent standards of 'good reasons' need to be invoked in a final adjudication of outcome? (Estlund 1997). Equating deliberative democracy with pure procedure is problematic for some commentators (Rawls 1997). However, should recourse be made to standards of assessment, the question then arises where do these standards come from and what role do they play in relation to the deliberative process?

Also raised is the extent to which a deliberative democracy implies an agreement or consensus. Advocates argue that commitment is to trying to reach an agreement rather than actually reaching an agreement. There is no implication of a shared community ethos. What is pertinent are the intentions of those participating in the process. 'To communicate means that we seek to understand and convince; to be rational means that we offer reasons that can be understood and can convince; to be in agreement means that we understand each other fully and have been freely convinced' (Chambers 1996: 119). Strategic or instrumental engagement is proscribed (Chambers 1996). Commitment is to a mutual consideration and reconsideration of positions held and reasons for this, with the intention of arriving at a course of action by making reasonable compromises in the deliberation process. It is not to conceive of the process as interest-based bargaining (Richardson 1997).[7]

'Reasonableness is a...central norm built into deliberative procedures' (Bohman and Rehg 1997: xxvii). Reasons must be advanced for supporting proposals, for criticizing them, and for deciding issues. Choices cannot be agreed because they are 'preferred'. As reasons are expressed and voiced, they are exposed to reason in the public forum of debate. Indeed, the argument is that only by engagement in public fora are rational capacities fully realized. The practice of reasoning enhances the process of deliberations, and thus, even though agreement might not be achieved, there is an increased understanding as positions are aired. Reason demands that explanations be given, that these appear 'reasonable' to those who request them, even where not accepted.[8] This invokes the competence basis of reasonableness, that which is an appropriate response within a particular context.[9] In giving reasons, one has to be aware that reasons have to be accepted by others as reasons.

Although not positioning his work directly in relation to deliberative democracy, Habermas's (1987) work on communicative rationality has been highly influential in this debate (Elster 1998). For Habermas, 'Communicative reason is directly implicated in social life processes insofar as acts of mutual understanding take on the role of a mechanism of coordinating action' (quoted in Flyvbjerg 2001: 90). Habermas's early work sought to explore the possibilities of the democratic formation of public opinion and its potency within political systems of domination.[10] He distinguishes communicative rationality or a communicatively achieved agreement from an instrumental or strategic use of language that produces domination through systematically distorted communication (Deetz 1992). Communicative reason is aimed at mutual understanding rather than purposively inducing others to adopt a particular position, that is, treating them as an end. The latter, strategic action, is where the intent is oriented to success in bringing about a desired response or effect, rather than engaging in mutual understanding and convincing through reason. What is required, therefore, is 'clarifying the presuppositions of the rationality of processes of reaching understanding, which are presumed to be universal because they are unavoidable' (quoted in Flyvbjerg 2001: 89).

Habermas sees reason as the intersubjective recognition of a validity claim. There is the assumption when engaging in communicative action that participants desire to reach an agreement. Communicative rationality thus aspires to offer a plausible reconstruction of the assumptions speakers must have and make in the attempt to communicate with one another. These are that individuals defend only what they understand or believe (rather than attempt to deceive), and respect the intent behind claims as being responsible and sincere even if the claims themselves are disputed. Thus, his model of rational discourse has four criteria that must be met relating to four shared domains: propositional truth (based on a shared external world); normative rightness or correctness (appeals to the norms of social relations); sincerity (accurately representing the speakers views); and intelligibility (of language, e.g. an avoidance of jargon). These factors will allow 'the force of the better argument' to emerge. In order to function, it implies certain procedural requirements: no one affected by discussion is excluded from it; there is the opportunity both to present and engage with others' claims; others' claims are taken seriously; there is a neutralization of power relations; and there must be no engagement with strategic manipulation.

Criticisms of deliberative democracy point to its idealism or utopianism, arguing that it ignores structured inequalities and economic and political domination; that divisions of opinion and position can reflect quite fundamental and diametrically opposed worldviews that are not amenable to reasoned discussion; and that institutionalized procedures are fundamentally designed to preserve the status quo and do not admit radical change. Also highlighted are procedural issues such as time constraints for discussion; that the structure and framework of discussions favours some positions over others; there are heroic demands or assumptions made of participants; that sharply differentiated capacities privilege some speakers over others; the difficulties of securing unanimity; and whether unanimity constitutes conformity rather than reasoned agreement (Johnson 1998). More cogently, perhaps, is its failure to articulate the practical steps required to secure its intentions.

Responses are that although the presentation of deliberative democracy may be ideal, and in large spheres of life, counterfactual, it is neither unthinkable nor absolutely divorced from experience (Michelman 1997). As an ideal, it requires the identification of power structures and social relations that prevent involvement in public debate and distort communication. The degree to which actual practice deviates from an ideal is indicative of the operation of power. As an aspiration, it offers a model for collective decision-making and as such, the foundation for critique of current configurations and an avenue of possible reform.

Collective reasoning and the 'collective good'

The deliberative view of the public good is of public reasoning establishing the grounds for decisions (Cohen 1997a). 'Collective or public good' is enhanced both through the deliberation of issues and the assumption that this will lead to enhanced decision-making, and also that the process of listening to others' reasons accords them the respect that is due oneself, treating the other as an end rather than a means to an end. Deliberative democracy is advanced as thus providing the virtues of being valuable morally and instrumentally worthwhile (Christiano 1997). The sense of 'common good' under this perspective is a position that emerges consequent upon the deliberation and the weighing of reasons. It is 'fashioned' rather than 'discovered', and as such is not absolute, but open to revisions as sentiments change. Re-evaluation of positions occurs over time. 'A general agreement can emerge as the product of many single conversations even when no single conversation ends in agreement' (Chambers 1996: 171).

Although deliberative democracy is put forward as an alternative to the view of politics as competition between private interests, deliberative rather than aggregative, it does not entail putting aside the personal in order to adopt an abstract or disembedded persona. The relationship between the individual and the collective may vary. In one form of collective reasoning, 'the cooperative product should be conceived as a common pool of reasons and arguments on the basis of which each participant can make up his or her mind about the question being addressed. That is, collective reasoning involves cooperation to create a common resource on which each can draw...to form an individual judgement' (McMahon 2001: 3). Reasons are the 'public good' that collective reasoning furnishes. This is distinct from collective reasoning where the evaluation of reasons is also cooperatively undertaken, and a collective judgement taken on the strength or efficacy of the reasons given. Collective rationality in this sense is 'a shared judgement with others' (Gaus 1997: 226).

The common good under this perspective is not conceived of as being the aggregate outcome of individuals' pursuing private interests that are antecedent to debate. Rather the emphasis is on the transformation of positions through public and rational discussion (Elster 1998). Discussions with

---

BOX 9.1. COMMUNICATIVE MEASURES?

There is a strong belief that performance measures will act as a stimulant to a communicative rationality, enhancing communication between agencies leading to more effective work organization. This is the 'theory' behind them:

Basically we see targets as a means to enforce cooperation between the agencies on securing targets. This is the rationale behind them. This is the rationale for cross agency system targets. The cross agency approach, targets, forces you to take a different perspective. It gets cooperation going. It forces you to find out where the problems lie and to try and deal with them. Targets have to have a stimulant effect: 'We know where we want to go'. This is the advantage of this.   (Policy)

We must learn to deal with cases in a more effective way. It is only worthwhile to do something if you make a difference in what you do. There is no point in having overarching aims and objectives if that's all they are. It is up to colleagues. Its purpose is to develop a common language for people to start thinking about what they actually do. Where you have performance indicators then you have conversations about what it is that you do. Where you have overarching performance indicators then you can have conversations about overall what it is that you do. You can reduce areas that are rubbing, but you can produce approaches that are better outcomes for society as a whole. Measures can provide the language necessary to have a conversation. You can discuss things in terms of 'this is what we wanted to achieve'. It is not necessarily to have a shared focus.   (Policy)

The important thing is management information. We want to get to a situation...the best thing is to get to a situation where there is the information and there is agreement that 'it is not very good is it?' You have to start talking to other agencies and your indicators help in the overall process.   (Policy)

Although, there was an agreement with a need for information and data as a basis for discussion, this did not translate into support for a system of measures and targets (the two were confused by all respondents and seen as synonymous):

You need to know 'this is how long it takes in the system'. Everyone is in agreement on this. You need to know how long it takes. If not, you're not going to stop the hold ups, the problems. You need to get information in order to understand the ways in which the system is driven. To work out who it's for, and what its focus is, and what the court process is. You need to ask what supports the core processes and this will allow you to deliver the process to the public. The process mapping produced a lot of interesting data. It's good to talk to parties in the system and get an understanding of what they've got to deal with.

(anonymous)

You have people on the Criminal Justice Board that run the organizations. It is a positive structure where we are able to say...ask: 'Is this what we want to do?' There is very much the view on the Board of 'how can we make things work better?' There is a strong feeling by those involved of, that they want to make it work better. There is a lot of good cooperation developing. It has top people sitting around a table saying 'how are we doing with this? This area is not so good here. Can you try and secure an improvement on this? If this requires that you work together then please get together and work this out'. There are more open minded approaches. There is quite a degree of enthusiasm about. But there is a question of how this filters through the ranks. The local CJ Board has helped in this, because it gets partners around a table. It gets data out on the table. And it's a forum for asking questions and it's a basis, an opportunity, for gaining commitment.

(anonymous)

BOX 9.1. (*continued*)

For front-line staff, measures were not seen as being part of the job:

We don't look at these figures. The only time we look at it is when we are researching for an argument for extra resources compared with others. It's useful from that point of view. I looked at them one year ago when I was making a staffing bid, arguing that resources had not kept up with workloads, caseloads.   (Court services)

However, there was some indication that measures were being used as the foundation of initiating debate rather than necessarily being seen as part of a strategy of systemic distortion:

We are now being much more transparent with numbers and performance measures. Previously the approach was that we should always try and present the best information. We needed to show that we were doing well . . . To present ourselves in the best light. For example, there was a thing about drunk driving. If numbers went up, all hell broke loose and we had to spin it, to put the best light on it. Now we present all the information, good as well as bad. But the argument is, 'this is what can be done within these resources'. Now the view is that if drunk driving is up, then put this information out and do a media issue on this and show people that there is a problem. Also put out information and say this is our performance with these resources. We are moving to a more informed debate. 'This is our performance in these areas with these issues. If you want us to do all these things, then they have to be resourced properly or we have to decide what the priorities are in all these initiatives.'   (Police)

---

others who are 'differently situated' from oneself, and with different points of view, provide the foundations of a process of learning (Christiano 1997). Participation is thus not just 'speaking', nor is it based on a formal equality and reciprocity. It requires a knowledge of histories and context with the situated knowledge that each brings being the basis for 'enlarging the understanding of everyone and moving them beyond their own parochial interests' (Young 1997: 399). It requires that participants are reflective rather than self-regarding, situating their own position in relation to the situated position of others. In doing so, there is recognition of the perspectival or partial view of each; being aware of reasons that are compelling to others; and pooling information with a view to trying to find an accommodation through public reasoning. This position denies a 'removed impartiality' in reasoning. Not for Young (1997), Rawls's veil of ignorance. Reasoning involves a relationship with identification: acknowledging the legitimacy of others to participate as oneself; considering what one's response would be as the recipient of the action being put forward (as oneself); and considering what one's response would be if one was in the place of those affected (as a specific other). Journeying through these positions is, it is argued, to move imperceptibly from a position of reasonableness as competence to one of reasonableness as fairness (Young 1997).[11] This emphasizes the formative power of the collective reasoning process (Braaten 1995).

The collective within organization studies

Consideration of the collective within organizations remains strangely absent. Strangely in the sense that organizations are identified as a type of collectivity: 'Organizations are first and foremost, collectivities' (Scott 1981: 79). They are 'a means of achieving the benefits of collective action in situations where the price system fails' (Arrow 1974: 33) (see Chapter 2). Mechanisms for addressing the reasoned or aggregate position of the collective, however, do not feature in organizational texts, and rarely in organizational practice. Organizations are private property. They are not democratic institutions. The question that a collective rationality raises, 'what is the position of the collective?, thus does not feature. Discussions of collective rationality are restricted to those 'types' of organizations where it might be more readily assumed given different ownership structures, as for example, political parties, trade unions and professional associations, feminist or cooperative organizations, public organizations, or political action groups (Davis et al. 2004; Lipset et al. 1962; Michels 1949; Rothschild Whitt 1979; Wilson 1995). Within private property, an individual rationality predominates. The organization is anthropomorphized and organizational action is a type of individual action (Albrow 1992/2002: 388). The collective is accommodated in the concept of culture. The contrast between the experience of organizations as a collective body and the inability to influence decisions having implications for the collective, remains the unspoken and unaddressed element of work experience.

Where a collective rationality is addressed, it is either as an aggregate of a number of isolated decisions or as the registering of a collective position. Both organizational ecology and institutional theory take a form of collective rationality as their starting point. Hannan and Freeman's (1977/2002: 122) work in population ecology raises the issue.[12] The collective rationality 'problem' they identify is that a strategy which is rational for a single decision-maker will not necessarily be rational if adopted by large numbers of decision-makers. Their ecological analysis is conducted at three levels, individual, population, and community. Events at one level have consequences at others. Although there is interdependence, population events are not reducible to the individual organization; community events are not reducible to population events. The 'environment' optimizes, it selects out, regardless of whether individuals consciously adapt or not. 'The problem of ecological adaptation can be considered a game of chance in which the population chooses a strategy (specialism or generalism) and then the environment chooses an outcome...So if there is rationality involved, it is the rationality of natural selection. Organizational rationality and environmental rationality may coincide in the instance of firms in competitive markets' (Hannan and Freeman 1977/2002: 129). If rationality operates, then it does so in different forms, 'It is unusual for individual rationality and environment or market rationality to lead to the same optima. When two rationalities do not agree we are concerned with the optimizing behaviour of the environment' (Hannan and Freeman 1977/2002: 129). Meyer and Rowan (1977), DiMaggio and Powell (1983) and institutional theorists also implicitly function with a concept of a collective rationality, in the sense that that which is rational is given or determined by the collective through the operation of rationalized myths (see Chapter 5).

Collective reasoning and practice

As McMahon (2001: 3) notes, 'collective reasoning about practical matters is especially germane to rational cooperation.' Within mainstream organizations, and in the absence of any explicit reference to the directive rights of private property and ownership, appeals to specialized knowledge and concerns for efficiency are raised as reasons why a more deliberative form of democracy would be impracticable. Just as Aristotle restricted deliberation to the 'wise, virtuous and well-off' (Bohman 1997: 324), so to do modern organizations. Collective decision-making is the responsibility of organizational 'leaders'. However, some of the claims for deliberative democracy, especially the efficacy and legitimacy of decision-making when participation is enhanced, have strong appeals within the management and organization literature. Collective reasoning has tended to be addressed either in a very individualized form, directed at the individual qua individual, rather than as a member of a collective, through communication, participation, and involvement, and organizational development (OD) schemes, or has been the province of industrial relations, addressed through trade union participation and collective bargaining. These two avenues promote different understandings of 'voice', participation, and involvement, and as a consequence, different understandings of the nature of the collective and any attempt at a collective rationality.

Trying to develop a 'collective' or 'communicative' rationality in organizations, a 'search for community', has exercised much time and many management initiatives (Jablin et al. 2001). The emphasis however has been under the broad umbrella of communication and participation programmes rather than more developed forms of industrial democracy (Webb and Webb 1920). Emphasis is on job enrichment, teamwork, participation and empowerment, quality circles, self-directed teams, QWL, TQM, BPR, 'systems' thinking, high-performance work systems, and high-performance organizations. These formalized programmes indicate quite restricted opportunities for engagement. Knights and McCabe (1999) illustrate how the hierarchical structure of organization and a preoccupation with profits remain unchallenged in a

TQM programme. Issues such as organizational structure and staffing are not open to discussion, and the problem-solving discourse reinforces rather than questions norms and values of the organization. More recently, knowledge management programmes have been developed with a 'collective' or 'communicative' end in view. Nonaka (1994: 247), for example, gives some 'field rules' for processes that help in knowledge creation. These are that participants should be able to express their ideas candidly and freely; that constructive criticism should be substantiated by reasoned arguments and be used to build a consensus; and negation for its own sake discouraged. Each programme brings with it a new jargon and with this new promises of effectiveness. Barley and Kunda (1992) and Ramsay (1977) illustrate how such programmes have a strong cyclical nature.

Some organizational behaviour interventions have had the explicit purpose of encouraging individuals to engage in 'full and frank' discussions with a view to improving communication within organizations, or to develop a new understanding of 'organizational reality'. Some of the experiments with T groups and behaviour modelling are in this light. T groups were introduced as an aid to successful communication, especially where there were obstacles to understanding human relations, that is, the ability to appreciate how others react to one's behaviour and the inability to gauge the state of relationships between both oneself and others, and of others. They were designed to increase an individual's sensitivity skills and enhance ability in interpersonal skills. Seven to ten people are introduced to a circle, where although there is a topic, there is no structure to the encounter. The aim is to engage in a frank and honest exchange of information that deals with issues of dependence and interdependence. Teambuilding exercises are also designed to encourage communication. Their focus is the development of 'interpersonal competence', increased understanding, fostering collaboration, conflict resolution, and 'inspiring a shared vision'. These programmes, and a number of other intervention techniques, come under the general rubric of OD.

Some approaches to OD are explicit in their understanding of it as a process designed specifically to help the organization through teaching individuals how to continuously improve their performance. Others present it more as a process of understanding, improving, and empowerment, portraying it in a more collaborative light (French and Bell 1999). Their focus is on uncovering the beliefs, values, and assumptions that underlie behaviour with the intent to change them. The emphasis is increased interaction, communication, participation, and understanding. Other programmes are less directive. One element of OD, for example, is action research, a highly participative process involving the consultant as co-learner in an iterative process of diagnosis and action. Its purpose is 'intentional collective action'. It is research focused, involving data collection, action planning, and feedback and analysis based on this. It varies dependent on whether it is diagnostic, participant, empirical, or experimental action research. Under some depictions, the participative aspect of a collaborative and iterative process of diagnosis and action is highlighted more than others, to the extent that in some understandings of the process, one of the foundations of action research is akin to democratic dialogue (Reason and Bradbury 2002).

A range of questions that might be addressed of any of these endeavours include issues about the degree of information people are given, the range of alternatives that are considered in the process, and the nature of the participation and decision-making process they permit and exclude. An evaluation of all these programmes using the distinction drawn by Habermas between strategic and communicative forms of action would have to be very sceptical of their communicative intent given their top-down instigation, highly structured nature and restricted range of debate, and the inequalities in power relationships. (Although this is not to deny that within such systems, there may be some opportunities for some process of deliberation to take place.)

While management texts are replete with suggestions for participation and involvement, recommendations for engagement and dialogue with representatives of collective organizations, trade unions or professional associations, are notable by their absence. The latter directly addresses the directive rights of ownership in their attempts to extend the concept of 'polis' to the employing organization. There is a 'ladder' of relationships reflecting different degrees of worker involvement and influence. These range from communication (involving the passing of information); involvement and consultation; participation; collective bargaining; extended collective bargaining to co-determination or joint regulation, the latter representing a form of industrial democracy. Consultation is the 'taking of counsel', seeking information or advice (*OED*). It is advisory in function. Participation is sharing in a common action (*OED*), a cooperative relationship. Joint participation is partnership aimed at enhancing efficiency and productivity, maintaining the status quo, but do not fundamentally challenge power relationships. Bargaining is haggling, a dispute over terms (*OED*). It is therefore implicitly or explicitly an adversary relationship. Collective bargaining may cover issues such as recruitment, training, deployment, income, benefits, and discipline. Extended collective bargaining includes discussions on corporate strategy issues. The institution of collective bargaining necessarily involves agreement on union recognition, the disclosure of information and the protection of union representation, shop stewards, convenors, and full-time union officials. It is to recognize the organization as a collective. In structures of industrial democracy, workers and shareholders have equal rights (and concomitant responsibilities) in law. It is a structure that aims to change the criteria of decision-making and the balance of power (Edwards 2003).

Managerial focus has been on fostering a form of 'communitarianism' rather than collectivism, a focus on task-centred participation through micro-level governance systems, rather than encouraging forms of representative engagement that directly exercise decision-making rights. Even those organizations that have traditionally functioned on the basis of collegiate decision-making, for example, universities or professionally based organizations, have seen such structures eroded in favour of more hierarchical and centralized decision-making structures. There is not only a democratic deficit in all organizations but also an increasingly limited sphere in which collective participation and decision-making may be practised.

Forester's (1983, 1993, 2000) work examines the extent to which communicative action is possible in organizations, whether it is possible to question statements in terms of their validity according to the criteria of communicative action (truth, legitimacy, sincerity, clarity), or whether there are systemic factors that impede this. Again debate is enjoined as to whether evaluation of communication should be in terms of an 'ideal' or whether response should be more pragmatic. Forester (1992) identifies systemic distortions as the division of labour that restricts access to information or dissipates it across organizational boundaries. This is contrasted with more deliberate or calculated distortions that are used to legitimate and perpetuate structures of inequality. Forester (1992) advocates a critical ethnography, tracing factual claims, claims to legitimacy, and expressive claims within an exchange, as a means of analysing relations of power and hegemony (the reproduction of social and political relations) and how these are specifically played out in practice. His focus is rationality, 'an interactive and argumentative process of marshalling evidence and giving reasons, a process that in principle minimizes excluding relevant information and encourages the testing of conjectures, a process that welcomes rather than punishes value enquiry' (Forester 2000: 6). As a method of analysis, it primes questions such as the extent to which there is disclosure of full information, whether there is suppression of certain issues and debates, and whether and to what extent there is coercion or intimidation in acceptance of positions. As Alvesson and Willmott (1996: 118) note, 'a developed capacity to question and discuss the rationality of significant statements can consequentially alter the way that these discourses act to maintain the position of a ruling managerial elite. This capacity can also provide a basis for the critique and transformation of organizational practice.'

Debates on collective rationality emphasize formal process. This has been criticized by Deetz (1992: 290) for being at the expense of what he terms momentary practice, the ongoing interactions, and the importance of the 'micro-practice of democracy', actions designed to enhance everyday communicative practice. 'Each time we say... "let me see if I understand your point correctly?", we are engaging in moral conversations of justification... it is the process of such dialogue, conversation, and mutual understanding, and not consensus, which is our goal.' Forester (2000) also emphasizes the importance of dialogical and argumentative processes and is critical of analyses 'inspired by liberal models of voice and empowerment [that] unwittingly reduce empowerment to "being heard"', and the neglect in any learning of local as well as expert knowledge. Participation is thus reduced to speaking, and learning to knowing. 'The transformation of the done-to into doers, spectators and victims into activist, fragmented groups into renewed bodies, old resignation into new beginnings, are lost from our view' (Forester 2000: 115). Forester (2000) also emphasizes the importance of learning that takes place in dialogical action, and the interrelationship between knowledge, power, voice, and growth. Participation may thus involve a change, a shift or adjustment, in an understanding not only of oneself but also more crucially one's position within structured conditions that form the basis of action.

Conclusions

Collective rationality informs a number of different understandings based on what constitutes a collective, that is, whether the collective is a substantive entity or an abstraction constructed through the aggregation of individuals. In one strand of debate, the lexicon is in terms of the recording and optimization of preferences, the recording of majority opinion as the foundation of a collective decision and position. In another, the question relates to the possibilities of publicly exercising reason and the practices that sustain this. It holds out the prospect of reaching a collective decision that represents in some form a collective 'will' reflective of a collective rationality. In terms of the original question of the role of reason in coordinating collective action, however, these two positions are in danger of prompting a cynicism either with the former, as votes may be manipulated for strategic advantage or voices remain unrepresented in majority decisions, or with the latter, as advocates for deliberative procedures are dismissed for idealism and naivety in ignoring the realities of gross inequities in power positions. This, however, would be to adopt a disembedded assessment of the question and to ignore the embodied reality of its practice. The exercise of collective rationality takes place in specific contexts, with specific individuals, having specific resources. The outcome and effect of these engagements are only known in practice. While there may be gross inequalities in power structures that heavily structure possibilities, these are engaged with in a multitude of circumstances, the overall outcomes of which are not given or prescribed.

10 Practical reason

Let us recap the argument. Why a focus on rationality? A focus on rationality allows us to escape the dominance of the focus on 'organizations'. Organization theory reflects modernity, not because its object, the bureaucratic organization, is the archetypical structure of modernity (although it is), but because of the style or mode of statement that informs its analysis: the antinomy of the transcendental subject and determined object. Thus, its focus is the anthropomorphized organization 'acting' in, or on, an environment, or management 'acting' on its behalf. However, as Weick (1969: 358) notes,

The word, organization, is a noun and it is also a myth. If one looks for an organization one will not find it. What will be found is that there are events, linked together, that transpire within concrete walls and these sequences, their pathways, their timing, are the forms we erroneously make into substances when we talk about an organization.

For this reason, he argues for a focus on organizing, stating that primarily, 'the activities of organizing are directed toward the establishment of a workable level of certainty' (Weick 1969: 91). A focus on organizing avoids theoretical consequences of conceptual models of organization: organization/environment, individual/organizational, and organization/society dichotomies, levels that are prized apart which are then required to be conjoined in the conception of the organization as the rational actor (Marsden 1993).

A focus on 'organization' highlights the presence or absence of the adjectival form, 'rational', the consequence of which are binary analyses that contrast the rational with the political; the rational and the emotional; and the rational and irrational. Rationality is thus constructed through, and known in, a hierarchical relation to an 'other'. The understanding of rationality depends on this preservation of a non-rational sphere. A focus on practice, organizing, directs analysis to 'forms' or 'types' of reasoning involved in organizing and moves from a dualistic set of categories to one that emphasizes multiplicity. It is this that allows for an analysis in terms of embedded layers of rationality.[1]

But how to engage with concept of rationality? Contrary to postmodernist interpretations, Foucault's work is relevant for the study of rationality in several respects. Wanting to avoid the futility of being 'for' or 'against' reason, Foucault argues for a focus on rationalities as they are experienced in critical domains. Not 'reason in general' but 'a very specific type of rationality' (Foucault 2002: 313). Foucault argues that rationalities, 'modes of thought', should be analysed in their own terms rather than being dismissed as the 'rationalizations' that accrue to powerful groups in the exercise of their interests. Focusing on the latter at the expense of the former is to fail to understand an important dimension of the operation of power and its disciplinary effects.

Foucault's work is also important in identifying various facets of rationality. He identifies three axes of a field or a domain: its savoir, the field of knowledge or 'science' that 'defines' the field; its connaissance, the systems that regulate its practice; and the way subjects understand themselves, or recognize themselves as subjects of the field. Applying this to organization studies, rationality can be identified as disembedded and disembodied, reflecting the savoir that constructs the field of knowledge; embedded and operational in specific locales that regulate its practice; or embodied, informing the way in which the subject understands himself or herself. Each of these different axes constitutes the operation of power/knowledge within the field. And, as knowledge regimes provide 'subject positions' from which the individual may speak, each of these rationalities entails that individuals 'position' themselves in different ways. The savoir of the field of organizations and management is the economic, bureaucratic, and technocratic rationalities that construct the position of a disembedded self. It is this self which adopts a disinterested overview. An embedded subject position informs and is informed by the institutional, contextual, and situational. Each outlines how rationality may be used in specific fields. An embodied rationality recognizes the rationality located in the body, which is accessed through physical awareness, feelings, and cognizance of seemingly insignificant 'irrationalities'. Each degree of embeddedness has implications for how it constructs the individual and produces different subject positions from which to speak. Each form of rationality informs what is legitimate and appropriate; rational, within its own sphere.

A focus on rationality and rationalities also provides an entrée for the individual as they approach organizations. The individual acts to make situations encountered rational, in the sense of their being open to reasons and an assessment of reason. Approaching organizations through an analysis of embedded modes of rationality is a means by which the individual may grasp the modalities of power that they encounter.

Practical concerns

This odyssey into rationality was initially stimulated by a desire to explain some of the deficiencies encountered with a 'rational' technique, performance measurement systems, and in particular, some of their 'irrational' consequences (Townley 2008).[2] Although performance measures have been part of the political agenda within the public sphere since their adoption in the post-Second World War period, they have failed to live up to their promise (National Audit Office 2001). Experiences in the private sector also indicate problems (Meyer 2002). Studies document the disappointments: distortions of operational goals and programmes; the creative reporting of measures; the encouragement of a 'measurement mentality' with the collection of information rather than knowledge and learning; the routinization of measures with little impact on policy; and irrational expectations of what targets may achieve (Carter et al. 1992; Paton 2003; Smith 1993).

Explanations for these outcomes point to the 'usual suspects': lack of support and resources for their implementation; insufficient time for their introduction; conflicting stakeholder demands; and institutional versus managerial requirements in their operation (refs). Rationalizations that might be offered as practice fails to conform to theory are those that accompany any unsuccessful introduction of a management technique and include faith ('there is no problem'); salvation ('it's the process that counts'); elaboration ('just you wait'); reversion ('back to basics'); and pitfalls ('it's them not us') (Mintzberg 1994). All of these have a degree of plausibility. But are we then, just then, faced with the eternal optimism of an administrative mind, and that next time lessons will be learnt?

In place of this, I offer an analysis in terms of conflicting rationalities that are brought into play in the attempt to flesh out what is involved in implementing a rational technology (Townley 2002*b*). With regard to performance measures, my argument is a simple one. Performance measures do not work. They are made to work (Townley 2004*b*; Townley and Doyle 2006; Townley et al. 2003). A performance measurement system is a theoretical construct. It is operationalized in a set of concrete practices. It has to be socially accomplished. Performance measures are recommended as a rational tool, part of the rational panoply of effective management and organizational functioning (Townley 2002*a*). Their purpose is clear; the means whereby this is achieved are not. Their recommendation lies in their rationality. No rational individual could deny that their objectives are desirable and rational. Ergo performance measures are rational.

And therein lies their difficulty.[3] Rationality does not inhere in an action, recommendation, tool, or policy. It is ascribed (Weber 1978). Rationality is ascribed by those who encounter a recommendation, tool, action, request, etc. on the grounds that it meets the requisite warranty for its operation (Toulmin et al. 1979). In other words, something is rational 'in context'. To become an acceptable and accepted technology, performance measures must be able to address reasons for their introduction. They are introduced to focus on 'what is the goal, purpose, objective of what we do?' (an economic rationality). But performance measures simultaneously prompt questions of 'what to measure?' (a bureaucratic rationality); 'how to measure accurately?'

BOX 10.1. 'IRRATIONAL' MANAGEMENT?

Performance measurement systems are rational procedures designed to achieve a number of objectives:

> to provide a 'clear public statement of what the Government is trying to achieve'
> to provide a 'clear sense of direction to delivery agents'
> 'used wisely', to provide a focus on delivering results in the form of improved services
> to provide 'a basis for monitoring what is and what isn't working'
> to 'ensure that good practice is spread and rewarded' and 'poor performance is tackled' and to ensure accountability to the public through regular reports   (PSAF 2003: 3)

The desired effects of such techniques will appear 'as if by magic'. Measures themselves are ascribed an agency that will effect change (see also Box 9.1):

> The targets will help eliminate the rubs...

Once spoken and after a moment of reflection, this remark was subsequently amended:

> ... The targets will measure the elimination of the rubs.   (Policy)

It is the attempted rationalization of a sphere that can only lead to a specific form of 'disenchantment':

> It's not immediately obvious why you get measures. But when you do, does anything change? Does anything improve?   (Social work)

(technocratic); how do these help me understand what my job is and know what to do?' (institutional and contextual rationalities); 'how does this help me now?' (a situational and embodied rationality); and 'how do we all understand what it is we're doing?' (a collective rationality). All these rationalities are brought into play to render 'rational' technologies rational. 'Rationality' is an activity. It is produced through, and in, action by those engaged in coming to terms with its operation (Flyvbjerg 1998).

The failure to recognize this means that the enchanted still informs a large element of management practice (Gambling 1984). For the rational image to accurately describe that which takes place in organizations, there has to be a suspension of belief, or rather a suspension of disbelief. 'Rational accounts' rely on a belief in the magical properties of rationality. They ignore reason as labour; the work in making or rendering something rational. The latter involves choosing the form of rationality from a range of repertoires, applying and measuring against appropriate warrants and forming a conclusion as to whether something is rational. This is an ongoing labour. As Foucault recognizes, rationality is hewn from 'unreason'. Learnt strategies or tactics are employed or worked upon to construct reason and to keep unreason at bay. There is work involved in being rational and ascribing rationality to something and what the empirical material sketches are the various labours that are engaged in, in hewing its form.

The argument put forward is that as a concept, a performance measurement system, can only be made to work because people imbue it with different understandings or rationalities, in order to make it work. The rationalities, in their various ways, function to facilitate coordinated action or activity. They ensure 'the establishment of a workable level of certainty' (Weick 1969: 91). Technologies are informed by the rationalities that operate within a particular field and are made rational through this. These rationalities may sometimes conflict, and take precedence at different times in the formulation and implementation process. Exhortations that often accompany their introduction, that performance measures must be 'owned' by the organization; must be credible; resist manipulation; lie within the control of the organization, etc. fail to capture the significance of their social accomplishment and in doing so easily become understood as being a technical exercise.

Practical rationalities

But what has been achieved through such a focus? First, it denies the sovereignty of reason. Rather, reason is an activity, a social practice. People have to learn to reason. They must know 'how' to be rational. Gauthier (1982) argues that the ability to choose which concept of rationality prevails is in itself an important element of being fully rational. 'A person who is not able to submit his connection of rationality to critical assessment . . . is rational only in a restricted and mechanical sense. He is a conscious agent, but not fully a conscious agent, for he lacks the freedom to make, not only his situation, but himself in his situation, his practical object' (Gauthier 1982: 103). Part of learning to reason is learning what reasons are deemed credible in what contexts, and conversely what types of reasoning are dismissed as lacking credibility. A practice-based view of reason, where reasons are grounded in social practices, introduces the concept of appropriateness. Reason as appropriateness or well-groundedness exploits the analogy between knowledge and rationality and also sees rationality as being experientially grounded (Audi 1990). Some reasons are more appropriate than are others in certain circumstances. Being rational is judged according to the norms of plausibility or acceptability in context. As Toulmin (2001: 21) notes, 'if we concentrate our attention exclusively on the propositions that figure in an argument while ignoring the situation in which it is presented, we can be described as viewing the argument from the strict standpoint of rationality.' Reasonableness, however, requires that we balance the formal structure of content with the situation of its presentation. An argument may be coherent and rational but inappropriate to the situation, and hence unreasonable. Equally, the argument may be appropriate to the context but inadequately formulated. Rationality must have both a formal (an internal coherence) and a substantive soundness (an appropriateness).

But this is not to argue that the forms of rationality coexist as equals. Far from it. Disembedded forms of rationality are highly privileged, particularly an economic instrumental reason, but also the scientific. Other forms, particularly the situational and embodied, are often marginalized and treated as 'irrational'. The elevation of a certain type of rationality and its ability to stand unquestionably as *the* form of rationality has denigrated other forms, particularly that known to the situated knowledges that inform daily practice, and the everyday certitude that gets things done. Although the disembedded, the embedded, and embodied are different forms of reason, it is not the case of one being superior to the other. Multiple rationalities, founded on Davidson's principle of interpretive charity, that is, the idea that one is 'acting rationally or reasonably' or 'one has a good reason for action' should emphasize 'uncertainty, disagreement and respect for the variety of reasonable opinions' (Toulmin 2001: 206). Politically, explanations for the failure to adopt a 'rational' technology or practice cannot take comfort in the asymmetry of one position being rational and the other not.

Nor is it to pose reason or rationality as distinct from, or the counter to, power (or its being the only form of power). The exercise of reason is inextricably linked to the operation of power. Forms of rationality operate as forms of power/knowledge. They have direct power/knowledge effects and consequences. A first step in highlighting the power effects of rationality in organization theory has been this excavation of its various manifestations, how they have been directed and used in organization studies, and how they are manifest in debates on the introduction of a particular management technology. It is the first stage of an archaeology of rationality in organization studies and how it has been constituted. These rationalities are presented as 'structures' or 'grammars'. They are vocabularies with rules of use, grammars that structure debate into certain considerations. The grammars that these rationalities provide, however, is not the playing out of a script. There are conflicts among different rationalities as well as contradictions within them. This enables strategies of choice to be adopted; not unlimited, but choice, nonetheless. The next step would be an analysis of how 'different power actors . . . operate in and through different rationalities' (Clegg 2002a: xi). Which rationalities gain ascendancy in which contexts, why, and with what effects? What constitutes the conditions within which certain types of rationality may be expressed? In other words, the next stage would be an analysis of the sovereign concept of power and a genealogy of how these rationalities are specifically played out in practice as certain agents privilege one form of rationality over another, or sedimented practices give a structural bias that gives one form of rationality prominence. Together, an archaeology and a genealogy would constitute the 'different foundations, different creations, different modifications in which rationalities engender one another, oppose and pursue one another' (Foucault 1983: 202).

The focus on rationalities is with the intention of avoiding the position of being 'for' or 'against' reason. But if rational argument is not extra-historical or rational according to a universalistic set of criteria, and reason is inextricably caught up with power, what of the possibilities of reason? What is reason's role? Foucault's position is not to operate 'outside' reason. It is not to reject reason. Reason is necessarily a tool of the trade, the necessary prerequisite of the presentation of a reasoned argument or defence. Reason 'succeeds' not through the force of a better argument, however, but because it is taken to be 'sound' at that time.[4] This is the sense of its being context dependent. But knowing what position is appropriate in given circumstances also lays the foundation of questioning why certain types of reasoning are dismissed as lacking credibility. The act of engaging reason is to challenge reasons. The function of critique is reflecting on reason's constraints. Reason and its historical forms are criticizable. This is the political project of critique.[5] Argumentation, challenging 'validity claims', and publicizing hidden disciplines all presuppose that criticisms and arguments will have weight. The debate is whether the exercise of critique is sufficient in itself or whether criticism has to have an 'emancipatory' force (Chambers 1996).[6] For Foucault, critique comes from method. Archaeology, the method of outlining what is permissible within a certain discourse, or that which sustains certain practices, provides for the possibility of the politics of new modes of thought and action. Critique for Foucault is 'Not "What can I know?" but rather, How have my questions been produced? How has the path of my knowing been determined? Not "What ought I to do?" but rather How have I been situated to experience the real?' (Bernauer 1990: 19). It is critique as 'deconstruction'. However, 'Critique does not have to be the premise of a deduction which concludes: this then is what needs to be done' (Foucault 1981 quoted in Philp 1985: 77).

Although the role of critique is political, grand schemes are eschewed because reason is embodied in social practices. The link between critique and practical activity is firm in Foucault's work; he writes,

if prisons and punitive mechanisms are transformed, it wont be because a plan of reform has found its way into the heads of the social workers; it will be when those who have to do with that penal reality, all those people, have come into collision with each other and with themselves, run into dead ends, problems and impossibilities, been through conflicts and confrontations; when critique has been played out in the real, not when reformers have realized their ideals.   (quoted in Philp 1985: 77)

Critique lies in specific experience. 'Criticism renders transparent what had previously been hidden, and in doing so initiates a process of self-reflection, in individuals or groups... a change in practice is a constitutive element of a change in theory' (Connerton 1980: 20).

But then, is everything reason? Davidson (1990) notes that psychoanalytical explanation extends the range of phenomena that may be subject to 'reason explanations'. Is the argument presented here equally all encompassing? Davidson (1990: 462) refers to this as the 'paradox of irrationality': 'if we explain it [irrationality] too well, we turn it into a concealed form of rationality; while if we assign incoherence too glibly, we merely compromise our ability to diagnose irrationality by withdrawing the background of rationality needed to justify any diagnosis at all'. Does rationality as a viable concept require a well-defined sphere that is external to it? As Swidler (1973: 42), in her analysis of Weber's concept of rationality, writes, 'there is always a sphere of social life which is non-rational, and it is on the preservation of this sphere that the rationality of the rest of the system depends.' Irrationality is usually taken to be the opposite of rationality, the absence of reason and understanding. It has been described as 'a failure of the house of reason: Irrationality appears only when rationality is evidently appropriate' (Davidson 1990: 458). Posing multiple rationalities does not deny that irrationality is an important concept. The 'irrational' is not a distinct province, however. Things are rational or irrational within their own sphere. The question then arises, how are these spheres integrated?

Practical reason

In the range of rationalities that constitute this working out of the contingent and particular to the total, one facet of reason has not been directly examined: practical reason, that which addresses the question: 'how do we make wise decisions?' In an eloquent passage, Clegg (2002*b*: xxviii) writes of the ethical import of organization theory:

> organization analysis implies a substantial moral responsibility...The responsibility should not be shrugged off lightly or reduced to a mere technical discourse...It should be acknowledged for what it is: a conversation with the living and the dead about those conditions of social existence that we imagine for the future, as well as a struggle to establish powers that can transcend those histories we inherit, in the service of those futures we can imagine.

The role of reason in guiding ethics is much debated. Reason's evolution gives much weight to moral positions as being distinct from reason, Hume's 'tis not contrary to reason to prefer the destruction of the whole world to the scratching of my finger' being a particularly extreme example of this (quoted in Cullity and Gaut 1997: 7). A Humean morality is neither rational nor irrational. It depends on motivation or passions. The link between reason and morality is limited to means. Reason is 'goal' directed not 'truth' directed. This leads to an 'ethical irrationality' that holds that there is no rational way of deciding between plural value commitments. A clash over ends and values are not amenable to being solved in a rational manner. 'Actions can be justified in terms of value judgements ... but every chain of reasoning eventually reaches some ultimate value judgement or value orientation that cannot be rationally justified' (Brubaker 1984: 99). This is Weber's ethical irrationalism.[7] 'Only in situations shielded from value conflict can choice be rational; between conflicting value commitments choice must be arbitrary' (Brubaker 1984: 60). This leads to a seemingly irrational position that fundamental choice depends on criterionless choice. It leads ultimately to the irrationality of an autonomous moral position, MacIntyre's (1981) emotivist or Taylor's (1995) subjectivist position. However, as Brubaker (1984: 101) points out, 'while fundamental choices cannot be rationally governed they can be rationally framed'. They are thus open to rational analysis for their logical implications and empirical consequences.

Kant's contribution was to argue that moral actions could be expressed in rational principles. Kant aligned morality with universalism: that which is ethical is that which is determined by rational, abstract, universal principles. Consistency and universalizability guarantee the correctness of the moral judgement. For Kant, something has value because it is the object of rational choice. It is what every other rational agent would choose and it should be willed as such, because rational beings act according to generalizable and universal principles. Moral requirements are the requirement of reason (moral rationalism); reasons are shared with other rational beings (the categorical imperative). Kant's call to universalism, however, appeals to the construction of a disembedded and disembodied logos, principles that hold true for all human beings indiscriminately, overcoming the particularities of the merely personal. As Young (1997) notes, however, universalism cannot eliminate the specificity and variability of the circumstances in which judgements must be made, that which makes the circumstances distinct. The attempt to do so not only devalues the difficulties that individuals face dealing with practical moral life but also 'imposes an impossible burden on reason itself' (Young 1987: 68).

An alternative to either an ethical irrationalism or a universalism is to be found in practical reason. Practical reason has several meanings in the literature. At its most literal, it refers to time- and situation-specific reasoning with the aim of achieving a practical outcome. Action that is a consequence of practical reasoning is action that is appropriate or reasonable at a particular time of action, that is, useful to realize an expressed aim. Practical reason, however, is more than this. It is a form of *phronesis*. The term derives from Aristotle who distinguishes between an intellectual understanding of theory or concept, an analytical scientific knowledge (*episteme*); techniques for dealing with practical problems, technical knowledge or know how (*techne*); and knowledge to know how to apply these knowledges in practical situations or circumstances in concrete cases dealing with actual problems (*phronesis*). All are guided by a broader wisdom, Sophia (Toulmin 2001: 190).[8]

Phronesis is understood as prudence or practical wisdom (Flyvbjerg 2001; Townley 1999). It is an instrumental rationality in the sense of being practical in its orientation of getting things done, but is balanced by the recognition that rationality encompasses context, judgement, experience, common sense, and intuition. This is not to argue that practical reason is of a different order from other forms of reasoning. *Phronesis*, and its Latinate term practical prudence (as in jurisprudence), involves judging an issue in relation to its 'case history', guided by an understanding of universal or general principles.[9] It is the balance between the reasonable judgements of the practitioner, and the formal computations of the rationally applied theorem, techne or instrumental knowledge. It is the rejection of a single set of criteria defensible across all contexts, but makes 'rational assessments stepping stones to reasonable decisions' (Toulmin 2001: 213). Theoretical reason should serve practical reason. Theorizing is but one form of practice alongside the other forms of practice that go into making a domain function (Toulmin 2001). From this, more, rather than less, knowledge contributes to a more rational and informed judgement. What is important are the 'complex particulars' reflected in the indeterminacy and multiplicity of contexts. The situation in which something takes place speaks to its 'rationality' as much as the general to which it might be referring. To use practical reason is therefore to judge in the light of all available and relevant information. It is a link between understanding and practice. It is through this daily working out of the relationship between the particular and contingent to a total position that reason is reaffirmed and itself constitutes the exercise of practical reason (Benhabib 1992).

Its method of development is experience. There is an emphasis on the concrete details of practical experience and practical wisdom is built up through reflection on experience. It does not 'devolve' from abstract knowledge; it does not argue from foundationalist assumptions. As an approach to what constitutes reason, it implies a toleration of ambiguity, complexity, uncertainty, and pluralism. 'Practical rationality depends far less on formulas and recipes than on a keen grasp of the particulars seen in the light of more general principles and goals' (Forester 2000: 33). It is the active, hard, work that is involved before 'decisions' are made, attentive listening, paying attention, teasing out issues, awareness, and engagement, not the following of rules or formula (Forester 2000; Weick 2001). The full exercise of rational powers requires life to be broad based, rather than narrowly exclusive, and thus able to draw upon a range of experiences to guide judgement (Homiak 2002).

To return to the pictorial dimension that illustrates the argument of the book, Picasso's *The Bull: Six States from One Stone* (see Figure 1.1). To engage in a disembedded rationality alone is to act as a homunculus. The 'rational' procedures that result furnish the irrational consequences and outcomes that is an oft-noted aspect of rationality, the consequences of actions in ways unforeseen by actors, the 'cunning of reason' (Hollis 1987). This is identified in Weber as the 'paradox of consequences': a formally rational system that does not lead to substantively rational outcomes.[10] It is reason as Simon's (1990: 191) 'gun for hire'.[11] It is the impartiality that informs the search for 'objective' knowledge, not restricted to being fair and considering others' needs as well as one's own, but impartiality as 'outside' or 'above' the situation about which one reasons (Young 1987). Equally, however, to be embedded and totally dependent on the situational, is not to see 'the big picture'.

A practical reason is the ability to retain the disembedded, embedded, and embodied dimensions of rationality and to incorporate or distil them into a unified understanding or picture. It is to be able to hold and see the interrelationships between all the dimensions of that with which there is engagement, the ability to see in the abstract the concrete and vice versa. It is informed by the knowledge of all subject positions, the disembedded, embedded, and embodied, to give a fully rounded interpretation of what suitable action should be. It is the combination of the disembedded 'knowing that', the epistemic knowledge that guides us; the contextual awareness of knowing how, a grounded awareness. It is 'knowing how', based on distilled reflective judgement of experience guided by a consideration of general principles. 'Phronesis requires an interaction between the general and the concrete; it requires consideration, judgement, and choice. More than anything else phronesis requires experience' (Flyvbjerg 2001: 57). It is to be able to make a judgement on a case using concrete, practical context-dependent knowledge informed by general principles. In this sense, it is allied to 'reason' as 'really knowing something'.

There are thus close links between practical reason and morality (Cullity and Gaut 1997). Reason is embodied in the playing out of specific social practices. This emphasizes not only its practical element but also its ethical dimension.[12] As Forester (2000: 6) notes, 'we learn in action not only about what works but about what matters as well.'[13] Practical wisdom lies in long experience and recognizes an everyday, interactional morality, where ethical issues are embedded in ongoing forms of social practice and experience. It is the morality of engaging with the specific, embodied, other. It is to understand 'the order of things', but in an embodied sense. 'We do not understand the order of things without understanding our place in it' (Taylor 1985: 142). It is an attempt to reintegrate the 'is' and the 'ought' of treating situations 'rationally (without distortion) and reasonably (without injustice)' (Toulmin 2001: 94).

BOX 10.2. PRACTICAL REASON AND THE SIGNIFICANCE OF THE EMBODIED OTHER

A failure to secure the effective functioning of the criminal justice system (CJS) impacts on those who encounter the service, employees, and ultimately the polis itself. For the vast majority of those who worked in it, the effective and efficient functioning of public service organizations is not only a political but also a moral obligation:

People do the job because they think it's important and worthwhile. They could probably earn far more money elsewhere, but they are here because they want to be there. It's an important and worthwhile job and they really like their work. (PFS)

The arguments that had most salience to those who worked in the CJS as to why there needed to be change were those that related to an idea of a specific other:

You have to remember that it's the most serious case in the world to the two witnesses and the accused, even at the District Court level. You must never forget this. It's the same for them as a murder in trial court. And they deserve the right for it to be handled in the best way that it can be. But the system will not really allow this to happen. The pressure of the case load does not permit this. (PFS)

The real indicators are the witness rooms and witness experiences, whether they get called or not and how long they wait. The measures that are important are not recognized.
(Court service)

The Justice Committee did some work in Glasgow on public views [on crime]. When the public is asked given a case of housebreaking, their response is 'prison'. But if you give them more details then their views change. The response is 'let's help them [the criminal] change'. It's a question of educating the population. (Social work)

As prosecutors, if we don't deal with the trivial stuff, who deals with it? It is not trivial to the people involved. It is too easy to see things as too trivial and it can seem like this is a court context. But it is arrogant of us to say we know what happens in your Scheme [housing estate], we need to see what happens in people's lives. (Sheriff)

An example of an effective approach is the Drug Courts, where the sentencer is involved. Usually the offender comes before different Sheriffs. Drugs treatment and testing was pioneered in the Sheriff courts. There are now specific drug courts. A judge and sheriff can instruct a Drug Testing and Treatment Order, which involves a commitment to the court, rehabilitation and random testing. They are brought back to the court on monthly basis. Drug courts take a long time. There are a series of appearances. But this builds up rapport with the punter. (Judge)

Reasons that 'made sense' for any suggested changes in process and procedure included broad principles such as a moral commitment to the CJS as a public good; what it is to live in a 'just' society; maintaining the ethos of CJS; protecting the accused; and preserving the integrity of CJS institutions. More often than not, however, it was the importance of lessening emotional distress; helping the vulnerable; giving protection from fear; helping people who are caught up by crime. These were deeply felt sentiments expressed by those working within it. These were factors that ensured that the existing 'system' functioned and that extra effort was forthcoming when things had to be made to work. But there was a deep scepticism of a rational

(*cont.*)

BOX 10.2. (*continued*)

performance measurement system, especially as it was seen as not being guided with a detailed knowledge of how the CJS operates:

You can't treat people like this. You can't treat people who work in the system, like this. You can't put people under this degree of stress. You can't impose targets unless you know how the system works. Once you know how the system works in detail, you know the work organization, then you can make changes. And to make changes without this information is immoral.   (anonymous)

This should not be taken to hide complacency. To be critical of the means chosen to secure a more effective functioning of CJS, overarching objectives and measures, is not to imply criticism of the ends. But it was the morality of the appeal to the specific other that guided decisions:

Basically we have taken a view that the Board is opposed to the development of targets. We don't want to be target driven. We are doing this for the benefit of the people involved *by* the system, not in the system. You should be able to see improvement without targets. Targets is not what's driving it. It's not why we're doing it. There were problems of which we were vaguely aware. We are now getting evidence. We can tackle these. I don't see this developing into a target driven system. This has been touched on in discussions but the agencies have set their face against this. This is not why we're doing this. It's important to be able to say, 'lets look at things strategically, we're about criminal justice at the end of the day, how do we achieve the final end'.

(Criminal Justice Board member)

It is interesting to note that improvements in the operation of the CJS came in response to recommendations for changes in High Court legal practice and procedure made by a senior judge, changes that are also percolating to Sheriff Courts. These changes addressed institutional and contextual reasons for change. Changes were also brought about through the findings of the mapping exercise that traced in detail how files circulate within and between the various agencies, thus addressing a situational and practical reason. Wisdom in these circumstances would indicate that measures should act as indicators of a 'direction of travel', part of the free circulation of information that informs practice in, and knowledge of, a sphere of activity, and never as a tightly connected cascade of targets and measures.

Conclusion

I wanted to do three things in this book: to introduce the different rationalities identified as operational within organization studies; to illustrate their use in some exemplars in the field of studying and understanding organizations and behaviour therein; and to illustrate their role in a practical example of the introduction of a 'rational' management tool, the introduction and use of performance measures in organizations. This is its theoretical intent. No doubt, it is between these three stools that the book will fall. For some, inadequate in its discussion of the various facets and dimensions of rationality; for others, paying insufficient attention to the subtleties of its use in organizational writings; and for others, ignoring some obvious elements of the role of performance measures and the empirical setting of the CJS. This is bound to be the case. A book that is at the same time modest and wildly ambitious could not do otherwise. Modest, because its intentions are to alert the reader to its possibilities; unmistakably ambitious in drawing upon such a broad canvas. I could offer some rational defence. Instead, I take comfort in a suitably trite aphorism of 'nothing ventured . . .'. It is a work in progress. It can be no other. But let us turn to its political endeavour. Its aim has been to give voice, to let 'real people' speak about 'real things', here, the introduction of a managerial technology that directly and concretely affects their working (and family) lives and the operation of a major institution in society. It is hoped that my approach has provided a framework and a vocabulary to make the operation of these processes and some of their 'irrationalities' more intelligible and understandable, more rational; and through this, to enable those working in organizations to address circumstances in which they find themselves and act upon this. As Flyvbjerg (1998: 229) notes, 'rational argument is one of the few forms of power the powerless still possess.' It is for the reader to judge the extent to which any of this has been accomplished. You decide.

APPENDIX

The criminal justice system (CJS) refers to an institution or a number of institutions and agencies that comprise a specific institutional field (Maguire et al. 2002). As an institutional field, it is asked to address and absorb a variety of discourses that coalesce around the concept of crime including statistics about crime (their collection, interpretation, significance, meaning etc.); people's experiences of crime; political positioning on crime; those who commit a crime; those who have a crime committed against them; crime as a social problem; crime as a social problem affecting certain socio-economic classes and circumstances (Hacking 1999). As crime has risen on the political agenda, so governments of all political persuasions have expressed increasing disquiet about the functioning of the CJS. In Scotland, there have been a number of reviews of various agencies and the CJS itself (Normand 2003; Bonomy 2002; McInnes 2004). Similar reviews have taken place in England and Wales and Northern Ireland (Auld 2001; National Audit Office 1999). Reviews of the CJS have indicated a number of issues: a lack of inter-agency communication; a failure of 'organizational empathy' (asking 'what does this mean for our partners?'); the lack of knowledge of each other's work; and insufficient direct contact between staff.

It is against this background that an initiative was proposed for the design of overarching objectives and targets for the CJS. The Normand Report (2003) had as its remit: 'Having appropriate regard to the interests of justice, to make proposals for the integration of the aims, objectives and targets of the principal agencies which make up the CJS in Scotland, in order to ensure the more efficient, effective and joined-up operation of the system and to secure delivery of the criminal justice priorities of the Scottish Executive.' The Normand Report (2003) recommended the establishment of a National Criminal Justice Board and Local Criminal Justice Boards to oversee the operation and performance of the CJS against overarching aims, objectives, and performance targets. Performance measures currently impact the police, prosecution, court service, and legal aid. Solicitors, advocates, the Sheriffs, and Judges (who also impact on the progress of cases) lie outside the purview of any performance target system. Research was conducted into responses to Normand's suggestions. Respondents were asked about their experience of performance measures within their own agencies, and their views on the likely impact of any overarching measures, and the role and functioning of the National Criminal Justice Board and Local Criminal Justice Boards. Most interviews however ranged far wider than the initial remit, with interviewees keen to talk in detail about the nature of their jobs and role and about broader issues and problems they saw facing the CJS.

Over eighty interviews were conducted with those involved with the CJS: members of the judiciary, sheriffs, prosecution service (PFS), police, advocates (barristers), defence agents (solicitors), legal aid, court service, prison service, social work, charities associated with the CJS, civil servants, and political representatives. The exceptions, it must be noted, were any interviews with victims of crime or convicted criminals.

Interviews were conducted in 2004 and generally lasted between one or two hours. Material is also drawn from attending both academic and practitioner conferences and workshops on the role of performance measures. Scotland is a small country. The CJS community is equally small with many known to each other. Thus, only the most general of identifiers have been used to identify the source of the quotes. (Policy, for example, refers to any senior organizational personnel whose principle activity is contribution to policy.) This is to preserve confidentiality and ensure anonymity. Occasionally, the term 'anonymous' has been used where it is believed an identifier would have allowed the organization or agency to be recognized. It must be remembered that the comments expressed are personal views. The quotations are not to be taken as verified practice, but are vignettes indicative of a rationality at work and must be read as such.

1 Foucault and rationality

1. Critics may argue that the economic definition of rationality is quite precise and quite precisely used. It should not therefore be set up as a paradigm for rationality. The argument that a discipline can maintain control of its boundaries is disingenuous. It assumes that disciplines are given (Abbot 1988*b*) and that boundaries are non-porous. Simon (1978*b*: 2) notes that 'rationality is economics' main export commodity in its trade with other social sciences'. The dominance of the neoclassical economics paradigm is seen in a number of disciplines, including public choice theory in political science and rational choice theory in sociology. Pfeffer's (1993) argument for an orthodoxy in organization studies was prompted by a concern with colonizing tendency of rational choice and its dominance in other areas. As I illustrate, avenues in organization theory criticize particular elements of the definition of rationality.

2. It should not be forgotten that the 'triumph of reason' coincided with the physical exclusion of women in the major European witch hunts in 1450–1750, which reached their height in 1560–1650. Estimates range from 900,000 to 3 million women being executed, mainly burnt at the stake (Barstow 1994).

3. Toulmin (1990, 2001) shows it is from the mid-sixteenth century that the balance in the rational/reasonable axis began to tip in favour of rationality, and theoretical abstraction starts to gain pre-eminence and replace what he terms the 'balance of reason', that is, multiple ways of thinking. The clash between rationality and reasonableness characterizes our understanding of reason and rationality since the seventeenth century and the rise of deductive techniques (Toulmin 2001).

4. It is a position that derives from Kant, 'man, and in general every rational being, exists as an end in himself' (quoted in Lukes 1973: 49).

5. Interestingly, the work that first adopted this approach makes no justification for its approach. It begins: 'Central to our thesis is the idea that "all theories of organization are based upon a philosophy of science and a theory of society"' (Burrell and Morgan 1979: 1). These are then categorized according to their assumptions of ontology, epistemology, human nature, and methodology.

6. Rationality has been identified as a concept that allows us to bridge a range of social science perspectives. For Hollis (1987: 7), it is 'the category which lets us make the most objective yet interpretive sense of social life' allowing hermeneutics and causality to be linked. I wish to avoid 'the tendency to think out a question of what something is in terms of the question of how it is known' (Taylor 1995: 34), and defend a focus on rationality as a concept that has the most intuitive purchase for the individual as an active, competent knower of enquiry.

7. Rationality is the province of many social science disciplines, philosophy, economics, sociology, and psychology. Within sociology, it has been considered by Weber, Habermas, and Mannheim. Schutz (1943) identifies scientific and everyday rationalities and Garfinkel (1960) identifies the scientific and common sense.

8. Simon (1997: 118), writing in 1947, commented, 'The central concern of administrative theory is the boundary between the rational and the nonrational aspects of human social behaviour.' For Simon, however, the non-rational was confined to intended and bounded rationality 'the behaviour of human beings who satisfice because they have not the wits to maximize'. In a paper in 1978, March expanded a framework of calculated rationality in relation to strategies of decision-making to include limited rationality, contextual rationality, game rationality, process rationality, adaptive rationality, selected rationality, and posterior rationality.

9. Within organization theory, rationality's relevance, with some exceptions (see Bryman 1984 for an interesting discussion), has been dismissed. Brunsson (1985) critiqued traditional understandings of decision rationality in favour of action rationality in his analysis of public sector organizations. Argyris (2004) makes reference to reason and rationalization in his work on single- and double-loop learning. Albrow (1997) considers the emphasis on rationality in some depictions of bureaucracy at the expense of considering the affective element of organizations. Halpern and Stern (1998) consider rationality and decision-making. Shenhav (1999) considers rationality in relation to an historical analysis of engineers and management.

10. Shenhav (1999: 197) makes the point that this is the consequence of Weber's translation into American sociology, where rationality 'rather than constituting an external object of study...has become the prism through which the (social) world is conceived and understood'.

11. For Foucault, there are regimes of truth, which function to give the true, but are themselves the operation of power/knowledge. Rationality is one such regime of truth.

12. Both Simons (1995) and Gutting (1990) identify a great endebtedness to Kant in Foucault's work, including, for Gutting (1990), the conception of philosophy as the critical use of reason, and for Simons (1995), the positive view of power, and the questioning of what limits to knowledge, should be resisted. Foucault, however, does not aim to identify universal structures of all knowledge and moral action, rather his focus is critique, analysing, and reflecting on limits and arbitrary constraints, and opening up the possibilities of practical critique and possible transgression. Simons (1995) also identifies the archaeological method, that is, an examination of 'the history of that which renders necessary a certain form of thought', as borrowed from Kant.

13. Unreason also incorporates indigence, laziness, vice, and madness. Disciplinary practices have since distinguished these and their different social connotations. In *Madness and Civilization*, Foucault identifies the period studied as introducing a caesura between reason and non-reason. This then becomes valorized through the depiction of the animality of madness and the immorality of the unreasonable. He writes, 'to observe madness is to place oneself on the side of reason—one would be better employed observing reason' (Sheridan 1980: 15).

14. Debates on rationality raise, as Hume recognized, the issue of the ontological unity of the self over time. Because rationality is constructed or characterized as a capacity to relate to the future, that is, embarking on a course of action over time based on declared preferences, this requires an individual to recognize ties both to a former and future self. The early recognition of rationality as constructing the self is not prominent in rational choice literature. It is, however, an approach that is found in some ethnographic studies: 'It is by virtue of mundane reason that "persons" or "individuals" are constituted' (Pollner 1987: 151).

15. Foucault identifies the individual as one of the prime effects of power. He writes, 'The individual is not to be conceived as a sort of elementary nucleus, a primitive atom, a multiple and inter material on which power comes to fasten or against which it happens to strike...The individual...is, I believe, one of its prime effects' (Foucault 1980: 98). Lukes (1973) portrays the links between rationality and individualism.

16. The identities that have been used to frame discussion are informed by Benhabib's (1987) distinction between the generalized and concrete other. Benhabib (1987) introduces this distinction as a means of critiquing an ethics of justice and rights based on universalistic ethical principles rather than a more contextualized moral reasoning arguing from the specificity of others, that formed the basis of the Kohlberg/Gilligan debate on moral reasoning. Drawing on a philosophical lineage of contractarian theory from Hobbes to Rawls, Kohlberg wishes to claim that 'a moral self is viewed as a disembedded and disembodied being' (Benhabib 1987: 81). Benhabib wishes to demonstrate that a more contextualized judgement Gilligan identified reflects a moral maturity rather than an immaturity. Benhabib identifies the latter as the 'concrete' other as distinct from the disembedded and disembodied that characterizes the generalized other of Kohlberg's position. Reference to disembedded, embedded, and embodied selves is also influenced by Taylor's (1989) reference to the 'disengaged reason' and 'disengaged self' in his discussion of Descartes's work. The terms individual, self, identity, subject, and subject position are used interchangeably. For Foucault, knowledge regimes provide 'subject positions' from which the individual may speak. The different rationalities construct these 'subject positions' in specific ways. The reference to 'self' reflects the influence of Benhabib and Taylor. Just as MacIntyre makes use of the concept of a 'character' as a means of examining 'the way moral and metaphysical ideas and theories assume through them an embodied existence in the social world' (MacIntyre 1981: 28), the terms are used as illustrative of a general argument, rather than with a high degree of precision from their theoretical antecedents.

17. Posing multiple rationalities as a mode of analysis has drawn some criticism. Archer (2000), for example, is critical of the various complements that have been added to *homo economicus*. This leads, in Archer's (2000: 44) terms, to 'incommensurable situational logics...These different men all harmoniously cohabiting the same body...all confined to separate spheres of action and supposed to know their own place. What is it that ensures the complements do know their proper place...what prevents one from usurping the other?' What is being proposed is not an, however, 'addition' or adaptation of *homo economicus*, rather it is more analogous to the position adopted by Knorr Cetina (1981) who identifies scientists acting variously as practical, indexical, analogical, socially situated, literary, and symbolic reasoners.

18. Foucault draws the distinction between the analytical and the critical (Foucault 2001). The first ensures a process of reasoning is correct, that is, a statement is rational or true in that it is concerned with the ability to gain access to the rational or to truth. The second asks 'what is the importance for the individual and society' of being 'rational', knowing how to be rational, of people acting rationally, and being able to recognize this' (Foucault 2001: 170). This he labels the critical tradition. Like the archaeological, it is concerned with discursive systems that sustain practices and the effects of this, not with the reality or otherwise of their referent, that is, the 'reality' of madness or disease for example. (Although this does not deny that the phenomena that has been problematized may have 'some real existent in the world' (Foucault 2001: 172).)

Part I Disembedded rationality

1. From these origins, the supremacy of individual reason became linked in France to debates on interests and rights; in Germany, to German idealism and Romantic notion of uniqueness, originality and self-realization. In America, it is an abstraction that incorporates the concepts of autonomy, privacy, and self-development, becoming linked to free enterprise, capitalism, and liberal democracy (Lukes 1973).
2. The term 'Enlightenment' covers a wide range of references including the *philosophes* of eighteenth-century France, the work of Hobbes through to Locke, Smith, and the Scottish enlightenment. It is used here as a recognizable shorthand rather than a strictly reliable designation.
3. The systematization of reason also helped privatize abstract thought, removing it from, or making it more independent of, institutional or organizational structures in which it might take place.
4. Biographical detail in Kant's being a recluse, in contrast to Descartes as a former soldier and 'man of action' and hence an emphasis on method, may be pertinent here.
5. As Gellner (1992) notes, there is an important levelling quality in posing a universal reason open to all, equally applicable to all subjects and objects of enquiry, that is the ultimate arbiter of 'truth', independently of a person, institution, or text. But the strictures of training, 'proper education', for attaining 'pure thought' ensures that institutionalization is not escaped altogether.
6. Specific groups being taken as paradigmatic cases for the human is largely unrecognized in this presentation of universal reason.
7. It is a form of rationality that may be used in support of, or in opposition to, existing power structures.

2 Economic rationality

1. Elster draws the distinction between what he terms thin and broad theories of rationality. Thin rationality concerns itself with the consistency of beliefs and desires, and the actions which stem from these. A 'thin' theory of rationality would thus not preclude suicide, homicide, or genocide from being 'rational' action. A broad theory of rationality requires more than acting consistently with beliefs and desires. It requires that the latter are 'rational in a more substantive sense' (Elster 1985: 1). A broad rationality examines the principles of belief acquisition and uses judgement and autonomy as criteria with which to evaluate rational action. Judgement is the extent to which beliefs are rational given the available evidence. Autonomy is indicated by not being influenced by conformity, 'sour grapes' ('adaptation of preferences to what is seen as possible'), counteradaptive preferences (the grass is greener), an obsession with novelty, and drives (drives shape desires, but are 'non-conscious psychic forces' focused on short-term pleasure), that is, not known to the individual (Elster 1985: 16). What Elster seems to be aiming at is a notion of 'correct reasoning', that is, a conscious and reflexive thought process, based on a theory of explanation, prediction, and 'control' of events in the understanding of 'how things work', and being able to articulate reasons

for a positions. An evaluation of the 'broad rationality' of beliefs and desires introduces complexities to the analysis of rational action that provides a bridge with the literature on culture. It requires an engagement with the concept of context that provides rationality its foundation (see Chapter 6).

2. Preferences should be transitive (preferring A to B and B to C, thus A to C), independent (of payoff for any other outcome), monotinicity (between the most and least preferred the most probable is chosen), and continuous (there is a balance between outcomes and preferences); see Halpern (1998).

3. The anthropomorphization of organizations has various manifestations. Most fundamentally, it is inscribed in law. Corporate actors are allowed to acquire rights and pursue interests (Marsden 1993). The anthropomorphization of organizations is also implicit in the literature on organizational identity.

4. Katz and Kahn (1966), following a Parsonian framework, identify productive/economic (business enterprise); maintenance (e.g. schools); adaptive (e.g. research institutes), and managerial/political (e.g. the state) organizations.

5. Blau and Scott (1962) identify beneficiaries as members (unions, clubs, professional associations); clients/public in contact (hospitals, schools, social services); owners/manager (firms, banks); and the public at large (fire, police, army, Inland Revenue).

6. Etzioni (1961) identifies coercive, remunerative, and normative types of regulation.

7. Woodward (1958) identifies types of technologies as single batch, craft, and large-scale production.

8. Ackoff (1970) identifies organizations based on their degree of homogeneity and heterogeneity (i.e. the relative balance of power of members versus the organization, a homogenous organization has more control over its members than they have over it, while in a heterogeneous organization members have greater control); and their modality, that is, the way that authority is distributed in an organization. This forms an elaborate unimodal homogenous organization (corporations, army, prisons, ships); homogenous multimodal organizations (multinational corporations and coalition governments); heterogeneous unimodal organizations (clubs, professional associations, political parties); and heterogeneous multimodal organizations (universities, employers confederations, congress, and communities).

9. For Mintzberg (1983), organizations fall into natural clusters or configurations depending on the balance between a strategic apex, operating core, technostructure, middle line, and support and how work is coordinated. This results in a simple structure; machine bureaucracy; professional bureaucracy; divisional form, and adhocracy.

10. Weber (1978: 48–9) defines organizations as: 'whether or not an organization exists is entirely a matter of the presence of a person in authority...More precisely it exists so far as there is a probability that certain persons will act in such a way as to carry out the order governing the organization; that is that persons are present who can be counted on to act in this way whenever the occasion arises'.

11. Simon (1959) identifies three features of decision-making that he finds missing in classical theory: setting an agenda of which decision are to be made when; factors that influence which problems are selected for attention; and how a problem is formulated or presented.

12. In Simon's original version, the boundedness of rationality is a useful, necessary contrivance by which rational beings let decisions beyond a certain range of interests take care of the themselves, or rather be taken care of by relying on organizational or environmental cues. The original idea comes from Barnard's 'zone of indifference', an area where authority has

no problems. 'Bounded rationality (at least in Simon's first formulation and in Barnard's concept of a zone of indifference) is an unfocused area of ideas and purposes. For each individual, it indicates a horizon of appropriate relief from vigilance and respite from choosing, without implying anything about incompetence' (Douglas 1995: 107). This subsequently developed into satisficing and bounded rationality. 'The scope of the wording suggested that bounded rationality is an aid to competent decision, since without being bounded, rationality cannot work at all...However, bounded rationality has come to mean merely the limits on cognitive competence' (Douglas 1995: 106).

13. Staw (1981/2002: 355) identifies consistency in a course of action as important for actors. Thus, both a prospective and retrospective rationality function in commitment decisions, and individuals may be motivated to rectify past losses as well as seek future gain. Commitment thus escalates beyond what would be warranted by the 'objective' facts of the situation. The past influences decision-making in that individuals are more likely to use exonerating rather than implicating information, thus the search for information is affected.

14. Brunsson (1985: 27) writes, 'organizations have two problems: to chose the right thing to do, and to get it done. There are also two kinds of rationality, corresponding to the two problems: decision rationality and action rationality.' Confusing the two can lead to the irrationality where decision-making is seen as being the sole purpose of a function with the assumption that action will follow. Brunsson's distinction has parallels with Simon's (1997) distinction between economic man and the administrator: between one who maximizes and one who 'looks for a course of action that is satisfactory or "good enough"'.

15. Money was identified by Weber as the most technically perfect measure because it allows the comparison of two unlike things on a scale common to both. It is a common yardstick for that which has 'value'. Thus, the 'value' of money is that it supplies the foundation of 'unambiguous' calculation. 'Uniform numerical statements become possible' (Weber 1978: 82). He writes, 'from a purely technical point of view, money is the most perfect means of economic calculation' (Weber 1978: 86). The formal rationality of economic action refers and relates to the extent of quantitative calculation (accounting) that is technically possible and actually applied.

3 Bureaucratic rationality

1. From this framework, the Aston School identifies personnel bureaucracies (high concentration of authority, low structuring of activities, examples would be central and local government); full bureaucracies (high authority and structured activities, units in large organizations); non-bureaucracies (low concentration and structure, small private companies); and workflow bureaucracies (low concentration of authority but highly structured activities, manufacturing organizations) (Pugh et al. 1968).

2. These dimensions are then tested against the impact of ownership, control, size, history, technology, independence (autonomy), and location, thus turning bureaucracy into a variable, that is, of organizations being more or less bureaucratic (Pugh et al. 1969).

3. Mintzberg (1983) identifies machine and professional bureaucracies; while the former are centralized and characterized by formalized procedures, functional grouping, and limited horizontal decentralization; the latter are characterized by vertical and horizontal decentralization, for example, hospitals.

4. These are characterized by lateral coordination and networks; cross functionality; teams or project groups; problems or people defining jobs; informed consensus rather than hierarchy; information sharing; influence based on the ability to persuade rather than an official positions of power and command; informed consensus rather than institutionalized authority and rules; integration based on interdependence and organization mission rather than the rational definition of offices; guidelines based on principles (i.e. reasons behind rules); and work based on expertise and temporary networks (Heckscher and Donnelson 1994).

5. Udy (1959) distinguishes between bureaucratic and rational elements in formal organizations and concludes that bureaucracy and rationality may be mutually inconsistent in the same formal organization. For Udy (1959), bureaucratic characteristics are dysfunctional for the institutionalization of rationality.

6. Themes of hierarchy, continuity, impersonality, and expertise link bureaucracy as a system of administration with bureaucracy as a type of political system. Arising in the eighteenth century as a theory of government, taking its name from the bureau, the writing table where officials worked, and in contrast to monarchy and aristocracy, bureaucracy proposes rule by officials or administrative elite (Beetham 1996). The division of labour refers to the division of governmental powers and their functionally restricted spheres of jurisdiction.

7. These are that a legal code can be established which can claim obedience from members of the organization; that the law is a system of abstract rules which are applied to particular cases, and that the administration looks after the interests of the organization within the limits of the law; that the person exercising authority also obeys this impersonal order; that only qua member does the member obey the law; that obedience is due not to the person who holds the authority but to the impersonal order that has granted him this position (Albrow 1970: 43–5).

8. These are that official tasks are organized on a continuous, regulated basis; that tasks are divided into functionally distinct spheres, each furnished with the requisite authority and sanctions; offices are arranged hierarchically, with rights of control and complaint being specified; the rules according to which work is conducted may be either technical or legal, but in both cases, trained individuals are necessary; the resources of the organization are quite distinct from those of private individuals; the office-holder cannot appropriate his office; administration is based on written documents which makes the office the centre of the modern organization; legal authority systems take many forms but are seen in their purest in a bureaucratic administrative staff (Albrow 1970: 43–5).

9. These are that staff members are personally free, observing only the impersonal duties of their offices; there is a clear hierarchy of offices; the functions of offices are clearly specified; officials are appointed on the basis of a contract; they are selected on the basis of a professional qualification; they have a monetary salary, graded according to position in the hierarchy. The official is free to leave the post and, in certain circumstances, he may be terminated; the official's post is his sole or major occupation; there is a career structure with promotion based on seniority or merit; the official may appropriate neither the post nor the resources that go with it; the official is subject to a unified control and a disciplinary system (Albrow 1970: 43–5; based on Weber 1978).

10. Rationality as a defence against uncertainty is a theme that pervades organizational studies. The contrast between rationality and uncertainty was explicitly adopted by Thompson (1967) as the dominant motif with which to analyse organizations. Placed within an analysis of rational and open systems, the former, the rational, emphasizes a determinate system that ensures prediction; the latter, an informal adaptive response, is based on the expectation

of uncertainty. 'One avoids uncertainty to achieve determinateness, while the other assumes uncertainty and indeterminateness ... Each ... leads to some truth, but neither alone affords an adequate understanding of complex organizations' (Thompson 1967: 8). He continues, 'The two strategies reflect something fundamental about cultures surrounding complex organizations—the fact that our culture does not contain concepts for simultaneously thinking about rationality and indeterminateness ... These appear to be incompatible concepts ... One alternative ... is the closed system approach of ignoring uncertainty to see rationality; another is to ignore rational action to see spontaneous processes' (1967: 10). Thompson's focus then becomes the reduction of uncertainty and its conversion to relative certainty.

11. Along with the rise of the legal systems and accounting, bureaucracy fulfils the requirement for calculability and the provision of predictability. The development of bureaucracy is identified by Weber as one facet, or one manifestation, of a broader process of rationalization. The latter encapsulates many different processes in different spheres of life, including a scientific rationality and technological innovation; the development of a universalistic rational law; dispassionate and impersonal administration and bureaucracy; calculated economic action, rational bookkeeping, and organization (Sayer 1992). Predictability and calculability through codification, systematization, and general 'disenchantment' characterize the development of rationalism in Western society. The formal rationality of economic action is introduced through rational economic calculation or accounting facilitated through money. Processes of classification and compilation characterize a rational legal system and a 'calculable' law. And the formal rationality of ruling or domination comes through bureaucracy. Calculable law, a functioning administrative environment, an accounting procedure that facilitates the operation of the market sphere and its calculability, rational technology, and technical knowledge all sustain a formal rationality that brings predictability to individuals' behaviour and actions, making actions both calculable and increasingly calculated (Sayer 1992).

12. The first is typified by the no-smoking rule which, despite signs, everyone ignores; the second are safety rules, respected by everyone; and the third, the no absenteeism rule, is imposed by management and resented by the workforce.

4 Technocratic rationality

1. 'To explain an action as resulting from an actor's reasons is to say that there is a sense in which these reasons are a cause of action' (Hindess 1987: 50). The definition of rational action places a strong emphasis on evidenced antecedent causality. It is not sufficient for me to believe that sticking a pin in a doll will kill someone for this to constitute rational action. The emphasis on antecedent causality influenced the decline of the belief in witchcraft, and the development of a distinct area of 'science'.

2. The translation loses the subtlety of meaning in that *techne*, in denoting 'know how' also denotes craft, and with this its links to art. It is the application of technical knowledge and skills, the bringing of something into being (Flyvbjerg 2001).

3. Thompson (1967) specifically addresses the relationship between beliefs and outcomes in his study of organizations and their technologies. He sees technical rationality as activity producing the desired outcome. This would require complete knowledge of cause and effect

relations and the knowledge and control of all relevant variables affecting this. For these reasons, Thompson sees technical rationality as achievable or perfected only within a closed system of logic. It is an abstraction. An automotive system is the closest example of an instrumentally perfect technology. Less-perfect technologies produce desired outcomes only some of the time, providing possible rather than probable success, for example, mental hospitals. In what he describes as patently imperfect technologies, beliefs are greater than outcomes, and he cites the example of the United Nations.

4. The parallels with Foucault (1977a: 228) are obvious: 'Is it surprising that prisons resemble factories, schools, barracks, hospitals which all resemble prisons?'

5. The essence of measurement is comparison and thus is distinct from counting. Measurement however, requires a standard, an abstraction. An abstraction has no natural base. It is Quetlet's 'average man' (Poovey 1993).

6. Representations may represent other representations. Sense may be conveyed by the spatio-temporal order of representations rather than resemblance or symbolization of an external object or 'reality' (Lynch and Woolgar 1990).

7. Despite a long history of antagonism technology and the technical also lay claim to the mantle of science. As Lynch (1982/2000: 289) explains, ' "Technical" is seen to be emblematic of a hardening or reification of the "body" of a discipline, since what was once the subject of widespread dispute, once a "revolution" was settled, was no longer as open to question and critical inquiry, but was instead taken up as the discipline's practices and tools by the second generation scientists.'

8. Canguilhem describes science as an exploration of the norm of rationality at work. His teacher was Bachelard; his student, Foucault. It is for these reasons that Gutting (1990) traces the debates about rationality in France through the studies of science and places Foucault's work within this tradition.

9. For MacIntyre, managerial expertise lies in the claims and aspiration to value neutrality, emanating from the division between fact and value in the seventeenth and eighteenth century. 'The manager treats ends as outside his scope; his concern is with technique, with effectiveness in transforming raw materials into final products, unskilled labour into skilled labour, investment into profits' (MacIntyre 1981: 30). The manager is the technocratic expert laying claim to two foundations of authority: 'one concerns the existence of a domain of morally neutral fact about which the manager is to be expert. The other concerns law-like generalizations and their applications to particular cases' (MacIntyre 1981: 79). These knowledge claims cannot be made good. 'Fortuna, the bitch-goddess of unpredictability cannot be dethroned' because of the unpredictable nature of radical conceptual innovation; the unpredictability of an individuals' future actions; the game theoretic nature of social life and the role of pure contingency in life.

10. As Ashmos and Huber (1987) indicate, the assumption that early theorists, who emphasized the 'rational model' of organizations associated with the 'closed system' approach, ignore the environment, is inaccurate. As is its obverse, that is, that open systems approaches first recognized the importance of the environment. The difference is one of emphasis and focus, the choice between internal structures and processes, or the identification of elements in the environment reflecting the broader nature of market circumstances. Closed is never in the sense of a self-referential system.

11. The 'standard of rationality for a technique' refers to the efficiency of a technique or means and, for Weber, is not the same as the technical rationality of an action. Nor is technical rationality synonymous with efficiency (Albrow 1970).

12. Guillen (1997/2002: 249) outlines scientific management's appeal to progressives to help solve social and industrial problems.

13. It is for these reasons that Hindess (1987) argues strongly that techniques and procedures are important objects of investigation by themselves. He identifies 'instruments' and 'representations of the world' employed in decision-making processes as laying the foundation of a critique of rational action and rational choice models that dominate politics.

14. Porter (1992: 52) uses the term calculation (as distinct from descriptive statistics and mathematization, the latter involving formula) to indicate the reduction of decisions 'to the comparison of numbers'. For Porter, the standardization of numbers provides one resolution of the problem of how to establish intersubjectivity. This can be achieved through routines and customs, local wisdom, or through tools of standardization and techniques. 'When meaning are not shared and face to face dialogue is impractical, rigid austere formalism may provide hope for settling contested issues.' It is 'way of forming ties across wide distances' (Porter 1992: 48). It allows for interaction between diversified societies and as such is a means of 'trading' (Galison 1999). Familiarity with numbers, and their legitimacy within certain domains, however, reflects historical and cultural circumstance (Cline Cohen 1999; Crump 1992). As Crump (1992: 34) notes, 'every language contains its own rules as to what can and cannot be counted.'

15. Rose (1999) contrasts a benign American history of the role of quantification in politics with a less optimistic European history. The reason for such a discrepancy lies in the political culture of quantification and its history. A large immigrant population in the USA placed a heavy emphasis on numeracy rather than language, the development of numerical skills, and spread of quantification in education, as an integrating mechanism (Cline Cohen 1999).

16. For Habermas (1971), the technocratic model of a scientized politics is the reduction of political power to rational administration. The role of the hermeneutic task is the reliable translation of scientific information into the language of practice and technical and strategic questions into practical questions.

17. Technocracy is defined as 'a system of social control based on scientific technical knowledge and instrumental rationality in decision-making. It involves highly systematized and codified forms of knowledge (science) and their systematic application in terms of technology, social engineering, information processing, decision making and work procedures' (Heydebrand 1979: 33).

18. A cost–benefit analysis was undertaken of the Pinto car petrol tank which was known to explode on collision. Although aware of the dangers, Ford initially took no action. A cost–benefit analysis of 600–700 deaths per year estimated compensation to be about $50m versus the $137m that would be the consequence of modifying the car design (Corbett 1994). In the case of the Holocaust, Bauman (1989: 197) cites the following example: 'A shorter, fully loaded truck could operate much more quickly. A shortening of the rear compartment would not disadvantageously affect the weight balance, overloading the front axle, because actually a correction in the weight distribution takes place automatically through the fact that the cargo in the struggle towards the back door during the operation is preponderantly located there. Because the connecting pipe was quickly rusted through the fluids, the gas should be introduced from above, not below. To facilitate cleaning, an eight to twelve inch hole should be made in the floor and provided with a cover opened from the outside. The floor should be slightly inclined, and the cover equipped with a small sieve. Thus all fluids would flow to the middle, the thin fluids would exit even during the operation, and thicker fluids could be hosed out afterwards.' As Bauman notes, 'The fact that the load consisted

of people about to be murdered and losing control over their bodies, did not detract from the technical challenge of the problem. [It had] to be translated first into the neutral language of car production technology before it could be turned into a "problem" to be "resolved".'

19. The separation between science and alchemy was not as delineated for Newton who has also practised alchemy.

20. In an influential paper, Merton (1936) refers to the latent consequences of purposive social action. This he attributes to (1) a lack of knowledge: while there may be ignorance, often it is not possible to obtain all the necessary knowledge, and even where there is knowledge of possibilities and some probabilities, this cannot be known in every case; (2) the influence of initial conditions: this makes the past problematic as a guide, there are also chance consequences that influence factors; (3) error: in appraising the current situation, the future situation, choice of action, execution of action, directed attention may lead to wish fulfilment and the neglect of other factors; (4) the imperious immediacy of interest: the concern with the immediate consequences precludes consideration of future or other concerns; (5) there are ramifications of the effects of action into other spheres because of the complex interaction of society; and (6) prediction influencing action: prediction becomes a new element in a concrete situation that changes the initial course of action.

21. Sensitivity to initial conditions and developments displaying path dependence were influential in determining their eventual success of VHS and the QWERTY keyboard despite their not being the superior technology (Frost and Egri 1991). Staw's (1981) work on the escalation of commitment to a course of action also illustrates the determining effects of initial conditions.

22. One simulation that takes its inspiration from complexity theory concerns the action of 'boids'. What are the rules that have to be generated to ensure that 'boids' will fly in a flock? A master plan with clear cut targets? Mission statements? Only three rules are needed: fly towards the middle of the group; fly at the same speed as the other boids, that is, match their velocities; fly near other boids. In other words, three simple rules can result in highly complex structures and complicated dynamics. Not only this, but also rules are local, or 'bottom up', based on boid-to-boid interaction and what the boid can do and see in the vicinity. The emphasis is on behaviour not the final result. Nothing was said about the overall shape or final result (Waldrop 1992). This emphasizes the importance of the situational (see Chapter 7).

23. Pettigrew criticizes conventional studies of change as being too rational. He argues for the need to 'challenge rational, linear, theories of planning and change where actions are seen as ordered and sequenced in order to achieve rationally declared ends and where actors behave mechanistically and altruistically in pursuit of organizational goals'. There is a need to capture the 'complex, the haphazard, and the often contradictory ways change emerges' (Pettigrew 1990/2000: 373).

24. The social studies of science is strongly influenced by Bloor's (1991) strong programme for the social studies of science which critiques the practice of referring to social factors when science is 'wrong' and assuming that when science is 'correct' it is rational. He argues that social factors influence both successful and unsuccessful outcomes.

25. The 'objectivity' of measures should not be viewed as representative of an objective 'truth' but as the exercise of power. 'Every measure as a social institution is an expression of a particular configuration of human relations...Kilograms and degrees were not given

by nature, but settled upon by scientists, industrialists, bureaucrats, citizens, kings and presidents' (Kula 1986: 101). What Kula (1986: 120) demonstrates is the transition from 'representational measures' with human associations, to 'abstract measures of convention, signifying nothing'. He details how, in order to function in widely divergent areas, measures have to become immutable, usually guaranteed by social control, supervision by authorities, or religious sanction.

Part II Embedded rationality

1. This is reflected in hierarchized oppositions between a seventeenth-century rationalism in opposition to a sixteenth-century renaissance humanism (Toulmin 1990), scientism and romanticism (Polanyi 1983), Enlightenment and Romantic ideologies (Bloor 1991). For Toulmin, renaissance humanism was informed by Aristotelian principles recognizing the circumstantial character of practical issues, their complexity and diversity, the particularity of human action. It recognized the importance of the oral, the particular, the local, and the timely (the rationality of a decision as highly contingent upon the moment), and implies a toleration of ambiguity, complexity, uncertainty, and pluralism. There was thus no requirement to generality or absolute certainty beyond the circumstances of the individual case. Abstraction necessarily involves omission, thus denying concrete diversity and the relevance of the particular. For Bloor, contrasting ideologies form archetypes that 'settle down in each of us and form a foundation and resource for our thinking' (Bloor 1991: 75). The methodological style of Romantic thought stressed the importance of the contextual, the concrete, and the historical; locally informed responses to situations. 'The particular case, provided it is viewed in all its concrete individuality, is thought of as more real than abstract principles' (Bloor 1991: 64). This forces the recognition of wholeness, intricacy, and the interconnection of social practices, their complexities. It is also recognized that social wholes cannot be understood as the collection or aggregation of their component or constituent parts, but have their own properties.

2. Evans-Pritchard (1976) was an anthropologist who studied the Azande investigating their beliefs in witchcraft and sorcery.

3. The question recalls Elster's argument that sticking a pin in a doll to bring about someone's death does not constitute rational action. Elster (1985a: 15) is anxious to exclude 'from the domain of the rational the rain dance of the Hopi', and 'consulting the horoscope before investing in the stock market'. It is interesting that he chooses and equates these two examples. While the latter might be dismissed as, if not irrational, then certainly superstitious in modern society; the former, both in terms of the activity's place and meaning within its society is of a different order altogether. A contextualist would argue that within its own context, it is a rational thing to do.

4. A 'bridgehead' would be the belief that people speak the truth, that there is a degree of coherence in their statements, and that there is an interdependence of beliefs. Other criteria might include: a quest for explanation; causal explanation; theoretical processes of abstraction and analysis; the use of theoretical models and analogies.

5. Relativism raises the issue of whether different groups order their experience according to different concepts, space, time, causation, identity, etc. (a conceptual relativism) or live in different worlds (a perceptual relativism) (Hollis 1982).

6. Criticism of a context-dependent concept of rationality is that it amounts to rationality as conformity to norms (Lukes 1970), thus either deeming rational any action that is not 'sociologically meaningless' (Jarvie and Agassi 1970). This would deny recognition of the social role of absurdity (Lukes 1970) or imply that thinking about a thing in a certain way could make it true (Hacking 1982*a*). (This is distinct from 'bringing' something into existence, the truth or falsehood of which must be contested.) If everything that is validated by the group is rational, on what grounds if any may one ascribe rationality? If all are rational, how might one account for contradictory positions? For others, the ubiquity of certain styles of reasoning, that is, the use of theory in explanation, prediction and belief, analogical, deductive and inductive inference in developing and applying theory, having stood the test of different social and historical contingencies, point to context-free styles of reasoning (Horton 1982). However, this position does recognize that the logic of the situation, the technical, social, and economic setting, explains different uses to which these skills are put.

7. The disembedded or disembodied self informs moral debate. 'The generalized other requires us to view each and every individual as a rational being entitled to the same rights and duties we would want to ascribe to ourselves. In assuming the standpoint, we abstract from the individuality and concrete identity of the other.' It is a position that informs Rawls's 'veil of ignorance' where one is asked to put oneself in the place of the other when making moral judgements about the suitability of a type of policy or practice. As Benhabib (1987) points out, however, the foundation on which the other is different from the self is thus obliterated. Without knowing the other, one cannot know what the situation would be for the other.

8. This is an argument that has parallels with the work of Schutz (1962) for whom, 'Man in daily life considers himself as the centre of the social world which he groups around himself in layers of various degrees of intimacy and anonymity' (Schutz 1962: 37). Schutz uses this organizing principle as a way of distinguishing between everyday and scientific rationalities.

9. This is not to argue that anything the individual claims as knowledge is thus true. Knowledge is verifiable according to the criteria of the community. It is thus non-arbitrary, non-subjective, and non-idiosyncratic (Longino 2002). The degree of 'objectivity' is dependent on the degree of argumentation and interrogation within the community, its degree of openness.

10. From this perspective, 'objective' becomes reformulated. Objectivity is a positioned rationality. It is not only accountability to the 'evidence', the veridical representation of the 'real world', but accountability is also to an epistemic community that is able to judge or evaluate it. It is a position that contests a correspondence theory of reality. Causes are but one form of evidencing reason. While in certain circumstances there is a practical verification (e.g. prediction of planetary motion) that is the 'test' of rational statements, most others are inherently perspectival.

11. For some, judging how something came to be taken as rational, that is, giving a sociological explanation is not the same as saying that beliefs are either true or rational. For others, there is no distinction between what are taken to be reasons and what really are reasons (Barnes and Bloor 1982). Lukes's (1982) 'resolution' of the debate was to isolate the discussion of rationality from statements relating to the existence of an independent reality, drawing the distinction between credibility (evidencing reasons) and validity (statements of cause). Rationality implies principles of logical consistency and coherence. Thus, actions and beliefs may be termed irrational if they break these principles. (For Lukes 1970, beliefs are irrational if they are illogical, inconsistent, or self-contradictory; partially or wholly false; non-sensical;

situationally specific or ad hoc; incorrectly held, that is, based on irrelevant considerations or insufficient evidence; unreflective or uncritically held; or contradict one or other of these criteria.) This is a different argument from that which has verifiability as a criterion of rationality. The latter would presume that the ascription of rationality has to make at least some reference to the explanatory basis of action tested against 'facts' or practical utility. It must be grounded in available evidence. [It is a distinction that has been labelled 'logical' versus 'scientific' (Winch 1970).] On the criteria of verifiability, the belief as to whether witchcraft is rational or irrational is governed by whether there are witches or not. While the Azande may be 'rational' in their belief in witches, given the coherence and consistency of the belief system itself; they may be less so in holding to a belief in witches per se, given that their actions are not causally efficacious. This criteria of rationality is heavily entwined with the scientific. Rationality involves reference to rational action as well as rational belief. Winch (1970), however, argues that there should not be an appeal to an independent or objective reality as what is taken as real depends on context and language use. Beliefs might be 'rational' in method and purpose, even if 'unscientific'. For Lukes, the criteria of truth (i.e. 'correspondence' with reality) and logic (i.e. logical relations between statements) are necessary criteria of rationality. Thus, though there are contextually dependent criteria for judging what counts as a 'good reason', this alone is not sufficient to satisfy a criteria of rationality. Reasons must be judged on both context-specific and context-independent grounds and both are relevant to judging whether a belief is rational or not (Lukes 1970). For critics, this evokes a correspondence theory of rationality.

12. It is a position that recognizes that the presentation of cases is in part dependent on the character of recipient audiences. Argument cannot be carried by fact or proof alone, but is influenced by its reception which is more akin to the Aristotelian position.

5 Institutional rationality

1. Rationalization thus encompasses the transition from a belief in spirits, to a belief in gods, and from thence to monotheism, and from magical divination to a belief in providence.

2. Thus, rationalization has been interpreted as the dynamic of capitalist development. Studies of rationalization highlight these points, for example, Thompson's (1967a) analysis of the rationalization of time; Marglin's (1974) details of the rationalization of space, Guillen's (1997) analysis of architectural space, and Braverman's (1974) presentation of the rationalization of knowledge in the labour process (Stark 1980). The essence of rationalization is that morality becomes detached from world views in which it was embedded and is placed in an autonomous sphere. It is this detachment from ethical value orientations that causes Weber to mistrust rationalization processes. Tambiah (1990) illustrates how the seventeenth century saw the gradual demarcation between religion and magic, with the former becoming more associated with a rational belief system and the latter deemed to involve rituals and manipulation.

3. Rationality is the control of actions by ideas: the wider an area over which conscious ideas have influence, the more rational a culture, society, or institution. Rationalization is the systematization of ideas and refers to the process by which ideas develop their own internal logic (Swidler 1973). It involves the clarification, systematization, and integration of ideas by

ordering discrete elements to make them more precise and internally consistent; integrating elements by finding a more abstract concept that relates them; and extending systems of ideas by increasing the range of cases to which they apply (Swidler 1973). Rationalization allows for a theoretical and a practical mastery of reality. It has an impetus of its own. The discipline of psychology, for example, may be the impetus for its techniques to be incorporated into personnel selection, with an increased professionalization and accreditation of an accompanying occupation, accompanied by training programmes, specialist personnel, and evaluators.

4. Although Weber identifies two great rationalizing forces in the extension of a market economy and bureaucratization, there is not a uniform, all pervasive universal law of rationalization (e.g. unlike the depiction of some presentations of globalization).

5. Value orientations are the inner properties of individuals, their beliefs, attitudes, and values. These are subjectively generated in the sense that they must be actively embraced and have a subjective validity. A shift in value orientations involves an internal reorientation. Value spheres reflect the values, norms and obligations of a distinct realm of activity, having an 'objective' existence (Brubaker 1984).

6. Conflict between value spheres is due to objective differences in the inner structure and logic of different forms of social action.

7. As Douglas (1987: 95) notes, 'Weber has taught us to see society in terms of institutional sectors that we know: these sectors are inhabited by priests, judges, intellectuals, elites, landowners, tenants, and outcasts ... problems of rationality are posed as problems that arise in the growth and conflict of these institutions.' Each social group generates its own view of the world, developing a thought style that sustains the pattern of interaction.

8. The existence of a substantive body of knowledge transmitted through systematized training; the certification of practitioners; broad social recognition of authority; and a commitment to a broader service enforced through a code of ethics are generally taken to be the defining characteristics of a profession (Abbot 1988*a*).

9. Toulmin et al. (1979) examine these fields of argument in relation to legal, scientific, artistic, managerial, and ethical spheres.

10. Neo-institutional theory is ambiguous in acknowledging its foundations in Weber's rationalization thesis, although they recognize the influence of Weber. The two germinal articles of neo-institutional theory (DiMaggio and Powell 1983; Meyer and Rowan 1977) draw strongly from Weber's work. Scott (1987) recognizes Weber as the premier influence on contemporary organization theory. Meyer (1992) locates his work within long-term processes of rationalization.

11. The problem for Meyer and Rowan (1977/2000: 276) is that this deviates from the lived experience of organizations where 'formal organizations are loosely coupled (structural elements are loosely linked to each other and activities); rules are violated; decisions unimplemented; or if implemented have uncertain consequences; technologies are of problematic efficiency; evaluation and inspection systems are subverted or rendered vague'. And yet formal organizations are 'endemic'. An explanation has to be offered that is not premised on the assumption that formal structures actually coordinate and control work.

12. As Barry and Hardin (1982: 370) note, 'The concept of rationality is pressed into service...in a desperate attempt to plug the gap left by the absence or weakness of social institutions of the traditional kind.' It is no coincidence that the appeal to performance management systems in the public sector has coincided with the undermining of professional

expertise that used to guide its operations, the denial of good faith assumptions, and public interest concerns in professional practice. A 'rational' practice or technology, that is, one devoid of 'substantive' content, holds out hopes of being neutral. For Barry and Hardin, rationality has thus become a default option in closing down arguments, requiring fewer presuppositions of an argument to be tested. Rationality, however, is being made to do an 'enormous amount of work'. 'The question is . . . whether the concept of rationality can stand the strain that this imposes on it' (Barry and Hardin 1982: 368).

13. As Meyer and Scott (1992: 201) note, a completely legitimate organization would be one about which no questions could be asked. Every goal would be 'specified, unquestionable'; every technical means, adequate with 'no alternative'; every human and external resource used 'necessary and adequate'; every aspect of the control system 'complete and without alternative'. Conflicts about goals, procedures, technologies, and resources prompt the demand for ever more elaborate documentation justifying activities. It is when these documents are compromises between legitimating authorities, that it becomes more and more difficult for those on the front line to link their activities to them.

14. Parsons (1956) distinguishes between the technical, managerial, and institutional roles in organizations. The technical refers to the sphere of work, those transformations that are required to turn inputs into outputs. Managerial roles are concerned with the control and coordination of resources and outputs, and ensuring that the technical is supported. Institutional roles engage with other organizations in the broader environment and represent the organization to outside bodies to ensure support in the wider community. It is a distinction that is carried over in some institutionalist analyses.

15. Technical systems, however, are themselves grounded in institutional requirements. There are a number of competing and inconsistent institutional rationalities, one of which is 'efficiency', others are purposefulness to external audiences. For this reason, Scott and Meyer (1994) distinguish between technical and institutional environments. In the former, a product or service is 'tested' in a market, in the latter institutional rules define meaning, patterns of appropriate activity, and the identity of actors. They constitute the purpose and legitimacy of organizations and professions and provide actors with reflexive depictions of their proper roles. Organizations are thus subject to strong or weak requirements in both, for example, strong technical and institutional requirements (e.g. airlines and banks); strong technical, weak institutional (manufacturing); strong institutional, weak technical (schools, mental health, churches, clinics); weak technical and institutional (personal service units).

16. The links between diffusion and legitimation are problematic. As DiMaggio (1991) notes, institutional theorists tend to emphasize legitimacy prior to diffusion, that is, practices are deemed to have legitimacy and are thus acquired. This underplays the extent to which the diffusion process itself legitimates that which is being diffused.

6 Contextual rationality

1. As Smircich (1983) notes, culture is used in anthropology as a 'foundational term' through which orderliness of social life is explained. Within organization studies, organizations are seen as analogous to culture in that they inform 'a particular structure of knowledge for knowing and acting' (1983/2002: 162). The adoption of culture from anthropology by organization studies has not gone uncriticized as being a concept of 'societal significance

in the context of life, death, kinship relations, religion, crime and punishment and ethnicity' to 'a form of anthropological kitsch' (Linstead and Grafton-Small 1992/2002: 229).

2. Given the retrospective nature of sense-making, Weick (1995: 189) is quite specific that 'Culture is what we have done around here, not what we do around here'.

3. A list of what is represented by culture, taken from Martin's (1992: 54) collection of various definitions, includes values, symbols, shared meanings, customs and traditions, historical accounts, norms, habits, expectations, rites, stories, myths, logos, heroes, verbal or physical artefacts, dress, office decore, and humour. Schein makes the distinction between levels of culture which include artefacts (visible organizational structures and processes); values (strategies, goals, and espoused justifications); and underlying assumptions (the unconscious taken-for-granted beliefs, habits of perception, thought and feeling that are the ultimate source of values and action).

4. The taxonomies are endless. For example, Handy (1989) identifies the power culture (watching the boss); task culture ('all hands on deck'); role culture (following procedures); and person culture (the importance of relationships).

5. Martin (1992) discusses degrees of integration, distinguishing between cultures where there is integration, differentiation, and fragmentation. This allows for ambiguity, conflict, and heterogeneity, in effect introducing the idea of nested cultures. While there may be an 'organization' with a particular 'ethos', within this there might be a variety of 'subcultures'. Consensus is thus reduced in scale, rather characterizing the subculture than a larger entity. It also differentiates 'official' culture as 'the system of meanings, values, and norms espoused by the managerial dominant coalition', and 'unofficial culture', 'the systems of meanings, values, and norms actually prevailing in the organization'.

6. It has led some to criticize it as a 'grab bag of norms, beliefs, values and customs' (Barley 1983/2002: 115). He continues, 'what does culture do? who shares it? of what is it composed? how are its parts structured and how does it work?' It is this critique that informs Barley's study of semiotics that raises 'background' assumptions into explicit focus. Pettigrew also describes culture as lacking analytical bite (1983/2002: 144).

7. As Linstead and Grafton-Small note (1992/2002: 230), through culture applied as a critical variable, 'the seemingly irrational could become rational and hence understandable by applying the correct techniques of interpretation, which was but a short step from making it manageable and amenable to assessment in terms of managerial goals'. 'Corporate culture' tries to influence perceptions and attitudes, as for example Van Maanen's (1991*b*) analysis of the role of screening, language, socialization, and emotional management at Disney. For Willmott (1993/2002: 274), 'Rejecting the view that the non-rational aspect of human organization must be eliminated (e.g. scientific management) or patronized (human relations) it is argued that these aspects can be legitimately and effectively colonized.' Willmott concludes, 'far from abandoning zweickrationalitat (instrumental rationality) corporate culturalism extends it to the affective domain'. In this, he is supported by the work of Barker (1993).

8. The problems of defining boundaries is exemplified by Alvesson (2003: 118). 'As with all cultural meanings, they are a mix of societal, industrial, organizational and group-level phenomena.'

9. Schein's (1994) definition focuses on a 'learning focus', identified as the external adaptation and internal integration of a group, and in doing so, provides some foundations for what was later to emerge in the communities of practice literature.

10. Turner (1973) also acknowledges that explanations, rationales, anecdotes, normative views, and myths would also be a feature of an industrial subculture.

11. Van Maanen and Barley (1984) take any activity used to make a living as work and thus an occupation. This is a broad definition of occupation not necessarily in keeping with the four criteria that they identify as the distinguishing characteristics of an occupational community. Thus, Van Maanen and Barley (1984) appear to distinguish between an occupation and an occupational community.

12. An important aspect of this autonomy is control of membership and their employment circumstances. Relative monopoly positions within the labour market are important criteria influencing these factors.

13. An element of an occupational group for Van Maanen and Barley (1984) is a claim to an institutional rationality. The examples they give are of air traffic controllers, police officers, taxi drivers, nurses, and emergency medical technicians, who 'all extol the virtues of service as an occupational creed'. With the exception of taxi drivers, the other groups can lay claim to the institutional rationale of public safety, security, and well-being within the purview of state responsibility for these issues.

14. A community of practice is defined as 'a set of relations among persons, activity and world, over time and in relation with other tangential and overlapping communities of practice' (Lave and Wenger 1991: 98). There is an issue as to whether a 'community of practice' entails co-presence. For Lave and Wenger, this is not necessarily the case. Factors that indicate a CoP include sustained mutual relationships; shared ways of doing things together; rapid flow of information; quick depictions of problems to be discussed and the absence of preambles; knowledge of others' abilities and knowledge; mutual identity construction; criteria for evaluation of actions and products; tools, representations, and other artefacts; shared stories and jokes; specific communication and jargon; membership 'styles'; and shared discourse or outlook (Wenger 1998: 125–6). The definition of a community of practice is problematic as Wenger (1998: 122) acknowledges. 'Should any work group be considered a community of practice? . . . Calling every imaginable social configuration a community of practice would render the concept meaningless.' Organizations are 'social designs directed at practice' (Wenger 1998: 241), that is, organizations 'bring together' different CoPs for a particular overall objective. Larger social configurations are referred to as constellations of practices.

15. For Brown and Duguid (1991: 48), a CoP may be 'nuclear physicists, cabinet makes, high school classmates, street-corner society.' Interestingly, one of the central elements of Frost et al's (1991) cultural analyses is an analysis of Whyte's 'Street Corner Society'.

16. Wenger directly addresses what he identifies as the differences between the CoP literature and the 'culture' literature. He argues that practice is more enterprise- and community-specific than culture. The claims for practices resonates with the claims for culture in terms of facilitating the resolution of conflicts, providing a communal memory, socializing newcomers, and providing an 'atmosphere' through stories, dramas, customs, etc. (Wenger 1998: 46). Given the nebulous definitions of some of these terms, particularly 'enterprise', debate is a little difficult. However, what seems to be the significant factor is the amount of direct engagement that takes place. CoPs depend on a frequency of interaction that definitions of culture do not require. Culture is rather a 'composite repertoire created by the interaction, borrowing, imposing, and brokering among constituent communities of practice' (Wenger 2003: 291). Wenger does however differentiate between shared meaning, a term he does not find useful, and a shared ownership of meaning. The latter is the ability

to negotiate a meaning in a given circumstance, that is, a competence in its use, rather than understanding exactly the 'same'.

17. It is debatable the extent to which the CoP literature has solved the problems noticed earlier as to whether a culture (or practice) defines a group (or community), or vice versa, or whether it falls into tautology. As Wenger notes, its terms predefine each other. While not all communities have practices, and not all practices create communities, a practice creates a community through mutual engagement, joint enterprise, and a shared repertoire. The terms are not very specific, being defined in terms of what they are not rather than what they are (see Wenger 1998: Chapter 2).

18. Wenger states that 'practice entails the negotiation of ways of being a person in that context' (2003: 149). This has similarities with earlier work on the negotiation of 'roles' in organizations, in that it entails ways of engaging in action with other people, accountability to the enterprise, and the negotiation of a repertoire.

19. The advantages that Gherardi and Nicolini (2002) claim for communities of practice as opposed to Schein's occupational subcultures is that there is not the assumption of shared meanings. Although different communities of practice have different understandings of how things work, the use of homonyms (same signifier, different objects) and decontextualization (same object, different terms) means that each 'can successfully talk about something without understanding each other' (2002: 430). It is the immediacy of the situated context (and often task) that allows communication to occur. It is an approach that emphasizes the role of the 'broker', those individuals who are able to communicate and translate between one practice and another, to span the boundaries between one meaning system and another.

20. An epistemic community is defined as a knowledge community whose shared meanings are broadened to include 'world views'. Thus, for example, 'Scientists keep watch over each other. Each scientist is both subject to criticism by all others and encouraged by their appreciation of him. This is how scientific opinion is formed . . . (Polanyi 1983: 72).

21. For Polanyi, 'consensus' can be achieved through criticism that may range from 'tussle' to 'mortal struggle'. He gives as examples literary and artistic circles and the contentious debates on merit that may occur there (Polanyi 1983: 84).

22. This reference to 'publicly demonstrable' is to distinguish the understanding of tacit from that used in Chapter 8 where it remains non-public, that is, it is knowledge given through the body and is known to the practitioner only.

23. Gherardi and Nicolini (2002) provide an example of the different contextual rationalities that inform the separate interpretations of safety and accidents given by engineers, site foremen, and the main contractors at a construction site. Foremen have an understanding of safety based on a relational rationality, gained from their role in trying to coordinate the temporal and spatial interdependency of bodies and equipments at the sites. This leads them to see accidents as inevitable, part of the order of things. Safety procedures try and minimize this. Engineers' understanding of safety is based on a technical rationality. Accidents should not happen. That they do is a failure of control, a lack of rules, or respect for rules. Site contractors' views of safety are based on an economic rationality, its likely impact on insurance, fines and work continuing, and their compatibility with safety costs.

24. Gabriel is keen to distinguish between narratives and stories. A narrative is 'a temporal chain of interrelated events or actions, undertaken by characters' (Gabriel 2004: 63). It implies sequence, and as a plot that ties sequences together becomes more apparent, then a narrative becomes a story. In the latter, there is attribution of motive, agency, causal connections,

responsibility, and a degree of providential significance. Stories allow a degree of license to the story teller. The 'truth' of the story is not its successful depiction of events, but in its 'meaning'.

7 Situational rationality

1. Schutz criticizes this model of rational action because it involves the actions of others; involves the self interpreting of the other's action as being rational and acting in a rational way, including involving knowledge of means, ends, and secondary results. 'This is a condition of ideally rational interaction because without such mutual knowledge I could not "rationally" project the achievement of my goal by means of the Other's co-operation or reaction...It seems that under these circumstances rational social interaction becomes impracticable even among consociates. And yet we receive reasonable answers to reasonable questions, our commands are carried out, we perform in factories and laboratories and offices highly "rationalized" activities' (Schutz 1962: 32). Schutz identifies scientific and everyday rationalities, Schutz' scientific rationality has four dimensions: a commitment to means–ends relations; semantic clarity and distinctiveness in relation to the situation; a clarity of rules of procedures; and acting according to a body of scientific knowledge.

2. Wright Mills is concerned to establish a sociological conception of motives and critique psychological understandings: 'The differing reasons men give for their actions are not themselves without reasons' (Wright Mills 1940: 904). He argues for an analysis of the situated actions of motives. We learn 'vocabularies of motive' appropriate to the situation in which we find ourselves. They are the 'typical vocabulary of motives of a situated action' (1940: 906).

3. Practical reason, for Garfinkel, is taken to be routine, semi-automatic, taken for granted, non-calculative reason. This understanding of practical reason, however, is not the same as *phronesis*, practical reason, to which we return in the final chapter.

4. Garfinkel identifies 'routine' as a necessary condition of rational action, and it is the stability of social routine that stimulates his future work in its disruption.

5. Interestingly, the validation Simon evokes for his description of bounded rationality is that it is recognizable from everyday life. 'Common sense', 'our picture of decision-making fits pretty well our introspective knowledge of our own judgemental processes' (Simon 1997: 119).

6. 'Common sense is shamelessly and unapologetically ad hoc. It comes in epigrams, proverbs, *ober dicta*, jokes, anecdotes, *contes morals*, a clatter of gnomic utterances, not in formal doctrines, axiomised theories or architectronic dogmas' (Geertz 1983: 90). He continues, 'If knowing chalk from cheese, a hawk from a handsaw, or your ass from your elbow...is as positive an accomplishment, if perhaps not so lofty a one, as appreciating motets, following a logic proof, keeping the Covenant, or demolishing Capitalism—as dependent as they are upon developed traditions of thought and sensibility—then the comparative investigation of "the ordinary ability to keep ourselves from being imposed upon by gross contradictions, palpable inconsistencies, and unmask'd impostures" (as a 1726 "Secret History of the University of Oxford" defined common sense) ought to be more deliberately cultivated' (Geertz 1983: 93).

7. Thinness is 'simpleness or literalness', 'being precisely what they seem to be, neither more nor less' (Geertz 1983: 89); immethodicalness is 'Not very regular and not very uniform' (Geertz 1983: 77). Elsewhere, he calls it 'ant heap' wisdom; while accessible is 'any person with faculties reasonably intact can grasp common-sense conclusions ... and indeed will not only grasp them but embrace them ... there are no acknowledged experts in common sense' (Geertz 1983: 91).

8. It is also to recognize the importance of talk in everyday interaction. Barnard (1995/2002: 283) writes, 'the need for expressing reasons is one of the most deep-seated of human necessities. To talk is largely to reason, and to reason is to talk. The fact that much reasoning and much talk is loose, incorrect and bad does not gainsay this view.'

9. Weick (1995: 188) goes on to say, 'If people want to share meaning, then they need to talk about their shared experience in close proximity to its occurrence and hammer out a common way to encode it and talk about it ... Recounting the details of the experience, without labelling it or summarizing it or categorizing it, is sufficient to establish a common referent. What people make of the referent individually is incidental.'

10. Weick's work is also informed by his early work on cognitive dissonance whereby an 'outcome' is made sensible by the construction of a plausible story or interpretation.

11. Weick's (1990: 55) apocryphal story is of soldiers lost in the mountains being successfully guided to safety with the aid of a wrong map.

12. Weick notes how strong identities or dense connections may, through the 'fallacy of centrality', deny the possibility of new interpretations and knowledge, a position that has some similarities with Granovetter's (1973) work on strong ties, and work in the social studies of science (Collins 1974).

13. Echoing this point, Weick notes 'managers keep forgetting that it is what they do, not what they plan, that explains their success. They keep giving credit to the wrong thing—namely the plan—and having made this error, they then spend more time planning and less time acting. They are astonished when more planning improves nothing' (Weick 1990: 55). This position is similar to Mintzberg's critique of strategic planning.

14. For Wenger, it is relationships with others that enable individuals to know what they know. 'In this sense, knowing is an act of participation in complex social learning systems' (1998: 29). Wenger identifies three structuring elements of social learning systems: communities of practice, boundary processes among communities, and identities shaped by participation in systems.

15. Subjective expected utility, for example, posits the individual as prospectively rational, that is, they seek to maximize future utility. 'Retrospective rationality' is not a feature of discussions of rational action, except in Staw's (1981) analysis of escalation of commitment where it is the desire to appear competent in previous actions. To the extent that situational rationality is recognized or incorporated into rational choice theory, it may be seen in the 'framing' in choice preference (Tversky and Kahneman 1990).

Part III The 'other' of reason

1. Weber did not dismiss that which was informed by the enchanted. He writes, 'magically motivated behaviour is relatively rational behaviour ... It follows rules of experience, though

it is not necessarily action in accordance with a means-end schema' (Weber 1978: 400). Weber's work outlines the rationalization of religious life through the belief in the existence of a pantheon of 'functional' gods, their anthropomorphization and delineation of jurisdictions to the emergence of monotheism, and a rationalized bureaucratic structure that attends this. His work describes the process of disenchantment that attends a growing rationalization, as magical divination gives rise to a belief in providence, a belief in spirits to a belief in gods, and the final segregation of a distinct sphere of religious beliefs, separate and distinct from other forms of social engagement.

2. The association of the body with the feminine was also reflected in the debates of Descartes and Bacon, whose work presented a conscious contest between the male and the female, a flight from association with the feminine, historically associated with 'unnatural' powers (Bordo 1987; Merchant 1980; Scheibinger 1989; for a critique, see Atherton 2002).

3. Although Augustine had claimed a sexual equality with regard to the capacity for reason, seeing woman as a rational spirit, physical differences between the sexes meant that woman was not as free to subordinate practical concerns to the contemplation of higher things.

4. This is the foundation of Bologh's (1990) aesthetic rationality, the recognition and response to beauty and attempts to re-create this in everyday existence.

8 Embodied rationality

1. It is interesting to note that one of the 'humiliations' in the Zimbardo experiments was forcing the male 'prison' inmates to wear short smocks with nothing underneath. The men had no experience of how to physically carry themselves in such attire that further added to their subordination (Haney et al. 1973).

2. This is not to deny that a birth and death are not highly socialized in terms of the practices and signification that surround them. Nor is it to deny that there is a material body afflicted by illness, disease, and biological processes. For women, menstruation, pregnancy, and menopause are processes that they are obliged to hide in organizations.

3. For Bourdieu, bodies bear the imprint of social class through shape and presentation, and reflect social location (i.e. 'distance from necessity').

4. Elias traces how behavioural codes impact the individualization and socialization of the body. Civilization refers to the degree of internal pacification in a society; its customs and their degree of refinement; and the degree of self-restraint and reflexivity that are required in social relations (Shilling 1993).

5. The influence of Parson's saw the organization as having the needs of adaptation (organization and environmental fit); goal (acquiring the resources for achieving this); integration (a focus on control and coordination); and latency (dealing with issues of motivation).

6. Open systems theory is heavily influenced by general systems theory and recognizes that the organization is affected by changes in the environment. External factors affect internal structures, for example, the degree of dependency on outside funding influencing authority relations within an organization.

7. Stimulating research into how the environment is known; what constitutes the environment (sets, networks, etc.); and definitions of types of environments (e.g. Emery and Trist 1965).

8. Organizational characteristics have therefore to be organized for success in dealing with environmental conditions, internal systems have to secure adaptation and goal attainment (e.g. Burns and Stalker 1961; Donaldson 1985; Lawrence and Lorsch 1967). Other concerns are the bridging and managing of critical boundaries, gate keepers, and boundary exchanges.

9. Hannan and Freeman (1977) develop a social Darwinism in their development of population ecology as an explanatory framework for the success of 'populations' of organizations in 'niches', their variation, selection, and retention.

10. As Pringle (1989/2001: 1271) notes, 'Far from being marginal in the workplace, sexuality is everywhere. It is alluded to in dress and self-presentation, in jokes and gossip, looks and flirtation, secret affairs and dalliances, in fantasy and in the range of coercive behaviours that we now call sexual harassment.'

11. For Williams and Bendelow (1998: xvi), 'Embodiment is reducible neither to representations of the body, to the body as an objectification of power, to the body as physiological entity, nor to the body as an inalienable centre of human consciousness.'

12. Elias makes the point that with the civilization of the body, there is a move from the 'expressive aspect to the experience aspect of corporeality' (Shilling 1993: 165). The ear and the eye are the dominant means through which this experience is mediated. Optocentrism, the primacy of the visual and the 'eye' as the predominant sense organ, is reflected in visualization technologies, visual metaphors, and perspectivism (Hoskin 1995), with its assumed neutrality of the disembodied observer. Vision however, as Harraway (1991: 194) notes, 'requires a politics of positioning; positioning implies responsibility. Vision is the power to see, thus struggles over what counts as rational accounts of the world are struggles over how to see.'

13. From this, Polanyi derives a model of social organization that operates at different levels, each level operating according to the 'rules' of that level, but also controlled by laws that form at a lower and higher level. The example he gives is of giving a speech, in which he identifies five levels: voice, words, sentences, style, and literary composition. The laws of phonetics, lexicography, grammar, stylistics, and literary criticism control each level, but each is controlled by its position within the comprehensive entity.

14. Polanyi argues strongly that subsidiary awareness, an awareness of the proximal, is not the equivalent of a preconscious or unconscious awareness. Awareness is subsidiary because of the function that it fulfils in relation to the main object of knowledge. It may thus be at any level of awareness.

15. The example given is of playing a game of chess, which operates on two levels, attention to the pieces but the necessary awareness of the game itself.

16. Polanyi notes that if we attend to something 'in particular', that is, not the comprehensive entity as a whole, this can become meaningless. The example he gives is of a word repeated several times that comes to lose its meaning. Although he also notes that in certain circumstances, for example, an analysis of a text, a close scrutiny of 'the particulars' can give a more enriched understanding.

17. Polanyi uses the concept of tacit knowledge, our awareness of the particulars, that are not yet fully integrated, as a solution to the contradiction or paradox of Plato's Meno, the experience of a problem and the search for a solution. 'Either you know what you are looking for, and then there is no problem; or you do not know what you are looking for, and then you cannot expect to find anything' (Polanyi 1983: 22).

18. The transmission of knowledge is predominantly tacit. Polanyi writes, 'We have seen that tacit knowledge dwells in our awareness of particulars while bearing on an entity which the particulars jointly constitute. In order to share this indwelling, the pupil must presume that a teaching which appears meaningless to start with has in fact a meaning which can be discovered by hitting on the same kind of indwelling as the teacher is practicing. Such an effort is based on accepting the teacher's authority' (Polanyi 1983: 61).

19. Laqueur (1987) illustrates how anatomy, physiology, and biology began to play a role in this process in the eighteenth century as the body changed from being a manifestation of identity to its basis.

20. Hume recognizes the important role of habit as being an equivalent authority to sovereign reason (Baier 2002).

21. The idea that men, following their own passion, might contribute to some overall common purpose of which they remain, as individuals, unaware was eventually expressed by Smith in *The Wealth of Nations*. It is in Smith's work that the pursuit of individual (material) self-interest becomes associated with the general (material) interest. It is however worth returning to Smith (quoted in Hirschman 1977: 239) on this question: 'individuals contribute to the general productiveness of society although their intent is to be only interested in their own gain...By pursuing his own interest he frequently promotes that of society more effectively *than when he really intends to promote it*' (emphasis added). Smith points to the accidental consequence of self-interested choices, decisions, and actions leading to a collective benefit. His comments reflect more on concepts of causality than the recommendation that individual rational action automatically leads to collective benefit.

22. It is relatively late in the evolution of thought that interest becomes focused on economic advantage.

23. Passion, unbridled or unruly passion, was dangerous and disruptive to the body politic. This is particularly true at court, where personal standing, one's own and others, was so precarious. Such uncertainty stressed the importance of the control of emotions, and court behaviour also required fine gradations according to status.

24. Charisma is the mobilization of action in mass organization and religious movements.

25. In cases of technical decision-making, that is, clear goals and courses of action, emotions cease to play this guiding role and may be quite disruptive.

26. Elster (1985b) distinguishes between interpersonally appropriate and intrapersonally appropriate. The first refers to the expectation that most people would behave similarly in such circumstances. The second is that which is consistent with an individual's responses in similar circumstances or 'intersituational consistency'. The example Elster (1985b: 385) gives is to be afraid in one situation but not in others that are known to be more objectively dangerous. Phobias would be 'inappropriate emotional reactions' and thus irrational.

27. From Aristotle, the virtues involve responding in an appropriate way. It is a vice to over indulge in pleasures or passions, but equally it is a vice not to engage in pleasure or not exhibit, for example, anger when there is reason to be angry (Homiak 2002). Reason does not suppress emotion and passion.

28. The role of the unconscious, although not termed such, has a long history. The origin of the term idiot, for example, is the individual who is ruled by the id. In Greek political theory, the idiot referred to the individual who was not able or eligible to participate as a citizen in

the polis (Deetz 1992). The association of being 'weak' or 'feeble minded' and the lack of a public role carrying over into gender politics.

29. This gives the distinction based on behaviour that is known to the self and that which is known to others, giving rise to the matrix of behaviour that is public (known to self and others); blind (unknown to self but known to others); hidden (known to self but not others); and unconscious (unknown both to self and others).

30. There is a strong association between irrationality and emotions. Freud, for example, places the emotions in the id, rather than the ego, their having the potential to disrupt personality, thus indicating irrationality's relation to madness (Barbalet 1998).

31. Diamond (1993: 70) notes that 'Psychodynamically, humour is a way of re-establishing ego (self-other) boundaries. It puts necessary distance and protection between oneself and one's internalization of others and the events that may consume them'.

32. Forming a committee, strict adherence to bureaucratic procedure, many committee meetings, collecting copious amounts of data are examples of such defensive ritualistic behaviour. In this sense, the technically rational gains its rationality from the psychic defence it provides. But it can inhibit learning and change (Diamond 1993).

33. These may include repression, regression (to an earlier stage, infantile of childish behaviour), sublimation (displacement), projection (externalized, e.g. paranoia), or introjection (internalized, e.g. neuroticism), reaction/formation (e.g. passive/aggressive behaviour), denial or rationalization, isolation (reflected in obsessional behaviour), and splitting (separation of the psyche into two parts, something is either all good or all bad).

34. As Jacques (1995: 344) writes, however, 'It is not necessary to look further a field than our Psychoanalytical Societies and Institutes to realize that the understanding of psychodynamics by the members of an organization, all of whom have been psychoanalyzed, can make no difference whatever to their degree of sophistication in effectively coping with their own organization.' He continues: 'this observation is not intended as a criticism of such organizations, but only to draw attention to the fact that psychoanalytic insights do not, and cannot, beget organizational knowledge or wisdom.'

35. Identified through behaviour that is, respectively, impulsive and unpredictable; focuses on rules, order, and control; disappears in a cohesive social role trying to achieve collective perfection; focuses on distinction, excellence, exploits, and achievements; and interested in collective welfare.

36. As Diamond (1993) notes of this type, there is usually a need to be surrounded by admiring and loyal subordinates.

37. Group dynamics may result in dependency (where the members feel they know nothing and see the leader as omniscient and omnipotent); pairing (awaiting a 'messiah' be this in the form of new technology, a new management team, the business plan, a new building, etc. which will 'solve' current problems and allow things to be resolved, or function smoothly); and fight/flight (the group creates a perceived 'enemy' but then dissipates as soon as this is vanquished). A group is more effective when working on a set task, that is, it functions as a work group to achieve a common task.

38. The functioning of this group inhibits independent thought, or any approach to decision-making, for example, by reliance on scientific data, which might diminish the leader. When the group rejects the leader for a failure to live up to expectations they then appoint 'another one who is their sickest member: a thorough-going psychiatric case' (de Board 1990: 39),

leading to an oscillation between the two, that might manifest itself in the splitting into two subgroups.

39. This mechanism based on hope in the future avoids the group having to face any difficult issues and delay painful decisions.

40. The 'leader' is the creature of the group, forced to identify enemies and lead the group against them.

41. This was based on an experiment on different ways of communicating information about food; a lecture with information; and a group-based discussion and a group decision to implement change based on this discussion. Lewin emphasizes the importance of group commitment. However, an important element here is the different role that reasoning plays in each context. In the group context, there is a significant role for reasons to be sought and given. A similar feature is evident in the autocratic, democratic, and laissez faire experiments in leadership styles.

42. Groups of seven to ten people sit in a circle and engage in unstructured discussion. A trainer assists in helping people to understand what is happening in the enfolding discussion and dynamic.

43. Davidson (1990) cites Freud's work and the Medea principle, the notion of a weakness of will causing one to act against one's better judgement. The latter is similar to rational choice theory's reference to *akrasia* (I might know that an extra glass of wine is one too many but it does not stop me at the time!). In the latter, this is explained as a conflict between long-term interests and short-term desires or wants. It does not require an unconscious to explain it.

9 Collective rationality

1. Rational action models cannot explain the presence of voluntary collective action or public goods in the absence of selective incentives or coercive measures. Either incentives must be provided by trying to introduce elements of divisibility or exclusivity, as for example, through private or communal property rights; or there is recourse to sanctions through an external authority (the 'State') for some public provision, legitimated through the concept of contract (on the grounds that it is rational to agree to be bound by authority in order to secure long-term interests of safety and security).

2. McMahon's position places a lot of importance on the assurance that others will participate in order to reduce individual costs. He thus invokes social norms, conventions, and the act of promising as providing assurances for cooperatively disposed people.

3. See Chapter 4, footnote 20.

4. Arrow's (1990) general possibility theorem illustrates the impossibility of satisfying everyone's individual interests through a mechanism of cumulative addition or aggregation. Applying the principles of unrestricted domain, that is, no limits on preferences or interests, anonymity (voters are treated equally), and neutrality (of voting procedure), there is no common good that is acceptable to all because there is no aggregation mechanism that would generate collective decisions.

5. These debates derive from Kant's original discussion on the 'public use of reason' (Gaus 1997). It takes as the basis of its discussion Kant's transcendental formula of public right

'all actions affecting the rights of other human beings are wrong if their maxim is not compatible with their being made public' (quoted in Elster 1998: 20).

6. Deliberative democracy does not presume direct democracy but allows for representation where constituents express and formulate opinions to representatives; where representatives are accountable to constituents through election, but have the ability to exercise judgement rather than being mandated (i.e. are open to persuasion through argument in the decision-making venue); and where decision-making follows discussion and debate. Nor does it deny the relevance of expert authority where this is supported by reasons rather than merely being claimed.

7. A focus on practical issues (what is to be done) tends to avoid disputes about ends and what 'ought' to be done, which oriented towards 'truth', is in danger of being unduly conflictual. Richardson (1997) gives the example of Roe v. Wade which adjudicated the abortion debate in the USA. While there are competing positions and no intention or desire to compromise on whether a foetus constitutes a person or not, the pragmatic decision to differentiate the pregnancy in terms of trimesters is continually open to contention. On occasions, where agreement is not forthcoming and when faced with the need for a decision, some form of voting procedure must occur (Cohen 1997*b*).

8. Reasonable in this sense is 'sufficiently credible to justify acceptance, assuming that a belief that violates clear maxims of logic or is based on manifestly bad evidence cannot be sufficiently credible' (Gaus 1997: 215). For Rawls, these are reasons that one can reasonably expect reasonable members of the collective group to accept. However, Rawls (1997) goes further than this arguing that those participating in public debate are constrained to put forward proposals in relation to the common good. 'Norms of reasonableness and reciprocity govern and limit the public use of reason by citizens in a pluralistic society' (Bohman and Rehg 1997: xvii). Others argue that this is an undue restraint on deliberation and self-interested claims are able to generate points of importance in debate.

9. This, of course, presupposes an ability to deliberate as well as an awareness of how reasons will be responded to, an awareness of what constitutes convincing as opposed to unconvincing reasons. This obviously relates to cognitive and communicative ability, intellectual and social capital.

10. Habermas recognizes asymmetrical access to 'the production, validation, steering and presentation of images'. Nonetheless, he believes that 'communicatively generated legitimate power can have an effect on the political system insofar as it assumes responsibility for the pool of reasons from which administrative decisions must draw their rationalizations' (Habermas 1987: 56). In Habermas's work, rationalization or the 'linguistification of the sacred', is understood as the unfettering of the rationality potential of action oriented to mutual understanding.

11. In this sense, Young (1997) sees deliberative democracy as a form of practical reason (see Chapter 10).

12. DiMaggio and Powell (1983) argue that Hannan and Freeman assume a system rationality rather than a collective rationality.

10 Practical reason

1. Boden's (1994: 185) analysis is perhaps the most elaborate analysis of 'rationality in action' and how it illuminates 'rationality writ large'. The latter she sees as a largely idealized

rationality that relies on everyday rationalities needed to make organizations happen. She poses the idea of reflexive layers of rationality, 'nested within one another', taking their meaning indexically from each other, and that are mutually elaborating (Boden 1994). However, she poses analysis in binary terms, between local and larger rationalities, formal versus a substantive rationality, or a reflexive tension between an ideal and practical action (Boden 1994: 190). Rather than pose analysis in binary terms, my approach has been to explicate a range of rationalities that represent different degrees of embeddedness within a context.

2. This section relies on Townley (2008).

3. Meyer and Rowan (1992: 95), commenting on the need for organizations to adopt rational myths pervasive in the environment in which they operate, note, 'Much of the irrationality of life in modern organizations arises because the organization itself must maintain a rational corporate persona.'

4. A shared understanding of reasons implies neither consensus nor their acceptance, merely the recognition of their force within certain contexts.

5. Critique first informed the judgement of ancient texts, that is, it was in the service of the church, and used to inform or justify the position of either humanist or reformer (Connerton 1980). The impact of the religious wars of the period saw its gradual dissociation from informing the understanding of revelation to its being distinct from this. Revelation and reason drew apart. Critique served the latter and no sphere was exempt from its use.

6. The position of Foucault and Habermas are not so distinct (Ashenden and Owen 1999) Habermas critiques the assumptions of a universalist, disembodied logos, a 'subjective' non-social concept of rationality, hence his position on the intersubjectivity of language and rationality. This is a position that Foucault also critiques. Habermas critiques the view of rationalization as the equivalent of instrumentalization. For Habermas, rationalization is a process of bringing the foundation of argument to light rather than its being hidden. Foucault does not admit to Habermas's position of being 'for' reason and does not have an emancipatory project.

7. Weber is very conscious of the limits of rationality as an organizing principle, 'only a narrowly defined class of problems—involving no conflict over ends or values—have objectively or technically rational solutions' (Brubaker 1984: 5). As most problems involve a clash over ends and values, as such they are not amenable to being solved in an objectively rational manner.

8. *Phronesis* appears in medieval Aristotelianism as *prudentia*, and was one of the four cardinal virtues (MacIntyre 1988). In this, that which is rational is that which is good for the agent to perform. Practical reason is in accordance with right reason and is directed towards the good (Cullity and Gaut 1997). Practical reason is thus substantive. It is to have correct vision, or moral discrimination.

9. Toulmin's argument is that a focus on rationality has been at the expense of considering reasonableness, and that the latter cannot be expected to meet the stringent requirements that are placed on the former. Rather than see the two as distinct, they are presented as a continuum of reason. Formal arguments derive from the application of rational techniques or the 'correct' interpretation of rules and procedures lie to the more 'rational', calculative end of the continuum, while the substantively rational, being more situated, lies closer to the 'reasonableness' end of the continuum.

10. An increasing calculative rationality can lead to substantive irrationality. Ritzer identifies the 'irrationality of rationality' (Ritzer 1996); 'hyperrationality' is where the four types of rationality (identified by Kalberg 1980: 231 from Weber's work), the formal, substantive,

practical, and theoretical, interact with one another to form a 'heightened, historically unprecedented level of rationality'. The most extreme example of this is Bauman's analysis of the Holocaust. Here rational, planned, scientifically informed, expert, efficiently managed, and coordinated systems based on a meticulous functional division of labour, and the dehumanization of the bureaucratic operation, eased the substitution of technical for moral responsibility that led to the final solution. In his analysis of the Holocaust, Bauman distinguishes between the rationality of the actor and the rationality of the action. In his analysis of the cooperation of the victims, Bauman illustrates how they were caught by their belief in deploying reason, that responding rationally to rational overtures in an irrational setting would lead rational outcomes. While their cooperation was not without rationality, 'save what you can' became a choice between a greater and a lesser evil. Sacrificing the few to save the many, involved cooperation and collaboration, and in the end provided no rational or moral safeguard against further demands. He states 'reason is a good guide for individual behaviour only on such occasions as the two rationalities [the actor and the action] resonate and overlap' (Bauman 1989: 149). The coincidence of the two rationalities does not depend on the actor, it depends on the setting of the action.

11. Herbert Simon (1990: 190) makes the point 'Reasoning processes take symbolic inputs and deliver symbolic outputs...Axioms and inference rules together constitute the fulcrum on which the lever of reasoning rests; but the particular structure of that fulcrum cannot be justified by methods of reasoning...Reason goes to work only after it has been supplied with a suitable set of inputs or premises' (Simon 1990: 191).

12. Flyvbjerg (2001) sees a strong link between Foucault's position and *phronesis* in Foucault's emphasis on the examination of micro-practices, specific practices, and technologies, and his analysis and understanding of power informed by an approach that focuses on 'how'. Foucault, however, would not ascribe to the moral position that accompanies *phronesis*.

13. As such, it does not require the choice between what Habermas (1992) terms Weber's 'false alternative', between a substantive and formal rationality.

☐ REFERENCES

Abbot, A. (1988a). *The System of Professions*. Chicago, IL: University of Chicago Press.

Abbot, A. (1988b). *Chaos of Disciplines*. Chicago, IL: University of Chicago Press.

Abell, P. (1992). 'Is Rational Choice Theory a Theory of Rational Choices', in J. Coleman and T. Fararo (eds.), *Rational Choice*. Newbury Park, CA: Sage, pp. 183–206.

Ackoff, R. (1970). *A Concept of Corporate Planning*. New York, NY: Wiley.

Albrow, M. (1970). *Bureaucracy*. London: Macmillian.

Albrow, M. (1987). 'The Application of the Weberian Concept of Rationalization to Contemporary Conditions', in S. Whimster and S. Lash (eds.), *Max Weber, Rationality and Modernity*. London: Allen and Unwin, pp. 164–82.

Albrow, M. (1992). '*Sine Ira et Studio*- or Do Organizations Have Feelings', *Organization Studies*, 13(3): 313–29, in Clegg (2002b: vol. 7, 377–92).

Albrow, M. (1997). *Do Organizations Have Feelings*. London: Routledge.

Aldrich, H. (1972). 'Technology and Organizational Structure: A Re-examination of the Findings of the Aston Group', *Administrative Science Quarterly*, 17: 26–42, in Clegg (2002a: vol. 2, 344–66).

Aldrich, H. and Pfeffer, J. (1976). 'Environments of Organizations', *Annual Review of Sociology*, 2: 79–105, in Clegg (2002a: vol. 3, 92–119).

Allmendinger, J. and Hackman, J. R. (1996). 'Organizations in Changing Environments: The Case of East German Symphony Orchestras', *Administrative Science Quarterly*, 41: 337–69, in Clegg (2002a: vol. 3, 217–52).

Alvesson, M. (2003). *Understanding Organizational Culture*. London: Sage.

Alvesson, M. (2004). 'Organizational Culture and Discourse', in D. Grant, C. Hardy, C. Oswick, and L. Putnam (eds.), *Handbook of Organizational Discourse*. Sage: London, pp. 317–36.

Alvesson, M. and Willmott, H. (1996). *Making Sense of Management*. London: Sage.

Amado, G. (1995). 'Why Psychoanalytical Knowledge Helps Us Understand Organizations', *Human Relations*, 48: 351–7.

Anthony, P. (1999). *Managing Culture*. Buckingham: Open University Press.

Anthony, L. and Witt, C. (eds.) (2002). *A Mind of One's Own: Feminist Essays on Reason and Objectivity*. Boulder, CO: Westview Press.

Archer, M. (2000). 'Homo Economicus. Homo Sociologicus and Homo Sentiens', in M. Archer and J. Tritter (eds.), *Rational Choice Theory*. London: Routledge, pp. 36–56.

Archer, M. and Tritter, J. (2000a). 'Introduction', in M. Archer and J. Tritter (eds.), *Rational Choice Theory. Resisting Colonization*. London: Routledge.

Archer, M. and Tritter, J. (eds.) (2000b). *Rational Choice Theory*. London: Routledge.

Arendt, H. (1967). *The Origins of Totalitarianism*. London: Allen and Unwin.

Argyris, C. (2004). *Reasons and Rationalizations: The Limits to Organizational Knowledge*. Oxford: Oxford University Press.

Arrow, K. (1974). *The Limits of Organization*. New York, NY: Norton.

Arrow, K. (1990). 'Values and Collective Decision Making', in P. Moser (ed.), *Rationality and Action*. Cambridge: Cambridge University Press, pp. 337–53.

Arrow, K. (1992). 'Rationality of Self and Others in an Economic System', in M. Zey (ed.), *Decision Making: Alternatives to Rational Choice Models*. Newbury Park, CA: Sage Publications, pp. 63–78.

Asch, S. (1951). 'Effects of Group Pressure Upon Judgments', in J. Ott (ed.), *Classical Readings in Organizational Behavior*. Belmont, CA: Wadsworth.

Ashenden, S. and Owen, D. (eds.) (1999). *Foucault Contra Habermas*. London: Sage.

Atherton, M. (2002). 'Gendered Reason and Cartesian Reason', in Anthony and Witt (eds.), pp. 21–37.

Audi, R. (1990). 'Rationality and Valuation', in P. Moser (ed.), *Rationality in Action*. Cambridge: Cambridge University Press, pp. 416–48.

Auld, Lord Justice (2001). *Review of the Criminal Courts of England and Wales*. London: HMSO.

Baier, L. (2002). 'Reclaiming Embodiment', in Anthony and Witt (eds.), pp. 38–52.

Barbalet, J. (1998). *Emotion, Social Theory and Social Structure*. Cambridge: Cambridge University Press.

Barker, J. (1993). 'Tightening the Iron Cage: Concertive Control in Self-Managing Teams', *Administrative Science Quarterly*, 38: 408–37, in Clegg (2002b: vol. 5, 180–210).

Barley, S. (1983). 'Semiotics and the Study of Occupational and Organizational Cultures', *Administrative Science Quarterly*, 24: 570–81, in Clegg (2002: vol. 7, 114–39).

Barley, S. (1986). 'Technology as an Occasion for Structuring: Evidence from Observations of CT Scanners and the Social Order of Radiology Departments', *Administrative Science Quarterly*, 31(1): 78–108, in Clegg (2002b: vol. 7, 393–211).

Barley, S. and Kunda, G. (1992). 'Design and Devotion: Surges of Rational and Normative Ideologies of Control in Managerial Discourse', *Administrative Science Quarterly*, 37: 363–99.

Barnard, C. (1938). *The Functions of the Executive*. Cambridge, MA: Harvard University Press.

Barnard, C. (1995). 'Mind in Everyday Affairs: An Examination into Logical and Non-Logical Thought Processes', *Journal of Management History*, 1(4): 7–27, in Clegg (2002a: vol. 1, 278–98).

Barnes, B. and Bloor, D. (1982). 'Relativism, Rationalism and the Sociology of Knowledge', in M. Hollis and S. Lukes (eds.), *Rationality and Relativism*. Oxford: Blackwell, pp. 21–47.

Barnes, B. and Edge, D. (eds.) (1982). *Science in Context*. Milton Keynes: Open University Press.

Barry, B. and Hardin, R. (1982). *Rational Man and Irrational Society?* Beverly Hills, CA: Sage.

Barstow, A. (1994). *Witchcraze*. London: Pandora.

Bartunek, J. (1984). 'Changing Interpretive Schemas and Organizational Restructuring: the Example of a Religious Order', *Administrative Science Quarterly*, 29: 355–72.

Bauman, Z. (1989). *Modernity and the Holocaust*. Cambridge: Polity Press.

Bauman, Z. (1993). *Modernity and Ambivalence*. Cambridge: Polity Press.

Baumard, P. (1999). *Tacit Knowledge in Organizations*. Thousand Oaks, CA: Sage.

Beetham, D. (1996). *Bureaucracy*. Minneapolis, MI: University of Minnesota Press.

Benhabib, S. (1987) 'The Generalized and the Concrete Other: The Kohlberg-Gilligan Controversy and Feminist Theory', in S. Benhabib and D. Cornell (eds.), *Feminism as Critique*. London: Polity Press, pp. 77–96.

Benhabib, S. (1992). *Situating the Self*. Cambridge: Polity Press.

Bernauer, J. (1990). *Michel Foucault's Force of Flight*. London: Humanities Press.

Bernstein, R. (1978). *The Restructuring of Social and Political Theory*. Philadelphia, PA: University of Pennsylvania Press.

Bernstein, R. (ed.) (1994). In *Habermas and Modernity*. Cambridge, MA: MIT Press.

Beynon, H. (1975). *Working for Ford*. Harmondsworth: Penguin.

Biagioli, M. (1999). *The Science Studies Reader*. New York, NY: Routledge.

Bion, W. (1961). *Experiences in Groups*. London: Tavistock.

Bittner, E. (1965). 'The Concept of Organization', *Social Research*, 32: 239–55, in Clegg (2002*a*: vol. 2, 76–87).

Bittner, E. (1967). 'The Police on Skid Row: A Study of Peace Keeping', *American Sociological Review*, 32(5): 699–715, in Salaman and Thompson, pp. 331–45.

Blau, P. (1955). *The Dynamics of Bureaucracy*. Chicago, IL: University of Chicago Press.

Blau, P. and Scott, W. (1962). *Formal Organizations: A Comparative Approach*. San Francisco, CA: Chandler.

Blauner, R. (1964). *Alienation and Freedom*. Chicago, IL: University of Chicago Press.

Bloor, D. (1991). *Knowledge and Social Imagery*. Chicago, IL: University of Chicago Press.

Bloor, D. (2002). *Wittgenstein, Rules and Institutions*. London: Routledge.

Boden, D. (1994). *The Business of Talk*. Cambridge: Polity Press.

Bogen, D. (1999). *Order Without Rules: Critical Theory and the Logic of Conversation*. Albany, NY: SUNY Press.

Bohman, J. (1992). 'The Limits of Rational Choice Explanation', in J. Coleman and T. Fararo (eds.), *Rational Choice Theory*. London: Sage, pp. 207–28.

Bohman, J. (1997). 'Deliberative Democracy and Effective Social Freedom', in Bohman and Rehg (eds.), pp. 321–48.

Bohman, J. and Rehg, W. (1997). *Deliberative Democracy: Essays on Reason and Politics*. Cambridge, MA: MIT Press.

Boje, D. (1995). 'Stories of the Storytelling Organization', *Academy of Management Journal*, 38: 997–1035, in Clegg (2002*b*: vol. 7, 29–66).

Bollas, C. (1987). *The Shadow of the Object: Psychoanalysis of the Unthought Known*. New York, NY: Columbia University Press.

Bologh, R. (1990). *Love or Greatness*. London: Unwin Hyman.

Bonomy, Lord (2002). *Improving Practice Review of the Practices and Procedures of the High Court*. Edinburgh: Scottish Executive, TSO.

Bordo, S. (1987). *The Flight to Objectivity*. Albany, NY: State University of New York.

Bourdieu, P. (1984). *Distinction*. London: Routledge.

Bowker, G. and Star, S. (2000). *Sorting Things Out*. Cambridge, MA: MIT Press.

Braaten, J. (1995). 'From Communicative Rationality to Communicative Thinking', in J. Meehan (ed.), *Feminists Read Habermas*. London: Routledge, pp. 139–61.

Brand, A. (1990). *The Force of Reason*. London: Allen and Unwin.

Braverman, H. (1974). *Labor and Monopoly Capital*. London: Monthly Review Press.

Brown, A. (1995). *Organizational Culture*. London: Pitman.

Brown, C. (1992). 'Organization Studies and Scientific Authority', in M. Reed and M. Hughes (eds.), *Rethinking Organization*. London: Sage, pp. 67–84.

Brown, J. and Duguid, P. (1991). 'Organizational Learning and Communities of Practice: a Unified View of Working, Learning and Innovation', *Organization Science*, 2(1): 40–56.

Brubaker, R. (1984). *The Limits of Rationality*. London: Allen and Unwin.

Brunsson, N. (1982). 'The Irrationality of Action and Action Rationality: Decisions, Ideologies and Organization Actions', *Journal of Management Studies*, 19(1): 29–44, in WOBS (2001: vol. 1, 245–61).

Brunsson, N. (1985). *The Irrational Organization*. New York, NY: Wiley.

Brunsson, N. (1989). *The Organization of Hypocrisy*. Chichester, NY: John Wiley.

Brunsson, N. and Olsen, J. (1997). *The Reforming Organization*. London: Routledge.

Bryman, A. (1984). 'Organization Studies and the Concept of Rationality', *Journal of Management Studies*, 21(4): 391–408.

Burns, T. (1963). 'Mechanistic Organismic Structures', in D. Pugh (ed.) (1982), pp. 43–55.

Burns, T. and Stalker, G. (1961). *The Management of Innovation*. London: Tavistock.

Burrell, G. (1984). 'Sex and Organizational Analysis', *Organization Studies*, 5(2): 97–118.

Burrell, G. (1992). 'The Organization of Pleasure', in M. Alvesson and H. Willmott (eds.), *Critical Management Studies*. London: Sage, pp. 66–89.

Burrell, G. and Morgan, G. (1979). *Sociological Paradigms and Organizational Analysis*. London: Heinemann.

Burris, B. (1993). *Technocratic Management at Work*. Albany, NY: SUNY Press.

Calas, M. and Smircich, L. (1996). 'Feminist Approaches to Organization Studies', in Clegg et al.

Camic, C. (1992). 'The Matter of Habit', in M. Zey, M. (ed.), *Decision Making*. Thousand Oaks, CA: Sage, pp. 185–232.

Carter, N., Klein, R., and Doey, P. (1992). *How Organizations Measure Success*. London: Routledge.

Chambers, S. (1996). *Reasonable Democracy: Jurgen Habermas and the Politics of Discourse*. Ithaca, NY: Cornell University Press.

Chan, A. (2003). 'The Case for Culture as Process', in R. Westwood and S. Clegg (eds.), *Debating Organization*. Oxford: Blackwell, pp. 311–20.

Child, J. (1972). 'Organizational Structure, Environment and Performance: The Role of Strategic Choice', *Sociology*, 6: 1–21, in Clegg (2002: vol. 2, 323–43).

Christiano, T. (1997), 'The Significance of Public Deliberation', in Bohman and Rehg (eds.), pp. 243–77.

Clawson, D. (1980). *Bureaucracy and the Labor Process*. New York, NY: Monthly Review Press.

Clegg, S. (1994). 'Max Weber and Contemporary Sociology of Organizations,' in L. Ray and M. Reed (eds.), *Organizing Modernity*. London: Routledge.

Clegg, S. (2002). 'Introduction,' in Clegg (2002a: vol. 1).

Clegg, S. (ed.) (2002a). *Central Currents in Organization Theory*, vols. 1–4. London: Sage.

Clegg, S. (ed.) (2002b). *Central Currents in Organization Theory*, vols. 5–8. London: Sage.

Clegg, S., Hardy, C., and Nord, W. (1996). *Handbook of Organizational Studies*. London: Sage.

Cline Cohen, C. (1999). *A Calculating People*. Chicago, IL: University of Chicago Press.

Coase, R. (1937). 'The Nature of the Firm', *Economica*, 4(16): 386–405, in Clegg (2002a: vol. 4, 151–66).

Code, L. (1993). 'Taking Subjectivity into Account', in L. Alcoff and E. Potter (eds.), *Feminist Epistemologies*. New York: Routledge.

Cohen, J. (1972). 'Max Weber and the Dynamics of Rationalized Domination', *Telos*, 14: 63–86.

Cohen, B. (1994). 'Newton and the Social Sciences, with Special Reference to Economics, or, the Case of the Missing Paradigm', in P. Mirowski (ed.), pp. 55–90.

Cohen, J. (1997*a*). 'Deliberation and Democratic Legitimacy', in Bohman and Rehg, pp. 67–92.

Cohen, J. (1997*b*). 'Procedure and Substance in Deliberative Democracy', in Bohman and Rehg (eds.), pp. 407–38.

Cohen, M., March, J., and Olsen, J. (1972). 'A Garbage Can Model of Organizational Choice', *Administrative Science Quarterly*, 17(1): 1–25.

Coleman, J. (1990). *Foundations of Social Theory*. Cambridge, MA: Harvard University Press.

Coleman, J. (1992). 'Introducing Social Structure to Economic Analysis', in M. Zey (ed.), pp. 265–72.

Coleman, J. and Fararo, T. (1992). *Rational Choice Theory: Advocacy and Critique*. Newbury Park, CA: Sage.

Collins, H. (1974). 'The TEA Set: Tacit Knowledge and Scientific Networks', in M. Biagioli (ed.), *The Science Studies Reader*. New York, NY: Routledge, pp. 95–110.

Collinson, D. (1988). 'Engineering Humor', *Organization Studies*, 9(2): 181–99.

Commons, J. (1934). *Institutional Economics*. Madison, WI: The University of Wisconsin Press.

Connerton, P. (1980). *The Tragedy of Enlightenment*. Cambridge: Cambridge University Press.

Cook, K. and Levi, M. (eds.) (1990). *The Limits of Rationality*. Chicago, IL: University of Chicago Press.

Cooke, M. (1997). *Language and Reason*. Cambridge, MA: MIT Press.

Corbett, J. (1994). *Critical Cases in Organization Behavior*. London: Macmillan

Courpasson, D. (2000). 'Managerial Strategies of Domination: Power in Soft Bureaucracies', *Organization Studies*, 21(1):141–61, in Clegg (2002*b*: vol. 5, 324–43).

Crossley, N. (1998). 'Emotion and Communicative Action', in G. Bendelow and S. Williams (eds.), *Emotions in Social Life*. London: Routledge, pp. 16–38.

Crozier, M. (1964). *The Bureaucratic Phenomenon*. London: Tavistock.

Crump, T. (1992). *The Japanese Numbers Game*. New York, NY: Routledge.

Cullity, G. and Gaut, B. (1997). *Ethics and Practical Reason*. Oxford: Oxford University Press.

Cyert, R. and March, J. (1963). *A Behavioural Theory of the Firm*. Oxford: Blackwell.

Czarniawska, B. and Sevon, G. (eds.) (1996). *Translating Organizational Change*. Berlin: de Gruyter.

Dale, K. (2001). *Anatomizing Embodiment and Organization Theory*. Basingstoke, Hampshire: Palgrave.

Dalton, M. (1959). *Men Who Manage*. New York, NY: Wiley.

Daston, L. (1992). 'Objectivity and the Escape from Perspective', *Social Studies of Science*, 20(4): 597–618.

Davidson, D. (1980). *Essays on Actions and Events*. Oxford: Oxford University Press.

Davidson, D. (1990). 'Paradoxes of Rationality', in K. Moser (ed.), pp. 449–64.

Davis, G., McAdam, D., Scott, W., and Zald, M. (eds.) (2004). *Social Movements and Organization Theory*. Oxford: Oxford University Press.

Dawson, S. (1996). *Analyzing Organizations*, 3rd edn. London: Macmillan.

Deal, T. and Kennedy, A. (1982). *Corporate Culture*. Reading, MA: Addisson Wesley.

De Board, R. (1990). *The Psychoanalysis of Organizations*. London: Routledge.

Deetz, S. (1992). *Democracy in the Age of Corporate Colonalization*. Albany, NY: NYU Press.

Derlien, H. (1999). 'On the Selective Interpretation of Max Weber's Concept of Bureaucracy', in P. Ahonen and K. Palonen (eds.), *Disembalming Max Weber*. Jyvaskyla, Findland: SoPhi, pp. 56–70.

Dewey, J. (1922). *Request for Certainty*. London: George Allen and Unwin.

Diamond, M. (1993). *The Unconscious Life of Organizations*. Westport, CT: Quorum Books.

DiMaggio, P. J. (1991). 'Constructing an Organizational Field as a Professional Project', in W. W. Powell and P. J. DiMaggio (eds.), *The New Institutionalism in Organizational Analysis*. Chicago: University of Chicago Press, pp. 267–92.

DiMaggio, P. and Powell, W. (1983). 'The Iron Cage Revisited: Institutional Isomorphism and Collective Rationality in Organization Fields', *American Journal of Sociology*, 48(2): 147–60, in W. Powell and P. DiMaggio (eds.), *The New Institutionalism in Organizational Analysis*. Chicago, IL: University of Chicago Press, pp. 63–82.

Donaldson, L. (1985). *In Defence of Organization Theory*. Cambridge: Cambridge University Press.

Donaldson, L. (1987). 'Strategy and Structural Adjustment to Regain Fit and Performance', *Journal of Management Studies*, 24(1): 1–24, in Clegg (2002*a*: vol. 2, 379–403).

Douglas, M. (1987). *How Institutions Think*. London: Routledge.

Douglas, M. (1995). 'Converging on Autonomy: Anthropological and Institutional Economics', in O. E. Williamson (ed.), *Organization Theory*. Oxford: Oxford University Press.

du Gay, P. (2000). *In Praise of Bureaucracy*. London: Sage.

Edwards, R. (1979). *Contested Terrain*. New York, NY: Basic Books.

Edwards, P. (2003). *Industrial Relations: Theory and Practice*. Oxford: Blackwell.

Eisen, A. (1978). 'The Meanings and Confusion of Weberian Rationality', *British Journal of Sociology*, 29(1): 57–70.

Eldridge, J. and Crombie, A. (1974). *A Sociology of Organizations*. London: Allen and Unwin.

Elias, N. (1978). *The Civilizing Process*. Oxford: Blackwell.

Ellul, J. (1964). *The Technological Society*. New York, NY: Vintage Books.

Elster, J. (1979). *Ulysses and the Sirens*. Cambridge: Cambridge University Press.

Elster, J. (1985*a*). *Sour Grapes*. Cambridge: Cambridge University Press.

Elster, J. (1985*b*). 'Sadder but Wiser? Rationality and the Emotions', *Social Science Information*, 24(2): 375–406.

Elster, J. (1986). 'Introduction', in J. Elster (ed.), *Rational Choice*. New York, NY: New York University Press, pp. 1–33.

Elster, J. (1990). 'When Rationality Fails', in K. S. Cook and M. Levi (eds.), *The Limits of Rationality*. Chicago: The University of Chicago Press.

Elster, J. (1998). 'Introduction,' in J. Elster (ed.), *Deliberative Democracy*. Cambridge: Cambridge University Press.

Emerson, J. (1973). 'Behaviour in Private Places', in G. Salaman and K. Thompson (eds.), *People and Organisations*. Milton Keynes: Open University Press, in WOBS (2001: pp. 35–48).

Emery, F. and Trist, E. (1965). 'The Causal Texture of Organizational Environments', *Human Relations*, 18: 21–32, in Clegg (2002*a*: vol. 3, 79–91).

Estlund, D. (1997). 'Beyond Fairness of Deliberation', in J. Bowham and W. Rehg (eds.), *Deliberative Democracy*. Cambridge, Mass: MIT Press, pp. 173–204.

Etzioni, A. (1961). *A Comparative Analysis of Complex Organizations*. New York, NY: Free Press.

Evans-Pritchard, E. (1976). *Witchcraft, Oracles and Magic Among the Azande*. Oxford: Oxford University Press.

Fayol, H. (1949). *General and Industrial Management*. London: Pittman.

Feldman, M. and March, J. (1981). 'Information in Organization as Signal and Symbol', *Administrative Science Quarterly*, 26: 171–86.

Ferguson, K. (1984). *The Feminist Case Against Bureaucracy*. Philadelphia, PA: Temple University Press.

Fineman, S. (ed.) (1993). *Emotion in Organizations*. London: Sage.

Fineman, S. (1996). 'Emotion and Organizing', in S. R. Clegg, C. Hardy, and W. R Nord (eds.), *Handbook of Organization Studies*. Thousand Oaks, CA: Sage, pp. 543–64.

Fineman, S. and Gabriel, Y. (2000). *Experiencing Organizations*. London: Sage.

Fischer, W. (1987). *Human Communication as Narration*. Greenville, SC: University of South Carolina Press.

Fischer, F. (1990). *Technocracy and the Politics of Expertise*. Newbury Park, CA: Sage.

Fish, S. (1980). *The Authority of Interpretive Communities*. Cambridge, MA: Harvard University Press.

Flam, H. (1990). 'Emotional "Man" II', *International Sociology*, 5(2): 225–34, in Clegg (2002*b*: vol. 7, 367–76).

Flyvbjerg, B. (1998). *Rationality and Power*. Chicago, IL: University of Chicago Press.

Flyvbjerg, B. (2001). *Making Social Science Matter*. Cambridge: Cambridge University Press.

Forester, J. (1983). 'Critical Theory and Organizational Analysis', in G. Morgan (ed.), *Beyond Method*. Beverley Hills, CA: Sage, pp. 234–46.

Forester, J. (1992). 'Critical Ethnography: On Fieldwork in a Habermasian Way', in M. Alvesson and H. Willmott (eds.), *Critical Management Studies*. London: Sage.

Forester, J. (1993). *Critical Theory, Public Policy and Planning Practice*. Albany, NY: NYU Press.

Forester, J. (2000). *The Deliberative Practitioner: Encouraging Participatory Planning Practices*. Cambridge, MA: MIT Press.

Foucault, M. (1967). *Madness and Civilization*. London: Tavistock.

Foucault, M. (1970). *The Order of Things*. London: Tavistock.

Foucault, M. (1972). *The Archeology of Knowledge*. London: Routledge.

Foucault, M. (1973). *The Birth of the Clinic*. London: Routledge.

Foucault, M. (1977*a*). *Discipline and Punish*. London: Allen Lane.

Foucault, M. (1977*b*). 'Nietzsche, Geneaology, History', in D. Bouchard (ed.), *Language, Counter-memory, Practice*. Ithaca, NY: Cornell University Press.

Foucault, M. (1978). *The History of Sexuality: Volume 1*. London: Penguin.

Foucault, M. (1980). 'Two Lectures', in C. Gordon (ed.), *Power/knowledge*. New York, NY: Pantheon Books.

Foucault, M. (1981). 'The Order of Discourse', in R. Young (ed.), *Untying the Text*. London: RKP.

Foucault, M. (1982*a*). 'The Subject and Power', in H. Dreyfus and P. Rabinow (eds.), *Michel Foucault: Beyond Structuralism and Hermeneutics*. Brighton: Harvester, pp. 208–26.

Foucault, M. (1982*b*). *Ce n'est pas une Pipe*. (Trans. by J. Harkness) Berkley, CA: University of California Press.

Foucault, M. (1983). 'Structuralism and Poststructuralism,' *Telos*, 55: 195–211.

Foucault, M. (1984*a*). 'What is Enlightenment?', in P. Rabinow (ed.), *The Foucault Reader*. London: Penguin, pp. 32–50.

Foucault, M. (1984*b*). 'Space, Knowledge and Power,' in P. Rabinow (ed.), *The Foucault Reader*. London: Penguin, pp. 239–56.

Foucault, M. (1986). *The Care of the Self: Volume 3, The History of Sexuality*. New York: Vintage.

Foucault, M. (1988). 'Practicing Criticism', in L. Kritzman (ed.), *Michel Foucault. Politics, Philosophy and Culture*. New York, NY: Routledge.

Foucault, M. (1990). *The Use of Pleasure: Volume 2, The History of Sexuality*. Harmondsworth: Penguin.

Foucault, M. (1991). 'Questions of method', in G. Burchell, C. Gordon, and P. Miller (eds.), *The Foucault Effect*. Hemmel Hempstead: Harvester, Wheatsheaf.

Foucault, M. (2001). *Fearless Speech*. Los Angeles, CA: Semiotexte.

Foucault, M. (2002). 'Omnes et singulatim: Toward a Critique of Political Reason', in J. Faubion (ed.), *Michel Foucault, Power, Essential Works of Foucault 1954–1984*. London: Penguin, vol. 3: 298–325.

Fox Keller, E. (1985). *Reflections on Gender and Science*. New Haven, CT: Yale University Press.

French, W. and Bell, C. (1999). *Organization Development*. New Jersey: Prentice Hall.

Friedland, R. and Alford, R. (1991). 'Bringing Society Back In: Symbols, Practices, and Institutional Contradictions', in W. Powell and P. DiMaggio (eds.), *The New Institutionalism in Organizational Analysis*. Chicago, IL: University of Chicago Press, pp. 232–66.

Frost, P. and Egri, C. (1991). 'The Political Process of Innovation', *Research in Organizational Behaviour*, 13: 229–95, in Clegg (2002*b*: vol. 5, 103–61).

Frost, P., Moore, L., Louis, M., Lundberg, C., and Martin, J. (eds.) (1991). *Reframing Organizational Culture*. Beverly Hills, CA: Sage.

Gabriel, Y. (1999). *Organizations in Depth*. London: Sage.

Gabriel, Y. (2004). 'Narratives, Stories, Texts', in D. Grant, C. Hardy, C. Oswick, and L. Putnam (eds.), *The Sage Handbook of Organizational Discourse*. London: Sage, pp. 61–79.

Galison, P. (1999). 'Trading Zone: Coordinating Action and Beliefs', in M. Baglioli (ed.), *The Science Studies Reader*. London: Routledge, pp. 137–60.

Gambling, T. (1984). 'Magic Accounting and Morale', *Accounting Organizations and Society*, 2(2): 141–51.

Garfinkel, H. (1960). 'The Rational Properties of Scientific and Common Sense Activities', *Behavioral Science*, 5: 72–83, in G. Delanty and P. Strydom (eds.), *Philosophies of Social Science*. Open University Press (2003), pp. 194–201.

Garfinkel, H. (1964). 'Studies of the Routine Grounds of Everyday Activities', *Social Problems*, 11: 225–50, in Clegg (2002*b*: vol. 6, 234–62).

Garfinkel, H. (1967). *Studies in Ethnomethodology*. Englewood Cliffs, NJ: Prentice-Hall.

Garfinkel, H. (1968). 'The Origins of the Term Ethnomethodology', in R. Turner (ed.), 1974. *Ethnomethodology*. Harmondsworth: Penguin.

Garfinkel, H. (1988). 'Evidence for Locally Produced, Naturally Accountable Phenomena of Order, Logic, Reason, Meaning, Method', *Sociological Theory*, 6: 103–9.

Gaus, G. (1997). 'Reason, Justification, and Consensus: Why Democracy Can't Have it All', in J. Bohman and W. Rehg (eds.), *Deliberative Democracy: Essays on Reason and Politics*. Cambridge, Mass: MIT Press, pp. 205–42.

Gauthier, D. (1982). 'Reason and Maximization', in Barry and Hardin, 85–106.

Gauthier, D. (1990). 'Maximization Constrained: The Rationality of Co-Operation', in P. Moser (ed.), pp. 315–36.

Gawande, A. (2001). *Complications*. New York, NY: Metropolitan Books.

Geertz, C. (1973). *The Interpretation of Cultures*. New York, NY: Basic Books.

Geertz, C. (1983). *Local Knowledge*. New York, NY: Basic Books.

Geertz, C. (1994). 'Thick Description', in M. Martin and L. McIntyre (eds.), *Readings in the Philosophy of Social Science*. Cambridge, MA: MIT Press.

Gellner, E. (1982). 'Relativism and Universals', in M. Hollis and S. Lukes (eds.), *Rationality and Relativism*. Oxford: Basil Blackwell, pp. 181–200.

Gellner, E. (1992). *Reason and Culture*. Oxford: Blackwell.

Geneen, H. (1984). *Managing*. New York, NY: Avon Books.

Gherardi, S. (2003). 'Feminist Theory and Organization Theory', in H. Tsoukas and C. Knudsen (eds.), *Oxford Handbook of Organization Theory*. Oxford: Oxford University Press.

Gherardi, S. and Nicolini, D. (2002). 'Learning in a Constellation of Interconnected Practices', *Journal of Management Studies*, 39(4): 419–36.

Giddens, A. (1994). 'Reason Without Revolution?', in R. Bernstein (ed.), *Habermas and Modernity*. Cambridge, MA: MIT Press, pp. 95–124.

Goffman, E. (1956). 'Embarassment and Social Organization,' *American Journal of Sociology*, 62: 264–71.

Goffman, E. (1969). *The Presentation of Self in Everyday Life*. Harmondsworth: Penguin.

Goldthorpe, J. (1998). 'Rational Action Theory for Sociology', *British Journal of Sociology*, 49(2): 167–92.

Gouldner, A. (1954). *Patterns of Industrial Bureaucracy*. New York, NY: Free Press.

Gouldner, A. (1955). 'Metaphysical Pathos and the Theory of Bureaucracy', *American Political Science Review*, 49: 496–507, in Clegg (2002*a*: vol. 1, 367–79).

Gouldner, A. (1959). 'Organizational Analysis', in R. Merton, L. Broom, and L. Cottrell (eds.), *Sociology Today*. New York, NY: Basic Books, pp. 400–28.

Granovetter, M. (1973). 'The Strength of Weak Ties', *American Journal of Sociology*, 78(6): 1360–80, Clegg (2002*b*: vol. 6, 3–21).

Granovetter, M. (1985). 'Economic Action and Social Structure: The Problem of Embeddedness', *American Journal of Sociology*, 91: 481–510, in Clegg (2002*a*: vol. 3, 363–89).

Green, D. and Shapiro, I. (1994). *Pathologies of Rational Choice*. New Haven, CT: Yale University Press.

Grey, C. (2005). *Studying Organizations*. New York, NY: Sage.

Grosz, E. (1993). 'Bodies and Knowledge', in L. Alcott and E. Potter (eds.), *Feminism and The Crisis of Reason*. New York, NY: Routledge, pp. 187–216.

Guillen, M. (1997). 'Scientific Management's Lost Aesthetic', *Journal of Management History*, 1(4): 682–715, in Clegg (2002a: vol. 1, 241–77).

Gulick, L. and Urwick, L. (1937). *Papers on the Science of Administration*. New York, NY: Columbia University Press.

Gutting, G. (1990). *Michel Foucault's Archeology of Scientific Reason*. Cambridge: Cambridge University Press.

Habermas, J. (1971). *Towards a Rational Society*. London: Heinemann.

Habermas, J. (1984). *The Theory of Communicative Action, Vol 1*. Boston, MA: Beacon.

Habermas, J. (1987). *The Theory of Communicative Action, Vol 2*. Boston, MA: Beacon.

Habermas, J. (1992). 'An Alternative Way Out of the Philosophy of the Subject', in *The Philosophical Discourse of Modernity*. Cambridge, MA: MIT Press.

Habermas, J. (1997). 'Popular Sovereignty as Procedure', in J. Bohman and W. Rheg (eds.).

Hacking, I. (1982a). *Language Truth and Reason*, in M. Hollis and S. Lukes (eds.), pp. 48–66.

Hacking, I. (1982b). 'Biopower and the Avalanche of Numbers', *Humanities in Society*, 5: 279–95.

Hacking, I. (1983). *Representation and Intervening*. Cambridge: Cambridge University Press.

Hacking, I. (1990). *The Taming of Chance*. Cambridge: Cambridge University Press.

Hacking, I. (1992). 'The Self Vindication of the Laboratory Sciences', in A. Pickering (ed.), *Science as Practice and Culture*. Chicago: The University of Chicago Press, pp. 76–98.

Hacking, I. (1999). *The Social Construction of What?* Cambridge, MA: Harvard University Press.

Hall, P. and Soskice, P. (eds.) (2001). *Varieties of Capitalism*. Oxford: Oxford University Press.

Halpern, J. J. (1998). 'Bonded Rationality', in J. J. Halpern and R. N. Stern (eds.), *Debating Rationality: Nonrational Aspects of Organizational Decision Making*. Ithaca, NY: Cornell University Press, pp. 219–38.

Halpern, J. and Stern, R. (1998). *Debating Rationality*. Ithaca, NY: Cornell University Press.

Handy, C. (1989). *Understanding Organizations*. Harmondsworth: Penguin.

Hanen, M. (1987). 'Feminism Reason and Philosophical Method', in W. Tomm (ed.), *The Effects Feminist Approaches on Research Methodology*. Waterloo, ON: Wilfrid Laurier University Press, pp. 31–50.

Haney, C., Banks, C., and Zimbardo, P. (1973). 'A Study of Prisoners and Guards in a Simulated Prison', *Naval Research Reviews*, Sept: 1–17, in WOBS (2001: vol. 4, 1663–79).

Hannan, M. and Freeman, J. (1977). 'The Population Ecology of Organizations', *American Journal of Sociology*, 82, 5: 929–64, in Clegg (2002a: vol. 3, 120–51).

Hannan, M. and Freeman, J. (1984). 'Structural Inertia and Organizational Change', *American Sociological Review*, 49(2): 149–64, in Clegg (2002a: vol. 3, 152–77).

Haraway, D. (1991). *Simians, Cyborgs and Women*. New York, NY: Routledge.

Hardin, G. (1968). 'The Tragedy of The Commons', *Science*, 19(2): 1243–8.

Harding, S. (1991). *Whose Science? Whose Knowledge?* Ithaca, NY: Cornell University Press.

Hassard, J., Holliday, R., and Willmott, H. (2000). *Body and Organization*. London: Sage.

Hasselbladh, H. and Kallinikos, J. (2000). 'The Project of Rationalization', *Organization Studies*, 21(4): 697–720.

Hatch, M. and Cunliffe, A. (2006). *Organization Theory*. Oxford: Oxford University Press.

Hearn, J. and Parkin, W. (1987). 'The Search for Literature', in J. Hearn and W. Parkin (eds.), *Sex at Work*. London: Prentice Hall, pp. 17–39, in WOBS (2001: vol. 2, 927–49).

Heckscher, C. (1995). 'Changing the Rules', in C. Heckscher (ed.), *White Collar Blues*. New York, NY: Basic Books, pp. 3–36, in WOBS (2001: vol. 1, 185–223).

Heckscher, C. and Donnelson, A. (eds.) (1994). *The Post Bureaucratic Organization*. Thousand Oaks, CA: Sage.

Henderson, L. and Mayo, E. (1936). 'The Effects of Social Environment', *Journal of Industrial Hygiene and Toxicology*, 18(7): 401–16, in Clegg (2002a: vol. 1, 299–313).

Heydebrand, W. (1979). 'The Technocratic Administration of Justice', *Research in Law and Sociology*, 2: 29–64.

Hill, S. (1988). *The Tragedy of Technology*. London: Pluto Press.

Hindess, B. (1987). *Choice, Rationality and Social Theory*. London: Unwin Hyman.

Hindmarsch, J. and Pilnick, A. (2007). 'Knowing Bodies at Work', *Organization Studies*, 28: 1395–416.

Hirsch, P. (1975). 'Organizational Effectiveness and the Institutional Environment', *Administrative Science Quarterly*, 20: 327–44, in Clegg (2002a: vol. 2, 253–73).

Hirschman, A. (1977). *The Passion and the Interests*. Princeton, NJ: Princeton University Press.

Hochschild, A. (1983). *The Managed Heart*. Berkeley, CA: University of California Press.

Hogarth, R. and Reder, M. (eds.) (1987). *Rational Choice: The Contrast Between Economics and Psychology*. Chicago, IL: University of Chicago Press.

Hollis, M. (1970). 'Reason and Ritual', in R. Wilson (ed.), *Rationality*. Oxford: Blackwell, pp. 221–39.

Hollis, M. (1982). 'The Social Destruction of Reality', in M. Hollis and S. Lukes (eds.), pp. 67–86.

Hollis, M. (1987). *The Cunning of Reason*. Cambridge: Cambridge University Press.

Hollis, M. and Lukes, S. (eds.) (1982). *Rationality and Relativism*. Cambridge, MA: MIT Press.

Holton, R. (1995). 'Rational Choice Theory in Sociology', *Critical Review*, 9(4): 519–37.

Homiak, M. (2002). 'Feminism and Aristotle's Rational Ideal', in Anthony and Witt (eds.), 2–30.

Hopfl, H. and Linstead, S. (1993). 'Passion and Performance', in S. Fineman (ed.), *Emotion in Organizations*. London: Sage.

Horkheimer, M. (1994). *Critique of Instrumental Reason*. New York: Continuum.

Horkheimer, M. and Adorno, T. (1995). *Dialectic of Enlightenment*. New York, NY: Continuum.

Horowitz, A. and Maley, T. (eds.) (1994). *The Barbarism of Reason*. Toronto: University of Toronto Press.

Horton, R. (1982). 'Tradition and Modernity Revisited', in M. Hollis and S. Lukes (eds.), *Rationality and Relativism*. Oxford: Basil Blackwell, pp. 201–60.

Hoskin, K. (1995). 'The Viewing Self and the World We View', *Organization*, 2(1): 141–62.

Hoskin, K. and Macve, R. (1986). 'Accounting and the Examination', *Accounting, Organisations and Society*, 2(2): 105–36.

Jablin, F., Putnam, L., Roberts, K., and Porter, L. (eds.) (2001). *The New Handbook of Organizational Communication*. Thousand Oaks, CA: Sage.

Jackall, R. (1988). *Moral Mazes: The World of Corporate Managers*. Oxford: Oxford University Press.

Jackson, M. (2000). *Systems Approaches to Management*. New York, NY: Plenum.

Jacoby, S. (1995). *Employing Bureaucracy*. New York, NY: Columbia University Press.

Jacques, E. (1995). 'Why the Psychoanalytic Approach to Understanding Organizations is Dysfunctional', *Human Relations*, 41(9): 343–57.

Jaffe, D. (2001). *Organization Theory*. New York, NY: McGraw Hill.

Jaggar, A. (1989). 'Love and Knowledge', *Inquiry*, 32: 51–76.

Jarvie, J. and Agassi, J. (1970). 'The Problem of the Rationality of Magic', in B. Wilson (ed.), pp. 172–93.

Jarzabkowski, P. (2005). *Strategy as Practice*. London: Sage.

Jensen, M. and Meckling, W. (1976). 'Theory of the Firm', *Journal of Financial Economics*, 3: 305–60.

Jick, T. (1979). 'Mixing Qualitative and Quantitative Methods: Triangulation in Action', *Administrative Science Quarterly*, 24: 602–11, in Clegg (2002*b*: vol. 7, 67–76).

Johnson, J. (1998). 'Arguing for Deliberation', in J. Elster (ed.), *Deliberate Democracy*. Cambridge: Cambridge University Press.

Kahneman, D. and Tversky, A. (1990). 'Prospect Theory', in P. Moser (ed.), 140–70.

Kalberg, S. (1980). 'Max Weber's Types of Rationality', *American Journal of Sociology*, 85(5): 1145–79.

Kallinikos, J. (1995). 'The Architecture of the Invisible', *Organization*, 2(1): 117–40.

Katz, D. and Kahn, R. (1966). *The Social Psychology of Organizations*. New York, NY: John Wiley and Sons.

Kerr, S. (1995). 'On the Folly of Rewarding A While Hoping for B', *Academy of Management Executive*, 9(1): 7–16.

Kets de Vries, M. and Miller, D. (1984). *The Neurotic Organization*. San Francisco, CA: Jossey-Bass.

Kieser, A. (1987). 'From Asceticism to Administration of Wealth', *Organization Studies*, 8(2): 103–23, in Clegg (2002*a*: vol. 1, 120–40).

Klamer, A. and Leonard, T. (1994). 'So What's an Economic Metaphor?', in P. Mirowski (ed.), pp. 20–54.

Klein, G. (1998). *Sources of Power*. Cambridge, MA: MIT Press.

Knight, J. and Johnson, J. (1997). 'What Sort of Equality Does Deliberative Democracy Require?', in Bohman and Rehg, pp. 279–320.

Knights, D. and McCabe, D. (1999). 'Are There No Limits To Authority?', *Organization Studies*, 20(2): 197–224, in Clegg (2002*b*: vol. 5, 246–72).

Knorr Cetina, K. (1981). *The Manufacture of Knowledge*. Oxford: Pergamon Press.

Knorr Cetina, K. (1999). *Epistemic Cultures*. Chicago, IL: Chicago University Press.

Kramer, P. (2003). 'The Virtue of Prudent Trust', in R. Westwood and S. Clegg (eds.), *Debating Organization*. London: Blackwell.

Kuhn, T. (1962). *The Structure of Scientific Revolutions*. Chicago, IL: University of Chicago Press.

Kula, W. (1986). *Measure and Man*. Princeton, NJ: Princeton University Press.

Langlois, R. (1986). *Economics as Process*. Cambridge: Cambridge University Press.

Langton, J. (1984). 'The Ecological Theory of Bureaucracy: The Case of Josiah Wedgwood and the British Pottery Industry', *Administrative Science Quarterly*, 29(3): 330–54, in Clegg (2002*a*: vol. 1, 166–91).

Laqueur, T. (1987). *Making Sex*. Cambridge, MA: Harvard University Press.

Lash, S. and Whimster, S. (eds.) (1987). *Max Weber, Rationality and Modernity*. London: Allen and Unwin.

Latour, B. (1983). 'Give Me a Laboratory and I Will Raise the World', in M. Biagioli (ed.) (1999). *The Science Studies Reader*. New York, NY: Routledge.

Latour, B. (1987). *Science in Action*. Cambridge, MA: Harvard University Press.

Latour, B. (1988). 'Drawing Things Together', in M. Lynch and S. Woolgar (eds.), *Representation in Scientific Practice*. Cambridge, MA: MIT Press.

Latour, B. (1999). *Pandora's Hope*. Cambridge, MA: Harvard University Press.

Latour, B. and Woolgar, S. (1979). *Laboratory Life*. Beverly Hills, CA: Sage.

Lave, J. (1986). 'The Values of Quantification', in J. Lave (ed.), *Power Action and Belief. A New Sociology of Knowledge?* London: Routledge, pp. 88–111.

Lave, J. and Wenger, E. (1991). *Situated Learning*. Cambridge: Cambridge University Press.

Law, J. (1986). 'On the Methods of Long-Distance Control: Vessels, Navigation and the Portuguese Route to India', in J. Law (ed.), *Power, Action and Belief: A New Sociology of Knowledge?*, *Sociological Review Monograph*. London: Routledge.

Lawrence, P. and Lorsch, J. (1967). *Organization and Environment*. Cambridge, MA: Harvard University Press.

Levine, D. (2005). 'The Corrupt Organization,' *Human Relations*, 58(6): 723–40.

Lewin, K. (1947). 'Group Decision and Social Change', *Human Relations*, 8: 356–89.

Linstead, S. and Grafton-Small, R. (1992). 'On Reading Organizational Culture', *American Psychologist*, 45(2): 109–19, in Clegg (2002*b*: vol. 7, 227–49).

Lipset, A., Trow, M., and Coleman, J. (1962). *Union Democracy*. Garden City, NY: Anchor Books.

Lloyd, G. (1995). *The Man of Reason*. London: Routledge.

Longino, H. (2002). *The Fate of Knowledge*. Princeton, NJ: Princeton University Press.

Luhmann, N. (1979). *Trust and Power*. New York, NY: Wiley.

Lukes, S. (1967). 'Some Problems about Rationality', *Archives of European Sociology*, VIII: 247–64.

Lukes, S. (1970). 'Some Problems about Rationality', in B. Wilson (ed.), pp. 194–213.

Lukes, S. (1973). *Individualism*. Oxford: Blackwell.

Lukes, S. (1982). 'Relativism in its Place', in M. Hollis and S. Lukes (eds.), pp. 261–305.

Lukes, S. (1991). 'The Rationality of Norms', *Archives of European Sociology*, 32: 142–9.

Lynch, M. (1982). 'Technical Work and Critical Inquiry: Investigations in a Scientific Laboratory', *Social Studies of Science*, 12: 499–533, in Clegg (2002*b*: vol. 6, 286–311).

Lynch, M. and Woolgar, S. (1990). *Representation in Scientific Practice*. Cambridge, MA: MIT Press.

Lyotard, J. (1984). *The Postmodern Condition*. Manchester: Manchester University Press.

MacIntyre, A. (1970). 'The Idea of a Social Science', in B. Wilson (ed.), pp. 111–30.

MacIntyre, A. (1981). *After Virtue*. London: Duckworth.

MacIntyre, A. (1988). *Whose Justice? Which Rationality?* Notre Dame, IN: University of Notre Dame Press.

Maguire, M., Morgan, R., and Reiner, R. (eds.) (2002). *The Oxford Handbook of Criminology*, 3rd edn. Oxford: Oxford University Press.

March, J. (1978). 'Bounded Rationality, Ambiguity and the Engineering of Choice', *Bell Journal of Economics*, 9(2): 582–608, in Clegg (2002*a*: vol. 4, 194–217).

March, J. (1981). 'Decisions in Organizations and Theories of Choice', in A. Van de Ven and W. Joyce (eds.), *Perspectives On Organizational Design and Behavior*. New York, NY: Wiley, pp. 201–44.

March, J. and Olsen, J. (1982). 'Organizational Choice Under Ambiguity', in *Ambiguity and Choice in Organizations*. Norway: Universeiktsforlaget.

March, J. and Simon, H. (1958). *Organizations*. New York, NY: Wiley.

March, J., Schultz, M., and Zhou, X. (2000). *The Dynamics of Rules*. Standford, CA: Stanford University Press.

Marcuse, H. (1964). *One-Dimensional Man*. Boston: Beacon Press.

Marglin, S. (1974). 'What Do Bosses Do? The Origins and Functions of Hierarchy in Capitalist Production', *Review of Radical Political Economics*, 6: 60–112, in Clegg (2002*a*: vol. 1, 43–83).

Marion, R. (1999). *The Edge of Chaos*. Thousand Oaks, CA: Sage.

Marsden, R. (1993). 'The Politics of Organizational Analysis', *Organization Studies*, 14(1): 93–124.

Marsden, R. and Townley, B. (1996). 'The Owl of Minerva: Reflections on Theory and Practice', in S. Clegg, C. Hardy, and W. Nord (ed.)

Martin, J. (1992). *The Culture of Organizations*. Oxford: Oxford University Press.

Martin, J., Feltman, M., Hatoh, M., and Sitkin, S. (1983). 'The Uniqueness Paradox in Organizational Stories', *Administrative Science Quaterly*, 28: 438–53.

Martin, P. (2002). 'Sensations, Bodies, and the "Spirit of a Place"', *Human Relations*, 55: 861–85.

Martin, J. and Frost, P. (1996). 'The Organizational Cultural War Games', in S. Clegg (ed.), *Handbook of Organization Studies*.

Maurice, M., Sorge, A., and Warner, M. (1980). 'Societal Differences in Organizing Manufacturing Units', *Organization Studies*, 1(1): 59–86, in Clegg (2002*a*: vol. 3, 297–323).

Mayntz, R. (1964). 'The Study of Organizations', *Current Sociology*, 13: 94–156, in Clegg (2002*a*: vol. 2, 88–151).

McCarl Nielsen, J. (1990). 'Introduction', in J. McCarl Nielsen (ed.), *Feminist Research Methods*. Boulder, CO: Westview Press, pp. 1–37.

McInnes, J. (2004). *The Summary Justice Review Committee Report to Ministers*. Edinburgh: TSO.

McMahon, C. (2001). *Collective Rationality and Collective Reasoning*. Cambridge: Cambridge University Press.

Meehan, J. (1995). *Feminist Read Habermas*. London: Routledge.

Menzies, I. (1970). *The Functioning of Social Systems as a Defense against Anxiety*. Centre for Applied Social Research. London: Tavistock.

Merchant, C. (1980). *The Death of Nature*. New York, NY: Harper Collins.

Merton, R. (1936). 'The Unanticipated Consequences of Social Action', *American Sociological Review*, 1(6): 894–904.

Merton, R. (1940). 'Bureaucratic Structure and Personality', *Social Forces*, 18(5): 560–8, in Clegg (2002*a*: vol. 1, 357–67).

Meyer, J. (1983). 'On the Celebration of Rationality', *Accounting, Organisations and Society*, 8: 235–40.

Meyer, J. (1992). 'Institutions and the Rationality of Formal Organizations', in M. Meyer et al. (eds.), *Environments and Organizations*. San Francisco, CA: Jossey-Bass, pp. 78–109.

Meyer, J. (1994). 'Rationalized Environments', in W. Scott and J. Meyer (eds.), *Institutional Environments and Organizations*. Thousand Oaks, CA: Sage, pp. 28–54.

Meyer, M. (2002). *Rethinking Performance Measurement*. Cambridge: Cambridge University Press.

Meyer, J. and Rowan, B. (1977). 'Institutionalized Organizations: Formal Structure as Myth and Ceremony', *American Journal of Sociology*, 83: 340–63, in Clegg (2002*a*: vol. 3, 274–96).

Meyer, J. and Rowan, B. (1992). 'The Structure of Educational Organizations', in J. Meyer and R. Scott (eds.), *Organizational Environments*. Newbury Park, CA: Sage.

Meyer, J. and Scott, R. (1992). 'Centralization and the Legitimacy Problems of Local Government', in J. Meyer and R. Scott (eds.), *Organizational Environments*. Newbury Park, CA: Sage.

Michelman, F. (1997). 'How Can the People Ever Make the Laws? A Critique of Deliberative Democracy' in J. Bohman and W. Rehg, pp. 145–72.

Michels, R. (1949). *Political Parties*. New York, NY: Free Press.

Miller, E. (1993). *From Dependency to Autonomy*. London: Free Association Books.

Mills, W. (1940). 'Situated Actions and Vocabularies of Motive', *American Sociological Review*, 5: 904–13, in Clegg (2002*b*: vol. 6, 183–92).

Mindlin, S. and Aldrich, H. (1975). 'Interorganizational Dependence', *Administrative Science Quarterly*, 20: 383–92, in Clegg (2002*a*: vol. 2, 367–78).

Mintzberg, H. (1983). *Designing Effective Organizations*. Englewood Cliffs, NJ: Prentice-Hall.

Mintzberg, H. (1994). *The Rise and Fall of Strategic Planning*. New York, NY: Free Press.

Mirowski, P. (1994*a*). 'Doing What Comes Naturally: Four Metanarratives on What Metaphors are For', in P. Mirowski (ed.), pp. 3–19.

Mirowski, R. (ed.) (1994*b*). *Natural Images in Economic Thought*. Cambridge: Cambridge University Press.

Molotch, H. and Boden, D. (1985). 'Talking Social Structure: Discourse, Domination and the Watergate Hearings', *American Sociological Review*, 50: 273–88, in Clegg (2002*b*: vol. 6, 312–35).

Moser, P. (1990). *Rationality in Action*. Cambridge: Cambridge University Press.

Mouzelis, N. (1975). *Organizations and Bureaucracy*. London: RKP.

Mueller, G. (1979). 'The Meaning of Rationality in the Work of Max Webber', *European Journal of Sociology*, 20: 149–71.

Mumby, D. (2004). 'Discourse, Power and Ideology', in D. Grant, C. Hardy, C. Oswick, and L. Putnam (eds.), *Handbook of Organizational Discourse*. Sage: London, pp. 317–36.

Mumby, D. and Putnam, L. (1992). 'The Politics of Emotion: A Feminist Reading of Bounded Rationality', *Academy of Management Review*, 17(3): 465–86, in WOBS (2001: vol. 3, 1244–66).

Munro, R. (1999). 'Power and Discretion', *Organization Studies*, 6(3): 429–50, in Clegg (2002*b*: vol. 5, 304–23).

Nagel, T. (1986). *The View From Nowhere*. Oxford: Oxford University Press.

National Audit Office (2001). *Measuring the Performance of Government Departments*. London: Stationary Office.

Nelkin, D. (ed.) (1984). *The Politics of Technical Decisions*. Thousand Oaks, CA: Sage.

Nelson, R. and Winter, S. (1982). *An Evolutionary Theory of Economic Change*. Cambridge, MA: Belknap.

Nicholson, L. (1999). *The Play of Reason*. Buckingham: Open University Press.

Nicolini, D., Gherardi, S., and Yanow, D. (2003). *Knowing in Organizations*. Armonk, NY: ME Sharpe.

Noble, D. (1992). *A World Without Women*. Oxford: Oxford University Press.

Nonaka, I. (1994). 'A Dynamic Theory of Organizational Knowledge Creation', *Organization Science*, 5(1): 14–37, in Clegg (2002*b*: vol. 8, 229–66).

Normand, A. (2003). *Proposals for the Integration of Aims, Objectives and Targets in the Scottish Criminal Justice System*. Edinburgh: Stationary Office.

Oakes, L., Townley, B., and Cooper, D. (1998). 'Business Planning as Pedagogy', *Administrative Science Quarterly*, 43: 257–92.

O'Connor, E. (1999). 'Minding the Workers: The Meaning of "Human" and "Human Relations"', in E. Mayo (ed.), *Organization*, in Clegg (2002*a*: vol. 1, 333–56).

Olson, M. (1971). *The Logic of Collective Action*. Cambridge, MA: Harvard University Press.

Orr, J. (1990). 'Sharing Knowledge, Celebrating Identity', in D. Middleton and D. Edwards (eds.), *Collective Remembering*. Newbury Park, CA: Sage.

Ouchi, W. (1980). 'Markets, Bureaucracies, and Clans', *Administrative Science Quarterly*, 25: 129–41, in Clegg (2002*a*: vol. 4, 295–308).

Parsons, T. (1956). 'Suggestions for a Sociological Approach to the Theory of Organizations–I', *Administrative Science Quarterly*, 1(1): 63–85, in Clegg (2002*a*: vol. 2, 24–39).

Parsons, T. (1959). *Economy and Society*. London: RKP.

Parsons, T. (1960). *Structure and Process in Modern Societies*. Glencoe, IL: Free Press.

Parsons, S. (2003). *Money and Rationality in Max Weber*. London: Routledge.

PASC (Public Administration Select Committee) (2002–2003). *On Target? Government By Measurement* (Fifth Report, vol. 1). London: House of Commons.

Paton, B. (2003). *Managing and Measuring Social Enterprises*. London: Sage.

Pennings, J. (1992). 'Structural Contingency Theory: A Reappraisal', *Research in Organizational Behaviour*, 14: 267–309.

Perrow, C. (1967). 'A Framework for the Comparative Analysis of Organizations', *American Sociological Review*, 32(2): 65–114, in Clegg (2002*a*: vol. 2, 197–215).

Perrow, C. (1979). *Complex Organizations*. New York, NY: Random House.

Perrow, C. (1986). 'Economic Theories of Organizations', *Theory and Society*, 15: 11–45, in Clegg (2002*a*: vol. 4, 244–71).

Perrow, C. (1999). *Normal Accidents*. Princeton, NJ: Princeton University Press.

Pettigrew, A. (1973). *The Politics of Organization Decision Making*. London: Tavistock.

Pettigrew, A. (1977). 'Strategy Formulation as a Political Process', *International Studies of Management and Organizations*, 1(2): 78–87, in Clegg (2002*a*: vol. 5, 43–9).

Pettigrew, A. (1979). 'On Studying Organizational Cultures', *Administrative Science Quarterly*, 24: 570–81, in Clegg (2002*b*: vol. 7, 140–51).

Pettigrew, A. (1990). 'Longitudinal Field Research on Change: Theory and Practice', *Organization Science*, 1(3): 267–92, in Clegg (2002*b*: vol. 6, 372–402).

Pfeffer, J. (1982). *Organizations and Organization Theory*. Marshfield, MA: Pitman.

Pfeffer, J. (1993). 'Barriers to the Advance of Organizational Science', *Academy of Management Review*, 18(4): 599–620, in WOBS (2001: vol. 2, 539–61).

Philp, M. (1985). 'Michel Foucault', in F. Skinner (ed.), *The Return of the Grand Theory in Human Sciences*. Cambridge: Cambridge University Press, pp. 65–82.

Pickering, A. (1992). *Science as Practice and Culture*. Chicago: University of Chicago Press.

Polanyi, M. (1983). *The Tacit Dimension*. Gloucester, MA: Doubleday.

Pollner, M. (1974). 'Mundane Reasoning', *Philosophy of Social Science*, 4: 35–54.

Pollner, M. (1987). *Mundane Reason*. Cambridge: Cambridge University Press.

Poovey, M. (1993). 'Figures of Arithmetic, Figures of Speech', *Critical Inquiry*, 19: 256–76.

Porter, R. (2000). *Enlightenment*. London: Penguin.

Porter, T. (1992). 'Objectivity as Standardization', *Annals of Scholarship*, 9: 19–59.

Porter, T. (1995). *Trust in Numbers*. Princeton, NJ: Princeton University Press.

Power, M. (1997). *The Audit Society*. Oxford: Oxford University Press.

Pringle, R. (1989). 'Bureaucracy, Rationality and Sexuality: The Case of Secretaries', in J. Hearn, D. Sheppard, O. Tancred-Sheriff, and G. Burrell (eds.), *The Sexuality of Organizations*. London: Sage, pp. 158–77, in WOBS (2001: vol. 3, 1267–86).

PSAF (2003). *The UK Government's Public Service Agreement Framework*. London: Treasury.

Pugh, D. (1966). 'Modern Organization Theory: A Psychological and Sociological Study', *Psychological Bulletin*, 66(4): 235–51, in Clegg (2002*a*: vol. 2, 175–96).

Pugh, D. (ed.) (1982). *Organization Theory: Selected Readings*. Harmondsworth: Penguin.

Pugh, D., Hickson, D., Hinings, C., MacDonald, M., Turner, C., and Lipton, G. (1963). 'A Conceptual Scheme for Organizational Analysis', *Administrative Science Quarterly*, 8: 289–315.

Pugh, D., Hickson, D., Hinings, C., and Turner, C. (1968). 'Dimensions of Organization Structure', *Administrative Science Quarterly*, 13(2): 65–114, in Clegg (2002*a*: vol. 2, 216–44).

Pugh, D., Hickson, D., Hinings, C., and Turner, C. (1969). 'The Context of Organizations Structure', *Administrative Science Quarterly*, 13(2): 91–114, in Clegg (2002*a*, 245–75).

Rafaeli, A. (2004). 'Emotion as a Connection of Artifacts to Organizations', *Organization Science*, 15(6): 671–86.

Ramsay, H. (1977). 'Cycles of Control: Worker Participation in Sociological and Historical Perspective', *Sociology*, 11(3): 481–506.

Rapoport, A. (1982). 'Prisoner's Dilemma—Recollections and Observations', in Barry and Hardin (eds.), pp. 71–84.

Rawls, J. (1971). *A Theory of Justice*. Oxford: Clarendon Press.

Rawls, J. (1997). 'The Idea of Public Reason', in Bohman and Rehg (eds.), pp. 131–44.

Ray, C. (1986). 'Corporate Culture: The Last Frontier of Control?', *Journal of Management Studies*, 23(3): 287–97, in Clegg (2002*a*: vol. 7, 196–205).

Ray, L. and Reed, M. (eds.) (1994). *Organizing Modernity*. London: Routledge.

Reason, P. and Bradbury, H. (eds.) (2002). In *Handbook of Action Research: Participative Inquiry and Practice*. London: Sage.

Reed, M. (1996). 'Organizational Theorizing: A Historically Contested Terrain', in Clegg et al. (eds.)

Richardson, H. (1997). 'Democratic Intentions', in Bohman and Rehg (eds.), pp. 349–82.

Riley, P. (1991). 'Cornerville as Narration', in R. Frost, L. Moore, M. Louis, C. Lundberg and J. Martin (eds.), *Reframing Organizational Culture*. London: Sage, pp. 215–22.

Ritzer, G. (1996). *The McDonaldization of Society*. Thousand Oaks, CA: Pine Forge Press.

Roethlisberger, F. and Dickson, W. (1939). *Management and the Worker*. Cambridge, MA: Harvard University Press.

Rorty, R. (1980). *Philosophy and the Mirror of Nature*. Oxford: Blackwell.

Rose, N. (1999). *Power of Freedom*. Cambridge: Cambridge University Press.

Rothschild Whitt, J. (1979). 'The Collective: An Alternative to Rational-Bureaucratic Model', *American Sociological Review*, 44: 509–27.

Roy, D. (1959). ' "Banana Time": Job Satisfaction and Informal Interaction', *Human Organization*, 18: 158–68, in Clegg (2002b: vol. 6, 212–33).

Ryle, G. (1949). *The Concept of Mind*. Chicago, IL: The University of Chicago Press.

Sahlin-Andersson, K. (1996). 'Imitating by Editing Success', in B. Czarniawska and G. Sevon (eds.), *Translating Organizational Change*. Berlin: de Gruyter, pp. 69–92.

Salaman, G. and Thompson, K. (eds.) (1973). *People and Organizations*. London: Longman.

Samuelson (1947). *Foundations of Economic Analysis*. Cambridge, MA: Harvard University Press.

Sayer, D. (1992). *Capitalism and Modernity*. London: Routledge.

Scarbrough, H. and Corbett, M. (1992). *Technology and Organization*. London: Routledge.

Schacht, T. (1992). *Nietzsche*. London: Routledge.

Schatzki, T., Knorr Cetina, K., and Von Savigny, E. (2001). *The Practice Turn in Contemporary Theory*. London: Routledge.

Scheff, T. (1992). 'Rationality and Emotion: Homage to Norbet Elias', in J. Coleman and T. Fararo (eds.), *Rational Choice Theory: Advocacy and Critique*. Newbury Park, CA: Sage, pp. 101–19.

Scheibinger, L. (1989). *The Mind Has No Sex?*. Cambridge, MA: Harvard University Press.

Schein, E. (1984). 'Coming to an Awareness of Organizational Culture', *Sloan Management Review*, 25: 3–16.

Schein, E. (1991). 'What is Culture?', in P. Frost, L. Moore, M. Louis, C. Lundbery and J. Martin (eds.), *Reframing Organization Culture*. London: Sage, pp. 243–53.

Schein, E. (1994). 'Organizational Culture', *American Psychologist*, 45(2): 109–19, in Clegg (2002b: vol. 7, 206–26).

Schön, D. (2000). *The Reflective Practitioner*. New York, NY: Basic Books.

Schott, R. (2002). 'Resurrecting Embodiment', in Antony and Witt (eds.), pp. 319–36.

Schutz, A. (1943). 'The Problem of Rationality in the Social World', *Economica*, 10(38): 130–49.

Schutz, A. (1962). *Collected Papers Vol. 11*. Martinus Nijhoff: The Hague.

Scott, R. (1981). *Rational, Natural and Open Systems*. Englewood Cliffs, NJ: Prentice Hall.

Scott, R. (1987). 'The Adolescence of Institutional Theory', *Administrative Science Quarterly*, 32(4): 493–511, in Clegg (2002a: vol. 2, 390–408).

Scott, J. (1992). 'Experience', in J. Butler and J. Scott (eds.), *Feminists Theorize the Political*. New York, NY: Routledge, pp. 22–40.

Scott, R. (1995). *Institutions and Organizations*. Thousand Oaks, CA: Sage.

Scott, M. and Lyman, S. (1968). 'Accounts', *American Sociological Review*, 33: 46–62.

Scott, R. and Meyer, J. (eds.) (1994). *Institutional Environments and Organizations*. Thousand Oaks, CA: Sage.

Seidler, V. (1994). *Unreasonable Men*. London: Routledge.

Selznick, P. (1948). 'Foundations of the Theory of Organization', *American Sociological Review*, 13: 25–35, in Clegg (2002a: vol. 2, 40–51).

Selznick, P. (1949). *TVA and the Grassroots*. Berkeley, CA: University of California Press.

Selznick, P. (1996). 'Institutionalism "Old" and "New" ', *Administrative Science Quarterly*, 41(2): 270–7, in Clegg (2002a: vol. 4, 111–19).

Sen, A. (1977). 'Rational Fools: A Critique of the Behavioral Foundations of Economic Theory', *Philosophy and Public Affairs*, 6(4): 317–44.

Sen, A. (1987). 'Economic Behaviour and Moral Sentiments', in A. Sen (ed.), *On Ethics and Economics*. Oxford: Blackwell.

Sevon, G. (1996). 'Organizational Imitation in Identity Formation', in B. Czarniawska and G. Sevon (eds.), *Translating Organizational Change*. Berlin: De Gruyter, pp. 49–67.

Shenhav, Y. (1999). *Manufacturing Rationality*. Oxford: Oxford University Press.

Sheridan, A. (1980). *Michel Foucault. The Will to Truth*. London: Routledge.

Shilling, C. (1993). *The Body and Social Theory*. London: Sage.

Sica, A. (1988). *Weber, Irrationality and Social Order*. Berkely, CA: University of California Press.

Simon, H. (1955). 'A Behavior Model of Rational Choice', *Quarterly Journal of Economics*, 69: 99–118.

Simon, H. (1957/1997). *Administrative Behavior*. New York, NY: Free Press.

Simon, H. (1959). 'Theories of Decision-Making in Economics and Behavioral Science', *The American Economic Review*, 49(3): 253–83, in Clegg (2002a: vol. 4, 167–93).

Simon, H. (1978a). 'Rationality in Psychology and Economics', in R. Hogarth and M. Reder (eds.), *Rational Choice*. Chicago, IL: University of Chicago Press.

Simon, H. (1978b). 'Rationality as Process and Product of Thought', *American Economic Review*, 68(2): 1–16.

Simon, H. (1989). *Reason in Human Affairs*. Oxford: Blackwell.

Simon, H. (1990). 'Alternative Visions of Rationality', in P. Moser (ed.), pp. 189–206.

Simon, H. (1991). 'Bounded Rationality and Organizational Learning', *Organization Science*, 2(1): 125–34, in Clegg (2002b: vol. 8, 49–62).

Simon, H. and Associates (1992). 'Decision Making and Problem Solving', in M. Zey (ed.), *Decision Making*. Newbury Park, CA: Sage.

Simons, J. (1995). *Foucault and the Political*. London: Routledge.

Smelser, N. and Swedberg, R. (eds.) (1994). *The Handbook of Economic Sociology*. Princeton, NJ: Princeton University Press.

Smircich, L. (1983). 'Concepts of Culture and Organizational Analysis', *Administrative Science Quarterly*, 28(3): 339–58, in Clegg (2002b: vol. 7, 152–74).

Smith, D. (1974). 'The Social Construction of Documentary Reality', *Sociological Inquiry*, 44(4): 254–68.

Smith, D. (1987). *The Everyday World in Problematic*. Boston, MA: Northeastern University Press.

Smith, D. (1990). *The Conceptual Practices of Power*. Toronto: University of Toronto Press.

Smith, P. (1993). 'Outcome Related Performance Indicators and Organizational Control in the Public Sector', *British Journal of Management*, 4(3): 135–52.

Sorge, A. (1991). 'Strategic Fit and the Societal Effect', *Organization Studies*, 12(2): 161–90, in Clegg (2002*a*: vol. 4, 3–30).

Stacey, R. (2000). *Strategic Management and Organizational Dynamics*. London: Prentice Hall.

Starkey, K. (1992). 'Durkheim and Organizational Analysis: Two Legacies', *Organization Studies*, 13(4): 627–42.

Staw, B. (1981). 'The Escalation of Commitment to a Course of Action', *Academy of Management Review*, 6: 577–87, in Clegg (2002*b*: vol. 7, 353–66).

Stinchcombe, A. (1990). 'Reason and Rationality', in Cook and Levi (eds.).

Strathearn, M. (1995). *The Relation. Issues in Complexity and Scale*. Cambridge: Prickly Pear Pamphlet.

Strauss, A., Schatman, L., Ehrlickh, D., Buchner, R., and Sashian, M. (1963). 'The Hospital and Its Negotiated Order', in Salaman and Thompson (eds.).

Suchman, L. (1987). *Plans and Situated Actions*. Cambridge: Cambridge University Press.

Suchman, L. (2003). 'Organizing Alignment', in D. Nicolini, S. Gherardi and D. Yanow (eds.), *Knowing in Organizations*. Armonk, NY: M. E. Sharpe.

Sudnow (1965). 'Normal Crimes', *Social Problems*, 12(3): 255–68. in Salaman and Thompson (eds.).

Sugden, R. (1991). 'Rational Choice' A Survey of Contributions from 'Economics and Philosophy', *The Economic Journal*, 101(409): 751–85.

Swedberg, R. (2003). *Principles of Economic Sociology*. Princeton, NJ: Princeton University Press.

Swidler, A. (1973). 'The Concept of Rationality in the Work of Max Weber', *Sociological Inquiry*, 43(1): 35–42.

Tambiah, S. (1990). *Magic, Science, Religion and the Scope of Rationality*. Cambridge: Cambridge University Press.

Taylor, F. (1911). 'Principles of Scientific Management', in D. Pugh (ed.) (1982), *Organization Theory*. Harmondsworth: Penguin, pp. 124–46.

Taylor, C. (1982). 'Rationality', in Hollis and Lukes (eds.), pp. 87–105.

Taylor, C. (1985). *Philosophy and the Human Sciences*. Philosophical Papers. Cambridge: Cambridge University Press.

Taylor, C. (1989). *Sources of the Self*. Cambridge, MA: Harvard University Press.

Taylor, C. (1995). *Philosophical Arguments*. Cambridge, MA: Harvard University Press.

Taylor, M. (1987). *The Possibility of Cooperation*. Cambridge: Cambridge University Press.

Thompson, E. (1967*a*). 'Time, Work-discipline, and Industrial Capitalism', *Past and Present*, 38: 56–97, in Clegg (2002*a*: vol. 3, 3–42).

Thompson, J. (1967). *Organisations in Action*. London: McGraw-Hill.

Tillyard, E. (1960). *The Elizabethan World Picture*. London: Chatto and Windsor.

Toulmin, S. (1990). *Cosmopolis*. Chicago, IL: University of Chicago Press.

Toulmin, S. (2001). *Return to Reason*. Cambridge, MA: Harvard University Press.

Toulmin, S., Rieke, R., and Janik, R. (1979). *An Introduction to Reasoning*. New York, NY: Macmillan.

Townley, B. (1995). 'Managing by Numbers', *Critical Perspectives on Accounting*, 6: 555–75.

Townley, B. (1997). 'The Institutional Logic of Performance Appraisal', *Organization Studies*, 18(2): 261–85.

Townley, B. (1999). 'Performance Appraisal and Practical Reason', *Journal of Management Studies*, 36: 287–306.

Townley, B. (2002*a*). 'Managing with Modernity', *Organization*, 9: 549–73.

Townley, B. (2002*b*). 'The Role of Competing Rationalities in Institutional Change', *Academy of Management Journal*, 45: 163–79.

Townley, B. (2004*a*). 'Organization Studies and Academic Boundaries: the Rationale of the Subject?', *Human Relations*, 57: 893–909.

Townley, B. (2004*b*). 'Managerial Technologies, Ethics and Management', *Journal of Management Studies*, 41: 425–45.

Townley, B. (2005*a*). 'Critical Views of Performance Measurement', in *The Encyclopaedia of Social Measurement*, vol. 1. Elsevier. pp. 565–71.

Townley, B. (2005*b*). 'La Place du Sujet dans la Theorie Organisationelle', in A. Hatchuel, E. Pezet, K. Starkey, and O. Lenay (eds.), *Gouvernement, Organisation et Gestion: l'Heritage de Michel Foucault*. Quebec: Les Presses de l'Universite de Laval, pp. 63–91.

Townley, B. (2005*c*). 'Neglecting Reason', *Organization*, 12: 938–42.

Townley, B. (2008). 'Performance Measurement Systems and the Criminal Justice System: rationales and rationalities', in J. Hartley, C. Skelcher, C. Donaldson, and M. Wallace (eds.), *Managing Improvement in Public Service Delivery: Progress and Challenges*. Cambridge: Cambridge University Press.

Townley, B., Cooper, D., and Oakes, L. (2003). 'Performance Measures and the Rationalization of Organizations', *Organization Studies*, 24(7): 1045–71.

Townley, B. and Doyle, R. (2006). 'Performance Measures', in G. Ritzer (ed.), *The Blackwell Encyclopaedia of Sociology*. Oxford: Blackwell.

Trice, H. and Beyer, J. (1984). 'Studying Organizational Cultures Through Rites and Ceremonies', *Academy of Management Review*, 9: 653–69.

Trigg, R. (1993). *Rationality and Science*. Oxford: Blackwell.

Trist, E. and Bamforth, K. (1951). 'Some Social and Psychological Consequences of the Longfall Method of Coal-Getting', *Human Relations*, 4(1): 3–38.

Tsoukas, H. (2005). 'Do We Really Understand Tacit Knowledge', in H. Tsoukas (ed.), *Complex Knowledge*. Oxford: OUP, pp. 141–62.

Turner, B. (1973). 'The Industrial Subculture', in G. Salaman and K. Thompson (eds.), Harlow, Essex: Longman.

Turner, B. (1984). *Body and Society*. Oxford: Blackwell.

Turner, B. (1986). 'Sociological Aspects of Organizational Symbolism', *Organization Studies*, 7(2): 101–15.

Tversky, A., and Kahneman, D. (1974). 'Judgment under Uncertainty: Heuristics and Biases', *Science*, 185: 1124–31.

Tversky, A. and Kahneman, D. (1990). 'Rational Choice and the Framing of Decisions', *Journal of Business*, 59: 4.

Udy, S. (1959). 'Bureaucracy and Rationality in Weber's Organization Theory', *American Sociological Review*, 24: 791–5.

Uzzi, B. (1997). 'Social Structure and Competition in Interfirm Networks: The Paradox of Embeddedness', *Administrative Science Quarterly*, 42: 35–67, in Clegg (2002*b*: vol. 6, 111–44).

Van Maanen, J. (1979). 'The Fact of Fiction in Organizational Ethnography', *Administrative Science Quarterly*, 24: 539–49, in Clegg (2002*b*: vol. 6, 539–71).

Van Maanen, J. (1991a). 'Fear and Loathing in Organization Studies', *Organization Science*, 6(6): 687–92, in WOBS (2001: vol. 2, 295–604).

Van Maanen, J. (1991b). 'The Smile Factory: Work at Disneyland', in P. Frost, L. Moore, M. Louis, C. Lundbery, and J. Martin (eds.), *Reframing Organizational Culture*. London: Sage: pp. 58–76, in WOBS (2001: vol. 3, 1542–60).

Van Maanen, J. and Barley, S. (1984). 'Occupational Communities', in B. Staw and L. Cummings (eds.), *Research in Organizational Behavior*, vol. 6. Greenwich, CT: Jai Press.

Van Maanen, J. and Pentland, B. (1994). 'Cops and Auditors: The Rhetoric of Records', in S. Sikin and R. Bies (eds.), *The Legalistic Organization*. Thousand Oakes, CA: Sage.

Wagner, P. (2000). 'Rational-Choice the Default Mode of Social Theory', in M. Archer and J. Tritter (eds.), *Rational Choice Theory. Resisting Colonization*. London: Routledge.

Waldrop, M. (1992). *Complexity*. New York, NY: Simon and Schuster.

Watson, T. (1994). *In Search of Management: Culture, Chaos and Control in Managerial Work*. London: International Thomson Business Press, pp. 29–57.

Webb, S. and Webb, B. (1920). *Industrial Democracy*. London.

Weber, M. (1948). *From Max Weber*, H. Gerth and C. Mills (eds.). London: Routledge.

Weber, M. (1978). In G. Roth and C. Wittich (eds.), *Economy and Society*. Berkeley, CA: University of California Press, vols 1, 2.

Weick, K. (1969). *The Social Psychology of Organizing*. Reading, MA: Addison-Wesley.

Weick, K. (1990). 'Cartographic Myths', in A. Huff (ed.), *Mapping Strategic Thought*. Chichester, NY: John Wiley.

Weick, K. (1993). 'The Collapse of Sensemaking in Organizations: The Mann Gulch Disaster', *Administrative Science Quarterly*, 38(4): 628–52, in Clegg (2002b: vol. 8, 3–28).

Weick, K. (1995). *Sensemaking in Organizations*. Thousand Oaks, CA: Sage.

Weick, K. (2001). *Making Sense of Organizations*. Oxford: Blackwell.

Weick, K. and Roberts, K. (1993). 'Collective Mind in Organizations: Heedful Interrelating on Flight Decks', *Administrative Science Quarterly*, 38: 357–81.

Weiss, R. (1983). 'Weber on Bureaucracy', *Academy of Management Review*, 8: 242–8

Wenger, E. (1998). *Communities of Practice*. Cambridge: Cambridge University Press.

Wenger, E. (2003). 'Communities of Practice and Social Learning Systems', in J. Nicolini et al. (eds.), pp. 76–99.

Wenger, E. and Synder, M. (2000) 'Communities of Practice', *Harvard Business Review*, Jan: 139–45.

Whitley, R. (1992). *European Business Systems*. London: Sage.

Williams, B. (1990). 'Internal and External Reasons', in P. Moser (ed.), pp. 387–97.

Williams, S. (1998). 'Modernity and the Emotions: Corporeal Reflections on the (Ir)rational', *Sociology*, 32(4): 747–69.

Williams, S. (2000). 'Is Rational Choice Theory Unreasonable', in Archer and Tritter (eds.).

Williams, S. and Bendelow, G. (1998). 'Introduction', in G. Bendelow and S. Williams (eds.), *Emotions in Social Life*. London: Routledge, pp. xv–xxi.

Williamson, D. (1993). 'Calculativeness, Trust and Economic Organization', *Journal of Law and Economics*, xxxvi: 453–86.

Williamson, O. (1975). *Markets and Hierarchies*. New York, NY: Free Press.

Williamson, O. (1981). 'The Economics of Organization: The Transaction Cost Approach', *American Journal of Sociology*, 87: 548–77, in Clegg (2002*a*: vol. 4, 218–43).

Williamson, O. (1995). *Organization Theory*. Oxford: Oxford University Press

Willmott, H. (1993). 'Strength is Ignorance, Slavery if Freedom: Managing Culture in Modern Organizations', *Journal of Management Studies*, 30(5): 515–52, in Clegg (2002*b*: vol. 7, 264–99).

Wilson, B. (ed.) (1970). *Rationality*. Oxford: Blackwell.

Wilson, H. (1973). 'Rationality and Decision in Administrative Science', *Canadian Journal of Political Science*, 6(3): 271–94.

Wilson, J. (1995). *Political Organizations*. Princeton, NJ: Princeton University Press.

Winch, P. (1970). 'Understanding a Primitive Society', in B. Wilson (ed.), pp. 78–111.

WOBS (Warwick Organizational Behaviour Staff) (eds.) (2001). *Organizational Studies: Critical Perspectives on Business and Management*. London: Routledge, vols. 1–4.

Woodward, J. (1958). *Management and Technology*. London: HMSO.

Young, I. M. (1987). 'Impartiality and the Civic Public: Some Implications of Feminist Critiques of Moral and Political Theory', in S. Benhabib and D. Cornell (eds.), *Feminism and Critique*. Minneapolis: University of Minnesota Press, pp. 56–95.

Young, I. M. (1997). 'Difference as a Resource for Democratic Communication', in Bohman and Rehg, pp. 383–406.

Zafirovski, M. (1999*a*). 'What is Really Rational Choice? Beyond the Utilitarian Concept of Rationality', *Current Sociology*, 47(1): 47–113.

Zafirovski, M. (1999*b*). 'Unification of Sociological Theory by the Rational Choice Model: Conceiving the Relationship between Economics and Sociology', *Sociology*, 33(3): 495–515.

Zey, M. (ed.) (1992*a*). In *Decision Making: Alternatives to Rational Choice Models*. Newbury Park, CA: Sage.

Zey, M. (1992*b*). 'Criticisms of Rational Choice Models', in M. Zey (ed.), *Decision Making: Alternatives to Rational Choice Models*. Newbury Park, CA: Sage.

Zey, M. (1998). *Rational Choice Theory and Organizational Theory: A Critique*. Thousand Oaks, CA: Sage.

Zouboulakis, M. (2001). 'From Mill to Weber: The Meaning of the Concept of Economic Rationality', *European Journal of Economic Thought*, 8(1): 30–41.

Zuboff, S. (1988). *In the Age of the Smart Machine: The Future of Work and Power*. Oxford: Heinemann.

Zysman, J. (1994). 'How Institutions Create Historically Rooted Trajectories of Growth', *Industrial and Corporate Change*, 3: 243–83, in Clegg (2002*a*: vol. 4, 31–66).

⬚ GLOSSARY

Advocate	A Lawyer or Barrister who argues before the High Court Counsel
Advocate depute	Prosecutes a case before the High Court
BCS	Battered Child Syndrome
Bonomy Report	A High Court judge, Lord Bonomy, conducted a study of High Court procedure, recommending changes
BPR	Business Process Reengineering
CJS	Criminal justice system
CJSW	Criminal Justice Social Work, social work with specific responsibility for the convicted
CPM	Cost Performance Management
CSO	Community Service Order, penalty in lieu of imprisonment
Defence agent	A solicitor who defends a case in court
High Court	A court which hears serious cases
HMIP	Her Majesty's Inspectorate of Prisons
IDP	Individual Development Plan
ITT	International Telephone and Telegraph
LCJB	Local Criminal Justice Board
Lord Advocate	Chief Law Officer
McInnes	Sheriff McInnes conducted a review into the functioning of the Sheriff Courts
MBO	Management by Objectives
NCJB	National Criminal Justice Board
'no pros'	no proceedings taken by the prosecution service on a police charge
Normand Report	A report into the functioning of the CJS recommending overarching objectives and measures and the establishment of the NCJB and LCJB
OD	organizational development
OED	Oxford English Dictionary
PASC	House of Commons Public Affairs Select Committee
PERT	Performance Evaluation Review Technique
PFS	Procurator Fiscal Service, responsible for conducting prosecutions
PPBS	Planning Programming and Budgeting System
Precognition	The taking of witness statements for use in court

PSA	Public Service Agreement
PSAF	Public Service Agreement Framework
QC	Queen's Council
QWL	Quality of Work Life
Sheriff	A judge who sits in the Sheriff court
Sheriff Court	A court which hears less serious cases
Sheriff Principal	Senior Sheriff within a Sheriffdom
Solemn cases	Cases heard before a sheriff court where there is a jury
Summary cases	Cases heard before a sheriff court without a jury
TQM	Total Quality Management
ZBB	Zero Based Budgeting

Scottish words

Feart	to be afraid
Haar	a dense sea fog
Neds	a colloquial term for a petty criminal

INDEX